Indigenous Knowledge of Namibia

EDITED BY

Kazhila C. Chinsembu, Ahmad Cheikhyoussef,
Davis Mumbengegwi, Martha Kandawa-Schulz,
Choshi D. Kasanda and Lawrence Kazembe

UNAM
PRESS
UNIVERSITY OF NAMIBIA

University of Namibia Press
www.unam.edu.na/unam-press
unampress@unam.na
Private Bag 13301
Windhoek
Namibia

First published: 2015

Copy-editor: Carole Roberts
Design and layout: Vivien Barnes, Handmade Communications
Cover design: Nambowa Malua
Maps: Carole Roberts
Printed by: John Meinert Printers, Windhoek

ISBN 978-99916-42-05-5

The information presented in this book is for research and academic purposes only. Medicinal properties mentioned in this book do not necessarily point to the clinical efficacy and safety of the plants. Readers should not use any information in this book for self-medication, therapy and consumption of plant materials, foods and drinks. The publisher, editors and authors will not be liable for claims arising from the application or misapplication of data from this book.

Responsibility for the correct orthography of indigenous language terms lies with the authors.

UNAM Press has no responsibility for the persistence or accuracy of URLs for external or third-party internet websites referred to in this publication, and does not guarantee that any content on such websites is, or will remain, accurate or appropriate.

Distributed nationally by Namibia Book Market: www.namibiabooks.com; email: contact@namibiabooks.com
In the rest of Southern Africa by Blue Weaver: www.blueweaver.co.za
Internationally by the African Books Collective: www.africanbookscollective.com

Contents

Acknowledgments

This book would not have been possible without the support received from Professor Frednard Gideon (Dean, Faculty of Science) and Dr Nelago Indongo (Director, Multidisciplinary Research Centre).

Photographs were supplied by the authors and Graham Alexander, Antje Burke, Dave Cole, Christopher Hines, Coleen Mannheimer, John Mendelsohn, Mark Paxton, Silke Rügheimer, George Sanzila and BCW van der Waal. UNAM Press acknowledges their support with gratitude.

Abbreviations and acronyms

°	degree(s)
%	per cent
ABS	access and benefit sharing
ad	*anno Domini* (number of years after the birth of Christ)
AIDS	acquired immunodeficiency syndrome
ALV	African leafy vegetables
AOAC	Association of Official Analytical Chemists
ART	antiretroviral therapy
ATCC	American Type Culture Collection
bc	number of years before the birth of Christ
BIKS	Bachelor of Indigenous Knowledge Systems
C	Celsius
CBNRM	community-based natural resource management
CDC	United States Centers for Disease Control and Prevention
CLM	Caprivi Liberation Movement
cm	centimetre(s)
CO_2	carbon dioxide
CRIAA SA-DC	Centre for Research Information Action in Africa Southern African Development and Consulting
CSIR	Council for Scientific and Industrial Research
DMSO	dimethyl sulfoxide
DNA	deoxyribonucleic acid
DPPH	2,2-diphenyl-1-picrylhydrazyl
DRST	Directorate of Research, Science and Technology (ME)
DST	Department of Science and Technology (South Africa)
e.g.	for example
EMIS	Education Management Information System
ENP	Etosha National Park
et al.	*et alii* (and others)
EU	European Union

EUR	Euro(s)
EVM	ethnoveterinary medicine
FAO	Food and Agriculture Organization of the United Nations
FMD	foot-and-mouth disease
g	gram(s)
GIBEX	Global Institute for Bioexploration
GIZ	Deutsche Gesellschaft für Technische Zusammenarbeit
GRN	Government of the Republic of Namibia
H_2O_2	hydrogen peroxide
ha	hectare(s)
HIV	human immunodeficiency virus
HWC	human–wildlife conflict
IBPC	Interim Bio-Prospecting Committee
IC_{50}	half maximal inhibitory concentration
IEK	indigenous ecological knowledge
IKS	indigenous knowledge systems
ILO	International Labour Organization
InWEnt	Capacity Building International, Germany
IBPC	Interim Bio-Prospecting Committee
IPTT	Indigenous Plant Task Team
LAB	lactic acid bacteria
µl	microlitre(s)
µg	microgram(s)
m	metre(s)
ME	Ministry of Education
MET	Ministry of Environment and Tourism
mg	milligram(s)
mℓ	millilitre(s)
mm	millimetre(s)
MoHSS	Ministry of Health and Social Services (Namibia)
MRC	Multidisciplinary Research Centre (UNAM)
NAD	Namibia Dollar
NANASO	Namibia Network of AIDS Service Organizations
NBC	Namibia Broadcasting Corporation
NBF	Namibia Biosciences Forum
NBRI	National Botanical Research Institute
NCI	National Cancer Institute (in the USA)
NEPAD	New Partnership for Africa's Development

NGO	non-government organization
NIKSO	National Indigenous Knowledge Systems Office
NLV	Namibian leafy vegetables
NPC	National Planning Commission
p.	page
PEPFAR	[USA] President's Emergency Plan for AIDS relief
pH	power of hydrogen ion concentration as a measure of acidity or alkalinity
pl.	plural
pp.	pages
RAEIN-Africa	Regional Agricultural and Environment Initiatives Network-Africa
RCT	rational choice theory
SANBio	Southern Africa Network for Biosciences
sing.	Singular
sp.	species (sing.)
spp.	species (pl.)
STAT3	signal transducer and activator of transcription 3
SWAPO	South West Africa People's Organization
TLC	thin-layer chromatography
UN	United Nations
UNAIDS	Joint United Nations Programme on HIV/AIDS
UNAM	University of Namibia
UNCED	United Nations Conference on Environment and Development
UNDP	United Nations Development Programme
UNESCO	United Nations Educational, Scientific and Cultural Organization
UNFCCC	United Nations Framework Convention on Climate Change
UNICEF	United Nations Children's Fund
USAID	United States Agency for International Development
USA	United States of America
USD	United States Dollar
VCF	veterinary cordon fence
WHO	World Health Organization
WIPO	World Intellectual Property Organization
ZMW	Zambian Kwacha

Introduction

Kazhila C. Chinsembu

Why this book, *Indigenous Knowledge of Namibia*? Nowadays, indigenous knowledge has gained prominence and attracted public interest due to its numerous applications in science and innovation: biotechnology, health, bioprospecting, pharmaceuticals, medicinal plants, agriculture, food preparation, mathematics, natural resource management, climate change and astronomy.

There are many niche players in the field of indigenous knowledge in Namibia and many studies being carried out. Thus, although not all aspects of Namibia's indigenous knowledge are covered in this book, most readers from various walks of life – laypersons, scholars and policy makers – will find this book a very useful companion. The content of this book serves as a good starting point, because 'we cannot go further into the future without looking deeper into the past' (anonymous).

Through their laboratory and scientific studies, the authors of this book serve as guides through the journey to discover and record the indigenous knowledge of Namibian society. More importantly, their individual and collective works endeavour to add value to Namibia's indigenous knowledge. The voyage and value addition are aimed at bringing greater clarity to some of the most perplexing aspects of indigenous knowledge in Namibia.

Authors are aware that local communities need to benefit from their indigenous knowledge. That being said, the aim of this book is not to appropriate the indigenous knowledge of local communities, as most indigenous knowledge is already in the public domain. Rather, in line with Namibia's National Programme on Research, Science, Technology and Innovation (NPRSTI), the aim of this book is to 'ensure that indigenous knowledge is properly documented' (NCRST, 2014, p.14).

Many definitions and connotations of indigenous knowledge are provided in this book. However, it is important to note that indigenous knowledge is the foundation of Namibian society, an information base which facilitates communication and decision-making. It is dynamic, being continuously influenced by internal creativity, experimentation and external contacts. Moreover, indigenous knowledge is the cornerstone of many modern-day innovations in science and technology. It is also a ready and valuable resource for sustainable and resilient livelihoods.

A brief historical background and context to this book is imperative. The idea to write this book was conceived by Professor Kazhila C. Chinsembu in January 2012. A proposal was made to the Faculty of Science Academic Board meeting, University of Namibia (UNAM), which approved the book project. An invitation was later extended to research staff in UNAM's Multidisciplinary Research Centre (MRC) who agreed to collaborate with academics from the Faculty of Science. This book is therefore a joint collaborative effort of the Faculty of Science and MRC.

To operationalize the book project, book chapters were drawn from presentations made during the 2nd Symposium, Indigenous Knowledge Systems (IKS): From Concepts to Applications, organised from 8 to 9 October 2012, by IKST Food and Beverages Programme of the Science, Technology and Innovation Division of MRC. This was followed by a Book Writers' Workshop to assist potential authors to draft and develop their book chapters.

Briefly, the book is arranged in 17 chapters. The first six chapters are devoted to the indigenous knowledge of medicinal plants for treating HIV/AIDS-related symptoms and diseases, malaria, cancer, and other microbial infections of humans and livestock. These are followed by chapters 7–10 which are assigned to indigenous foods, and chapters 11–13 that espouse the indigenous knowledge used to cope with human–wildlife conflicts and floods, as well as that which underpins the nexus of gender, climate change and management of natural resources.

Chapter 14 unravels the indigenous knowledge of the Mafwe ethnic group. Chapter 15 speaks to the challenges of harmonising modern education with that of the indigenous San people of Namibia. Chapter 16 urges a new rationalization of adolescent customary and initiation ceremonies in response to the HIV/AIDS pandemic. Chapter 17 sums it all up, offering a compelling argument for universities and other institutions of higher learning to rise to the occasion and integrate indigenous knowledge into existing or new degree programmes.

In Chapter 1, Chinsembu unpacks the indigenous knowledge of plants used to manage HIV/AIDS. Since Namibia is a diamondiferous country, Chinsembu introduces the term 'green diamonds' to refer to all the medicinal plants used in the management of HIV/AIDS in Namibia. Chinsembu agrees that while Namibia has made remarkable progress in the provision of antiretroviral therapy (ART) to HIV/AIDS patients, the country's ART programme is threatened by diminishing financial resources.

Given this shortcoming, there is reason to evaluate elements of traditional medicine, particularly medicinal plants and other natural products, that can yield effective and affordable therapeutic agents for conditions related to HIV/AIDS. Unfortunately, knowledge of ethnomedicines for HIV/AIDS is still vague and not well documented. Besides the problem of documentation, laws and administrative structures, public trust, and the lack of recognition of traditional healers continue to hamper the integration of traditional medicines within modern ART programmes. So, in Chapter 1, Chinsembu describes a contextual model for initiating collaboration with traditional healers as well as the repertoire of putative anti-HIV plants whose chemical constituents are being evaluated for possible development into novel antiretroviral drugs for AIDS.

Chapter 1 is part of a fresh corpus of scholarly works that draws on new empirical evidence about the medicinal efficacy of plants against HIV infection. This work overthrows the long-standing notion held by the medical and pharmaceutical fraternities that the crude aqueous extracts of medicinal plants, as used by traditional healers, are ineffective against HIV. Yet, most importantly, the antimicrobial and anti-HIV ethnobotanical data suggest an opportunity for inventing new drugs from Namibian flora.

Chapter 2, by Du Preez, Nafuka, Mumbengegwi and Bock, is on the indigenous knowledge of medicinal plants used to treat symptoms of malaria. Although malaria is on the decline in Namibia and the country is moving towards elimination of the disease by 2020, the authors contend that local communities continue to use traditional medicines to manage the disease. Ethnomedicinal plants are used to treat malaria-like symptoms in regions where the disease is endemic.

The authors are careful to state that it is premature to conclude that herbal medicines can be used as effective antimalarials, for several reasons. Most of the literature on medicinal plant remedies in Namibia lacks detail and specificity, including locality, abundance and plant parts used; mode of preparation, dosage and period of treatment; and the active components present in plants. In this chapter, the authors present data from investigations on antiplasmodial properties of selected Namibian plants. The authors conclude that the presence of compounds with antiplasmodial action strongly supports the traditional use of the plants for managing malaria symptoms.

The authors of Chapter 3, Dushimemaria, Mumbengegwi and Bock, detail the different plants used by ethnic groups in Namibia as medicinal remedies for alleviation of cancer symptoms. The authors present results on the phytochemical screening of local plant materials for anticancer properties. The presence of antiprotease activities and phytochemicals such as coumarins, anthraquinones, alkaloids, triterpenoids and flavonoids justifies the use of these medicinal plants in the management of cancer in Namibia and beyond.

Chapter 4 analyses the indigenous knowledge of medicinal plants used for the treatment of microbial infections. Mumbengegwi, du Preez, Dushimemaria, Auala and Nafuka, using phytochemical screening of extracts, show the presence of classes of compounds associated with antimicrobial activity against oral pathogens, enterobacteria, food-borne and other opportunistic pathogens.

Chapter 5 is about the exciting field of ethnoveterinary medicine (EVM). In this chapter, Chinsembu showcases the indigenous knowledge of plants used to treat livestock diseases. The rationale for EVM is simple. Small-scale and resource-poor livestock farmers cannot afford expensive synthetic pharmaceutical drugs. Therefore, they draw on their indigenous knowledge to unlock the power of EVM plants to treat animal diseases. However, there is no ethnoveterinary pharmacopeia and data on ethnoveterinary usage of plants are still sparse. In Chapter 5, ethnobotanical data from Namibia are briefly discussed within the prism of current knowledge of EVMs in selected African countries such as Botswana, Côte d'Ivoire, Ethiopia, Kenya, Nigeria, South Africa and Zambia.

Chapter 6 illustrates that indigenous knowledge is not just old-fashioned 'stuff' for the older folks. Kasanda and Kapenda, working with Junior High School learners in the Omusati and Oshana regions, show that high-school learners hold differing levels of knowledge on the use of traditional medicinal plants in curing common ailments and diseases. Female learners tend to be more knowledgeable of the traditional medicinal plants and their uses within their environment than male students. Interestingly, the majority of learners in this study are in favour of tuition on the use of traditional medicinal plants forming part of the science curriculum in Namibia. In retrospect, the authors also deduce that making the learners aware of the important use of medicinal plants will help preserve the plants for use by future generations.

In Chapter 7, Mushabati, Kahaka and Cheikhyoussef show that African leafy vegetables (ALVs) contain phytochemicals with medicinal value. Antimicrobial activities of the ALVs also confirm the urgent need to promote the consumption of ALVs as nutraceuticals, foods that provide medicinal or health benefits, including the prevention and treatment of diseases.

Heita and Cheikhyoussef in Chapter 8 delve into the indigenous knowledge of fermented milk products. The chapter focuses on three traditionally fermented milk products, namely *omashikwa*, *mabisi* and *mashini ghakushika* which are common in north-central and north-eastern Namibia. The authors isolate and identify key lactic acid bacteria (LAB), and analyse the physicochemical properties of the traditional milk products. Their results show the great potential in the microflora of these milk products, which can be used to control the fermentation process and thus extend the shelf life of most traditionally fermented milk products in Namibia.

Chapter 9 is about *oshikundu*, an indigenous, non-alcoholic fermented beverage. Here, the authors Embashu, Cheikhyoussef and Kahaka report on the physicochemical and nutrient content of this indigenous beverage. The importance of this research is to provide fresh insights into the possibility of extending the shelf life of *oshikundu*.

Whenever you need an indigenous food delicacy from Namibia, consider eating the African bullfrog. In Chapter 10, Okeyo, Kandjengo and Kashea appeal to our appetites. The authors dissect the indigenous knowledge surrounding the

Aawambo consumption of the giant African bullfrog *Pyxicephalus adspersus*, which besides being a source of food, has medicinal uses as well. They also mention the indigenous practices for the treatment of *oshiketaketa* infections. Various folklore beliefs, observations by local people on the propagation of the frogs, and future multidisciplinary research recommendations are presented.

Indigenous knowledge shapes our coping and response strategies. Chapter 11 weaves together the indigenous knowledge used in the management of human–wildlife conflicts along the borders of an important national park in Namibia. Lendelvo, Angula and Mfune report findings of a study which investigated how both commercial and communal area farmers living around Etosha National Park use their indigenous knowledge in dealing with human–wildlife conflicts. The study revealed that farmers are aware of problem animals and identify them through their spoor, calls and behaviour. The authors conclude that the indigenous knowledge of farmers in the vicinity of Etosha National Park has shaped local human–wildlife conflict management responses.

Coping with floods can be a daunting task. Understanding the indigenous coping strategies of the Basubiya people on the flooded plains of the Zambezi River is an even more daunting task. But, in Chapter 12, Mbukusa helps readers to understand how the Basubiya people know the scale of the floods that surround them, what makes them enjoy the time of flooding, how they cope during the floods, and whether they will ever move from the floodplains to higher grounds. The author asserts the need for government policy makers and disaster management agencies to understand the indigenous knowledge and coping skills of the Basubiya in order to improve future flood management operations.

Chapter 13 provides a lens through which we can view and bring into sharp focus the gender–climate-change nexus. The authors, Siyambango, Kanyimba and Mufune (now deceased, may his soul rest in peace), examine the significance of indigenous knowledge, highlight some areas of climate-change vulnerability and resilience in which indigenous knowledge is relevant, and suggest a mechanism to make it explicit in rural Namibia. The chapter is largely conceptual or even contextual as it examines issues of climate change especially impacting girls and women in rural Namibia. The authors use several examples to interrogate a gendered approach in coping with climate-change-induced environmental and natural resources management issues such as drought, fetching water and firewood, subsistence livestock and crop agro-ecosystems, and the use of scarce medicinal plant resources to survive the threats of water- and vector-borne diseases.

In Chapter 14, Lilemba and Matemba, on reclaiming indigenous knowledge in Namibia's post-colonial curriculum, use the Mafwe people as a case study. The authors argue that during Namibia's colonization by Germany and South Africa, missionaries and colonial powers regarded the indigenous system of education as barbaric and an obstacle to the spread of Christianity and Western culture. Yet, before the advent of Eurocentric education, African communities used their indigenous knowledge-based education systems to survive many odds. Nowadays, scholars on indigenous knowledge are using systematic enquiry about indigenous philosophical ideas and issues that frame contemporary indigenous thought, perspective, and worldview. The authors suggest that African riddles, folklores and proverbs can be used to impart knowledge and skills to younger generations as this is compatible with modern western education. They urge that Namibian school curricula should also include indigenous knowledge to enhance learning and teaching.

Chapter 15 examines the case of the San people of Namibia. In this chapter, Mashego-Brown and Haihambo confront the developmental issues facing the San of Namibia. While the authors provide a hint of the 'pot-holed' road to de-marginalization and formal education, they also admit the San do and will generally remain poor because their children do not attend school to a satisfactory level – a warning sign that the San will remain inferior to other ethnic groups who use education as a pathway to poverty alleviation. The chapter reveals that amongst the San culture is inclusive in nature and those affected by HIV are accepted.

Mashego-Brown and Haihambo find the San of Namibia to be at a crossroads because amongst these indigenous people, some want to maintain their indigenous culture and indigenous education. They also want to maintain their indigenous health practices and direct dependency on the immediate environment for survival. But, ironically, another section wants to move with the times, to leave their indigenous culture behind, and to retain only part-time cultural practices compatible with modern education and practices.

In Chapter 16, Haihambo explores the messages communicated to adolescents and young adults during traditional initiation ceremonies and premarital counselling in Namibia. The main aim is to determine the degree to which such messages are adapted to national HIV/AIDS response strategies. Using research studies on the Aawambo, Ovaherero, Ovahimba and Damara ethnic groups, the author takes an ethnocentric walk and revisits the indigenous 'curricula' used by the various ethnic groups to advise adolescents on how to lead adult lives in a particular cultural context. As she found out, it would seem that because such curricula have been transmitted from generation to generation, the curricula are still so rigid that they exclude new developments such as HIV/AIDS, not to mention gender equality. The author recommends that traditional practices should evolve with the times and should therefore incorporate HIV content in their indigenous life skills and counselling programmes.

Finally, Chapter 17 urges the integration of indigenous knowledge into university studies. The authors, Grace Chinsembu and Miriam Hamunyela, investigate the perceptions of lecturers towards integrating indigenous knowledge into the university curriculum, showing that most lecturers support the concept. However, the challenges of integrating it into the curriculum include the following: unskilled person-power, lack of documentation, the non-scientific nature of indigenous knowledge, and different cultural backgrounds of students and lecturers. Despite these shortcomings, and given the strong paradigm shift to indigenous knowledge, the authors urge the University of Namibia either to integrate it into existing curricula or to implement new indigenous knowledge degree programmes and courses.

Indigenous Knowledge of Namibia is an important book that rekindles our interest in documenting indigenous knowledge because the libraries of this tacit knowledge are usually older people who are not part of educational establishments. As efforts are being made to mainstream indigenous knowledge into formal education, there is a need to document available indigenous knowledge in order to ensure its effective instruction, learning and preservation. This book is a modest effort to document Namibia's indigenous knowledge in a single corpus.

In conclusion, the editorial team thanks all the indigenous knowledge holders, the man and woman in the village, without whom this book would still be a figment of our imaginations. Be that as it may, the opinions and interpretations expressed in various chapters of the book are those of the respective authors, and not of the chief editor, assistant editors or the institutions they represent. Many thanks for reading *Indigenous Knowledge of Namibia*.

Reference

NCRST [National Commission for Research, Science and Technology]. (2014). *The National Programme on Research, Science, Technology and Innovation (NPRSTI)* 2014/15 to 2016/17. Windhoek: Author.

1

Bioprospecting for 'green diamonds': Medicinal plants used in the management of HIV/AIDS-related conditions

Kazhila C. Chinsembu

I believe that while scientific research is necessary to improve the way in which our natural resources are exploited ... our people must not be completely disowned ... of resources that they have possessed for generations. It will be a sad day when the medicinal formulas of devil's claw are patented by big pharmaceutical companies and thereby become depleted and unavailable to the natural owners of the resource. (His Excellency Dr Sam Nujoma, Founding President of Namibia at a symposium on devil's claw, as reported by Wickham, 2001.)

INTRODUCTION

Namibia first described four cases of acquired immunodeficiency syndrome (AIDS) from infection by human immunodeficiency virus (HIV) in 1986 (GRN, 2002). Since then, many Namibians have continued to witness the multi-faceted impacts of HIV/AIDS in their households and neighbourhoods. By 2002, AIDS was the 'number one' killer, accounting for almost 51% of all deaths (GRN, 2002). In 2014, the overall prevalence of HIV in Namibia was 16.9% (GRN, 2014). In order to win the battle against the devastating effects of HIV/AIDS, some Namibians are turning to indigenous knowledge on two fronts: to use it to foster local understanding of HIV infection and AIDS-related symptoms, and in the use of medicinal plants to manage opportunistic infections related to AIDS. In many parts of Namibia, indigenous knowledge is now the cornerstone of resilient households and communities that continue to defy the impacts and shocks of HIV/AIDS.

This chapter is a modest attempt to showcase local knowledge of plant remedies used for managing HIV-related diseases and symptoms in Namibia. To help put it in perspective, the chapter first describes the HIV/AIDS scenario in Namibia, which includes the indigenous names and terms related to HIV infection and AIDS, and describes the challenges facing antiretroviral therapy (ART). It then goes on to examine the prospects for using ethnomedicines in Namibia and the processes for initiating collaboration with traditional healers. Finally, the chapter focuses on ethnobotanical surveys of plants used to treat the symptoms and opportunistic infections related to HIV/AIDS in Zambezi (formerly Caprivi) and Ohangwena regions of Namibia. This chapter is an extension of the rich vein of publications based on previous fieldwork in north-eastern Namibia.

HIV/AIDS SCENARIO IN NAMIBIA

Namibia has a generalized HIV/AIDS epidemic. By 2001, there were about 230,000 people between the ages of 15 and 49 living with HIV/AIDS – out of Namibia's small population of 2.1 million people at that time (GRN, 2002). By the year 2008, the number of people infected with HIV was 204,000; 14,000 new HIV infections were diagnosed during that year alone, giving a rate of 38 new diagnoses per day (GRN, 2008a). The national HIV prevalence rate increased from 17.8% in 2009 to 18.8% in 2010 (GRN, 2010). HIV/AIDS accounted for almost half of all adult deaths in 2006, and caused life expectancy (at birth) to decrease from 62 years in 1996 to 44 years in 2006 (Family Health International, 2007). Geographically, the prevalence of HIV/AIDS is higher in north-eastern (more than 25%) than southern (4%) Namibia.

By 2014, the average national HIV prevalence rate among pregnant women attending antenatal clinics was 16.9% (GRN, 2014); this was a slight reduction from the national average of 18.2% in 2012 (GRN, 2012). A diagram showing the average national HIV infection rates among pregnant women attending antenatal clinics from 1992 to 2012 is shown in Figure 1.1.

A confluence of geopolitical, biological, socio-economic, behavioural and cultural factors drives the HIV epidemic in the Zambezi Region. Katima Mulilo is a major hub that links five countries: Angola, Botswana, Namibia, Zambia and Zimbabwe. The Trans-Caprivi Highway passes through Katima Mulilo, bringing heavy traffic to and from these countries in southern Africa. Truckers, merchants and migrant workers are serviced by a booming commercial sex industry at this border town (GRN, 2008b).

Other factors that have silently conspired to fuel the HIV/AIDS epidemic in Katima Mulilo are: low frequency of circumcision, high levels of poverty, low levels

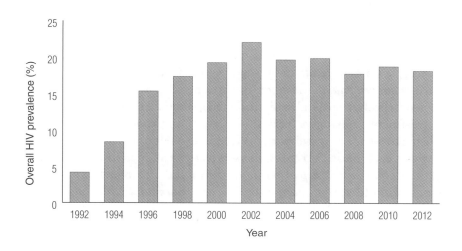

FIGURE 1.1: HIV infection rates of pregnant women attending antenatal clinics. Adapted from GRN, 2012.

of condom use, early sexual debut, multiple sexual partners, and a strong belief in witchcraft (GRN, 2008b; Chinsembu, 2009).

Many traditional healers work as diviners and sorcerers conducting diagnostic and healing rituals using beads known as the *ndaula*. The Lozi people of Zambezi Region have very strong beliefs in the use and effectiveness of herbal remedies. Furthermore, most inhabitants of Zambezi Region think that HIV/AIDS is spread through *mulaleka*, a witchcraft practice believed to force someone to have sex with another person without any physical contact (Chinsembu, 2009). Such beliefs detract from HIV/AIDS prevention and treatment and are used as an excuse for high HIV infections in Katima.

Local Namibian names for HIV infection and AIDS

In the Zambezi Region, the region hardest hit by the AIDS pandemic in Namibia, HIV-infected persons are referred to as 'prostitutes'. People often use the phrase *butuku bwa sihule* meaning 'disease for prostitutes' and the words *mbushahi, ndarabangwa* and *buhure*, which connote a person is promiscuous (Chinsembu, Shimwooshili-Shaimemanya, Kasanda, & Zealand, 2011). The AIDS condition is also called *kibutu bwa masapo* (bone disease), *simbandembande* (fish eagle), *mamuingelele* (disease that takes everything or everyone), *mashinya bomu* (disease that destroys without mercy) and *mapilelo* (place where people are saved).

In northern Namibia, Chinsembu et al. (2011) documented that the Aawambo are shrewd when it comes to talking about HIV/AIDS. Many people call AIDS 'four letters', *ekiya* (thorn), *katanga kamufifi* (hot ball), *owayapa* (HIV-infected), *ekululume* (denoting that one is a 'real man' if they are infected), *tondo* (testes), *omudimba* (corpse) and *okapendi* (underwear). Other Oshiwambo terminologies are: *ombuto* (virus), *omuntu talumbu nombuto* (infected person), *okuyina* (already infected), *okwayapa* (somebody that is already infected), *omukwati gwepango* (somebody receiving treatment), *shinangele* (very thin person) and *kaavulika* (somebody who does not listen to advice or is stubborn). AIDS is also referred to as: *osuvi, obustanga* or *odjou* (which each mean AIDS), *oshimbebe* (very weak), *oshinkapa* (very weak or disabled), *aantu mboka yeli kepango* (on antiretroviral treatment), *idisa* (disease), *omukithi* or *kakithi* (disease), *masipa* (bones) and *kuundanda une* (of four letters, AIDS) (Chinsembu et al., 2011).

These cultural references to HIV and AIDS are shared and communicated to promote individual and societal adjustment to the epidemic. The slang and derogatory appellations to HIV/AIDS also show that the local connotations are dynamic and subject to continuous modification in response to the changing epidemic. At the same time, derogatory names reflect the social stigma related to the syndrome.
Lay people recognise HIV/AIDS through certain symptoms. Typical symptoms of HIV/AIDS are herpes zoster, oral candidiasis, eczema, sexually transmitted infections, skin rashes, malaria, headaches, tuberculosis, weight loss, flu, fever, diarrhoea, coughing and swollen glands. Non-typical symptoms of HIV/AIDS are red lips, impaired vision, red eyes, big head, small pox, stress, unfriendliness, painful joints, change in body colour, stiff neck, high blood pressure, dizziness and loss of hair (Chinsembu et al., 2011).

Challenges facing antiretroviral therapy in Namibia

In 2006, the United Nations High-Level Meeting on HIV/AIDS in New York hailed Namibia's AIDS treatment programme as the best in southern Africa (GRN, 2009). At the end of August 2009, there were approximately 70,000 Namibians on antiretroviral treatment (ART) (Chinsembu, 2009), but this number was expected to escalate to 122,300 by 2014 (GRN, 2009). The projection was a slight underestimate. The United States of America President's Emergency Plan for AIDS Relief (PEPFAR) assisted the Namibian Government in treating 126,779 HIV-positive people in 2013 (PEPFAR, n.d.). During the 2008/09 financial year, the total cost of ART in Namibia was NAD148 million (approximately USD14.7 million, at the 2009 exchange rate) (GRN, 2009). The Global Fund and the United States Centers for Disease Control and Prevention (CDC) financed 68% of this cost through donations; the Namibian Government subsidised 23% of the cost; the Clinton Foundation, 8%; and Supply Chain Management Systems contributed the remaining 1% (GRN, 2009). Through PEPFAR, Namibia has received over US$800 million for HIV/AIDS activities since its inception in 2004 (PEPFAR, n.d.).

Although Namibia has made remarkable progress in the provision of ART to those in need, the country's antiretroviral programme is like a candle in the wind as it battles to glimmer against the inevitable possibility of dying from another form of AIDS, 'acquired income deficiency syndrome' (Chinsembu, 2009). I have genuine concerns that Namibia's free, public-sector ART programme is not sustainable due to its heavy reliance on donor funds. Besides funding, access to ART in Namibia is challenged by low levels of human and infrastructural resources required to provide services particularly in the pre-ART and ART clinics (GRN, 2009). Specifically, more trained professionals are needed to provide pharmaceutical services, as well as doctors, clinical officers and nurses in hospitals, health centres and clinics. Health facilities that provide ART services also need to be renovated in order to adequately accommodate patients. Furthermore, Namibia's sparsely distributed population requires a fully decentralized and community-based model supported by strong policies and leadership from the central level to provide full ART services to the rural population.

Insufficient numbers of skilled technical personnel and limited managerial capacity at all levels (McCourt & Awases, 2007) have impaired the challenges of decentralization, and access to services remains a herculean obstacle for those living in sparsely populated areas. As a country with one of the highest Gini coefficients and levels of income disparity in the world (UNDP, 2000), Namibia's household poverty and nutrition scenarios also pose major questions to ART access, adherence and success.

Clinically, ART is still associated with acute side effects, which now cause new forms of stigma. For example, ART has been associated with liver burnout and the development of lipodystrophy, which is characterized by peripheral fat loss (lipoatrophy) and central fat accumulation. This may result in emaciated and sunken facial pads, skinny arms and legs, pot-bellies and 'buffalo humps', leaving patients inviting serious stigma (Lindegaard, Keller, Bruunsgaard, & Pedersen, 2004). Thus, while hailing antiretroviral drugs as critically important in prolonging and improving the quality of the lives of HIV/AIDS patients, current drug protocols still have many challenges, including resistance, toxicity, limited availability, and lack of any curative effect, as ARVs do not eliminate HIV from the body (Vermani & Garg, 2002). It goes without saying that limitations of conventional ART continue to promote the use of ethnomedicines for the management of HIV/AIDS in Namibia.

PROSPECTS FOR THE USE OF ETHNOMEDICINES TO MANAGE AIDS

Most HIV/AIDS-infected persons that need treatment can access ART from local hospitals and health centres, but several constraints of the ART programme compel many HIV-infected Namibians to use herbal plants to manage HIV/AIDS-related opportunistic infections (Chinsembu, 2009). Others use herbal plants to offset side effects of ART. While the use of ethnomedicines to manage HIV/AIDS is gaining public interest in Namibia, harmonization with official HIV/AIDS policy remains a sensitive and contentious issue. It is sensitive because traditional medicines can easily become a scapegoat for denial and inertia to make ART more accessible, as was the scenario during former President Thabo Mbeki's period in office in South Africa. The use of ethnomedicines to manage HIV/AIDS is contentious because in many resource-poor settings in sub-Saharan Africa, government-sponsored ART programmes discourage the use of traditional medicines, fearing that the efficacy of antiretroviral drugs may be inhibited by traditional medicines, or that their interactions could lead to toxicity (Hardon et al., 2008). Reliance on traditional medicines could also lead to a discontinuation of ART (Langlois-Klassen, Kipp, Jhangri, & Rubaale, 2007). Accordingly, Chinsembu (2009) concluded that many African governments, including Namibia, still have contradictory attitudes towards traditional medicines for the management of AIDS, discouraging it within their ART programmes, and supporting it within their initiatives of public health and primary healthcare.

Despite this grey area in ART and public health policies, the World Health Organization (WHO) recommends that traditional healers be included in national responses to HIV/AIDS (Homsy et al., 2004). As early as 1989, WHO had already stated in a memorandum the need to evaluate ethnomedicines for the management of HIV/AIDS: 'In this context, there is need to evaluate those elements of traditional medicine, particularly medicinal plants and other natural products, that might yield effective and affordable therapeutic agents. This will require a systematic approach.' (WHO, 1989).

The significance of investing in the value-addition and high growth sectors of biotechnology and ethnophytomedicines is also articulated by the African Biosciences Initiative (African Biosciences Initiative, 2005) and in the founding document of the New Partnership for Africa's Development, NEPAD (NEPAD, 2001). These documents commit to the principle of shifting gears and powering the African continent from 'farmer' to 'pharma'. To politically promote this commitment on the continent, the Organization of African Unity (now the African Union) heads of state declared the period 2000–2010 as the Decade of African Traditional Medicine. The Director General of the WHO consequently declared 31 August as African Traditional Medicine Day (Homsy et al., 2004). Further to these declarations, the Eastern and Southern Africa Regional Initiative on Traditional Medicine and

AIDS convened a consultative meeting in May 2003. All these efforts demonstrate the need to mainstream and institutionalize traditional medicine into the formal healthcare delivery system.

Collaboration with traditional healers

Puckree, Mkhize, Mgobhozi and Lin (2002) urged healthcare professionals to be proactive in integrating traditional healing with 'western' medicines in order to promote health for all. Although there are a good number of reports on traditional uses of plants to treat various illnesses, Chinsembu and Mutirua (2008) bemoaned that knowledge of ethnomedications for HIV/AIDS was not well documented. Two other barriers also continue to hamper the integration of traditional medicines with modern conventional medicines. The first is that traditional remedies have neither been rigorously validated nor properly standardized. They are also poorly prepared, packaged and preserved. These drawbacks limit the use of traditional medicines for the treatment of HIV/AIDS (Kayombo et al., 2007). The second obstacle relates to the collaboration between traditional healers and biomedical scientists and how it can be initiated, operationalized and sustained. Here, the concern is how to initiate collaboration between two healthcare systems that differ in the theory of the cause and management of the disease (Kayombo et al., 2007).

In spite of the above-mentioned dilemma, collaboration is essential given the changing HIV epidemic and the dynamic relationship between the two health sectors (Mills et al., 2006). Experts recommend that healthcare providers should open channels of collaboration with traditional healers (Banda et al., 2007; GRZ, 2008). However, initiating collaboration – and sustaining it – is not as easy as academic literature suggests. Traditional healers are often secretive, cagey and suspicious of biomedical scientists. They are also reluctant to engage with scientists for fear of losing their trade secrets. In fact, if collaboration between traditional healers and biomedical scientists is to become meaningful, systematic and careful steps should be followed (Kayombo et al., 2007; Chinsembu, 2009).

Many Namibian traditional healers are living repositories and reservoirs of knowledge on indigenous plants and their properties for treating opportunistic AIDS-related infections. Other traditional healers, however, are charlatans. Collaboration with these genuine traditional healers should be open and carefully and individually determined. Given some benefit of the doubt, Namibian traditional healers present possible leads for the identification of novel anti-HIV active compounds.

Despite the potential to isolate new anti-HIV agents from Namibian medicinal plants, there is little engagement of traditional healers by the scientific community. As a result of this collaborative vacuum, bioprospecting for ethnomedicinal plants with anti-HIV compounds is difficult, and many traditional medicines used by healers to treat HIV/AIDS-related opportunistic infections are not scientifically validated.

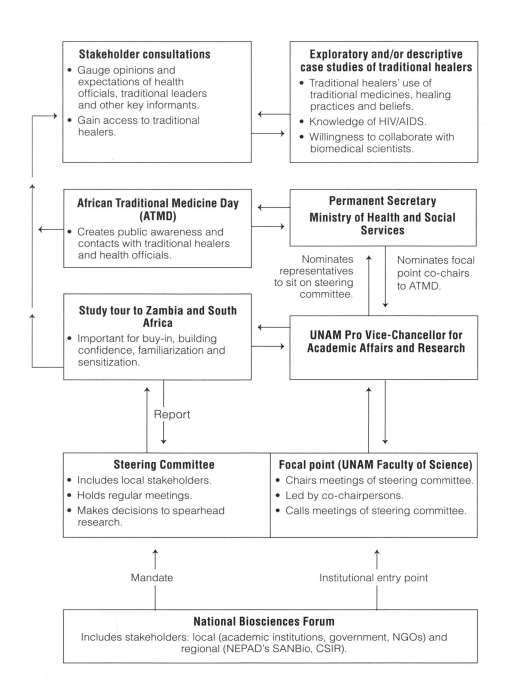

FIGURE 1.2: The five-stage contextual model used to initiate collaboration with traditional healers in Namibia. (Reproduced from Chinsembu, 2009.)

NEPAD's Southern Africa Network for Biosciences (SANBio) has launched a flagship project to validate traditional medicines for the affordable treatment of HIV/AIDS. Under this initiative, they are working with a traditional healer from Zambia (Dr Ludwig Sondashi), scientists from the Council for Scientific and Industrial Research (CSIR) in Pretoria (South Africa), and scientists and officials from Zambia to validate the Sondashi formula (SF-2000), a four-plant powder that is used to manage AIDS.

The collaborative framework between the various players in this initiative was documented by Chinsembu (2009), where he also described a model for the Namibian situation, as summarised below.

A model for collaboration with traditional healers in Namibia

Chinsembu (2009) described a model of collaboration between Namibian traditional healers and scientists at the University of Namibia (UNAM) so that local plants and ethnomedicines containing anti-HIV compounds can be identified and subjected to scientific validation.

Five main institutions or actions are used to initiate collaboration, namely: (1) the National Biosciences Forum (NBF); 2) a multi-stakeholder steering committee with UNAM as the focal point; (3) a study tour to institutions in Zambia and South Africa where validation of traditional medicines for HIV/AIDS was being undertaken; (4) commemoration of African Traditional Medicine Day; and (5) consultations with various stakeholders in the project area. A diagram of this model is shown in Figure 1.2.

National Biosciences Forum

The NBF of local and regional stakeholders established a multi-stakeholder steering committee mandated to guide research towards the validation of traditional medicines for the treatment of HIV/AIDS-related opportunistic infections in Namibia with UNAM's Faculty of Science as the focal point of the steering committee.

Steering committee and UNAM focal point

The following organizations are represented on the steering committee: the Centre for Research Information Action in Africa Southern African Development and Consulting (CRIAA SA-DC); the Health Professions Councils of Namibia; the Ministry of Agriculture, Water and Forestry (Directorates of Research and Forestry, as well as the National Botanical Research Institute (NBRI), and the Indigenous Plant Task Team (IPTT); the Ministry of Education; the Ministry of Health and Social Services; the Namibia Chamber of Commerce and Industry; the Namibia Network of AIDS Service Organizations (NANASO); the Namibia Traditional

Healers Association; the Regional Agricultural and Environment Initiatives Network-Africa (RAEIN-Africa); the Polytechnic of Namibia; and UNAM. The role of UNAM as the focal point is to call and chair steering committee meetings.

Steering committee meetings help to identify and gauge stakeholder expectations and concerns. For example, some members of the steering committee are against the idea of setting up a national pharmacopoeia of plants used to treat HIV/AIDS and related opportunistic infections. They are also sceptical of UNAM's links with NEPAD's SANBio and the CSIR. This scepticism is often centred on the controversial issues of biopiracy, intellectual property rights and benefit sharing. To clarify the situation, a study tour to Zambia and South Africa was undertaken to find out how the two countries had dealt with these sensitive issues.

Study tour to Zambia and South Africa

For a long time, many traditional healers in Zambia claimed 'cures' for HIV/AIDS. However, these claims had not been subjected to scientific validation. In November 2005, a five-month clinical trial to validate traditional medicines used to treat HIV/AIDS was started in Lusaka by the Ministry of Health. The objective of the trial was to evaluate for efficacy of the formulations, and to identify changes in the physical and clinical status of HIV-positive volunteers.

Three herbal formulations – Sondashi, Mayeyanini and Mailasine – were tested in 12, 11 and 9 HIV-positive adult volunteers, respectively. It was not known whether the volunteers had previously been on conventional ART. Their CD4 counts were determined at the onset of the trial and then at later dates. The formulations were also tested for any enhancements with conventional antiretroviral drugs. The trial ended in April 2006.

According to Dr Patrick Chikusu, principal investigator of the study, the results of that trial showed that all three formulations had promising anti-HIV activity. Patients' CD4 counts increased and their viral loads decreased somewhat during the course of the trial, although these differences were not found to be statistically significant by the University of Zambia's School of Medicine. In spite of this, the Sondashi formula was found to be the most-promising formulation for further testing (Chinsembu, 2009).

Sondashi, a former government minister and constitutional lawyer with a PhD, created the Sondashi herbal formula. He first used it to treat his sick son (Chinsembu, 2009). At that time, Dr Sondashi tried several herbal formulas, but his son died. He then created the four-plant powder, which he used to treat relatives with HIV/AIDS. He found that the powder was effective against HIV/AIDS-related opportunistic infections. He now uses this powder to treat hundreds of AIDS patients at his clinic in Lusaka. Patients take the Sondashi powder four times a day by dissolving it in a glass of cold water. In August 2008, a bottle of herbal powder cost ZMW160,000 (equivalent to NAD380.95, at that time); a patient needs four bottles of the medication per month.

Following the promising results of the trial in Lusaka, NEPAD's SANBio put the Sondashi herbal formulation through further testing to validate it. Laboratory tests conducted at the CSIR laboratories in Pretoria, South Africa, and in Switzerland, found SF-2000 to be efficacious against HIV. A pill using the four-plant formula has been produced, which will go into the first phase of clinical trials in Zambia in the near future (Chinsembu, 2009).

Collaboration between the South African and Zambian stakeholders led to the formation of a consortium, which has provided a smart example for the collaboration of traditional healers and scientists in Namibia. Of particular interest is that the CSIR has legal frameworks that guide their collaboration with the holders of indigenous knowledge and traditional healers, including heads of agreements with clauses on commercialization and benefit sharing, publications, patents, and the formation of databases. In South Africa, for example, the government issues a bioprospecting permit only when a benefit-sharing agreement is in place. Such benefits are usually given to communities, led by trust committees formed by traditional healers. CSIR enters into agreements with trust committees, or with individual traditional healers. The principle of prior informed consent is also followed (Chinsembu, 2009).

During bioprospecting, traditional healers are provided with a budget to help cover costs incurred during plant collection. These monies do not constitute sale of plant materials, otherwise traditional healers would forego future benefits. Sample delivery notes are used whenever plant materials are handed over to the CSIR. According to CSIR collaborative frameworks, a patent is a publication, and traditional healers are not part of the patent (Chinsembu, 2009). Traditional healers are, however, entitled to benefits before patenting.

Validation of the Sondashi formula at the CSIR brought a special challenge because the collaborative process involves stakeholders from another country, Zambia. The process is also complicated by the trans-boundary shipment of plant materials. A different model of collaboration has therefore been used to circumvent these challenges, which involves a consortium of institutional stakeholders, managed by a steering committee, including a lawyer.

The consortium enters into various agreements, such as a consortium agreement encompassing all stakeholders, a memorandum of agreement with the individual traditional healer, and a material transfer agreement with the Zambian Government.

Information regarding the modalities of collaboration between South Africa and Zambia, in general, and CSIR, NEPAD's SANBio and Dr Sondashi, in particular, helped enrich the understanding of Namibia's representatives of the requirements to develop a framework for collaboration in Namibia.

African Traditional Medicine Day

Commemoration of the sixth African Traditional Medicine Day in August 2008 was the first of its kind in Namibia (Chinsembu, 2009). Meetings of the organizing committee were held at the headquarters of the Ministry of Health and Social Services in Windhoek. They provided an important forum for the chairperson of the steering committee (this author), other stakeholders and traditional healers to interact. The meetings also provided an opportunity to inform members of the organizing committee about UNAM's new mandate and initiative to validate traditional medicines for the treatment of HIV/AIDS in Namibia.

African Traditional Medicine Day helps to create public awareness of traditional medicines. Public awareness campaigns are conducted through television, radio, newspapers, exhibitions of traditional medicines, displays of publications on traditional medicines, and releases of press statements. Under the theme, 'the role of traditional health practitioners in primary healthcare', celebrations of this sixth commemorative day provided the public with a rare glimpse into the work of traditional healers. This way, many traditional healers also felt that they made an important contribution to public health.

Official commemorations were held in Windhoek, the capital city of Namibia, while those for the seventh African Traditional Medicine Day (August 2009) were held in Rundu, Kavango East Region. During the Rundu celebrations, traditional healers exhibited their ethnomedicines, and explained to the public the medicinal properties of the various plants. This author gave a keynote presentation in Rundu, which was televised by the national broadcasting corporation.

Stakeholder opinions of traditional healers in northern Namibia

Stakeholders in northern Namibia, such as health officials and traditional leaders, have 'mixed' opinions about traditional healers, in general, and validation of ethnomedicines used for HIV/AIDS treatment, in particular. Health officials such as the regional directors of health and primary healthcare administrators are negative about traditional healers. In the northern Namibian town of Oshakati, one primary healthcare official remarked: 'I do not trust these people.' However, 90% of the stakeholders are quite eager to work with UNAM to validate traditional healers' ethnomedicines because 'it is necessary to throw out the bad herbs and promote the good ones.' They are also keen to learn about the outcome of the scientific validation of the Sondashi formula from Zambia.

Community leaders such as headmen and regional health administrators are more positive about traditional healers in their communities. Thus, they form the best entry points to traditional healers willing to collaborate with UNAM scientists.

Challenges facing collaboration with traditional healers in Namibia

Frameworks of collaboration

King (2005) has reviewed the conceptual elements necessary to initiate collaboration between traditional healers and biomedical scientists in the management of HIV/AIDS in Africa. Following the efforts of King, several country-specific models of collaboration between biomedical and traditional health practitioners in the field of HIV/AIDS management have been articulated. Later, Kayombo et al. (2007) scrutinized King's (2005) conceptual elements of collaboration and examined their practical appropriateness in initiating collaboration in Tanzania.

Protocols for controlled clinical evaluation of traditional medicines for HIV/AIDS treatment have been known for many years (Chaudhury, 2001), yet such models do not adequately address the initial but critical stages of collaboration between biomedical scientists and traditional healers. Notably, the protocols pay more attention to clinical practice than the administrative structures required to precede the process of scientific validation.

The contextual model presented here describes distinct administrative structures and processes that address the unique challenges found at the interface between biomedical science and traditional medicine. This is important because the best practice models of the Joint United Nations Programme on HIV/AIDS (UNAIDS) emphasize that sensitivity to the political, environmental, cultural and economic contexts is crucial to the success of collaborative interventions (King, 2006).

Laws, administrative structures and public trust

Traditional medicine is an area of active research and public discourse. Lebeau (1998) studied the practice of traditional medicine in Namibia. However, as early as 1993, WHO had already tried to partner with traditional healers in the management of HIV/AIDS (Boadu, 1993). The Traditional Health Council of Namibia was established in March 1996, under the Allied Health Services Professions Act of 1993 (Act No. 20 of 1993). The council was mandated to register traditional healers in Namibia and instil professionalism in their practice.

In 2004, the Allied Health Services Professions Act of 1993 was replaced by the Allied Health Professions Act (Act No. 7 of 2004), and the Traditional Health Council was subsequently dissolved. A Traditional Healers Bill has since been proposed, but it is still under discussion and not yet enacted into law. The Bill provides for the establishment of the Traditional Health Practitioners Council of Namibia. These dynamics have left many Namibian traditional healers in a legal quagmire and lacuna. Needless to say that the practice of traditional medicine in Namibia now faces a crisis having a lack of official government and 'day-time' recognition while, as one traditional healer in Ogongo puts it, 'in the night, big men from Windhoek come to see me to get treatment for erectile dysfunction.'

In retrospect, it seems the dissolution of the Traditional Health Council of Namibia was not just a legal technicality or coincidence. For a long time, government has been concerned about traditional healers that claim to cure HIV/AIDS, yet have turned the AIDS epidemic into a cash cow. This unscrupulous practice has become known as 'AIDS opportunism' and 'AIDS entrepreneurship' (Richter, 2003).

The dissolution of the Traditional Health Council of Namibia was also caused by the loss of public confidence in traditional healers, especially after media reports that HIV-infected adults had sex with minors, ostensibly because they were instructed by their traditional healers that sex with virgins would cure HIV/AIDS (Ahmad, 2001). The same author wrote that the Namibian Government threatened to prosecute healers. Unscrupulous Namibian traditional healers thus turned the HIV/AIDS epidemic into a profitable enterprise as well as a moral minefield, tarnishing the public image of traditional medicine practice.

Since these developments have also brought stigma to genuine traditional healers, UNAM and other research institutions willing to initiate collaboration with traditional healers have to tread very carefully. Such careful collaboration will help ensure that future flashpoints of conflict between traditional healers and their biomedical counterparts are minimised. In South Africa, friction between biomedicine and ethnomedicine is largely due to two factors: firstly, biomedical scientists are frustrated with traditional healers who claim to cure HIV/AIDS and, secondly, traditional healers do not refer their HIV-positive clients to hospital before their immune systems have completely broken down (Richter, 2003).

In the same vein, traditional healers in Namibia discourage the access of HIV/AIDS patients to conventional antiretroviral drugs. Not surprisingly then, the work of traditional healers is seen as being counter-productive to policies for the provision of antiretroviral therapy and invites the conspicuous wrath of government officials and cooperating partners (Kamwi, Kenyon, & Newton, 2006). Against this backdrop, Namibian traditional healers treating HIV/AIDS-related conditions have become officially isolated, making it extremely difficult to initiate collaboration with scientists.

Chinsembu (2009) argued that the Traditional Health Council of Namibia was abolished for five reasons: (1) charlatan traditional healers that claim AIDS cures; (2) public outrage against traditional healers that encourage sex with minors or virgins as a cure for AIDS; (3) lack of referral of HIV/AIDS patients to hospitals; (4) potential friction with donors supporting conventional ART programmes; and (5) fears of non-compliance to conventional ART programmes. These five reasons form part of the obstacle in the way of initiating collaboration with traditional healers in Namibia.

Bioprospecting versus benefits: The devil is in the details

Namibia is the driest country south of the Sahara Desert and its ecosystems are fragile and susceptible to disturbance (Barnard & Shikongo, 2000). Consequently, it is not surprising that traditional communities and authorities are concerned about the management of the country's natural resources. Falk (2009) stated that Namibia's customary norms control access to resources, limit their extraction, regulate the technologies of resource use, and prescribe clear consequences for non-compliant behaviour.

The sustainable use of Namibia's biodiversity is also enshrined in the country's constitution. Article 95 of Namibia's Constitution states that:

> The state shall actively promote and maintain the welfare of the people by adapting policies aimed at … the maintenance of ecosystems, essential ecological processes and biological diversity of Namibia and utilization of living natural resources on a sustainable basis, for the benefit of all Namibians, both present and future. (Barnard & Shikongo, 2000.)

Although Namibia's economy is largely dependent on diamond mining, biodiversity and medicinal plants, in particular, are viewed as the country's 'green diamonds'. Consequently, the Namibian Government has instituted the National Biodiversity Programme, the IPTT and the Interim Bio-Prospecting Committee (IBPC), which are mandated by Cabinet to deal with matters relating to indigenous plants, indigenous knowledge, genetic resources, and access and benefit sharing (ABS). A Bill on ABS was drafted (du Plessis, 2007), but technical questions remain unanswered, and by 2014, the draft bill had not yet been passed into law.

Despite the lack of specific and enforceable legislation related to bioprospecting and ABS, the Namibian Government is aware of the value of the country's medicinal plants. This realization stems from the fact that trade in medicinal plants forms a 'hidden economy' that supports self-dependent plant gatherers, street vendors and healers, and the income-generating strategies of rural households (Reihling, 2008).

Namibia is also home to highly commercialized medicinal plants, such as devil's claw (*Harpagophytum procumbens*) but, as aptly expressed by Stewart and Cole (2005), the devil is in the details. By 1981, Namibia (then South West Africa, as it was called under South African apartheid administration), exported 200 tonnes of devil's claw per year. Exports of the plant tubers were estimated at 600 tonnes in 1998, and four years later, Namibia exported in excess of 1,000 tonnes per year. Ever since Namibian plants, such as devil's claw and *Hoodia* spp., entered the speculative marketplace of bio-capital, the country's political leadership has awakened to the potential of bioprospecting, scientific validation and commercialization of indigenous medicinal plants (Chinsembu, 2009).

Speaking at a symposium on devil's claw in 2001, Namibia's founding President, His Excellency Dr Sam Nujoma, said:

> I believe that while scientific research is necessary to improve the way in which our natural resources are exploited … our people must not be completely disowned … of resources that they have possessed for generations. It will be a sad day when the medicinal formulas of devil's claw are patented by big pharmaceutical companies and thereby become depleted and unavailable to the natural owners of the resource. (Wickham, 2001.)

Still, such noble statements have not insulated local plant gatherers from the exploitation of middlemen and foreign pharmaceutical companies.

Despite the end of apartheid in 1990 with Namibia's independence, rural gatherers of devil's claw do not meaningfully benefit from the lucrative bio-trade in this plant product, whose sales in Germany soared to EUR30 million in 2001 (equivalent to NAD250 million, at that time). Finkelberg, a German pharmaceutical company, patented a purified extract of devil's claw (Reihling, 2008), but as Namibia's founding president feared, the people of Namibia were not addressed through patent negotiations. Up to the time of writing this chapter, Namibia had still not benefited from the large commercial success of this drug in Germany, where it has become the third-most frequently used natural drug. It is shameful that a 50-g extract of devil's claw in tablet form fetches more than EUR25 overseas, but Namibian gatherers in Okakarara are paid a paltry 30–40 (Namibian) cents per kilogram of dried tubers, equivalent to EUR0.02–0.03, at 2014 exchange rates (Stewart & Cole, 2005).

The case of devil's claw demonstrates that Namibians have not meaningfully benefited from bioprospecting and commercialization of their medicinal plants. It is within this prism of economic dispossession that the entry point for research into traditional medicines in Namibia is confronted by moral and economic persuasions. Therefore, the scientific validation of traditional medicines should be initiated in a very responsible and transparent manner.

There is a looming danger that UNAM researchers may be seen to be mediating and colluding with the interests of foreign commercial entities and capital. To avoid such pitfalls, UNAM should tread carefully. It is therefore very important that UNAM strikes an understanding with capable authorizing institutions. In this respect, our collaborative model provides for transparent mechanisms and monitoring from key stakeholders in government ministries, watchdog institutions, such as IBPC and IPTT, academia and non-government organizations (NGOs). The role of NGOs is crucial to the success or failure of collaboration.

Recognition of traditional healers

In our contextual collaborative model, the fourth process involves celebrations of African Traditional Medicine Day. This process provides a strong link that helps to popularize the use of traditional medicines, as well as changing the public image of traditional healers. The commemorations allow interactions between government and WHO officials, traditional healers and the steering committee (Chinsembu, 2009). Commemorating this day is a sign that government is changing its negative attitude to traditional healers and could leverage pressure on Parliament to pass the bill on traditional medicines (Chinsembu, 2009). On the other hand, health officials are still very sceptical about traditional medicines. They only soften their hard stance when pressed by the knowledge that most pharmaceutical drugs are in fact derived from the indigenous knowledge of plants.

The distinction between herbalists and diviners has, however, become blurred. Many traditional healers are both herbalists and diviners, treating both the patient's physical and spiritual needs. With an incurable condition such as AIDS, the spiritual aspects of treatment are very important. Yet, to many health officials, it is the diviners that make the profession of traditional medicine look suspicious and bogus. This is especially so because, during the apartheid era, the work of diviners was prohibited under the Witchcraft Suppression Act of 1957 and the Witchcraft Suppression Amendment Act of 1970 (Chinsembu, 2009). This Act, formulated during the apartheid era, is currently still in force in Namibia, putting diviners at risk of arrest if they practise openly. As diviners have not only an ethnobiological role in relieving the symptoms of AIDS but also can offer spiritual counselling, the law needs to decriminalise their work.

Since traditional healers are the first point of call for many sick people in north-eastern Namibia, it is important that both traditional healers and conventionally trained health officials find common ground for collaboration (Chinsembu, 2009). Synergy between conventionally trained doctors and traditional healers would improve healthcare delivery in Namibia. In South Africa, traditional healers play a crucial role in strengthening and supporting national responses to HIV/AIDS. Indeed, many trained doctors now recognize traditional healers as potential allies in the fight against HIV/AIDS.

ETHNOBOTANICAL SURVEYS

Namibia has a rich diversity of plants and a long tradition of ethnomedicinal usage of plants. Overall, plant life in Namibia comprises 4,483 plant taxa, 63 orders, 195 families and 1,127 genera (Klaassen & Kwembeya, 2013).

Undoubtedly, this rich Namibian plant diversity presents a tremendous resource from which to tap traditional medicines, including for the treatment of HIV/AIDS.

The indigenous knowledge of medicinal plants, coupled with a history of safe use and ethnopharmacological efficacy, provides a fast approach to producing new drugs from novel plant-based anti-HIV agents. This new approach is known as 'reverse pharmacology' (Kaya, 2009). It is important for us to search for novel antiretroviral agents that can be added to or replace the current arsenal of drugs against HIV. We can only do this if genuine traditional healers and holders of indigenous knowledge are called upon to divulge the various plants used as ethnoremedies for treating HIV/AIDS-related infections.

Traditional healers in the Zambezi and Ohangwena regions of Namibia participated in surveys to identify the different plants used to manage HIV/AIDS-related conditions (Chinsembu & Hedimbi, 2010; Hedimbi & Chinsembu, 2012). Information about traditional healers working in the field of HIV/AIDS was first obtained from local government and community leaders, such as the regional HIV/AIDS coordinators, the chairpersons of local traditional healers' associations, and relevant regional and district hospital officers through snowball sampling. These officials also assisted with English–Lozi and English–Oshiwambo translations.

Once the objectives of the research had been explained to traditional healers, and other people knowledgeable on indigenous plants, consenting participants were engaged in semi-structured interviews. During the discussions, information on the local names of plants, and plant parts used to treat various opportunistic infections related to HIV/AIDS, were recorded. Traditional healers also guided field trips to collect plant specimens, which were later identified at UNAM.

Plants for managing HIV/AIDS-related conditions in Zambezi Region

In Katima Mulilo, Zambezi Region, a total of 72 plants from 28 families are used to treat AIDS-related illnesses. Some of the scientific names and families of these plants, together with the diseases that they treat, are listed in Table 1.1 (adapted from Chinsembu & Hedimbi, 2010). The most frequently cited medicinal plant families – in decreasing order – are Combretaceae, Anacardiaceae, Fabaceae and Ebenaceae. Most of the medications are made from the leaves of the plants, followed by bark and roots. Fruits and seeds are rarely mixed into herbal formulations.

Several traditional healers and people in Zambezi Region use herbal plants to treat AIDS-related conditions, such as herpes zoster (shingles), diarrhoea, tuberculosis, meningitis, fungal infections, including thrush caused by *Candida albicans*, malaria, skin rashes, vomiting and coughs. In Katima Mulilo, herpes zoster is generally treated with several plants, including *Aloe zebrina*, *Capparis tomentosa*, and *Syzygium guineense* (see Table 1.1 for details).

Diarrhoea is one of the most prevalent conditions during AIDS. Several different plant species used to manage diarrhoea in Katima Mulilo were documented (see Table 1.1 for details). Many plant species are also used to treat oral candidiasis in

TABLE 1.1. Plants used to treat HIV/AIDS-related conditions in Katima Mulilo, Zambezi Region

Family	Scientific name	siLozi name	Parts used	Disease conditions treated
Anacardiaceae	*Lannea schweinfurthii* (Engl.) Engl. var. *stublmanii* (Engl.) Kokwaro	rungomba	roots	herpes zoster, herpes simplex, cryptococcal meningitis, skin infections, tuberculosis, skin rashes, herpes zoster, herpes simplex, chronic diarrhoea
	Lannea zastrowiana Engl. & Brehmer	kangawa	leaves, roots	herpes zoster, herpes simplex, cryptococcal meningitis, skin infections, tuberculosis, skin rashes, herpes zoster, herpes simplex, chronic diarrhoea
	Sclerocarya birrea (A.Rich.) Hochst. subsp. *caffra* (Sond.) Kokwaro	mulula	root bark	candidiasis, diarrhoea
	Searsia tenuinervis (Engl.) Moffett	rungomba	bark	herpes zoster, herpes simplex, cryptococcal meningitis, skin infections, tuberculosis, skin rashes, herpes zoster, herpes simplex, chronic diarrhoea
Annonaceae	*Annona stenophylla* Engl. & Diels subsp. *nana* (Exell) N.Robson	malolo	roots	herpes zoster, cryptococcal meningitis, skin infections
	Xylopia L. spp.	situnduwanganga	roots	stomachache, flatulence, malaria
Asphodelaceae	*Aloe zebrina* Baker	chiforoforo	leaves	herpes zoster (shingles)
Bignoniaceae	*Kigelia africana* (Lam.) Benth.	mupolota	bark, fruit	herpes simplex, diarrhoea
Bombacaceae	*Adansonia digitata* L.	mubuyu	leaves, bark, roots	malaria, dysentery, diarrhoea
Burseraceae	*Commiphora africana* (A.Rich.) Engl. var. *africana*	mubobo	roots	swollen pancreas
Capparaceae	*Capparis tomentosa* Lam.	ntulwantulwa	roots	skin rashes, tuberculosis, cryptococcal meningitis, oral candidiasis, herpeszoster, herpes simplex, chronic diarrhoea
Chrysobalanaceae	*Parinari curatellifolia* Planch. ex Benth.	mubula	bark, roots	skin rashes, tuberculosis, chronic diarrhoea, herpes zoster, herpes simplex
Clusiaceae	*Garcinia livingstonei* T.Anderson	mukononga	bark, roots	tuberculosis, chronic diarrhoea, cryptococcal meningitis, herpes zoster, herpes simplex, skin rashes

continues

Table 1.1 continued

Family	Scientific name	siLozi name	Parts used	Disease conditions treated
Combretaceae	*Combretum collinum* Fresen. subsp. *ondongense* (Engl. & Diels) Okafor	muzwili	leaves	chronic diarrhoea
	Combretum platypetalum Welw. ex M.A.Lawson subsp. *platypetalum*	mububu	leaves	malaria, diarrhoea
	Terminalia sericea Burch. ex DC.	muhonono	leaves, bark, roots	tuberculosis, cryptococcal meningitis, tuberculosis, diarrhoea
Cucurbitaceae	*Cucumis africanus* L.f.	katende konnsa	roots	malaria
Dracaenaceae	*Sansevieria* Thunb. spp.	–	leaves	pain, inflammation
Ebenaceae	*Diospyros mespiliformis* Hochst. ex A.DC.	muchenje	bark, leaves	malaria
Euphorbiaceae	*Antidesma rufescens* Tul.	–	roots	tuberculosis, chronic diarrhoea, oral candidiasis
	Croton gratissimus Burch. var. *gratissimus*	mukena	bark	diarrhoea, lack of appetite, anaemia
Fabaceae	*Abrus precatorius* L. subsp. *africanus* Verdc.	isunde	leaves, roots, bark	oral candidiasis, ulcer boils
	Acacia erioloba E.Mey.	mukotokoto	bark	malaria
	Acacia erubescens Welw. ex Oliv.	mukotokoto	bark	malaria
	Acacia nigrescens Oliv.	mukotokoto	bark	malaria
	Albizia anthelmintica (A.Rich.) Brongn.	muhoto	leaves	stomachache
	Dalbergia melanoxylon Guill. & Perr.	mukelete	leaves	backache, joint aches
	Dichrostachys cinerea (L.) Wight & Arn.	museselele	bark, leaves	herpes zoster, oral candidiasis
	Guibourtia coleosperma (Benth.) J.Léonard	muzauli	bark	malaria
	Pterocarpus spp.	mulombe	leaves, stems	dysentery, diarrhoea

continues

Table 1.1 continued

Family	Scientific name	siLozi name	Parts used	Disease conditions treated
Malvaceae	*Hibiscus sabdariffa* L.	sindambi	leaves	chronic diarrhoea
Moraceae	*Ficus burkei* (Miq.) Miq.	mukwiyu	bark, roots, leaves	lack of appetite, malaria
Moringaceae	*Moringa ovalifolia* Dinter & A.Berger	moringa	leaves	vomiting, diarrhoea
Myrtaceae	*Psidium guajava* L.	mu-quava	leaves	tuberculosis, chronic diarrhoea
	Syzygium cordatum Hochst. ex C.Krauss subsp. *cordatum*	musheshe	leaves, bark	herpes zoster, herpes simplex, skin rashes
	Syzygium guineense (Willd) DC. subsp. *barotsense* F. White		bark	diarrhoea, coughs
Olacaceae	*Ximenia americana* L. var. *americana*	mukauke	root bark	candidiasis
Oleaceae	*Schrebera alata* (Hochst.) Welw.	mulutuluha	roots	skin rashes
Polygalaceae	*Securidaca longipedunculata* Fresen.	muinda	leaves, bark, roots	cryptococcal meningitis, oral candidiasis, coughs
Rubiaceae	*Canthium* Lam. spp.	mubilo	bark, roots, leaves	cryptococcal meningitis,oral candidiasis
	Vangueria infausta Burch. subsp. *infausta*	mubila	bark, roots, leaves	cryptococcal meningitis,oral candidiasis
Tiliaceae	*Grewia avellana* Hiern., *G. bicolor* Juss. var. *bicolor*, *G. falcistipula* K.Schum., *G. flava* DC.	muzunzunyani	bark, roots, leaves	chronic diarrhoea

Katima Mulilo: *Sclerocarya birrea*, *Capparis tomentosa*, *Antidesma venosum*, *Ximenia americana*, *Abrus precatorius* and *Vangueria infausta*. While *Ximenia americana* is used to treat skin rashes and toothache in Katima Mulilo, Vermani and Garg (2002) reported that the same plant is a remedy for contagious diseases, stomach complaints and worm infestations in India.

Malaria, a common condition among AIDS-patients in Katima Mulilo, is managed with several plant species. Some of these plants are also used to treat malaria in other countries such as Nigeria (Kayode, 2006; Muazu & Kaita, 2008), Cameroon (Titanji, Zofou, & Ngemenya, 2008), Kenya (Njoroge & Bussmann, 2006); fig species are also used to treat malaria and lack of appetite in Ethiopia and Cameroon (Techlehaymanot & Giday, 2007; Titanji et al., 2008; Jernigan, 2009); while *Moringa* reduces vomiting and diarrhoea in Ethiopia (Mesfin, Demissew & Teklehaymanot, 2009).

Our results show that traditional healers manage several AIDS-related conditions using a single plant species. This is not surprising given that single plant species can contain several chemical compounds that can curtail several infections and/or conditions. On the other hand, many traditional healers also use several plant species to manage the same illness. Local knowledge of the medicinal uses of plants is dynamic and varies according to healers, prevalent disease conditions and availability of plant species.

Plants for managing HIV/AIDS-related conditions in Ohangwena Region

In Ohangwena Region, a total of 34 plant species in 19 different families are used to manage HIV/AIDS-related opportunistic disease conditions (see Table 1.2, adapted from Hedimbi & Chinsembu, 2012). The most frequently cited medicinal plant families – in decreasing order – are Fabaceae, Combretaceae, Convolvulaceae, Molluginaceae and Olacaceae. Furthermore, a total of 19 different HIV/AIDS-related conditions are treated with herbal plants.

Most of the ethnomedicinal plants in Ohangwena Region are used to manage gonorrhoea, coughing, syphilis, diarrhoea, headache, eczema and wounds. About half of all the ethnomedications are made from leaves; while a third are derived from the bark. Almost a quarter of the remedies are derived from plant stems, and less than five per cent of all medications are from fruits. Roots account for 15% of total plant parts used in remedies. It is urged that the roots should be cautiously harvested because uncontrolled digging of these can lead to the death of the plant, as can harvesting of bark.

Hedimbi and Chinsembu (2012) found that several plants have indigenous names that connote their specific ethnomedicinal properties and applications. For example, *Corchorus tridens*, a herbal remedy for genital ulcerative disease, is locally known as *okalyaoipute*, which translated from Oshiwambo literally means 'wound eater'.

TABLE 1.2: Plants used to treat HIV/AIDS-related infections in Ohangwena Region

Family	Scientific name	Oshiwambo name	Plant parts used	Disease conditions treated
Anacardiaceae	*Ozoroa schinzii* (Engl.) R. Fern. & A.Fern.	oshifiku	stems, fruit, leaves	diarrhoea
Apocynaceae	*Gomphocarpus tomentosus* Burch.	etamupya	stems, leaves	syphilis, gonorrhoea
Asparagaceae	*Asparagus bechuanicus* Baker.	okawekamuthithi	whole plant	eczema
Asteraceae	*Litogyne gariepina* (DC.) Anderb.	odivadiva	leaves	syphilis wounds
Bignoniaceae	*Rhigozum brevispinosum* Kuntze	ngandu	all plant parts	syphilis
Boraginaceae	*Heliotropium supinum* L.	ohanauni	any plant part	tumours, wounds
Capparaceae	*Boscia albitrunca* (Burch.) Gilg & Gilg-Ben.	omunghudi	leaves, bark	syphilis
Combretaceae	*Combretum collinum* Fresen. subsp. *ondongense* (Engl. & Diels)	omupupuaheke	roots	coughs
	Combretum imberbe Wawra	omukuku	bark	gonorrhoea
Convolvulaceae	*Jacquemontia tamnifolia* (L.) Griseb.	okatangaela	whole plant	headaches
	Xenostegia tridentata (L.) D.F.Austin & Staples	okashila konhoka	whole plant	headaches
Cucurbitaceae	*Acanthosicyos naudinianus* (Sond.) C.Jeffrey	katangakamufifi	fruit	gonorrhoea
Fabaceae	*Acacia ataxacantha* DC.	omukoro	bark	pneumonia
	Bobgunnia madagascariensis (Desv.) J.H.Kirkbr. & Wiersema	omumonga	bark, stems, roots	diarrhoea
	Erythrophleum africanum (Welw. ex Benth.) Harms	omupako	leaves	gonorrhoea, headaches
	Otoptera burchellii DC.	omalakaka	leaves	diarrhoea
	Piliostigma thonningii (Schumach.) Milne-Redh.	omutuutuu	roots, bark	coughs
	Pterocarpus angolensis DC.	uguva	bark	coughs
	Senna italica Mill.	okatundangu	whole plant	abscesses
	Senna occidentalis (L.) Link	omutiweyoka	leaves	coughs
	Vigna lobatifolia Baker	omuyimbo	roots	herpes
Gisekiaceae	*Gisekia pharnacioides* L.	omundjulu	whole plant	parasitic worms, diarrhoea
Lamiaceae	*Clerodendrum ternatum* Schinz	oshanyu	leaves, bark	eczema
Molluginaceae	*Limeum fenestratum* (Fenzl) Heimerl	oluide	stems, leaves	coughs
	Limeum viscosum (J.Gay) Fenzl	oluide	leaves	coughs

continues

Table 1.2 continued

Family	Scientific name	Oshiwambo name	Plant parts used	Disease conditions treated
Olacaceae	*Ximenia americana* L.	oshimbyu	leaves, stems	gonorrhoea
	Ximenia caffra Sond.	ompeke	leaves, stems	gonorrhoea
Poaceae	*Chrysopogon nigritanus* (Benth.) Veldkamp	omanenge	roots	gonorrhoea
Polygalaceae	*Securidaca longipedunculata* Fresen.	omutiwongobe	roots, bark	gonorrhoea, syphilis
Rhamnaceae	*Ziziphus mucronata* Willd.	omukekete	bark, leaves	gonorrhoea
Solanaceae	*Solanum delagoense* Dunal	onululu	roots, leaves	coughs
Sterculiaceae	*Waltheria indica* L.	oshihakulamesho	stems	syphilis
Tiliaceae	*Corchorus tridens* L.	okalyaoipute	stems, leaves	genital ulcers caused by syphilis, or chancroid

Litogyne gariepina, a treatment for syphilitic wounds, is locally known as *odivadiva* (meaning 'fast wound healer'), while *Heliotropium supinum*, another plant with wound-healing properties, is locally known as *ohanauni*, meaning 'wound disperser'.

Other Oshiwambo plant names are associated with the severity of the condition they treat. For instance, in the Ohangwena Region, the plant *Senna occidentalis* is made into a medication for coughs, yet it is known as *omutiweyoka*, loosely translated as 'snakebite medicine' or antidote for snakebites. Ironically, in Oshiwambo parlance, the severity of coughing in HIV/AIDS patients is synonymous to the danger posed by a snakebite; hence the name 'snake antidote plant' for *S. occidentalis*.

Many phytochemical and pharmacological profiles of *Senna occidentalis* show a wide range of chemical compounds, including anthraquinones, which have significant antibacterial, antifungal, laxative, analgesic and diuretic properties. This wide range of properties makes *S. occidentalis* a suitable remedy for many illnesses. Interestingly, our finding that *S. occidentalis* is a cough remedy in the Ohangwena Region is similar to ethnomedicinal knowledge from Nigeria and Asia where *Senna obtusifolia* is also used to treat coughs (Guo, Chang, Yang, Guo, & Zheng, 1998). In Mozambique, *Cassia abbreviata* alleviates eye infections, stomachache and diarrhoea (Ribeiro, Romeiras, Tavares, & Faria, 2010). The efficacy of *S. occidentalis* varies according to geographical location and season.

The plant species *Xenostegia tridentata*, also known as *okashila konhoka* (small, black mamba's tail) is used to treat chronic headaches whose pain is symbolically comparable to a black mamba snakebite. Another local plant, *Rhigozum brevispinosum*, known as *ngandu* (meaning crocodile), is used to treat syphilis, a stigmatized sexually transmitted disease that is metaphorically likened to someone caught by a crocodile (Hedimbi & Chinsembu, 2012). Earlier, Chinsembu and co-workers found a similar kind of symbolism in the Zambezi Region where HIV/AIDS is known as *simbandembande*, the siLozi name for the fish eagle. The Lozi believe that AIDS quickly takes people's lives away, just as quickly as the eagle picks fish from the river (Chinsembu et al., 2011).

The plant species *Solanum delagoense*, is locally called *onululu* (meaning 'bitter'); it is a herbal remedy for coughing. The use of bitter ethnophytomedications is a popular means of managing coughs in Namibia and beyond. Again, although the plant species *Securidaca longipedunculata* treats gonorrhoea and syphilis, it is locally known as *omutiwongobe or muinde,* meaning 'cattle medicine'. This is indicative that *S. longipedunculata* is an ethnoveterinary medication for cattle – probably to increase libido in bulls used for breeding. In South Africa, *S. longipedunculata* is used to treat erectile dysfunction in men.

While inhabitants of the Ohangwena Region in northern Namibia use *Acacia ataxacantha* to manage pneumonia, the same plant is a remedy for dysentery in Nigeria (Olowokudejo, Kadiri, & Travih, 2008). This finding suggests that *A. ataxacantha* has antibacterial properties. Hedimbi and Chinsembu (2012) stated that *Acanthosicyos naudinianus*, called the 'gemsbok cucumber' in Namibia, is a moisture-bearing wild plant and strong ecological competitor of the medicinal plant *Harpagophytum procumbens* (commonly known as devil's claw). Although the gemsbok cucumber is eaten as food, it is also a phytomedication for treating gonorrhoea, cancer, and many AIDS-related symptoms. *Acanthosicyos naudinianus* contains cucurbitacin B which gives the fruits a bitter taste (Hedimbi & Chinsembu, 2012). It is also incorporated into the hunting arrow poison used by the San people of southern Africa.

In Ohangwena Region, the leaves and bark of *Boscia albitrunca* (the shepherd's tree) are used to manage syphilis (Hedimbi & Chinsembu, 2012). Yet, in Mozambique, the leaves of *B. albitrunca* are used to treat diarrhoea and haemorrhoids (Ribeiro et al., 2010). In Tanzania, the same plant is a therapy for skin rashes, candidiasis, throat infections and malaria. Another plant that shows widespread ethnomedicinal usage is *Ximenia americana*. The bark and leaves of *X. americana* are used to lessen the symptoms of gonorrhoea in the Ohangwena Region. However, *X. americana* is also a remedy for candidiasis in the Zambezi Region and skin rashes in Tanzania (Chinsembu & Hedimbi, 2010). The widespread ethnomedicinal usage of *X. americana* suggests that this plant contains several active compounds which are responsible for its purported efficacy.

In the Ohangwena Region, *Clerodendrum ternatum* is herbal medication for treating eczema. It is also used to manage sexually transmitted infections, gastrointestinal disorders and pneumonia. In India, China, Thailand, Korea and Japan, *Clerodendrum* is used to treat several diseases such as syphilis, typhoid, cancer, jaundice and hypertension (Shrivastava & Patel, 2007). These authors state that various species in the genus *Clerodendrum* contain phenolics, steroids, di- and tri-terpenes, flavonoids and volatile oils.

CONCLUSION AND LOOKING AHEAD

Three main aspects of indigenous knowledge are discussed in this chapter: (1) the various indigenous names and appellations that local people use to describe their understandings of HIV infection and AIDS; (2) the experiences – including a model of initiating collaboration between traditional healers and biomedical scientists; and (3) the use of indigenous knowledge in conducting ethnobotanical surveys to identify medicinal plants used in the management of HIV/AIDS-related opportunistic infections.

The use of indigenous knowledge helps people to form strategies for interpreting local phenomena through the prism of what they already know. The formation of such strategies related to the perception and prevention of HIV/AIDS risk is important for individuals to form local meanings of the HIV/AIDS epidemic. Discussing AIDS, in ways that local people can relate to, helps them to face up to the pandemic. Similarly, the language used to describe people living with HIV and the symptoms that they associate with AIDS are part of society's hidden, but educative, curriculum through which the AIDS epidemic is locally understood.

That said, local terminologies associated with HIV/AIDS are meant to protect individuals by way of instilling fear. Sometimes, local descriptions of HIV/AIDS convey subtle messages, for example, when referring to a person perceived to have been infected by the virus. The use of certain metaphors very often reflects local perceptions of HIV/AIDS. Within these confines, many interventions may have failed to stem HIV/AIDS infection rates because they are not anchored on the local knowledge of the disease.

In terms of collaboration, the model presented here emphasises that deliberate steps can initiate cooperation between biomedical researchers and traditional healers. In Namibia there is no legislation on bioprospecting and benefit sharing, and research institutions have no prior national mandate to initiate work on scientific validation of traditional medicines. Therefore, participatory forums of stakeholders, including potential authorizing bodies and government watchdog committees, should be constituted to ensure a transparent and responsible research ethic on collaboration and scientific validation of ethnomedicines. In Namibia, the NBF created a transparent entry point for UNAM to initiate collaborative efforts to validate traditional medicines used in the treatment of HIV/AIDS.

Indigenous knowledge can help pinpoint medicinal plants effective in managing HIV/AIDS-related conditions. Several Namibian plants treat conditions such as herpes zoster, diarrhoea, coughs, tuberculosis and meningitis, which are often associated with HIV/AIDS. Yet, in spite of the knowledge many traditional healers hold, there is a need to educate them about the potential danger of wiping out some of the over-exploited medicinal plant species, especially by harvesting their roots and bark.

Regional differences in the ethnomedicinal usage of plants have been found in Namibia. For example, while *Securidaca longipedunculata* is used to alleviate the symptoms of syphilis and gonorrhoea in Ohangwena Region, it is used to ameliorate the symptoms of cryptococcal meningitis, oral candidiasis and coughs in Zambezi Region. Some species in the genus *Acacia* treat herpes zoster in Zambezi, but relieve pneumonia in Ohangwena. Similar regional differences apply to plants belonging to the genera *Combretum* and *Pterocarpus*. In Zambezi Region, plants in the genus *Combretum* provide important phyto-therapies for malaria, diarrhoea, meningitis and tuberculosis, but the same *Combretum* plants are used as a treatment for coughs and gonorrhoea in Ohangwena Region. *Pterocarpus* is a medication for dysentery and diarrhoea in Zambezi, but it also a medication for coughs in Ohangwena. These regional differences demonstrate the dynamic nature of phyto-medicinal innovations based on indigenous knowledge.

Currently, UNAM is conducting the scientific validation of Namibian plants at the CSIR laboratories in Pretoria, South Africa. This process is authorized by a material transfer agreement from the NBRI and an export permit from the Ministry of Environment and Tourism. UNAM has also signed a memorandum of understanding with the CSIR. All these documents delineate the various issues pertaining to intellectual property rights and ABS.

Interestingly, preliminary results show that some of the extracts of the plants used as ethnomedications for HIV/AIDS-related conditions in Namibia have greater efficacy than the AIDS drug nevirapine. Cytotoxicity experiments also indicate that some of the extracts are less toxic in human cell lines. Active compounds from these plants are being identified and will be patented for future development into new drugs for treatment of HIV/AIDS. Looking ahead, all these research efforts will soon put Namibia's unknown 'green diamonds' on the world stage.

References

African Biosciences Initiative. (2005). *Business plan 2005–2010*. Pretoria, South Africa: Office of Science and Technology, NEPAD.

Ahmad, K. (2001). Namibian government to prosecute healers. *The Lancet, 357*(9253), 371.

Banda, Y., Chapman, V., Goldenberg, R. L., Stringer, J. S., Culhane, J. F., Sinkala, M., …Chi, B. H. (2007). Use of traditional medicine among pregnant women in Lusaka, Zambia. *Journal of Alternative and Complementary Medicine, 13*(1), 123-127.

Barnard, P., & Shikongo, S. T. (2000, May). *Namibia's national report to the Fifth Conference of Parties on Implementation of the Convention on Biological Diversity*. Namibian National Biodiversity Programme, Directorate of Environmental Affairs, Ministry of Environment and Tourism.

Boadu, S. O. (1993). *Involving traditional healers in the AIDS campaign: Is true partnership possible?* Paper presented at the International Conference on AIDS (WHO/GPA, NACP), Windhoek, Namibia, 9: 127 (abstract no. wS-D24-5). Retrieved from http://gateway.nlm.nih.gov/MeetingAbstracts/ma?f=102202766.html

Botsaris, A. S. (2007). Plants used traditionally to treat malaria in Brazil: the archives of Flora Medicinal. *Journal of Ethnobiology and Ethnomedicine, 3*, 18. doi:10.1186/1746-4269-3-18

Chaudhury, R. R. (2001). A clinical protocol for the study of traditional medicine and human immunodeficiency virus-related illness. *Journal of Alternative and Complementary Medicine, 7*(5), 553-566.

Chinsembu, K. C. (2009). Model and experiences of initiating collaboration with traditional healers in validation of ethnomedicines for HIV/AIDS in Namibia. *Journal of Ethnobiology and Ethnomedicine, 5*, 30. doi:10.1186/1746-4269-5-30

Chinsembu, K. C., & Hedimbi, M. (2010). An ethnobotanical survey of plants used to manage HIV/AIDS opportunistic infections in Katima Mulilo, Caprivi region, Namibia. *Journal of Ethnobiology and Ethnomedicine, 6*, 25. doi:10.1186/1746-4269-6-25

Chinsembu, K. C., & Mutirua, T. (2008). *Validation of traditional medicines for HIV/AIDS treatment in Namibia* (a report of the study visit to Zambia and South Africa). Windhoek, Namibia: University of Namibia.

Chinsembu, K. C., Shimwooshili-Shaimemanya, C., Kasanda, C. D., & Zealand, D. (2011). Indigenous knowledge of HIV/AIDS among high school students in Namibia. *Journal of Ethnobiology and Ethnomedicine, 7*, 17. doi:10.1186/1746-4269-7-17

Du Plessis, P. (2007, November). *Indigenous knowledge and biotrade.* Paper presented at the National Biosciences Forum and Validation of Traditional Medicines Workshop, Windhoek, Namibia.

Falk, T. (2009). Biodiversity and the ancestors: Challenges to customary and environmental law [Review of the book *Biodiversity and the ancestors: Challenges to customary and environmental law*, edited by M. O. Hinz & O. C. Ruppel.] *Namibian Law Journal, 1*(1), 113-116. Retrieved from http://www.namibialawjournal.org.na/pnTemp/downloads_upload/Journal/falk.pdf

Family Health International. (2007). *Implementing AIDS prevention and care project, 2000–2007* (IMPACT Project Final Report for Namibia). Windhoek, Namibia: Author.

GRN [Government of the Republic of Namibia]. (2002). *The national strategic plan on HIV/AIDS: Third medium term plan, 2004–2009.* Windhoek, Namibia: Directorate of Special Programmes, Ministry of Health and Social Services.

GRN [Government of the Republic of Namibia]. (2008a). *Report on the 2008 National HIV Sentinel Survey: HIV prevalence rate in pregnant women, bi-annual survey, 1992–2008*. Windhoek, Namibia: Ministry of Health and Social Services.

GRN [Government of the Republic of Namibia]. (2008b). *HIV/AIDS in Namibia: Behavioural and contextual factors driving the epidemic*. Windhoek, Namibia: Ministry of Health and Social Services, USAID Namibia, MEASURE Evaluation.

GRN [Government of the Republic of Namibia]. (2009). *United Nations General Assembly Special Session (UNGASS) on HIV and AIDS country report: Reporting period 2008–2009*. Windhoek, Namibia: Directorate of Special Programmes, Ministry of Health and Social Services.

GRN [Government of the Republic of Namibia]. (2010). *Report on the 2010 National HIV Sentinel Survey*. Windhoek, Namibia: Ministry of Health and Social Services.

GRN [Government of the Republic of Namibia]. (2014). *Report on the 2014 National HIV Sentinel Survey*. Windhoek, Namibia: Ministry of Health and Social Services.

GRN [Government of the Republic of Namibia]. (2012). *Report on the 2012 National HIV Sentinel Survey*. Windhoek, Namibia: Ministry of Health and Social Services.

GRZ [Government of the Republic of Zambia]. (2008). Guidelines for research in traditional medicines in Zambia. Lusaka: Ministry of Health.

Guo, H. Z., Chang, Z. Z., Yang R. J., Guo, D., & Zheng, J. H. (1998). Anthraquinones from hairy root cultures of *Cassia obtusifolia*. *Phytochemistry, 49*(6), 1623-1625.

Hardon, A., Desclaux, A., Egrot, M., Simon, E., Micollier, E., & Kyakuwa, M. (2008). Alternative medicines for AIDS in resource-poor settings: Insights from exploratory anthropological studies in Asia and Africa. *Journal of Ethnobiology and Ethnomedicine, 4*, 16. doi:10.1186/1746-4269-4-16

Hedimbi, M., & Chinsembu, K. C. (2012). Ethnomedicinal study of plants used to manage HIV/AIDS-related disease conditions in the Ohangwena Region, Namibia. *International Journal of Medicinal Plant Research, 1*(1), 004-011.

Homsy, J., King, R., Tenywa, J., Kyeyune, P., Opio, A., & Balaba, D. (2004). Defining minimum standards of practice for incorporating African traditional medicine into HIV/AIDS prevention, care and support: A regional initiative in eastern and southern Africa. *Journal of Alternative and Complementary Medicine, 10*(5), 905-910.

Jernigan, K. A. (2009). Barking up the same tree: A comparison of ethnomedicine and canine ethnoveterinary medicine among the Aguaruna. *Journal of Ethnobiology and Ethnomedicine, 5*, 33. doi:10.1186/1746-4269-5-33

Kamwi, R., Kenyon, T., & Newton, G. (2006). PEPFAR and HIV prevention in Africa [letter]. *The Lancet, 367*(9527), 1978-1979.

Kareru, P. G., Gachanja, A. N., Keriko, J. M., & Kenji, G. M. (2008). Antimicrobial activity of some medicinal plants used by herbalists in Eastern Province, Kenya. *African Journal of Traditional, Complementary and Alternative Medicine*, 5(1), 51-55.

Kaya, H. O. (2009). Indigenous knowledge (IK) and innovation systems for public health in Africa. In F. A. Kalua, A. Awote, L. A. Kamwanja, & J. D. K. Saka (Eds.), *Science, technology and innovation for public health in Africa* (pp. 95-109). Pretoria, South Africa: NEPAD Office of Science and Technology.

Kayode, J. (2006). Conservation of indigenous medicinal botanicals in Ekiti State, Nigeria. *Journal of Zhejiang University SCIENCE B, 7*(9), 713-718.

Kayombo, E. J., Uiso, F. C., Mbwambo, Z. H., Mahunnah, R. L., Moshi, M. J., & Mgonda, Y. H. (2007). Experience of initiating collaboration of traditional healers in managing HIV and AIDS in Tanzania. *Journal of Ethnobiology and Ethnomedicine*, 3, 6. doi:10.1.186/1746-4269-3-6

King, R. (2005). *Collaboration with traditional healers on prevention and care in sub-Saharan Africa: A practical guideline for programs.* Geneva, Switzerland: UNAIDS.

King, R. (2006). *Collaborating with traditional healers for HIV prevention and care in sub-Saharan Africa: Suggestions for programme managers and field workers.* UNAIDS Best Practice Collection. Geneva, Switzerland: UNAIDS.

Klaassen, E. S., & Kwembeya, E. G. (Eds.). (2013). *A checklist of Namibian indigenous and naturalised plants. Occasional Contributions No. 5.* Windhoek, Namibia: National Botanical Research Institute.

Langlois-Klassen, D., Kipp, W., Jhangri, G. S., & Rubaale, T. (2007). Use of traditional herbal medicine by AIDS patients in Kabarole District, western Uganda. *American Journal of Tropical Medicine and Hygiene*, 77(4), 757-763.

Lebeau, D. (1998). Urban patients' utilization of traditional medicine: Upholding culture and tradition. Windhoek, Namibia: University of Namibia.

Lindegaard, B., Keller P., Bruunsgaard, G., Gerstoft, J., & Pedersen, B. K. (2004). Low plasma level of adiponectin is associated with stavudine treatment and lipodystrophy in HIV-infected patients. *Clinical and Experimental Immunology, 135*(2), 273-279. doi: 10.1111/j.1365-2249.2004.02367.x

Maggs, G. L., Craven, P., & Kolberg, H. H. (1998). Plant species richness, endemism and genetic resources in Namibia. *Biodiversity and Conservation, 7*(4), 435-446.

McCourt, W., & Awases, M. (2007). Addressing the human resources crisis: A case study of the Namibian health service. *Human Resources for Health*, 5(1), 1-35. doi: 10.1186/1478-4491-5-1

Mesfin, F., Demissew, S., & Teklehaymanot, T. (2009). An ethnobotanical study of medicinal plants in Wonago Woreda, SNNPR, Ethiopia. *Journal of Ethnobiology and Ethnomedicine*, 5, 28. doi:10.1186/1746-4269-5-28

Mills, E., Singh, S., Wilson, K., Peters, E., Onia, R., & Kanfer, I. (2006). The challenges of involving traditional healers in HIV/AIDS care. *International Journal of STD and AIDS*, *17*(6), 360-363.

Muazu, J., & Kaita, A. H. (2008). A review of traditional plants used in the treatment of epilepsy amongst the Hausa/Fulani tribes of northern Nigeria. *African Journal of Traditional, Complementary and Alternative Medicines*, *5*(4), 387-390.

NEPAD [New Partnership for Africa's Development]. (2001). *The New Partnership for Africa's Development: Founding document, Abuja, Nigeria*. Pretoria, South Africa: Author.

Njoroge, G. N., & Bussmann, R. W. (2006). Diversity and utilization of antimalarial ethnophytotherapeutic remedies among the Kikuyus (Central Kenya). *Journal of Ethnobiology and Ethnomedicine*, *2*, 8. doi:10.1186/1746-4269-2-8.

Olowokudejo, J. D., Kadiri, A. B., & Travih, V. A. (2008). An ethnobotanical survey of herbal markets and medicinal plants in Lagos State of Nigeria. *Ethnobotanical Leaflets*, *12*, 851-865.

PEPFAR [USA President's Emergency Plan for AIDS Relief]. (n.d.). *PEPFAR Namibia: Small grants*. Retrieved from http://photos.state.gov/libraries/namibia/19452/public/PEPFAR_fact_sheets.pdf

Puckree, T., Mkhize, M., Mgobhozi, Z., & Lin, J. (2002). African traditional healers: What health care professionals need to know. *International Journal of Rehabilitation Research*, *25*(4), 247-51.

Reihling, H. C. W. (2008). Bioprospecting the African Renaissance: The new value of *muthi* in South Africa. *Journal of Ethnobiology and Ethnomedicine*, *4*(9). doi:10.1186/1746-4269-4-9

Ribeiro, A., Romeiras, M. M., Tavares, J., & Faria, M. T. (2010). Ethnobotanical survey in Canhane village, district of Massingir, Mozambique: Medicinal plants and traditional knowledge. *Journal of Ethnobiology and Ethnomedicine*, *6*, 33. doi:10.1186/1746-4269-6-33

Richter, M. (2003). *Traditional medicines and traditional healers in South Africa: Discussion paper prepared for the Treatment Action Campaign and AIDS Law Project*. Retrieved from http://www.tac.org.za/Documents/ResearchPapers/Traditional_Medicine_briefing.pdf

Shrivastava, N., & Patel, T. (2007). *Clerodendrum* and healthcare: An overview. *Medicinal and Aromatic Plant Science and Biotechnology*, *1*(1), 142-150.

Stewart, K. M., & Cole, D. (2005). The commercial harvest of devil's claw (*Harpagophytum* spp.) in southern Africa: The devil's in the details. *Journal of Ethnopharmacology*, *100*(3), 225-236.

Teklehaymanot, T., & Giday, M. (2007). Ethnobotanical study of medicinal plants used by people in Zegie Peninsula, Northwestern Ethiopia. *Journal of Ethnobiology and Ethnomedicine, 3,* 12. doi:10.1186/1746-4269-3-12

Titanji, V. P. K., Zofou, D., & Ngemenya, M. N. (2008). The antimalarial potential of medicinal plants used for the treatment of malaria in Cameroonian folk medicine. *African Journal of Traditional, Complementary and Alternative Medicines, 5*(3), 302-321.

UNDP [United Nations Development Programme]. (2000). *Namibia Human Development Report, 2000.* Windhoek, Namibia: UNDP Namibia Country Office.

Vermani, K., & Garg, S. (2002). Herbal medicines for sexually transmitted diseases and AIDS. *Journal of Ethnopharmacology, 80*(1), 49-66.

WHO [World Health Organization]. (1989). In vitro screening of traditional medicines for anti-HIV activity: Memorandum from a WHO meeting. *Bulletin of the World Health Organization, 67*(6), 613-618.

Wickham, L. (2001). Devil's claw – the herbal solution to the north–south divide? *PositiveHealthOnline, 68.* Retrieved from http://www.positivehealth.com/article/herbal-medicine/devil-s-claw-the-herbal-solution-to-the-north-south-divide

2

Indigenous use of plants to treat malaria and associated symptoms

Iwanette du Preez, Sylvia Nafuka, Davis R. Mumbengegwi & Ronnie Böck

INTRODUCTION

Malaria, an infectious disease caused by *Plasmodium* parasites, remains a public health concern in many sub-Saharan countries. In Namibia, malaria claimed over 100 lives in 2011 alone (WHO, 2012). However, Namibia achieved a remarkable reduction in the number of cases between 2000 and 2011 (WHO, 2012). The number of confirmed (out- and in-patient) cases decreased from 477,786 in 2000 to 133,464 in 2008 (MoHSS, 2010), and further to 3,163 cases in 2012. Moreover, malaria deaths have dropped tremendously from 679 in 2000 to 199 in 2008 (MoHSS, 2010), and further to 45 in 2011 and four in 2012. This success story implies that Namibia is heading towards the elimination of malaria, with less than one case per 1,000 people per year (WHO, 2010). However, in 2013 a rise in the number of malaria cases was reported (4,745 cases), as well as in the number of reported deaths (21) (MoHSS, 2014).

Although the incidence of malaria has decreased in Namibia in recent years, many people are at risk of contracting the disease. Malaria often requires hospitalization for extended periods of time and can lead to the loss of life. Furthermore, it has been found that uncomplicated and severe malaria negatively affects cognition and behaviour of sufferers, and impairs school performance in children (Fernando, Rodrigo, & Rajapakse, 2010). Pregnant women who contract malaria tend to give birth to infants with a low birth weight, which leads to high infant mortality (Breman, 2001). Sachs and Malaney (2002) argue that malaria is one of the major barriers to improving health conditions and economic development in many developing countries. It should be noted that the Namibian Government has provided substantial funds for controlling malaria. In 2011, it provided 90% of the funds used for malaria vector control and malaria treatment in Namibia, with the balance from international donors (WHO, 2012).

Antimalarials are fundamental to any approach in attempting to reduce deaths by malaria (White, 2008). However, reports on the failure of treatment with antimalarial drugs such as chloroquine and sulphadoxine-pyrimethamine have been documented (Elamin, Elabadi, & Mohamad, 2007). Furthermore, not all communities accept or can afford allopathic medicine, preferring to use traditional medicines. As a result, increasing focus is being placed on medicinal plants as complementary or alternative medicines for the treatment of malaria. Such efforts are further encouraged by the isolation of currently used allopathic antimalarial drugs from plants, and the synthesis of analogues of plant compounds (Meunier, 2012). A well-known example of such compounds is artemisinin, isolated from *Artemisia annua*, a shrub which is used for the synthesis of artemisinin-based combination therapies – currently a first-line treatment for malaria in Namibia (Krishna, Uhlemann, & Haynes, 2004). Artemisinin was discovered following leads provided by the use of the plant in folk medicine to treat malaria, indicating that plants remain an important source of potential antimalarials.

Namibia has a rich diversity of plants (Cowling & Hilton-Taylor, 1994), with many species occurring in the malaria-endemic regions of the country. Some communities in these regions rely on ethnomedicinal plants for their primary healthcare needs and use herbal remedies to treat malaria-like symptoms, reinforcing the need to integrate traditional therapies with modern medicine to eliminate malaria. However, before plants can be established as complementary or alternative medicines for malaria, they need to be scientifically validated as safe and effective (Wang, Hao, & Chen, 2007).

This chapter presents an overview of the current malaria status in Namibia; available malaria prevention and treatment strategies; the use of traditional medicines in the form of plants to control and treat the disease in endemic regions; and the phytochemical composition and biological activity of some of the plants used traditionally. Lastly, we discuss research gaps and the way forward to discovering and developing drugs in Namibia.

AN OVERVIEW OF MALARIA

Malaria is a disease caused by protozoan parasites of the genus *Plasmodium*. According to Singh and Daneshvar (2013), five species of *Plasmodium* cause the disease in humans, namely, *P. falciparum, P. malariae, P. vivax, P. ovale* and *P. knowlesi*. *Plasmodium falciparum* is the most lethal parasite of the five as it causes the highest rates of complications and mortality (Rao, Kumar, Joseph, & Bulusu, 2010). Infection by this parasite can lead to death within hours to days (Trampuz, Jereb, Muzlovic, & Prabhu, 2003). Most malaria infections (80%) and mortalities (90%) are caused by *P. falciparum* in Namibia, and in the rest of sub-Saharan Africa. Female *Anopheles* mosquitoes transmit the *Plasmodium* parasites. Three species of vectors are found in Namibia, namely *Anopheles arabiensis, A. gambiae* and *A. funestus* with the most prevalent ones being *A. gambiae* and *A. funestus* (MoHSS, 2010; WHO, 2012).

Typical clinical symptoms of children and adult patients with uncomplicated malaria include fever and vomiting. Other clinical manifestations include headaches, chills, and muscle aches (Bannister & Mitchell, 2003; Krause, 2007). In pregnant women, symptoms typically include anaemia and hyperglycaemia, and, variably, paroxysms, fever, enlargement of the spleen, a combination of diarrhoea and vomiting, and convulsions. Clinical features of severe malaria in children include impaired consciousness (prostration or coma), seizures, respiratory distress, severe anaemia, hypoglycaemia, metabolic acidosis and hyperlactataemia (Crawley, Chu, Mtove, & Nosten, 2010).

Since malaria is a clinical disease, an individual can only be diagnosed with malaria when a proper medical examination is carried out using rapid diagnostic tests or microscopy. Communities and traditional healers in various cultures, however, rely on their knowledge of malaria symptoms and its aetiology. The Aawambo typically diagnose malaria by the presence of fever and chills; as a result, they have a misconception that malaria is caused by cold weather. According to a survey on traditional healers and community use of traditional medicine in Namibia, in the Aawambo culture a person can contract malaria by walking in the morning dew, eating cold food, swimming in cold water and playing or staying out in the cold (MoHSS & UNICEF, 2000). As a result, they emphasize that individuals should keep warm in order to prevent malaria. It is interesting to note, that although the cause is mistaken, by wearing warm clothing they will prevent contracting malaria.

Malaria prevention in Namibia

In Namibia, malaria transmission is prevented both at household and national level using different interventions. At the household level, individuals that live in malaria endemic regions use external barriers against mosquito bites at night, such as sleeping under insecticide-treated nets, using mosquito repellents, and wearing long-sleeved clothing. Individuals in such areas might also remove standing water from the proximity of their homestead, as these serve as breeding sites for mosquitoes. Some communities in rural areas of malaria-endemic regions use plants as mosquito repellents, for example, *Acrotome inflata*, locally known as *etwelakuku*. This plant gives off a peculiar scent, which mosquitoes do not tolerate. At night, individuals place the freshly uprooted plant in the bedroom hanging from the roof. The amount used and how effective it is depends on the size of the bedroom, as well as the personal experience of the individual who uses it.

At the national level, the World Health Organization (WHO) has stipulated various approaches for malaria endemic countries to adopt, which integrate preventative measures and chemotherapy (WHO, 2009). These include:

1. vector control through the use of insecticide-treated nets;
2. vector control through indoor residual spraying and, in some specific settings, larval control;
3. chemoprevention for the most vulnerable population groups, particularly pregnant women and infants.

A cross-border initiative called Trans-Kunene Malaria Initiative was established in 2009 to evaluate and monitor cross-border malaria transfer between Angola and Namibia.

Malaria treatment

Chemoprevention of malarial infections is considered important in the control of malaria in endemic areas and in the elimination of the disease (White, 2008). Malaria treatment has become somewhat of a problem because of the emergence of parasites resistant to former first-line antimalarials (Heelan & Ingersoll, 2001), such as chloroquine and sulphadoxine-pyrimethamine (Ekland & Fidock, 2007). Over the years, both drugs have lost effectiveness: chloroquine is now ineffective in almost every part of the world (Jiang, Joy, Furuya, & Su, 2006), and drug resistance to sulphadoxine-pyrimethamine (introduced in 1977) is developing (Eriksen et al., 2008). World Health Organization (WHO) has advised all endemic countries to adopt early and accurate diagnosis and appropriate treatment of malaria (WHO, 2009). These include:

1. the use of microscopy or rapid diagnostic tests to confirm malaria diagnosis for every suspected case;
2. timely treatment with antimalarial medicines appropriate for the parasite species and in accordance with documented drug resistance.

Currently used allopathic antimalarial drugs are divided into several categories: quinolones, atovaquones, antifolates and artemisinins (Cunha-Rodrigues, Prudêncio, Mota, & Haas, 2006). Quinine, an alkaloid, was isolated directly from *Cinchona* spp. in 1820 and became the lead compound from which quinolones were derived. Chloroquine, the most famous antimalarial of this group, was the only drug used in pure form to treat malaria for more than a hundred years. Other constituents of this group are amodiaquine, piperaquine, primaquine and mefloquine. The quinolones act mostly during the blood stage of the parasite's life cycle, but some are said to act during the liver stage as well (Srinivasa et al., 2012). However, resistance of *P. falciparum* to chloroquine was reported as far back as the 1950s in Thailand and Colombia, and has since spread throughout the world (Baird, 2005). Today, at the advice of WHO, the use of chloroquine for *P. falciparum* malaria has been withdrawn.

Another group of antimalarials, artemisinin, has become the essential part of uncomplicated and severe malaria treatment throughout the world. According to White (2008), artemisinin is a sesquiterpene that was isolated from a Chinese ethnomedicinal plant, *Artemisia annua*, in 1971. Many derivatives are now synthesized from this compound. Artemisinin and all its derivatives kill *P. falciparum* at all stages of its life cycle by interacting with haem to produce carbon-centred free radicals that alkylate proteins and damage the parasites (de Ridder, van der Kooy, & Verpoorte, 2004). This class of sesquiterpenes has been deployed over the past decade on a large scale (Bosman & Mendis, 2007).

An artemisinin-based combination therapy, artemether-lumefantrine is the current first-line treatment for uncomplicated malaria in Namibia. For severe or complicated malaria parenteral (intravenous or intramuscular injection) quinine is administered and then taken orally once the patient's condition improves. Chemoprophylaxis is only recommended for certain groups of people, including non-immune individuals living in and travelling to malaria endemic areas for short periods of time (MoHSS, 2005). In such cases, mefloquine and doxycycline (in the case of mefloquine-contra-indicated patients) are endorsed as the prophylactic drugs. For pregnant women, presumptive prophylactic treatment or intermittent preventive treatment in the form of sulphadoxine-pyrimethamine is prescribed by the current malaria policy (MoHSS, 2010). This regime is only administered during the first and second pregnancies and, recently, due to low levels of malaria prevalence, it is no longer recommended. Sulphadoxine-pyrimethamine is also administered to infants of 2–6 months as a first-line drug and quinine as the second-line drug (MoHSS, 2005).

Despite the efficacy and relatively safety of most available chemotherapies, there is still a growing concern about potential problems of acquired resistance. The widespread resistance of *Plasmodium* parasites, especially *P. falciparum*, can give rise to malaria mortality and morbidity, and contribute negatively to the socio-economic status of a country (Nchinda, 1998; Schlagenhauf & Petersen, 2009). Reduced sensitivity of *P. falciparum* to the current first-line artemisinin-based combination therapy has been reported (Batista, De Jesus Silva, & De Oliviera, 2009).

The development of a vaccine against malaria is taking place worldwide (Heelan & Ingersoll, 2001). The synthesis of an effective one, would be an important breakthrough in the fight against this disease. Until then, efforts in the search for new potential antimalarials are ongoing.

TRADITIONAL MEDICINES

WHO defines traditional medicine as 'the overall knowledge, skills, and practices based on the theories, beliefs, and experiences indigenous to different cultures, whether explicable or not, used in the maintenance of health, as well as in the prevention, diagnosis, improvement or treatment of physical and mental illness' (WHO, 2005). Traditional medicine in the form of medicinal plants and other natural products plays a great role in the management of diseases and various ailments in many cultures worldwide (Hoareau & Da Silva, 1999). In fact, 80% of people in developing countries still rely on traditional medicine for their primary healthcare needs.

Some communities have been using traditional medicine for centuries, which has resulted in it being considered safe and effective. In a bygone era, communities used plant resources by trial and error and, as a result, discovered which plants are effective and safe for use in the treatment of various ailments. Consequently, over time knowledge developed that correlated the effectiveness of traditional medicines in treating certain diseases and conditions. For instance, over generations people have established that potent ethnomedicinal plants are likely to have an odour and bitter taste. It has been shown that alkaloids, a class of compounds with these properties, are therapeutic for many diseases (Saxena, Saxena, Nema, Singh, & Gupta, 2013).

In an African context, indigenous knowledge about traditional healing is closely guarded in families, with the knowledge holder passing it on to an apprentice within the family. Traditional healing has many intricacies and nuances, which differ between cultures. There are, however, usually two consistencies: the view that the universe can explain the cause, diagnosis and treatment of the disease, and the cultural context in which the disease is diagnosed and treated. Some plants might have been found useful in treating a specific infirmity in some cultures, but the usage might not have been found in another (Balick, Elisabetsky, & Laid, 1996).

In Namibia, von Koenen (2001) has shown that traditional healers are divided into two categories, namely those that consult spirit mediums, ancestral spirits and magic to gain supernatural powers that enable them to heal; and those that simply use herbs without any spiritual association to treat various conditions. The latter are known as herbalists. Those that use mediums are considered unscrupulous by their communities, because apart from treating diseases they are perceived to cast possibly harmful spells in order to diagnose the aetiology of the diseases. In many cultures, people are encouraged to avoid such treatment. Herbalists, on the other hand, are perceived as safe because they only provide herbal remedies and recipes based on the symptoms provided by their patients.

Medicinal plants are prepared in a variety of ways ranging from teas, decoctions, poultices, tinctures, and steam baths, to using the fumes from glowing embers as inhalants. Others are dried, pulverized and mixed with oils or petroleum jelly and applied externally; and ground fresh or dried leaves can be administered as an enema.

The use of ethnomedicinal plants is gaining momentum as nature-based drugs grow in popularity and because many effective drugs, such as paclitaxel, artemisinin, quinine and morphine, were originally isolated from plants.

Ethnomedicinal plants and drug development

Medicinal plants possess substances that can be used for therapeutic purposes or contain precursors for chemo-pharmaceutical semi-synthesis, which are produced by the plant as defence-mechanisms (Kayani, Masood, Achakzai, & Anbreen, 2007). Tuulikki (2003) reported that some of these compounds produce a bitter taste and may be poisonous, which consequently deter browsers and herbivores from eating the plant. In addition, some of the secondary metabolites fight microbial infections of the plant caused by bacteria, fungi and parasites. In essence, some of these secondary metabolites are potent to human pathogens as well. Well-known examples of such secondary metabolites include alkaloids, phenolic compounds, terpenoids, steroids, saponins and tannins (Cowan, 1999).

The search for or selection of plants with potent secondary metabolites as potential, natural-compound-based drugs involves three approaches (Silva et al., 2013). The first approach is random sampling, which involves the collection of plants found in any geographical location without regard to their taxonomic relations, ethnomedicinal uses or other intrinsic qualities. The advantage of this approach is that it includes a wide variety of plants, thereby increasing the chance of discovering lead compounds or scaffolds for drug development. It is, however, usually accompanied by low rate of success.

The second approach is the ethno-directed sampling approach, in which plant species are selected for testing according to their use by community members and traditional healers for medicinal purposes. To date this approach has been responsible for bringing a high proportion of plant-based drugs and herbal medicines to the market. According to de Ridder et al. (2004), artemisinin was isolated from *Artemisia annua* and its antiplasmodial properties discovered using this approach.

The third approach is the targeted or chemotaxanomic approach, whereby essential characteristics and aspects of the plants such as taxonomy, phytochemistry, phylogeny and ecology are considered before plants are collected.

In the second approach which is commonly used, ethnobotanical studies are used to acquire information about useful medicinal plants. Following the leads provided by knowledge holders and or traditional healers, plants are collected and identified.

After plants have been collected, extracts are prepared using solvents of varying polarity. These extracts are tested, using phytochemical screens, for pharmacological activity based on the use of the plant in folk medicine. Plants that show significant activity are subjected to bioactivity-guided fractionation, which identifies potent fractions of the plant extracts based on their biological activity. The fractions are further fractionated until the biologically active phytochemicals are isolated and purified. Lastly, the structures of the pure substances are determined and the compounds identified. These compounds might not be the actual drugs, but they can serve as precursors for chemical modification, or scaffolds, for the synthesis of more potent drugs. In many cases, a single compound might not be as effective as the whole plant extracts from which they are isolated. In such cases, natural-products chemists use them in combinations to improve their effectiveness.

Namibian medicinal plants

Vegetation distribution in Namibia is dictated by the climate, which also determines malaria transmission and epidemiology. The northern regions of Namibia have the highest annual average rainfall in the country, with Zambezi having more than 550 mm, Kavango East having 450–600 mm and Omusati having 350–450 mm per year (Mendelsohn, Jarvis, Roberts, & Robertson, 2002). These regions are also known for their relatively high density and variety of vegetation. These regions also have a high incidence of malaria compared to the rest of the country. Many people living in these regions use ethnomedicinal plants for treating various diseases and conditions, including malaria and malaria-associated symptoms. They prefer to use plants to conventional medicines because they are easily accessible, readily available and affordable, and because these ethnomedicines have been used for generations, they trust the safety, efficacy and identity of these plants (Bussmann, 2013).

Indigenous knowledge about medicinal plants is typically retained by the elderly in the community and is only passed on to their children that are interested in continuing with the craft. The increase in westernized lifestyles among young people has, however, led them to question and lose interest in traditional healing. As a result, the knowledge is at risk of being lost. According to information communicated in a field survey for this project, the influence of Christianity has also caused communities to abandon practising traditional medicine, as it is perceived as witchcraft or divination. Therefore, it is imperative that indigenous knowledge is documented before it is lost. In response to this concern, a number of ethnobotanical studies have been conducted in order to document indigenous knowledge pertinent to medicinal plants in Namibia (von Koenen, 2001; Chinsembu & Hedimbi, 2010; Cheikhyoussef, Shapi, Matengu, & Mu Ashekele, 2011). Further studies required to validate the uses of these plants include botanical identification, phytochemical analysis and pre-clinical studies.

Some groups have been relying on traditional medicines to cure malaria-associated symptoms for thousands of years (Mohammed, 2010). These remedies are taken in a wide range of forms, but mostly as decoctions. The plants are pulverized into smaller pieces or powder, boiled in water and then administered orally. Other forms of treatments include infusions, inhalation of smoke or vapour, applying the plant material into incisions made in the skin and/or onto the skin surface, or simply by sniffing the powder made from the relevant plant part. For example, some traditional healers in the country administer a decoction of the leaves of *Guibourtia coleosperma* to patients with malaria symptoms. In some instances, the head of the patient is covered with a blanket over a bowl of leaves in boiling water to allow inhalation of herbal vapour (MoHSS & UNICEF, 2000). The Aawambo use herbal enemas that have strong laxative and emetic effects on patients.

The use of plants varies among different cultures. A plant may be used medicinally in one community and not at all in another, or for different ailments. For instance, local inhabitants of the Tsumkwe area of Otjozondjupa Region use *Rhigozum brevispinosum* as digging sticks and ornaments (Leffers, 2003), whereas this same plant is used to treat ailments such as headaches in Oshikoto Region (du Preez, Mumbengegwi, & Böck, 2010) and syphilis in Zambezi Region (Cheikhyoussef, Mapaure, & Shapi, 2011). *Dicerocaryum eriocarpum*, commonly known as devil's thorn, is used to treat chest and abdominal pains where it is found. A single plant may even have multiple uses in the same area. For example, in Tsumkwe area, a leaf

FIGURE 2.1:
Vahlia capensis, a plant used in traditional treatments in northern Namibia against fever, a prominent symptom of malaria. (© Coleen Mannheimer.)

FIGURE 2.2:
Nicolasia costata is
used in combination
with *Vahlia capensis* to
treat fever in northern
Namibia. (© Iwanette
du Preez.)

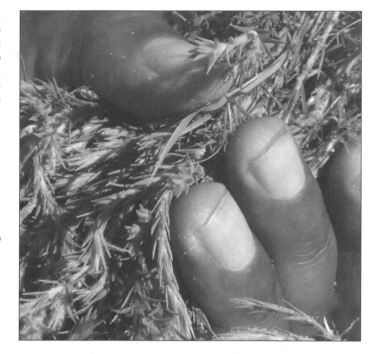

FIGURE 2.3:
*Dicerocaryum
eriocarpum* used in
traditional remedies
in northern Namibia
to treat abdominal
pain, one of many
symptoms of malaria.
(© Iwanette du Preez.)

FIGURE 2.4:
Guibourtia coleosperma is used as a traditional remedy in northern Namibia against malarial headaches. (© Silke Rügheimer.)

FIGURE 2.5: *Diospyros mespiliformis*, a conspicuous plant in the northern parts of Namibia, is used in traditional treatments as an antipyretic. (© Coleen Mannheimer.)

FIGURE 2.6: *Mundulea sericea* is used to treat malaria in traditional medicine practice in northern Namibia. (© Silke Rügheimer.)

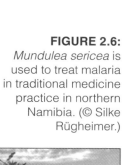

infusion of *Acrotome inflata* is used to cure coughing and the flower heads are burnt to ward off mosquitoes (Leffers, 2003).

Traditional medicine sometimes requires only one plant species. In other therapies, plants are used in combination with two or more plants. *Vahlia capensis* and *Nicolasia costata*, for example, are used together to treat fever. In allopathic medicine, combination therapy (or polytherapy) is also recommended in the treatment of malaria. This similarity in allopathic and traditional medicine serves to increase efficacy and reduce the emergence of resistant malaria parasites.

VALIDATION OF THE USE OF NAMIBIAN ETHNOMEDICINAL PLANTS FOR MALARIA

Ethnobotany

Six plants, namely *Vahlia capensis*, *Nicolasia costata*, *Dicerocaryum eriocarpum*, *Guibourtia coleosperma*, *Mundulea sericea* and *Diospyros mespiliformis* (Figures 2.1–2.6), were selected in order to validate their uses in the treatment of malaria and associated symptoms. Three criteria were used in the selection of these plants species:

1. they are used to treat malaria-associated symptoms in the traditional setting; i.e. following an ethnopharmacological approach;
2. they are presently abundant in malaria areas of Namibia to ensure sustainable harvesting; and
3. they have not previously been screened for antiplasmodial properties.

Vahlia capensis (Vahliaceae; Figure 2.1), a few- or several-stemmed plant, is known as *namushinga* in Oshiwambo. It is an annual herb that is 7–38 cm tall and has stems and leaves that usually have sparse to dense hairs, which terminate in glands, but are occasionally glabrous. *Vahlia capensis* is used in combination with *Nicolasia costata* (Asteraceae; Figure 2.2) for the treatment of fever by locals in Ofilu village, in the Oshikoto region of Namibia. The aerial parts of both plants are placed in hot water for inhalation purposes. A blanket is placed over the head and resulting steam is breathed in for a therapeutic effect. *Nicolasia costata*, an annual herb as well, creeps along the ground and has narrow elongated leaves arranged spirally around the stem. It is known as *okadimba* in Oshiwambo.

Dicerocaryum eriocarpum (Pedaliaceae; Figure 2.3) is known locally as *okalyata*. It is also known as devil's thorn due to its circular fruit with slightly raised central portions, imitating thorn-like structures. *D. eriocarpum* is an annual herb, which creeps along the ground, and is used traditionally to alleviate abdominal pains. Powdered roots are prepared in a decoction and then drunk.

Guibourtia coleosperma (Fabaceae; Figure 2.4) is a well-known tree that can reach 20 m in height and is known as *ushivi* in Rumanyo. In Kavango East Region, the leaves and roots are boiled and the patient undergoes a steam bath at regular intervals during the night. In between these sessions, drums are beaten and the *mahamba* (medicine dance) is performed. Scrapings of the plant's roots are rubbed all over the patient's body. This treatment is used for general debility, malaria, psychosis and depression. For headaches of unknown origin, the bark, root bark and resin are pounded and mixed with hot water for repeated steam baths.

Diospyros mespiliformis (Ebenaceae; Figure 2.5), an African ebony tree, is commonly known as *omwandi* by the Aawambo and jackal-berry in English. In Namibia, the jackal-berry is abundant on the Cuvelai floodplain, and in the Okavango and Zambezi regions. The tree grows on river banks, floodplains and around pans in the Cuvelai (Curtis & Mannheimer, 2005). The Aawambo use the leaves, twigs and bark as a remedy for ringworm, leprosy, fever, dysentery and as a treatment for wounds (von Koenen, 2001).

Mundulea sericea (Fabaceae; Figure 2.6) can grow up to 7.5 m high and is used in the treatment of malaria. According to von Koenen (2001), the Aawambo administer a shoot extract as an enema to treat the disease. Alternatively, the root is dried, crushed, pulverized and strewn over glowing embers, to be used as a smoke bath by the patient while covered by a blanket. *Mundulea sericea* is also used by the Himba to treat lice infestations, and furunculosis. The Damara use it to treat burns.

The ethnobotanical information on these plants is summarized in Table 2.1, below.

Phytochemistry

The overall 'chemical fingerprint' or 'chemical profile' of a plant is determined by using phytochemical screens. Thin-layer chromatography was used to isolate and separate different antimalarial compounds in the extracts of the six plants under investigation, suggesting where potential antiplasmodial activity might be found. The plants were tested for five known antimalarial compounds – alkaloids, anthraquinones, coumarins, flavonoids and terpenoids. The chemical profiles of the organic extracts from these plants are given in Table 2.1.

The organic extracts of the whole plant of *V. capensis* tested positive for alkaloids and coumarins. Organic extracts of the foliage of *N. costata* showed the presence of alkaloids, coumarins and terpenoids. Root extracts – aqueous and organic – of *D. eriocarpum* indicated the presence of alkaloids, anthraquinones, coumarins, flavonoids and terpenoids; interestingly, lower levels of the compounds were detected in the aqueous extracts than in the organic extracts.

Phytochemical screening of *G. coleosperma* leaves indicated the presence of alkaloids, anthraquinones, flavonoids, alkaloids and coumarins, and the absence of terpenoids. The bark, however, was positive for terpenoids, as well as alkaloids. The roots were

TABLE 2.1: Ethnobotanical information on selected medicinal plants used by traditional healers to treat malaria and associated symptoms in Namibia

Family	Species	Local name	Plant part used	Ailment	Traditional preparation
Vahliaceae	*Vahlia capensis*	*namushinga*	whole plant	fever	steam bath (placed in hot water, covered with blanket and vapour inhaled)
Asteraceae	*Nicolasia costata*	*okadimba*	whole plant	fever	steam bath (placed in hot water, covered with blanket and vapour inhaled)
Pedaliaceae	*Dicerocaryum eriocarpum*	*okalyata*	roots	abdominal pain	dried and pound into powder, boiled in water and aqueous extraction is drunk
Fabaceae	*Guibourtia coleosperma*	*ushivi*	bark, roots, leaves and resin	headaches, malaria	plant parts pounded, mixed with hot water and used as steam bath
	Mundulea sericea	*omumbanganyana*	roots	malaria	pulverized roots are strewn over glowing embers and the smoke is inhaled under a blanket
			shoots	malaria	water extract is given as enema
Ebenaceae	*Diospyros mespiliformis*	*omwandi*	leaves, twigs and bark	fever	water extract is given orally

positive for anthraquinones, only. Phytochemical analysis of *M. sericea* shoots revealed the presence of all five classes of antiplasmodial compounds, while leaves showed flavonoids and terpenoids only.

The presence of alkaloids, anthraquinones and terpenoids was observed in the leaves of *D. mespiliformis*, while the roots showed the presence of alkaloids, anthraquinones, terpenoids and coumarins and the absence of flavonoids.

Pharmacological activity

The plants were screened for antimalarial activity using an *in vitro* model. This involved growing the parasites in human peripheral (red blood) cells in cell culture flasks at 37 °C. The antimalarial activity of plant extracts at various concentrations was assessed by determining a reduction in the number of parasitized red blood cells in the samples after 24 hours, compared to the control.

Table 2.3 shows the change in parasitaemia of the *P. falciparum* 3D7 strain over 24 hours whilst incubated with plant extracts from *V. capensis*, *N. costata*, *D. eriocarpum*, *G. coleosperma*, *D. mespiliformis* and *M. sericea*. The concentrations at which the growth

TABLE 2.2: Classes of antimalarial compounds found in organic extracts of plants using thin-layer chromatography.

Plant	Part used	Alkaloids	Anthraquinones	Coumarins	Terpenoids	Flavonoids
				Class of antimalarial compounds		
Vahlia capensis	aerial parts	+	–	++	–	–
Nicolasia costata	aerial parts	+	–	+	+	–
Dicerocaryum eriocarpum	roots	++	++	++	+	++
Guibourtia coleosperma	bark	+	–	–	+	–
	leaves	+	+	+	–	+
	roots	–	+	–	–	–
Mundulea sericea	leaves	–	–	–	+	+
	shoots	+	+	+	+	+
Diospyros mespiliformis	leaves	+	+	–	+	–
	roots	+	+	+	+	–

+ indicates presence and relative concentration of the compound
– indicates absence of the compound

TABLE 2.3: Antimalarial activity exhibited by organic plant extracts

Plants	Plant parts	IC_{50} (µg/mℓ)
Vahlia capensis	whole plant	93.29
Nicolasia costata	whole plant	86.63
Dicerocaryum eriocarpum	roots	63.17
Guibourtia coleosperma	bark	3.57
	leaves	3.00
	roots	3.85
Mundulea sericea	leaves	3.95
	shoots	3.46
Diospyros mespiliformis	leaves	3.47
	roots	3.22

of parasites was inhibited by 50% (i.e. the half maximal inhibitory concentration, or IC_{50}) for *V. capensis*, *N. costata* and *D. eriocarpum* were 93.29, 86.63, 63.17 µg/mℓ mℓ, respectively, indicating that the amounts of *V. capensis* and *N. costata* required for effective parasite inhibition activity was ~1.5 times more than that of *D. eriocarpum*.

IC_{50} for *G. coleosperma*, *D. mespiliformis* and *M. sericea* were less than 5 µg/mℓ for all plant parts tested indicating they were at least ten times more potent than the other three plants.

For *in vitro* studies, plant extracts with IC_{50} values less than 10 µg/mℓ are considered having good activity. Those with IC_{50} values of 10–50 µg/mℓ are considered moderate, those with IC_{50} values of 50–100 µg/mℓ low, and those with IC_{50} values of greater than 100 µg/mℓ are considered inactive (Basco et al., 1994; Dolabela et al., 2008). Thus, as potential antimalarials, *G. coleosperma*, *D. mespiliformis* and *M. sericea* exhibit high activity. The other three have low activity; however, the crude extracts of these plants are therapeutically meaningful, validating their traditional use. This is because even in those showing low activity, it is likely that the active components in the plant extracts are present in very low concentrations and form part of complex mixtures with many other compounds within the extract (Batista et al., 2009).

INFORMATION GAP

Very little information exists on the use of ethnomedicinal plants in Namibia (Mapaure & Hatuikulipi, 2007) and what is there lacks detail. Plant names are sometimes given in either their vernacular or as scientific names, not both, and the exact illnesses for which the medicinal plants are used are not properly described. Local communities often describe illnesses by the ailments they cause, for example 'stomach problems', which can be misinterpreted.

Malaria is a clinical diagnosis. Traditional healers, however, diagnose patients based on the symptoms and might actually be treating malaria. Most of the plants they use have not been documented, neither have they been tested against *Plasmodium* parasites *in vitro* or *in vivo*, but are reported in some of the literature to treat ailments similar to the symptoms of malaria.

CONCLUSION AND RECOMMENDATIONS

It is very important that indigenous knowledge about medicinal plants is systematically documented. Research should focus on evaluating the safety and efficacy of medicinal plants used in folk medicine, and validating ethnomedicines against various pathogens and diseases. This study has contributed to the assessment of possible therapeutic properties of Namibian plants against malaria. The extracts of all six plants tested revealed the presence of known classes of antimalarial bioactive compounds and therefore were then screened for *in vitro* antimalarial activity. They all showed antiplasmodial activity.

The presence of compounds that have antimalarial and antiplasmodial properties strongly supports the argument that the traditional use of these plants is rational. In addition, the presence of these compounds also raises safety concerns because side effects of these compound classes are known, and they can be coded based on their cytotoxicity levels. More information about the active components of these plant extracts can assist in preparing them, as they may be enhanced or lost under certain preparation methods.

The antimalarial activity exhibited by these plants also supports the importance of using an ethnopharmacological approach in screening plants as potential sources of antimalarials. In conclusion, this study has illustrated the value of traditional knowledge in the fight against malaria. The validation of plants used by indigenous populations in Namibia will facilitate on-going efforts to eliminate malaria within the country by providing treatment to isolated, rural populations that do not necessarily have access to, or do not believe in, conventional medicines.

It is recommended that plants used to treat symptoms of malaria, or malaria itself, in a traditional setting should be documented, screened to validate their use, tested for safety, and registered with the Ministry of Health and Social Services in Namibia as alternative treatments for malaria. This may contribute to the integration of complementary or alternative medicines into public health services. Further studies should also be conducted to identify the active components of validated plant extracts as these may potentially be developed into pharmaceutical products for the treatment of malaria.

References

Baird, B. K. (2005). Effectiveness of antimalarial drugs. *New England Journal of Medicine, 352*(15), 1565-77.

Balick, M. J., Elisabetsky, E., & Laid, S. A. (1996), *Medicinal resources of the tropical forest, biodiversity and its importance to human health* (1st ed.). New York, USA: Columbia University Press.

Bannister, L., & Mitchell, G. (2003). The ins, outs and roundabouts of malaria. *Trends in Parasitology, 19*(5), 209-213.

Basco, L., Mitaku, S., Skaltsounis, A. L., Ravelomanantsoa, N., Tillequin, R., Koch, M., & Le Bras, J. (1994). *In vitro* activities of fluoroquinoline and acridone alkaloids against *Plasmodium falciparum. Antimicrobial Agents and Chemotherapy, 38*(5), 1169-1171.

Batista, R., De Jesus Silva Junior, A., & De Oliveira, A. B. (2009). Plant-derived antimalarial agents: New leads and efficient phytomedicines. Part II. Non-alkaloidal natural products. *Molecules, 14*(8), 3037-3072.

Bosman, A., & Mendis, K. N. (2007). A major transition in malaria treatment: The adoption and deployment of artemisinin-based combination therapies. *The American Journal of Tropical Medicine and Hygiene, 77*(Suppl. 6), 193-197.

Breman, J. G. (2001). The ears of the hippopotamus: Manifestations, determinants, and estimates of the malaria burden. *American Journal of Tropical Medicine and Hygiene, 64*(Suppl. 1-2), 1-11.

Bussmann, R. W. (2013). The globalization of traditional medicine in northern Peru: From shamanism to molecules. *Evidence-Based Complementary and Alternative Medicine, 2013*, 1-46.

Cheikhyoussef, A., Mapaure, I., & Shapi, M. (2011). The use of some indigenous plants for medicinal and other purposes by local communities in Namibia with emphasis on Oshikoto Region: A review. *Research Journal of Medicinal Plants, 5*(4), 406-419.

Cheikhyoussef, A., Shapi, M., Matengu, K., & Mu Ashekele, H. (2011). Ethnobotanical study of indigenous knowledge on medicinal plant use by traditional healers in Oshikoto Region, Namibia. *Journal of Ethnobiology and Ethnomedicine, 7*(10), 1-11.

Chinsembu, K. C., & Hedimbi, M. (2010). Ethnomedicinal plants and other natural products with anti-HIV active compounds and their putative modes of action. *International Journal for Biotechnology and Molecular Biology Research, 1*(6), 74-91.

Cowan, M. M. (1999). Plant products as antimicrobial agents. *Clinical Microbiology Reviews, 12*(4), 564-582.

Cowling, R. M., & Hilton-Taylor, C. (1994). Patterns of plant diversity and endemism in southern Africa: An overview. In B. J. Huntley (Ed.), *Botanical Diversity in Southern Africa. Strelitzia 1* (pp. 31-52). Pretoria, South Africa: National Botanical Research Institute.

Crawley, J., Chu, C., Mtove, G., & Nosten, F. (2010). Malaria in children. *The Lancet, 375*(9724), 1468-1481.

Cunha-Rodrigues, M., Prudêncio, M., Mota, M. M., & Haas, W. (2006). Antimalarial drugs – host targets (re)visited. *Biotechnology Journal, 1*(3), 321-332.

Curtis, B., & Mannheimer, C. (2005). *Tree Atlas of Namibia*. Windhoek, Namibia: National Botanical Research Institute.

De Ridder, S., van der Kooy, F., & Verpoorte, R. (2004). *Artemisia annua* as a self-reliant treatment for malaria in developing countries. *Journal of Ethnopharmacology, 120*, 302-314. doi:10.1016/j.jep.2008.09.017

Dolabela, F. M., Oliveira, S. G., Nascimento, M. J., Peres, J. M., Wagner, H., Povoa, M. M., & Oliveira, A. B. (2008). *In vitro* antiplasmodial activity of extract and constituents from *Esenbeckia febrifuga*, a plant traditionally used to treat malaria in the Brazilian Amazon. *Phytomedicine, 15*, 376-372. doi:10.1016/j. phymed.2008.02.001

Du Preez, I., Mumbengegwi, D., & Böck, R. (2010). Validation of ethno-medicinal plant knowledge in the Oshikoto Region through botanical identification and biological assessment of its value as complementary medicine for malaria. Proceedings of the 1st Biennial National Research Symposium, 15–17 September 2010, Windhoek, Namibia.

Ekland, E. H., & Fidock, D. A. (2007). Advances in understanding the genetic basis of antimalarial resistance. *Current Opinion in Microbiology, 10*(4), 363-370.

Elamin, S. B., Elabadi, E. K., & Mohamad, T. A. (2007). Efficacy of chloroquine and sulfadoxine–pyrimethamine mono-combined therapy against falciparum malaria. *Eastern Mediterranean Health Journal, 13*(1), 25-34.

Eriksen, J., Mwankusye, S., Mduma, S., Veiga, M. L., Kitua, A., Tomson, … Warsame, M. (2008). Antimalarial resistance and DHFR/DHPS genotypes of *Plasmodium falciparum* three years after into sulphadoxine-pyrimethamine and amodiaquine in rural Tanzania. *Transactions of the Royal Society of Tropical Medicine and Hygiene, 102*(2), 137-142.

Fernando, S., Rodrigo, C., & Rajapakse, S. (2010). The 'hidden' burden of malaria: Cognitive impairment following infection. *Malaria Journal, 9*(366), 1-11.

Heelan, J. S., & Ingersoll, F. W. (2001). *Essentials of human parasitology*. Delmar, USA:. Thomas Learning.

Hoareau, L., & Da Silva, E. (1999). Medicinal plants: A re-emerging health aid. *Electronic Journal of Biotechnology, 2*(2), 56-70.

Jiang, H., Joy, D. A., Furuya, T., & Su, X.-Z. (2006). Current understanding of molecular basis of chloroquine-resistance in *Plasmodium falciparum*. *Journal of Postgraduate Medicine, 52*(4), 261-7.

Kayani, S. A., Masood, A., Achakzai, A. K. K., & Anbreen, S. (2007). Distribution of secondary metabolites in plants of quetta-balochistan. *Pakistan Journal of Botany, 39*(4), 1173-1179.

Krause, P. J. (2007). Malaria (*Plasmodium*). In R. E. Behrman, R. M. Kliegman, & H. B. Jenson (Eds) *Nelson textbook of paediatrics* (18th ed.) (pp. 1477-1485). Philadelphia, USA: WB Saunders.

Krishna, S., Uhlemann, A., & Haynes, R. K. (2004). Artemisinins: Mechanisms of action and potential for resistance. *Drug Resistance Updates, 7*(4-5), 233-244.

Leffers, A. (2003). Gemsbok bean & kalahari truffle: Traditional plant use by Ju|'hoansi in north-eastern Namibia. Windhoek, Namibia: Macmillan Education Namibia.

Mapaure, I., & Hatuikulipi, T. (2007). Namibia's indigenous knowledge system: IKS literature review report on the use of plants for medicinal and other purposes by local communities in Namibia. Unpublished report. Windhoek, Namibia: University of Namibia.

Mendelsohn, J., Jarvis, A., Roberts, C., & Robertson, T. (2002). *Atlas of Namibia: A portrait of the land and its people.* Cape Town: David Philip Publishers.

Meunier, B. (2012). Towards antimalarial hybrid drugs. In J.-U. Peters (ed.) *Polypharmacology in drug discovery* (5th ed., pp. 423-439). Hoboken, New Jersey, USA: John Wiley & Sons. doi: 10.1002/9781118098141.ch21

MoHSS [Ministry of Health and Social Services]. (2005). *National malaria policy.* Windhoek, Namibia: Directorate of Special Programmes.

MoHSS [Ministry of Health and Social Services]. (2010). *Malaria Strategic Plan 2010– 2016.* Windhoek, Namibia: Author.

MoHSS [Ministry of Health and Social Services]. (2014). *Vector-borne diseases control programme annual report* (p. 22). Windhoek, Namibia: Author.

MoHSS, & UNICEF [Ministry of Health and Social Services, & United Nations Children's Fund]. (2000). *Survey on traditional healers and community use of traditional medicine in Namibia.* Windhoek, Namibia.

Mohammed, M. S. A. (2010). Traditional medicinal plants and malaria in Africa. In N. H. Juliani (Ed.), *African natural plant products: New discoveries and challenges in chemistry and quality* (Chapter 12). Washington DC, USA: American Chemical Society Symposium Series.

Nchinda, T. C. (1998). Malaria: A reemerging disease in Africa. *Emerging Infectious Diseases, 4*(3), 398-403.

Rao, A., Kumar, M. K., Joseph, T., & Bulusu, G. (2010). Cerebral malaria: Insights from host–parasite protein–protein interactions. *Malaria Journal, 9*(5), 155. doi: 10.1186/1475-2875-9-155.

Sachs, J., & Malaney, P. (2002). The economic and social burden of malaria. *Nature, 415,* 685-680. doi:10.1038/415680a

Saxena, M., Saxena, J., Nema, R., Singh, D., & Gupta, A. (2013). Phytochemistry of Medicinal Plants. *Journal of Pharmacognosy and Phytochemistry 1*(6), 168-182.

Schlagenhauf, P., & Petersen, E. (2009). Antimalaria drug resistance: The mono-combi-counterfeit triangle. *Expert Review of Anti-infective Therapy, 7*(9), 1039-1042.

Silva, A. C. O., Santana, E. F., Saraiva, A. M., Coutinho, F. N., Castro, H. R. A., Pisciottano, M. N. C., Amorim, E. L. C., & Albuquerque, U. P. (2013). Which approach is more effective in the selection of plants with antimicrobial activity? *Evidence-Based Complementary and Alternative Medicine, 2013,* 1-9. doi:10.1155/2013/308980

Singh, B. & Daneshvar, C. (2013). Human infections and detection of *Plasmodium knowlesi. Clinical Microbiology Reviews, 26*(2), 165-84. doi:10.1128/CMR.00079-12

Srinivasa B., Reddy, T., Sujith, M., Kumar, S., Babu, A. N., Rao, N. R., & Manjunathan, J. (2012). Malarial drugs got resistance. *International Journal of Pharmaceutical and Biomedical Research 3*(4), 213-215. Retrieved from http://www.pharmscidirect.com.

Trampuz, A., Jereb, M., Muzlovic, I., & Prabhu, R. M. (2003). Clinical review: Severe malaria. *Critical Care, 7*, 315-323. doi:10.1186/cc2183

Tuulikki, R. (2003). *Defences and responses: Woody species and large herbivores in Africa savannas* (Unpublished PhD thesis). Swedish University of Agricultural Sciences, Uppsala, Sweden.

Von Koenen, E. (2001). *Medicinal, poisonous and edible plants of Namibia* (Vol. 4). Windhoek & Göttingen, Namibia & Germany: Klaus Hess Publishers.

Wang, M.-W., Hao, X., & Chen, K. (2007). Biological screening of natural products and drug innovation in China. *Philosophical Transactions of the Royal Society, Biological Sciences, 362*(1482), 1093-1105. doi: 10.1098/rstb.2007.2036

White, N. J. (2008). The role of anti-malarial drugs in eliminating malaria. *Malaria Journal, 7*(Suppl 1), S8. doi: 10.1186/1475-2875-7-S1-S8

WHO [World Health Organization]. (2005). National policy on traditional medicine and regulation of herbal medicines: Report of a WHO global survey World Health Organization (p. 156). Geneva.

WHO [World Health Organization]. (2009). *World malaria report, 2009*. Geneva, Switzerland: Author.

WHO [World Health Organization]. (2010). Ministry of Health and Social Services launches Malaria Elimination Campaign on World Malaria Day 2010 (Newsflash). WHO Country Office, Windhoek, Namibia.

WHO [World Health Organization]. (2012). *World Malaria Report, 2012*. Geneva, Switzerland: Author.

3

Indigenous knowledge of medicinal plants used for the treatment of cancer

Florence Dushimemaria, Davis R. Mumbengegwi & Ronnie Böck

BACKGROUND

The global burden of cancer continues to increase in both developed and developing countries. This is largely attributed to a growing aged population as both the numbers of people and life expectancies increase. Another important factor is the adoption of lifestyles that increase the risk of developing cancer (Jemal et al., 2011). Lifestyle choices, such as smoking tobacco, consuming alcohol, being physically inactive and eating unhealthily, contribute to the upsurge in cancer cases. Siegel, Naishadham and Jemal (2012) estimated that about 1,638,910 new incidences of cancer and about 577,190 deaths due to cancer occurred worldwide in 2012. They further estimated that 56% of the cancer cases and 64% of cancer-related deaths occurred in developing countries (Jemal et al., 2011), indicating that the developing world is gradually having to shoulder more of the burden and where cancer survival rates tend to be lower.

The most common form of cancer in females is breast cancer, which accounted for 1,383,500 new cases in 2008, while lung cancer is the leading cause of morbidity in males, with 1,095,200 new cases estimated for 2008 (Jemal et al., 2011). These trends are similar in developed and developing countries (Jemal et al., 2011).

The Namibian National Cancer Registry (2011) reported a total of 6,363 neoplasms between 2006 and 2009. Of these, just over half (50.4%) were diagnosed in females. Within the four-year period, breast (27.6%) and cervix (17.1%) carcinomas were the most prevalent in females, while Kaposi sarcoma (22.1%) and prostate (19.2%) cancers were the most common malignancies in males. This marked a remarkable increase in the incidence of almost all types of cancer (>280 more cases per year) since the previous report (Namibian National Cancer Registry, 2009).

Namibia is one of the countries severely affected by the HIV (human immunodeficiency virus) and AIDS (acquired immunodeficiency syndrome) crisis, which has grown to a full-blown epidemic since the first diagnosed case in 1986. Estimates suggest that between 210,000 and 290,000 people in Namibia were infected with HIV by the end of 2013 (UNAIDS, 2013). They have an increased chance of developing Kaposi sarcoma, eye cancer and non-Hodgkin's lymphoma (Namibian Cancer Registry, 2011). Kaposi's sarcoma is now the leading cause of morbidity due to cancer in men and the third-most common cancer in women in Namibia. However, since the introduction of highly active antiretroviral therapies (Jemal et al., 2011) with increased coverage (Chinsembu & Hedimbi, 2010), the rate of increment of the three HIV-associated cancers has declined considerably, in Namibia and elsewhere.

In Namibia, the World Health Organization (WHO) reported that the proportion of Namibia's population living in urban areas had increased steadily from 28% in 1990 to 37% in 2009 (WHO, 2011). The report further notes that Namibians have high rates of alcohol consumption (about 6.5 ℓ of pure alcohol per annum) and tobacco use (24.1% of males and 9.5% of females use tobacco-derived products). WHO (2011) also reported a physician and nurse/midwife density of 3.7 and 27.8 per 10,000 people, respectively, for the period 2000–2010 for the country's population of 2.2 million people. These low rates of qualified healthcare personnel in Namibia are, however, higher than in many developing countries.

ETHNOMEDICINES

Plants have been used for the treatment of different ailments in humans and animals from time immemorial, according to archaeological records (Day, 2013). WHO (2002) estimates that over 80% of rural and urban African populations use plant-based products for primary healthcare. Users of these traditional medicines often self-medicate. There is a widespread misconception about the safety of medicinal plants and derived herbal supplements with many users of herbal products believing that the components of traditional medicines have undergone a long period of evaluation in nature. 'Natural', however, does not necessarily mean 'safe'. Furthermore, it is imperative that traditional healers have a good understanding of the plants they use and can identify them. For example, a Chinese weight-loss remedy caused serious renal failure among users because a nephrotoxic plant, *Aristolochia fangchi* was substituted for *Stephania tetrandra* or *Magnolia officinalis* (Nortier et al., 2000; Vivekanand, 2010). Nevertheless, an increased usage of traditional medicine or complementary and alternative medicine is observed in countries such as China, Chile and Colombia, amongst others. In Chile and Colombia, over 71% and 40% of the population, respectively, depend on traditional or nonconventional means for primary healthcare provision.

Medicinal plants as a source of anticancer medicines: A Western paradigm

In 1955, the National Cancer Institute (NCI) in the United States of America (USA) was formed with the sole mandate to screen plant samples for possible anticancer properties with applications in the fight against cancer. Since then, the NCI has provided resources for the preclinical screening and clinical development of compounds and materials. Over 60,000 plant samples have been collected and a repository of over 120,000 extracts for analysis has been established. This has contributed immensely to the discovery and development of many commercially available anticancer agents. In addition, more than 500,000 chemicals – both synthetic and natural – have been screened for antitumour activity with models ranging from *in vivo* murine tumours to human tumour xenografts in immunodeficient mice and isolated human tumour cell lines. An estimated 50% of new drugs marketed between 1981 and 2006 show that some owe their origin in one way or another to natural sources.

In India, about 70% of the population relies on the use of plants or traditional medicinal plants for healthcare (Sen, Chakraborty, & De, 2011), while 40% of all delivered healthcare in China is through non-conventional medicine. In these cultures, the plants to be used, the mode of preparation and dosage for each individual ailment are described. This is known as ethnomedicine or, more commonly, traditional medicine.

Ethnomedicine comprises embedded practices found in a defined area, region, or ethnic group, which may be unique and relate to the use of plants, herbs, rituals, spirits and religious beliefs as a way of life. Another name used to refer to other less-conventional methods of providing healthcare is 'alternative medicine'. This umbrella term includes unconventional forms of medicine such as Ayurveda or traditional Chinese medicine. Acupuncture has its origins with the Chinese; Unani has its origins about 2,500 years ago from the teachings of the Greek philosopher Hippocrates, and is widely practised in the Middle East and southern Asia (Lone et al., 2012); Kampo practices originated from the Japanese adaptation of traditional Chinese medicine during the 7th and 8th Centuries.

Although mainstream health practitioners discourage or shun the use of traditional or alternative medicines for primary healthcare (Barbee, 1986), many patients still seek less-orthodox doctors for treatment. Traditional medicine can be organized and well recorded, such as Ayurveda or Chinese medicine, but it can also take the form of practices passed down from one generation to the next and, as a result, is poorly recorded. In Africa and South America, documentation of the different traditional healing practices is poor as shown by the lack of information in comparison to other practices. Moreover, the chemical- and pharmacological-based evidence of the use of documented plants has been given little attention.

THE SIGNIFICANCE OF MEDICINAL PLANTS FOR CANCER TREATMENT

The use of traditional medicine is widespread in developing nations, while complementary and alternative medicines are gaining acceptance in developed countries. WHO hosted the first strategic meeting on traditional medicine in Geneva in 2002 (WHO, 2002) at which member countries deliberated the safety, efficacy, availability, access and quality of traditional, as well as complementary and alternative, medicines.

Many anticancer compounds have been discovered from plants of higher order (Farnsworth, Akerele, Bingel, Soejarto, & Guo, 1985; Schwartsmann et al., 2002; Shoeb, 2006; Patel, Das, Prakash, & Yassir, 2010; Agarwal, Majee, & Chakraborthy, 2012; Ghosh, Pal, Prusty, & Girish, 2012), some having been discovered through the NCI. Nirmala, Samundeeswari and Sankar (2011) discuss different plant-derived anticancer compounds, many of which are from well-known phytochemical classes such as stilbenes, flavonoids, triterpenes, coumarins and anthraquinones, but the majority appear to be alkaloids. In depth studies have revealed chemical components responsible for the observed activities and elucidated the structure of these active constituents.

Taxol (see Figure 3.1a), derived from the Pacific yew *Taxus brevifolia* (Guo, Kai, Jin, & Tang, 2006) acts by inhibiting mitosis during the cell cycle. Other products – such as ellipticine (Figure 3.1b), an alkaloid (Shi et al., 1998) – act by intercalating into DNA (deoxyribonucleic acid) and inhibiting topoisomerase and are active against a range of cancer types (Nirmala et al., 2011). Examples such as harringtonine (Figure 3.1c) and homoharringtonine, derived from *Cephalotaxus harringtonia* and two other related species, are active against leukaemia while another compound, colchicine, is active against both solid and leukaemic carcinomas. Shoeb (2006) reported active compounds, montamine and schischkinnin that were derived from *Centaurea montana* and *Centaurea schischkinii*, against colon cancer, however, the mechanism of action is not yet known (Nirmala et al., 2011).

Smith (1895) described the shrub *Sutherlandia frutescens*, known as the 'cancer bush' and which is found in Namibia and its neighbouring countries, as a viable candidate plant for the cure of malignant tumours, as it is effective when used topically or orally. *Sutherlandia frutescens* is also useful in the treatment of opportunistic infections in people living with HIV/AIDS (Otang, Grierson, & Ndip, 2012). Brown, Heyneke, Brown, van Wyk and Hamman (2008) alluded strongly to the long-standing use of *S. frutescens* against malignancies in South Africa. Despite the South African government's recommendation that *S. frutescens* should be used for the treatment of different ailments, including HIV (Mills, Cooper, Seely, & Kanfer, 2005), no clinical trials are currently underway on this plant, as far as we are aware (Minocha et al., 2011).

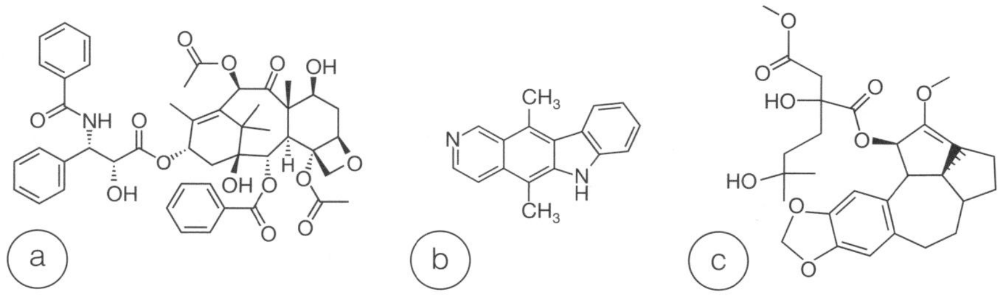

FIGURE 3.1: Chemical structures of anticancer compounds derived from plants: (a) Taxol, (b) ellipticine and (c) harringtonine.

Significance of plants for the treatment of cancer in Namibia

Namibia has a rich heritage of plants, both vascular and non-vascular. Curtis and Mannheimer (2005) describe about 408 indigenous, large, woody plant species found in Namibia. The indigenous people of Namibia use the abundant natural plant heritage for food, medicines, construction, and production and trading of curios.

Von Koenen (2001) depicts many traditional therapeutic practices in different communities in Namibia. His book describes a variety of plants and their uses and preparation for remedies, as well as their distributions in Namibia. Several other publications focus on the ethnomedicinal uses of Namibian plants by individual cultures, such as van den Eynden, Vernemmen and van Damme (1992) on the Topnaar community and Rodin (1985) on the Kwanyama. To date, there is no publication on the ethnomedicinal use of indigenous plants for the cure of or palliative care in cancer management in Namibia. This chapter addresses this gap by extracting existing knowledge from published sources, unpublished information from surveys and laboratory experiments currently underway, with particular emphasis on medicinal indigenous plants with potential for use in palliative care and treatment of cancer.

Namibian plants with potential for use in palliative care of cancer

Powell, Mwangi-Powell, Kiyange, Radbruch and Harding (2011) note a disregard and misconception of palliative care among experts – nurses, doctors, policy makers and other service providers – and the general public. Palliative care is a multifaceted discipline that draws from a range of expertise from diagnosis of the disease to the end of life. It continues to be administered to relieve pain, provide psychosocial support, and manage the side effects of treatment for individuals suffering from life-threatening illnesses such as cancer.

Pain management for cancer patients is an important aspect of palliative care. Van Dyk, Small and Zietsman (2000) reported that in the past, nurses and other health professionals in the Namibian health system often did not encourage patients to talk about their pain, let alone treat it. Dushimemaria and Mumbengegwi (pers. comm.) found that palliative care in Namibia focused mainly on pain management with painkillers such as morphine, but did not integrate psychosocial, spiritual, emotional or the effective management of side effects arising from treatments such as chemotherapy. Sadly, adequate palliative care is often mistaken for home-based care or end-of-life care, which would be followed by death in many instances (Powell et al., 2011).

Harpagophytum procumbens (Figure 3.2) is useful as an analgesic to provide pain relief in rheumatism, pregnancy and other afflictions such as gastrointestinal problems of the kidney, liver and pancreas (von Koenen, 2001), so has potential use for palliative care in cancer. Different preparations such as powders, ointments and teas are already in use, both within Namibia and beyond. An ointment containing *H. procumbens* can be used as a vulnerary, although caution should be taken in long-term or high-dosage use because it can result in internal organ damage or even cancer (von Koenen, 2001). A number of plants are known to be used as analgesics by various communities in Namibia, as listed in Table 3.1.

Nausea is an ever-present side effect of many chemotherapeutic drugs. As part of palliative care, nausea management is very important. One naturalised plant used to treat nausea in various ethnic groups is *Argemone ochroleuca* (Figure 3.3), which is also an opium-related analgesic. Furthermore, the plant has been found to contain berberine and several other toxic alkaloids and, hence, usage is subject to caution (von Koenen, 2001). The Ovahimba use the pale phloem of *Berchemia discolor* to prepare a remedy for nausea. The pulp is pounded and boiled in preparing this potent remedy. A study on *B. discolor* led to the isolation of five prenylated flavonoids, which also displayed cytotoxic activity against cancer cell lines (Chin et al., 2006). *Cyperus articulatus*, a member of the Cyperaceae family, has use in the treatment of nausea, as well as a sedative in cases of colic and toothache. A tea prepared from the stems and leaves of *Dombeya rotundifolia* is also effective against nausea. *Hypoestes forskaolii*, *Imperata cylindrica* and *Lophiocarpus polystachyus* are additional indigenous plants from which a root decoction is employed against nausea.

Namibian plants described as possessing curative properties against cancer

Arundo donax, also known as the giant reed, is a perennial grass and is claimed to confer anticarcinogenic properties in Namibia (von Koenen, 2001). In northern Pakistan, the plant is used as a diaphoretic to treat ailments such as fevers, headaches

TABLE 3.1: Indigenous Namibian plants used by different local communities as analgesics.

Family	Plant	Vernacular name	Language
Amaranthaceae	*Aerva leucura*	*eiso-lonhangu*	Oshikwanyama
Amaryllidaceae	*Ammocharis coranica*	*goen|a'ana*	!Kung
	Boophone disticha	*gifbol, malgif*	Afrikaans
Anacardiaceae	*Ozoroa schinzii*	*biatata*	!Kung
Apocynaceae	*Pergularia daemia*	*eumbanyanda*	Otjihimba
	Tavaresia barklyi	*olukatai*	Oshindonga
Asphodelaceae	*Aloe esculenta*	*endombwe*	Rukwangali
Asteraceae	*Helichrysum tomentosulum*	*ongwambundu*	Otjiherero
	Kleinia longiflora	*orukwasena*	Otjihimba
Bignoniaceae	*Catophractes alexandri*	*!ai!ari-se*	!Kung
Boraginaceae	*Ehretia rigida*	*horotos*	Khoekhoegowab
	Heliotropium ciliatum	*etadido*	Oshindonga
Caryophyllaceae	*Pollichia campestris*	*||nauha||hâb*	Khoekhoegowab
Chenopodiaceae	*Chenopodium ambrosioides*	*sinkingbossie*	Afrikaans
Colchicaceae	*Ornithoglossum calcicola*	*gelbes Vogelzunglein*	German
	Ornithoglossum dinteri	*braunes Vogelzunglein*	German
Crassulaceae	*Kalanchoe brachyloba*	*ondjize ongeama*	Otjiherero
Cucurbitaceae	*Cucumis meeusei*		
	Cucumis metuliferus	*dz'aa!'hau*	!Kung
Ebenaceae	*Diospyros lycioides*	*muncuvu*	Thimbukushu
Euphorbiaceae	*Antidesma rufescens*	*ofufe*	Oshikwanyama
	Croton megalobotrys	*grootkoorsbessie*	Afrikaans
	Ricinus communis	*omumunu*	Otjiherero
Fabaceae	*Baphia massaiensis*	*n!u'uri*	!Kung
	Cassia abbreviata	*omutangaruru*	Otjihimba
	Dichrostachys cinerea	*mweghe*	Thimbukushu
	Elephantorrhiza suffruticosa	*omumbala ndongo*	Oshindonga
	Erythrophleum africanum	*mupako*	Rugciriku
	Rhynchosia caribaea	*mughomo*	Rugciriku
Hyacinthaceae	*Dipcadi glaucum*	*murere*	Rugciriku
Lamiaceae	*Acrotome inflata*	*etwelakuku*	Oshikwanyama
	Clerodendrum ternatum	*sanyu*	Rukwangali
	Stachys spathulata	*omuwahe*	Otjiherero
Malvaceae	*Sida ovata*	*okanangola*	Oshikwanyama
Menispermaceae	*Cissampelos mucronata*	*murasanyka*	Thimbukushu
Myrothamnaceae	*Myrothamnus flabellifolius*	*teebossie*	Afrikaans
Nymphaeaceae	*Nymphaea nouchali*	*g|hoa*	!Kung
Olacaceae	*Ximenia americana*	*kakukuru*	Rukwangali

continues

Table 3.1 continued

Family	Plant	Vernacular name	Language
Papaveraceae	*Argemone ochroleuca*	*bloudissel*	Afrikaans
Pedaliaceae	*Harpagophytum procumbens*	*elyata*	Oshikwanyama
Polygalaceae	*Polygala schinziana*	*kanjengena*	Rugciriku
	Securidaca longipedunculata	*omdiku*	Oshikwanyama
	Oxygonum dregeanum	*oshikanda chefuma*	Oshindonga
Rhamnaceae	*Ziziphus mucronata*	*mukeke*	Thimbukushu
Rubiaceae	*Ancylanthos rubiginosus*	*ghutono*	Thimbukushu
	Gardenia brachythamnus	*mukova*	Rugciriku
Scrophulariaceae	*Jamesbrittenia atropurpurea*	*Saffran*	German
Solanaceae	*Solanum dinteri*	*okandumbwiriri*	Otjiherero
Strychnaceae	*Strychnos spinosa*	*omuuni*	Oshikwanyama

FIGURE 3.2: *Harpagophytum procumbens,* popularly known as devil's claw. Fruiting body with sharp, re-curved hooks above, and flowers, right. (© Dave Cole.)

FIGURE 3.3: The opium-related *Argemone ochroleuca* finds application as an analgesic within the Ovahimba culture of Namibia. (© Silke Rügheimer.)

and sweating (Murad, Ahmad, Gilani, & Khan, 2011). *Corallocarpus welwitschii* is another plant used in combination with *Marsdenia macrantha* and *Litogyne gariepina* (Figure 3.4 b) for the treatment of cancer of gynaecological orientation. *Corallocarpus welwitschii* is locally known as *ohona* or *omufifimano* by the Ovaherero and Aakwanyama, respectively. *Litogyne gariepina*, also known as *odivadiva* among the Aakwanyama and Aandonga, is crushed, dried or pulverized with two other plants in a cancer tonic. The tonic, or plant extract, is then administered to a patient for a period of six weeks, after which improvement is expected.

Many plants used medicinally are also claimed to be toxic (Figure 3.5). *Gymnema sylvestre* is also said to be a poisonous plant in Namibia and finds use as a remedy for snakebites; Angolans claim the plant to be a potent anticancer medicine. Another indigenous plant, which has therapeutic properties against external cancer although

FIGURE 3.4: A decoction prepared from a combination of (a) *Corallocarpus welwitschii* (© Silke Rügheimer) and (b) *Litogyne gariepina* (© Coleen Mannheimer) is used for the treatment of gynaecological cancers.

Medicinal plants as anticancer medicines: An eastern paradigm

Traditional Chinese medicine has developed over thousands of years. It has a holistic approach to prevent and cure illness and disease in that it does not just look at the etiology of a disease and the treatment, but also the interaction between mind, body and environment. Practitioners believe humans are interconnected with nature and affected by its forces, therefore health and disease relate to the balance or imbalance of the body's functions. All illnesses, including cancer, can be treated through a combination of practices that may include using herbal remedies as well as by restoring the balance of energies. The process of diagnosis involves looking at the patient as a whole and the environment they live in. For this reason, Western methods are not as suitable in evaluating how effective Chinese medicine is for treating or preventing cancer, compared to allopathic medicine. Chinese medicine is tailored to each patient, so it cannot be tested by giving a group of patients the same treatment regime. There is, however, some evidence that plants used in Chinese medicine may help to treat cancer or to control symptoms or side effects.

FIGURE 3.5:
Some renowned poisonous plants, (a) *Gymnema sylvestre* (© Coleen Mannheimer) and (b) *Ranunculus multifidus* (© FR de Villiers on 1419694977, iSpot), which are used as anticancer medicinals.

it is poisonous, is *Ranunculus multifidus* (Figure 3.5b). It is known as *kankerblare* in Afrikaans. Its leaves are crushed and applied for many external afflictions, such as mumps, wounds, warts, haemorrhoids and cancer.

Dianthus namaensis, known in Afrikaans as *grasangeliertjie*, is used to alleviate pain (Figure 3.6a). It has many uses, but among Coloureds it is a principal medicinal plant, and its root is used for wounds and as a dressing for boils. In addition, *D. namaensis* is used to alleviate cancer, poisoning, stomachache and, more generally, for weakness and as an analgesic.

According to von Koenen (2001), Coloureds claim a root preparation of *Osteospermum muricatum*, also known as *okahue* by the Ovaherero of Namibia, can be used for the treatment of stomach cancer (Figure 3.6b). Externally, the plant's flowers and leaves cause an allergic reaction of itching to the skin. The plant is widely spread among Namibia's varied vegetation.

FIGURE 3.6:
Dianthus namaensis (a) and *Osteospermum muricatum* (b) are used to alleviate pain and stomach cancer, respectively. (© Silke Rügheimer.)

FIGURE 3.7:
(a) Flowers of
*Sutherlandia
frutescens*, a
renowned medicinal
plant with different
applications within
the traditional
settings of southern
Africa (© Silke
Rügheimer); and
(b) fruiting structure
of *Gomphocarpus
fruticosus* claimed
to cure skin
cancer (© Coleen
Mannheimer).

FIGURE 3.8:
For any swellings or
hard lumps suspected
to be tumours,
Cucumis metuliferus
melon and water
infusion is taken orally
twice daily. (© Coleen
Mannheimer.)

Sutherlandia frutescens, or *kankerbos*, is traditionally used in dilute forms for internal cancer, and other ailments, such as chickenpox, influenza and rheumatism (Figure 3.7a). Internationally, the plant has attracted the attention of several scientists, especially in the management of opportunistic infections related to HIV/AIDS (Otang et al., 2012).

Gomphocarpus fruticosus, a member of the Asclepiadaceae family is an indigenous plant that local Damara claim can cure skin cancer (Figure 3.7b). Its leaves are used to prepare a tincture, which is used to rub down the patient's body together with additional plant leaves. Next, the body is covered using a blanket, and healing can be expected.

Several other plants are claimed by different ethnic groups to cure tumours. The people in the Kavango regions cut up the melon of *Cucumis metuliferus* (Figure 3.8), locally known as *ruputwi* and *dz'aa!'hau* by Mbukushu and !Kung San people, respectively. The cut melons are then prepared using heat and a little water. The resulting infusion is then taken twice a day to achieve curative results when one has what they perceive to be tumours. Here, it is worth noting that *C. metuliferus* belongs to the Cucurbitaceae family, which is a source of the famous tetracyclic triterpenoid compounds that are antiproliferative on various cancer cell lines by acting via the oncogenic pathway STAT3 (signal transducer and activator of transcription 3; Nirmala et al., 2011).

Heliotropium supinum (Figure 3.9) is used in a remedy for the treatment of solid metastases; the Aakwanyama call it *ohanauni*, and chop up the plant to prepare a tincture for tumours. The Ovaherero claim that a hot dressing prepared from the leaves of *Solanum lichtensteinii* (Figure 3.10) helps with external tumours. The plant is known as *umundumburiri* or *omutimburiri* by the Ovaherero, while the Ovahimba of the northern Opuwo area call this medicinal plant *omundumbwiriri*.

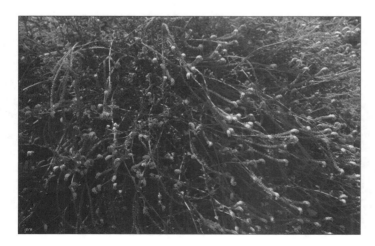

FIGURE 3.9: *Heliotropium supinum* is used by the Aakwanyama to prepare a decoction used against any type of tumour. (© Eitan f, Wikimedia Commons.)

Validation of antineoplastic properties of selected Namibian plants

In Namibia, many researchers have published on the ethnomedicinal practices of various ethnic groups. Researchers such as Cheikhyoussef, Mapaure and Shapi (2011), du Preez et al. (2011), Chinsembu, Hedimbi and Mukaru (2011) and von Koenen (2001) have documented indigenous uses of plants for food and medicinal purposes in various regions of the country by different ethnic groups. These endeavours have made the cultural heritage practised in some regions of Namibia, such as Oshikoto, Zambezi, and Kavango East and Kavango West, known. Sources cited in this work show that much of the indigenous knowledge of the different Namibian communities is known, however, there is room for greater awareness. This can be achieved through frequent and in-depth studies looking at the pattern of indigenous plant use for different ailments.

FIGURE 3.10:
A hot poultice preparation of *Solanum lichtensteinii* leaves is used by the Ovaherero for external tumours. (© Coleen Mannheimer.)

FIGURE 3.11:
Colophospermum mopane is used locally to prepare a remedy for treating 'swollen testes'. (© Silke Rügheimer.)

Sometimes, the plant parts, application or even the plant changes over time. For instance, Leger (1997) reported a list of 110 plants that were in use by the San; years later, Leffers (2003) described 238 species of plants used by the same community. This illustrates a perfect example of the need for continued documentation of indigenous knowledge. These changes are partly due to the fact that traditional medicine is not governed by logic, but is also influenced by spirits and magic (Morelli et al., 1983).

Du Preez et al. (2011) conducted an ethnomedicinal survey of Zambezi Region by conducting interviews with traditional knowledge-holders in a bid to compile a database of traditional plants used within the region for different infirmities. These and the above-mentioned sources are based on putative uses of the different plants. However, this work (du Preez et al., 2011), lead to an investigation into science-based evidence on the traditional use of plants for the treatment of cancer-like symptoms and ailments. Based on the surveys of ethnomedicinal practices, five plants, locally known as *mukonangwe, mungongo, mopane, muwowo, muputwi* and other additional plants were selected. These plants were processed and analysed in preliminary chemical-based studies in order to find out their potential as herbal supplements for alleviation of cancer.

Firstly, a field trip was conducted to collect the plants. Voucher specimens were prepared by pressing leaves and fruits, where available, of the different plants in a plant press. The specimens were sent to the Namibian National Botanical Research Institute (NBRI) for identification. They were identified as *Colophospermum mopane* (mopane) (Figure 3.11), *Schinziophyton rautanenii* (*mungongo*) (Figure 3.12), *Acanthosicyos naudinianus* (*muputwi*) (Figure 3.13 (a and b), *Capparis tomentosa* (*mukonangwe*) (Figure 3.13 c) and *Commiphora africana* (*muwowo*). In addition to these, several other plants were added to the study, including several *Commiphora* species (*C. pyracanthoides* and *C. anacardiifolia* amongst others), *Lessertia benguellensis* and *Moringa ovalifolia*.

FIGURE 3.12:
Local traditional knowledge-holders identified *Schinziophyton rautanenii* as a potent treatment for 'small sores all over the body'. (© Silke Rügheimer.)

FIGURE 3.13:
Plants collected
to investigate their
potential anticancer
properties: (a)
*Acanthosicyos
naudinianus*, locally
known as an anti-
inflammatory, © Silke
Rügheimer (fruit); (b)
© Antje Burke (plant);
and (c) *Capparis
tomentosa*,
© Christopher Hines.

The plant samples were then dried and assayed to determine their phytochemical properties. An ethanolic extract was prepared from each plant, which was used in the GIBEX (Global Institute for Bioexploration) screens-to-nature assay. A colorimetric test was used to determine the antioxidant potential of each plant extract, while a gelatin-coated film was used to determine the protease inhibition potential.

Proteases, especially matrix metalloproteinases (MMPs), are enzymes that are localised in the extracellular matrix and serve the purpose of cleaving adherent protein structures outside the cell, thereby dislodging it. In the case of cancer, MMPs have been implicated in facilitating the multistep process of invasion, metastasis and angiogenesis, which are all crucial steps in cancer progression (Gialeli, Theocharis, & Karamanos, 2011). Antioxidants are molecules that protect biological molecules, such as DNA, from oxidative damage resulting from reactive oxygen and nitrogen (Serafini, Villano, Spera, & Pellegrini, 2006). In fact, antioxidants are considered beneficial in the prevention of cancers that result from mutations in the cell's genetic material.

Table 3.2 shows the GIBEX-screen-to-nature assay results. Very good antioxidant potential was indicated in almost all plant specimens, while varying degrees of antiprotease activity was also demonstrated. Antioxidant activity is common in most plants (Narayanaswamy & Balakrishman, 2011), and also found common in the plants that were screened. Antiprotease activity is a component of a nonspecific defence system that exists in vertebrates and serves to protect against invading pathogens (Rao & Chakrabarti, 2004), such as *Salmonella* spp., which have been implicated in causing gallbladder cancer (Crawford et al., 2010). In addition, the discovery that the malignant nature of certain cancers is caused by the expression of certain proteolytic enzymes has raised the need for therapeutic entities with antiprotease activity in the treatment of cancer (Rakashanda, Rana, Rafiq, Masood, & Amin, 2012).

The plant extracts were screened using thin-layer chromatography. This technique detects the different phytochemical compounds that are found in plant extracts. Thin-layer chromatography separates a mixture based on two properties: the polarity of the compound as well its adsorption to the stationery phase. Roots, bark and leaves were the main plant parts used to prepare extracts for screening. Varied phytochemicals found in different plant tissue also imply that sustainable means of harvesting can be employed by local people to meet the same purpose since shoots, leaves and bark samples constitute a similar phytochemical profile as roots.

Table 3.3 shows the different phytochemical compounds detected in the nine Namibian indigenous plants analysed. These plants show the presence of various phytochemical compounds, such as alkaloids, flavonoids and triterpenoids. Phytochemical compounds such as alkaloids, phenolic acids, triterpenoids, etc. have been shown to confer anti-inflammatory (Bellik et al., 2013) and analgesic (Ojieh, Adegor, & Lawrence, 2013) properties, which are beneficial to combat cancer and

TABLE 3.2: Preliminary screening of Zambezi plants for anticancer activities.

Plant	Plant part	Antioxidant	Antiprotease
Colophospermum mopane	bark	+++	+++
	roots	+++	+++
Lessertia benguellensis	leaves	++	+++
Schinziophyton rautanenii	roots	+++	+++
	bark	+++	+++
Acanthosicyos naudinianus	tubers	+++	+
	shoots	+++	−
Commiphora africana	twigs	+++	+++
	roots	+++	+++
Commiphora pyracanthoides	twigs	+++	−
Commiphora anacardifolia	leaves	+++	++
	twigs	+++	+++
Commiphora spp.	twigs	+++	+++
	leaves	+++	+++
Capparis tomentosa	roots	+++	+++
	shoots	+++	+++
Moringa ovalifolia	leaves	+++	−
	twigs	+++	−

++++   very high presence   +++ high presence   ++ moderate presence   + present   − absent

TABLE 3.3: Compounds found in plants from Zambezi using thin-layer chromatography.

Plant	Plant part	Coumarin	Alkaloid	Flavonoid	Triterpenoid	Anthraquinone
Colophospermum mopane	bark	++	+	+	+++	−
	roots	+	+	+	++++	+++
Lessertia benguellensis	leaves	+	+	+	++	++++
Schinziophyton rautanenii	roots	++	+	+	+++	−
	bark	++	+	+	+++	−
Acanthosicyos naudinianus	tubers	−	+	−	−	+
	shoots	+	+	+	+	++
Commiphora africana	twigs	−	−	−	+	+
	roots	+	+	+	+	++
Commiphora pyracanthoides	twigs	+	+	+	++	++
Commiphora anacardifolia	leaves	−	+	+	+++	++++
	twigs	+	+	+	+++	++
Capparis tomentosa	roots	+	+	−	++	−
	shoots	+	+	−	++	++
Moringa ovalifolia	leaves	+	+	+	++++	+++
	twigs	−	+	++	++++	++

++++   very high presence   +++ high presence   ++ moderate presence   + present   − absent other diseases. The numerous bands indicate that different compounds of a particular phytochemical are present in the plant extract, as depicted in the relative abundance in Table 3.3 (++++ being very high; +, low; and −, absent). The presence of certain compounds is beneficial since it increases the chances of the presence of a bioactive molecule or molecules acting in synergy (Wagner & Ulrich-Merzenich, 2009).

Table 3.3 shows that phenolic compounds (coumarins, flavonoids and anthraquinones) were the predominant compounds in the plants tested, in comparison to alkaloids and triterpenoids. The roots and shoots of *A. naudinianus* depicted alkaloids, which was a finding consistent with the observation that the plant had a bitter astringent compound during plant harvesting and processing. The presence of phenolic compounds such as coumarins, flavonoids and anthraquinones could be responsible for the observed antioxidant activity in Table 3.2 due to their hydrogen-donating ability (Narayanaswamy & Balakrishnan, 2011).

Bernard and Olayinka (2010) reported on the antiproliferative, anti-inflammatory and antioxidant properties of cucurbitacins and triterpenoids, isolated from plants of the Cucurbitaceae family, to which *A. naudinianus* belongs. Fernandes, Cromarty, Albrecht and Janse van Rensberg (2004) showed the antioxidant potential of *Sutherlandia frutescens,* an important basis for South African traditional medicinal practices. In addition, the plant extracts appear to possess antioxidant properties that are important in preventing certain chronic diseases such as cancer (Farombi, 2004). Demonstration of these various bioactive compounds helps validate the use of the plants within traditional settings.

SUSTAINABLE DEVELOPMENT OF TRADITIONAL MEDICINES

Despite the increased number of publications on traditional medicines in different parts of the world (Hedberg & Staugard, 1989; Arnold et al., 2002), many individuals – health workers, medical doctors, service providers and members of the general public – are antagonistic towards the use of traditional medicines. These individuals do not appreciate the value of the traditional ethnomedicinal knowledge held within Namibian cultures, and that it is slowly being lost. Holders of traditional knowledge on practices and plant use for the treatment of different ailments, including cancer, are not always forthcoming with their knowledge, sharing it only with selected people orally, hence exacerbating the loss of this knowledge from the community. Documentation of traditional medicinal knowledge is key to preventing its loss and is the first step to commercial development of traditional medicine and the establishment of intellectual property rights for knowledge-holders. Together with valorization, these two processes are important in reducing the stigma and the misunderstanding that the general populace has towards the use of these traditional ethnomedicinal methods of treatment. They also add value to the medicine because the plant material source becomes linked to known qualities – in this case, their effectiveness as an anti-cancer treatment or usefulness in palliation of cancer symptoms. Furthermore, once the efficacy, mode of action and safety of these medicinal anticancer plants have been determined, stigma will dissipate and provisions can be made to facilitate their inclusion into mainstream medicines. However, documentation and valorization of indigenous knowledge is a long and expensive process taking up to 15 years and costing up to USD1 billion (Baxter et al., 2013).

The two steps involved in developing traditional medicines for mainstream use can be done separately, with documentation being conducted more broadly and valorization being performed on selected cancer treatments based on their potential for commercialization to recoup the costs of the process. Another consideration could be local or national demand for the particular treatment and its sustainability, which might lead to integration into primary healthcare for cancer as an alternative treatment.

In Namibia, there is a lengthy referral process in the formal healthcare system that patients have to endure before receiving a formal diagnosis and the necessary treatment for cancer. This is largely due to limited conventional drugs and healthcare personnel that can operate from remote health facilities (Tabuti, Hassan, Pateh, & Mahomoodally, 2014). Documentation and valorization of traditional ethnomedicines will help towards creating awareness of effective plant resources that are available in different rural communities and, in that way, healthcare provision would become more accessible and affordable to people living in these communities.

Conservation of these valuable plant resources is, however, of utmost importance to ensure their sustainable utilization. Loots (2005) describes a number of Namibian plants near extinction or under some form of threat that could result in loss of species. Okigbo, Eme and Ogbogu (2008) discuss the concern for conservation of African medicinal plants, including the possible loss of biodiversity; validation and documentation of traditional medicinal practices or knowledge; and bringing forth the issue of intellectual property rights.

Harmonizing intellectual property rights and the conservation of natural resources are important aspects of the development of novel drug compounds in developing countries (Swanson, 1995). Export of raw plant materials through bio-trade might create a steady source of revenue for Namibia, but valorization, documentation and development of ethnomedicines can be of greater economic benefit to local communities in Namibia. For instance, export of devil's claw *Harpagophytum procumbens* attracts markets and international recognition in Western countries (Maggs, Craven, & Kolberg, 1998). The plant is an important basis of traditional medicinal practices in South Africa, Botswana and Namibia, and is endemic to the Kalahari Desert. Development of devil's claw within Namibia would add value to the final product and attract revenue directly into the Namibian economy. Additionally, the scientific, evidence-based screening of traditional plants can lead to the discovery of novel drug entities for ailments, both locally and globally, and income-generating opportunities (Cotton, 1996), and contribute to the documentation and validation of traditional knowledge on medicinal plants.

CONCLUSION

Namibia is a country with diverse ecological systems giving rise to great biodiversity, and with a population of diverse cultures, which have developed medicine practices that rely on plants for primary healthcare. Some plants are well known for their medicinal properties and are well documented, but many are not. They also have not been valorized as being effective against cancer-related ailments, despite their use for generations in local communities. There is recognition that this knowledge is underutilized because of changing lifestyles related to urbanization, stigmatization of traditional medicines and reliance on allopathic medicine. This knowledge is becoming lost because it is passed on orally and younger generations have less interest in it. Formal documentation is urgently required.

The global trend of using complementary medicines, including herbal treatments, for chronic and terminal illnesses such as cancer, has resulted in renewed interest in ethnomedicinal plants. This presents economic opportunities for communities who have knowledge of the plants in their areas that can be used for cancer treatment or palliation. The documentation of this knowledge is even more important so that it is acknowledged that these communities hold intellectual property rights for these plant-based treatments; valorization will further strengthen their claims to such intellectual property rights. The information in this chapter highlights that some of the plants used not only alleviate pain in palliative treatment of cancer, but might also be useful in the treatment of several forms of the disease. The valorization of these plants should be considered for their possible integration into mainstream primary healthcare. Such steps in showing traditional healthcare options are effective would also reinforce the pride in communities associated with their cultural practices.

A plethora of practices are already in place within Namibian ethnic groups pertaining to the treatment of cancer-like conditions, as well as a number being used to palliate the symptoms of it. Documentation and scientific validation of traditional treatments not only preserves this knowledge, but also increases its value to the benefit of local communities with respect to healthcare and socioeconomic benefits. Namibia's rich heritage of traditional medicines is an important building block for bioprospecting new medicines to treat cancer and to generate intellectual property rights on the use of plants for the development of pharmaceuticals and credible herbal supplements.

References

Agarwal, N., Majee, C., & Chakraborthy, G. S. (2012). Natural herbs as anticancer drugs. *International Journal of PharmTech Research*, *4*(3), 1142-1153.

Arnold, T. H., Prentice, C. A., Hawker, L. C., Snyman, E. E., Tomalin, M., Crouch, N. R., & Pottas-Bircher, C. (2002). *Medicinal and magical plants of Southern Africa: An annotated checklist. Strelitzia, 13.* Pretoria, South Africa: National Botanical Institute.

Barbee, E. L. (1986). Biomedical resistance to ethnomedicine in Botswana. *Social Science and Medicine*, *22*(1), 75-80.

Baxter, K., Horn, E., Gal-Edd, N., Zonno, K., O'Leary, J., Terry. P. F., & Terry, S. F. (2013). An end to the myth: There is no drug development pipeline. *Science Translational Medicine*, *5*(171), 1-4. Retrieved from http://stm.sciencemag.org/content/5/171/171cm1.full.pdf

Bellik, Y., Boukraa, L., Alzahrani, H. A., Bakhotmah, B. A., Abdellah, F. A., Hammoudi, S. M., & Iguer-Ouada, M. (2013). Molecular mechanism underlying anti-inflammatory and anti-allergic activities of phytochemicals: An update. *Molecules*, *2013*(18), 322-353.

Bernard, S. A., & Olayinka, O. A. (2010). Search for a novel antioxidant, anti-inflammatory/analgesic or anti-proliferative drug: Cucurbitacins hold the ace. *Journal of Medicinal Plants Research*, *4*(25), 2821-2826.

Brown, L., Heyneke, O., Brown, D., van Wyk, J. P. H., & Hamman, J. H. (2008). Impact of traditional medicinal plant extracts on antiretroviral drug absorption. *Journal of Ethnopharmacology*, *119*(3), 588-592.

Cheikhyoussef, A., Mapaure, I., & Shapi, M. (2011). The use of some indigenous plants for medicinal and other purposes by local communities in Namibia with emphasis on Oshikoto Region: A review. *Research Journal of Medicinal Plant*, *5*(4), 406-419.

Chin, Y-W., Mdee, L. K., Mbwambo, Z. H., Mi, Q., Chai, H-B., Cragg, G. M., Swanson, S. M., & Kinghorn, A. D. (2006). Prenylated flavonoids from the root bark of *Berchemia discolor*, a Tanzanian medicinal plant. *Journal of Natural Products*, *69*(11), 1649-1652.

Chinsembu, K. C., & Hedimbi, M. (2010). An ethnobotanical survey of plants used to manage HIV/AIDS opportunistic infections in Katima Mulilo, Caprivi region, Namibia. *Journal of Ethnobiology and Ethnomedicine*, *6*, 25. doi:10.1186/1746-4269-6-25

Chinsembu, K. C., Hedimbi, M., & Mukaru, C. W. (2011). Putative medicinal properties of plants from the Kavango Region, Namibia. *Journal of Medicinal Plants Research*, *5*(31), 6787-6797.

Cotton, C. M. (1996). *Ethnobotany: Principles and applications.* Chichester, England: John Wiley and Sons. ▾

Crawford, R. W., Rosales-Reyes, R., Ramirez-Aguilar, M. L., Chapa-Azuela, O., Alpuche-Arand, C., & Gunn, J. S. (2010). Gallstones play a significant role in *Salmonella* spp. Gallbladder colonization and carriage. *Proceedings of the National Academy of Sciences, 107*(9), 4353-4358.

Curtis, B., & Mannheimer, C. (2005). *Tree atlas of Namibia.* Windhoek, Namibia: National Botanical Research Institute.

Day, J. (2013). Botany meets archaeology: People and plants in the past. *Journal of Experimental Botany, 64*(S1), 1-12.

Du Preez, I., Nepolo, E., Siyengwa, R., Shapi, M., Cheikhyoussef, A., & Mumbengegwi, D. (2011). *Study on indigenous medicinal knowledge in Caprivi Region: Field trip report.* Windhoek, Namibia: Multidisciplinary Research Centre, University of Namibia.

Farnsworth, N. R., Akerele, O., Bingel, A. S., Soejarto, D. D., & Guo, Z. (1985). Medicinal plants in therapy. *Bulletin of the World Health Organization, 63*(6), 965-981.

Farombi, O. E. (2004). Diet-related cancer and prevention using anticarcinogens. *African Journal of Biotechnology, 3*(12), 651-661.

Fernandes, A. C., Cromarty, A. D., Albrecht, C., & Janse van Rensburg, C. E. (2004). The antioxidant potential of *Sutherlandia frutescens. Journal of Ethnopharmacology 95*(1), 1-5.

Ghosh, S., Pal, S., Prusty, S., & Girish, K. V. S. (2012). Curcumin and cancer: Recent developments. *Journal of Research in Biology, 2*(3), 251-272.

Gialeli, C., Theocharis, A. D., & Karamanos, N. K. (2011). Role of matrix metalloproteinases in cancer progression and their pharmacological targeting. *FEBS [Federation of European Biochemical Societies] Journal, 278*(1), 16-27.

Guo, B. H., Kai, G. Y., Jin, H. B., & Tang, K. X. (2006). Taxol synthesis. *African Journal of Biotechnology, 5*(1), 15-20. DOI: 10.5897/AJB2006.000-5002

Hedberg, I., & Staugard, F. (1989). *Traditional medicinal plants: Traditional medicine in Botswana.* Gaborone, Botswana: Ipeleng Publishers.

Jemal, A., Bray, F., Center, M. M., Ferlay, J., Ward, E., & Forman, D. (2011). Global cancer statistics. *CA. Cancer Journal for Clinicians, 61*(2), 69-90. doi: 10.3322/caac.20107

Leffers, A. (2003). *Gemsbok bean & kalahari truffle: Traditional plant use by Ju|'hoansi in north-eastern Namibia.* Windhoek, Namibia: Macmillan Education Namibia.

Leger, S. (1997). *The hidden gift of nature: A description of today's use of plants in West Bushmanland (Namibia).* Windhoek, Namibia; ded, German Development Service and Ministry of Environment and Tourism.

Lone, A. H., Ahmad, T., Anwar, M., Sofi, G., Imam, H. & Habib, S. (2012). Perception of health promotion in Unani herbal medicine. *Journal of Herbal Medicine, 2*(1), 1-5.

Loots, S. (2005). *Red Data Book of Namibian plants. SABONET Report, 38.* Windhoek and Pretoria: Southern African Botanical Diversity Network.

Maggs, G. L., Craven, P., & Kolberg, H. H. (1998). Plant species richness, endemism and genetic resources in Namibia. *Biodiversity and Conservation, 7*(4), 435-446.

Mills, E., Cooper, C., Seely, D., & Kanfer, I. (2005). African herbal medicines in the treatment of HIV: *Hypoxis* and *Sutherlandia.* An overview of evidence and pharmacology. *Nutrition Journal, 4*, 19-24.

Minocha, M., Mandava, N. K., Kwatra, D., Pal, D., Folk, W. R., Earla, R., & Mitra, A. K. (2011). Effect of short term and chronic administration of *Sutherlandia frutescens* on pharmacokinetics of nevirapine in rats. *International Journal of Pharmaceutics, 413*(1), 44-50.

Morelli, I., Bonari, E., Pagni, A. M., Tomei, P. E., Menichini, F., & Amadei, L. (1983). *Selected medicinal plants.* Rome, Italy: FAO.

Murad, W., Ahmad, A., Gilani, S. A., & Khan, M. A. (2011). Indigenous knowledge and folk use of medicinal plants by the tribal communities of Hazar Nao Forest, Malakand District, North Pakistan. *Journal of Medicinal Plants Research, 5*(7), 1072-1086.

Namibian National Cancer Registry. (2009). *Cancer in Namibia, 2000–2005.* Windhoek, Namibia: Cancer Association of Namibia.

Namibian National Cancer Registry. (2011). *Cancer in Namibia, 2006–2009.* Windhoek, Namibia: Cancer Association of Namibia.

Narayanaswamy, N., & Balakrishman, K. P. (2011). Evaluation of some medicinal plants for their antioxidant properties. *International Journal of PharmTech Research, 3*(1), 381-385.

Nirmala, M. J., Samundeeswari, A., & Sankar, P. (2011). Natural plant resources in anti-cancer therapy – a review. *Research in Plant Biology, 1*(3), 1-14.

Nortier, J. L., Martinez, M. M., Schmeiser, H. H., Arlt, V. M., Bieler, C. A., Petein, M., Depierreux, M. F., de Pauw, L., Abramowicz, A., Vereerstraeten, P., & Vanherweghem, J. L. (2000). Urothelial carcinoma associated with the use of a chinese herb (*Aristolochia fangchi*). *The New England Journal of Medicine, 342*(23), 1686-1692.

Ojieh, A. E., Adegor, E. C., & Lawrence E. O. (2013). Preliminary phytochemical screening, analgesic and anti-inflammatory properties of *Celosia isertii. European Journal of Medicinal Plants, 3*(3), 369-380.

Okigbo, R. N., Eme, U. E., & Ogbogu, S. (2008). Biodiversity and conservation of medicinal and aromatic plants in Africa. *Biotechnology and Molecular Biology Reviews, 3*(6), 127-134.

Otang, W. M., Grierson, D. S., & Ndip, R. N. (2012). Ethnobotanical survey of medicinal plants used in the management of opportunistic fungal infections in

HIV/AIDS patients in the Amathole District of the Eastern Cape Province, South Africa. *Journal of Medicinal Plants Research, 6*(11), 2071-2080.

Patel, B., Das, S., Prakash, R., & Yassir, M. (2010). Natural bioactive compounds with anticancer potential. *International Journal of Advances in Pharmaceutical Sciences, 1*, 32-41.

Powell, R. A., Mwangi-Powell, F. N., Kiyange, F., Radbruch, L., & Harding, R. (2011). Palliative care development in Africa: How can we provide enough quality care? *BMJ Supportive & Palliative Care, 1*(2), 113-114.

Rakashanda, S., Rana, F., Rafiq, S., Masood, A., & Amin, S. (2012). Role of proteases in cancer: A review. *Biotechnology and Molecular Biology Reviews, 7*(4), 90-101.

Rao, V. Y., & Chakrabarti, R. (2004). Enhanced anti-proteases in *Labeo rohita* fed with diet containing herbal ingredients. *Indian Journal of Clinical Biochemistry, 19*(2), 132-134.

Rodin, R. J. (1985). *The ethnobotany of the Kwanyama Ovambos.* Kansas, USA: Allen Press, Inc.

Schwartsmann, G., Ratain, M. J., Cragg, G. M., Wong, J. E., Saijo, N., Parkinson, D. R., Fujiwara, Y., Pazdur, R., Newman, D. J., Dagher, R., & Di Leone, L. (2002). Anticancer drug discovery and development throughout the world. *Journal of Clinical Oncology, 20*(18 Suppl.), 47S-59S.

Sen, S., Chakraborty, R., & De, B. (2011). Challenges and opportunities in the advancement of herbal medicine: India's position and role in a global context. *Journal of Herbal Medicine, 1*(3), 67-75.

Serafini, M., Villano, D., Spera, G., & Pellegrini, N. (2006). Redox molecules and cancer prevention: The importance of understanding the role of the antioxidant network. *Nutrition and Cancer, 56*(2), 232-240.

Shi, L. M., Fan, Y., Myers, T. G., O'Connor, P. M., Paull, K. D., Friend, S. H., & Weinstein, J. N. (1998). Mining the NCI anticancer drug discovery databases: Genetic function approximation for the QSAR study of anticancer ellipticine analogues. *Journal of Chemical Information and Computer Sciences, 38*(2), 189-199.

Shoeb, M. (2006). Anticancer agents from medicinal plants. *Bangladesh Journal of Pharmacology, 1*(2), 35-41. doi: 10.3329/bjp.v1i2.486

Siegel, R., Naishadham, D., & Jemal, A. (2012). Cancer statistics, 2012. *CA: A Cancer Journal for Clinicians, 62*(1), 10-29. doi: 10.3322/caac.20138

Smith, A. (1895). *A contribution to South African materia medica.* South Africa: Lovedale Mission Press.

Swanson, T. M. (Ed.). (1995). *Intellectual property rights and biodiversity conservation: An interdisciplinary analysis of the values of medicinal plants.* United Kingdom: Cambridge University Press.

Tabuti, J. R. S., Hassen, I. E., Pateh, U. U., & Mahomoodally, M. F. (2014). Recent advances towards validating efficacy and safety of African traditional medicines. *Evidence-based Complementary and Alternative Medicines*. Retrieved from http://dx.doi.org/10.1155/2014/260567

UNAIDS [United Nations Programme on HIV and AIDS]. (2013). *HIV and AIDS estimates*. Retrieved from http://www.unaids.org/en/regionscountries/countries/namibia

Van den Eynden, V., Vernemmen, P., & van Damme, P. (1992). *The ethnobotany of the Topnaar*. Gent, Belgium: University of Gent.

Van Dyk, A. S. B., Small, L. F., & Zietsman, A. (2000). The pain experience and its management in cancer patients during hospitalisation (in Namibia). *Health SA Gesondheid*, *5*(4), 19-26.

Vivekanand, J. H. A. (2010). Herbal medicines and chronic kidney disease. *Nephrology*, *15*(s2),10-17.

Von Koenen, E. (2001). *Medicinal, poisonous and edible plants in Namibia*. Windhoek & Göttingen, Namibia & Germany: Klaus Hess Publishers.

Wagner, H., & Ulrich-Merzenich, G. (2009). Synergy research: Approaching a new generation of phytopharmaceuticals. *Journal of Natural Remedies*, *9*(2), 121-141.

WHO [World Health Organization]. (2002). *WHO traditional medicine strategy, 2002–2005*. Geneva, Switzerland: Author. Retrieved from http://whqlibdoc.who.int/hq/2002/who_edm_trm_2002.1.pdf

WHO [World Health Organization]. (2011). *World health statistics, 2011*. Geneva, Switzerland: Author. Retrieved from http://www.who.int/whosis/whostat/EN_WHS2011_Full.pdf

4

The use of traditional medicinal plants as antimicrobial treatments

Davis R. Mumbengegwi, Iwanette du Preez, Florence Dushimemaria, Joyce Auala & Sylvia Nafuka

INTRODUCTION

The scourge of microbial infections

Microbial infections are a major cause of morbidity and sometimes mortality, especially in developing countries such as Namibia. Severe poverty is the root cause of this undesirable situation as it leads to malnutrition, inadequate sanitation and consumption of unclean food and drink. This, compounded by lack of education and access to primary healthcare, results in infections by microorganisms such as viruses, bacteria, fungi and protozoa (Table 4.1).

The most vulnerable to infectious diseases caused by microbial agents are children under the age of five, where 66% of deaths in this age group are a result of such diseases; 34% of all deaths are attributed to infectious diseases. This was underscored by WHO's (World Health Organization's) Regional Director for Africa, Luis Gomes Sambo, in 2011 when he said 63% of deaths on the continent were caused by microbial infections, with HIV/AIDS accounting for 38.5% of these (Anon, 2012). Thus, the most vulnerable groups are young children and individuals whose immune systems are compromised by HIV infection (Table 4.2).

Community-acquired bacteraemia is a major cause of death in children at rural sub-Saharan district hospitals. A study by Berkley et al. (2005) showed that 12.8% of infants younger than 60 days had bacteraemia. *Escherichia coli* and group b streptococcus were the predominant infectious agents. In those older than 60 days, 5.9% were infected with *Streptococcus pneumoniae*, *Salmonella* species, *Haemophilus influenzae* or *E. coli*. In Gambia, children under five years have a 2.5% risk of

TABLE 4.1: Numbers of deaths by different causes in the developing world.

	Number of deaths (in thousands) per age group					
	5–14	**15–44**	**45–59**	**60+**	**All ages**	**Total**
Infections						
Respiratory	2,710	244	139	78	813	3,984
Diarrhoeal	2,474	210	97	30	54	2,865
Tuberculosis	71	151	696	534	526	1,978
Malaria	632	153	109	22	12	928
Tetanus	450	28	10	8	8	504
Pertussis	277	44	–	–	–	321
HIV	56	10	162	14	6	248
Meningitis	130	60	28	7	8	233
Syphilis	77	–	103	10	–	190
Other	434	226	180	94	94	1,028
Sub-total	7,311	1,126	1,524	797	1,521	12,279
Other causes						
Perinatal	2,402	–	–	–	–	2,402
Congenital	503	42	43	5	–	588
Pregnancy-related	–	12	408	7	–	427
Injury	487	407	1,683	381	462	3,420
Cancer	43	64	411	967	2,211	3,696
Cardiovascular	122	80	540	1,368	6,908	9,018
Chronic respiratory	156	50	90	222	1,818	2,336
Other	556	296	674	709	1,676	3,911
Sub-total	**4,269**	**951**	**3,849**	**3,659**	**13,075**	**25,799**
Total	**11,580**	**2,077**	**5,373**	**4,456**	**14,596**	**38,078**

Adapted from Hesketh and Zhu (1997).

TABLE 4.2: Estimates of mortality in children under five in sub-Saharan Africa.

Cause of death	Africa (%)	Global (%)
Acute respiratory infection	16	18
Diarrhoeal disease	14	15
Malaria	22	10
Measles	8	5
HIV or AIDS	8	4
Neonatal	13	23
Other	19	25
Total	**100%**	**100%**
	4.5 million people	**10.9 million people**

Adapted from Mulholland and Adegbola (2005).

acquiring an invasive bacterial infection with 28% of those dying from bacteraemia when admitted. Malaria is one of the major infectious diseases, globally, together with tuberculosis and HIV/AIDS (Coppi, Cabinian, Mirelman, & Sinnis, 2006). Of an estimated 225 million cases, globally, malaria caused 781,000 deaths in 2009 (Ku et al., 2011; USAID, 2011). Every year, 90% of malaria cases occur in sub-Saharan African countries (Mohammed, 2009), causing a mortality rate of over one million people, mainly children under the age of five years and pregnant women (Rosenthal, 2003; Ogunlana, Ogunlana, & Ademowo, 2009; Ku et al., 2011). Eight per cent of paediatric hospital admissions in Mozambique had bacterial infections, with *Salmonella* and *Pneumococcus* being isolated in 26% and 25% of all cases, respectively (Sigauque et al., 2009). Case-fatality from bacteraemia was 12% and accounted for 21% of hospital deaths; in addition, resistance to commonly used antibiotics was high in isolated *Salmonella*, *H. influenzae*, and *E. coli* (Sigauque et al., 2009). Bacterial meningitis is also a major global threat; a study in Gambia estimated that 2% of all children die of the disease before they reach the age of two (Adjogble et al., 2007).

Most microbial infections are treatable and are preventable. Yet they continue to be a public health concern, particularly food-borne diarrhoeal diseases and respiratory infections, which are life-threatening. Others are a cause of morbidity reducing the quality of life, such as periodontal diseases and other communicable opportunistic infections, especially in immune-compromised individuals; emerging diseases also contribute to morbidity rates (Azevedo, Prater, & Hayes, 2010). A lack of resources limits the availability of adequate sanitation, clean food and water, immunization, healthcare and medicines. As part of achieving Vision 2030, Namibia seeks to reduce morbidity and mortality of all preventable diseases.

A review of 22 studies conducted in Africa involving 58,296 patients revealed that 13.5% of adults and 8.2% of children had blood infections. Seventy per cent had malaria but, of the rest, more than half had *Salmonella* infections followed by *Staphylococcus aureus* then *E. coli* (Reddy, Shaw, & Crump, 2010). Food-borne pathogens are a major cause of concern in all parts of the world; there are 31 different pathogens known to cause food-borne illnesses (CDC, 2011). *Salmonella* spp., *S. aureus* and *E. coli* O157:H7 are generally the top five agents responsible for the majority of food-borne illnesses, hospitalizations and deaths (CDC, 2011). *Staphylococcus aureus* are gram-positive bacteria that can be found in the soil, on the skin or mucous membranes of humans, and on the bodies of animals (van Huyssteen, 2008). It causes skin infections under moist conditions or when diseases, surgical wounds or intravenous devices have breached the skin. Ninety per cent of all osteomyelitis and septic arthritis cases are of staphylococcal origin. *Staphylococcus aureus* also causes diarrhoea, pneumonia and destructive endocarditis (Gillespie & Bamford, 2007). *Escherichia coli* is the predominant gram-negative organism living in the intestines of humans and animals and is known to cause diarrhoea and urinary tract infections. Cholera is a major food-borne infection with Africa contributing more than 80% of cholera cases worldwide (Naidoo & Patric, 2002).

Over 750 species of microorganisms inhabit the oral cavity, including *Candida albicans*, and *Niesseria*, *Lactobacillus* and *Staphylococcus* spp. (Avila, Ojcius, & Yilmaz, 2009). Whilst not all are harmful, conditions in the oral cavity such as poor dental hygiene and age can cause biofilms to form, which may contain pathogens that cause dental problems. Periodontal diseases and dental caries are two common dental problems caused by microorganisms; up to 90% of school children have a prevalence of dental caries and the majority of adults are also affected (Palombo, 2011). *Candida*, *Cryptococcus* and *Tinea versicolor* are chronic fungal infections often acquired by immune-compromised patients. *Candida* forms part of the normal microflora of the skin, gastrointestinal tract and female genital tract, however, the overgrowth of *Candida* leads to thrush and vaginitis. Protozoan diseases are caused by plasmodia, *Leishmania* and *Trypanosoma*, with the most prevalent being malaria caused by *Plasmodium* spp.

Common microbial infections in Namibia

HIV/AIDS is the underlying cause of death due to microbial infections; others include tuberculosis, and diarrhoeal diseases that are typically caused by *Salmonella* and *Streptococcus* spp. (Table 4.3). Malaria and lower respiratory tract infections are also important. Malaria, which was the cause of most febrile illnesses in 2005, has declined by over 97% in Namibia with 62.2 cases per 1000 people and 9.6 deaths per 1000 being reported in 2009 (MoHSS, 2010). Most febrile cases are now a result of microbial infections, especially pneumonia and septicaemia (L. Haidula, National Case Manager, National Vector-Borne Disease Control Programme, MoHSS, personal communication, October 2011).

TABLE 4.3: Top ten causes of deaths in Namibia.

Cause	%
HIV/AIDS	51
Perinatal conditions	4
Cerebrovascular disease	4
Tuberculosis	4
Ischaemic heart disease	4
Diarrhoeal disease	3
Malaria	3
Violence	2
Lower respiratory tract infections	2
Road traffic accidents	2

Source: WHO (2003)

Namibia had an outbreak of cholera in Omusati and Kunene regions in 2007/08 when 250 cases were reported. *Vibrio cholerae* was the cause of the outbreak and isolates showed resistance to streptomycin, although they were susceptible to most antibiotics such as tetracycline, ampicillin, kanamycin, ciprofloxacin and chloramphenicol (Smith, Keddy, & de Wee, 2008).

Medicinal use of plants

In Africa and elsewhere in the world, phytomedicines were used for hundreds of years to treat various ailments long before the introduction of modern medicine. Herbal medicines are still widely used in many parts of the world, especially in areas where people do not have easy access to modern medicines. According to the World Health Organization (WHO), 60%–90% of Africa's population relies on medicinal plants to totally or partially meet their health needs (WHO, 2003). Traditional medicine in China accounts for about 40% of the total medicinal consumption, with the country having virtually two health systems (Hesketh & Zhu, 1997; WHO, 2003). In India and Chile, 65% and 71% of the population, respectively, meet their primary healthcare needs using traditional medicines (WHO, 2003).

Plants are a rich resource for traditional medicines and modern pharmaceuticals, and provide chemical compounds, which are templates for synthetic drugs (Hammer, Carson, & Riley, 1999). Plants have a wide variety of secondary metabolites, such as tannins, terpenoids, alkaloids and flavonoids, which have antimicrobial properties (Khullar, 2010). It has been estimated that only 14%–28% of higher plant species are used medicinally and that 74% of pharmacologically active, plant-derived components were discovered based on their ethnomedicinal use (Ncube, Afolayan, & Okoh, 2008). Plants' secondary metabolites probably evolved as defence mechanisms against predation by microorganisms, insects and herbivores. Some plant compounds used for their odours and flavours (terpenoids) and pigments (quinones and tannins) have medicinal properties (Arif et al., 2009).

Drug discovery from the indigenous knowledge of medicinal plants has evolved to include different scientific disciplines and various methods of analysis. The documentation and validation process starts with the collection and identification of plant(s) of interest, based on this knowledge. Plants with known biological activity in ethnomedicinal settings for which active compound(s) have not been isolated (e.g., traditionally used herbal remedies), or randomly collected taxa, are candidates for screening. Scientists prepare extracts from the plant materials and subject these extracts to biological screening in pharmacologically relevant assays to ascertain activity. Natural-product chemists then isolate and characterize the active compound(s) through bioassay-guided fractionation. The activity of the characterized compounds is then linked to their structure, forming the basis of drug development.

Cheikhyoussef, Shapi, Matengu and Mu Ashekele (2011) found that 36.4% of the 753 plant species found in the Oshikoto Region are used for medicinal purposes. They are used for various infections caused by microbial agents, such as diarrhoeal and skin diseases. Rural communities still mainly depend on locally available plants for oral hygiene because of their proximity, availability and reliability (David, Famurewa, & Olawale, 2010). Chewing sticks (plants) provide mechanical stimulation to the gums, whilst also killing harmful microorganisms present in the mouth (Muhammad & Lawal, 2010). HIV/AIDS patients are highly susceptible to opportunistic infections and suffer from chronic diarrhoea caused by intestinal infections (Yoda et al., 2011). Plant sources are unexploited sources of alternative cures and remedies for emerging diseases, opportunistic infections of HIV-positive patients (Govindappa, Kumar, & Santoyo, 2011) and as a means to control the increasing occurrence of antimicrobial resistance (Bessong & Obi, 2006; Chinsembu, 2009; Chinsembu & Hedimbi, 2010; Sawhney, 2012).

Studies on the roots, stems, leaves, seeds, flowers and fruits of many plants have found that these possess antimicrobial characteristics (Anburaja, Nandagopalan, & Marimuthu, 2011), which are effective against various pathogens, such as those that cause food-borne diseases. Leaf extracts of the plant *Senna siamae* (the kassod tree, which is native to south and south-east Asia) are traditionally used for treating infectious diseases and have been found to possess antibacterial properties against *Salmonella typhi* (Doughari & Okafor, 2008). Stem-bark extracts of *Ziziphus mucronata* (buffalo thorn; indigenous to Namibia) were tested against medically important pathogens such as *E. coli* and *S. aureus* and were found to have significant antimicrobial activity against both bacteria (Olajuyigbe & Afolayan, 2012). The control of microbial infections by using plants with antibiotic properties might mitigate the development of antibiotic resistance through the isolation and identification of secondary metabolites produced by plants and their use as active principles in medicinal preparations (Ncube, Finnie, & van Staden, 2010).

There are a number of plants that are used as chewing sticks in Namibia (Muhammad & Lawal, 2010). *Diospyros lycioides* (Cai, Wei, van der Bijl, & Wu, 2000) is well known among the Aawambo as *oshimumu* and is widely used as a chewing stick in northern Namibia. In fact, it is widely sold in markets throughout the country. Cai et al. (2000) reported on its significant antibacterial activity against *Streptococcus mutans*, *S. sanguinis*, *Porphyromonas gingivalis* and *Prevotella intermedia*. *Colophospermum mopane* is also used as chewing sticks in the northern regions of Namibia. Other plants used for oral hygiene in Namibia are *Croton gratissimus*, *Barleria prionitoides*, *Ocimum americanum*, *Harpagophytum zeyheri*, *Azima tetracantha* and *Artemisia afra*.

There are several classes of compounds that are associated with antimicrobial activity and these can be used as a 'fingerprint' to identify plants with the potential to kill microorganisms. Alkaloids are heterocyclic nitrogen compounds that are commonly isolated from the plants of the Ranunculaceae, or buttercup family

(Khullar, 2010). They are commonly found to have antimicrobial properties. Their activity is probably due to their ability to complex with extracellular and soluble proteins, and bacterial cell walls. Lipophilic flavonoids may also disrupt microbial membranes (Cowan, 1999). Terpenes are essential oil fractions that carry the fragrance of plants. These oils are secondary metabolites that are highly enriched in compounds based on an isoprene structure. Terpenene (terpenoid) activity has been demonstrated against bacteria, fungi, viruses, and protozoa (Cowan, 1999).

Despite the enormous pressures of managing diseases and the abundance of plant species in Namibia, little has been done to document the use of indigenous Namibian plants as antibacterial alternatives. This chapter highlights the valorization of indigenous knowledge of some medicinal plants through the determination of their antimicrobial properties by the University of Namibia. The plants investigated and the methods used follow below, as well as the results, which provide a foundation for further studies on the potential antimicrobial uses of these medicinal plants.

METHODOLOGY

The plants tested

Four plant species were collected and tested for antimicrobial properties: *Dichrostachys cinerea*, *Searsia tenuinervis*, *Tarchonanthus camphoratus* and *Pechuel-loeschea leubnitziae*. A short description of each follows below.

Dichrostachys cinerea is a plant used in Namibia as a chewing stick, as well as for treating dysentery, stomachache and various inflammatory conditions. The plant is also found throughout the tropical parts of Africa, from Sudan in the north to South

FIGURE 4.1:
A flowering *Dichrostachys cinerea* plant (Fabaceae: Mimosoideae).
(© Silke Rügheimer.)

FIGURE 4.2:
Leaves of the Kalahari currant, *Searsia tenuinervis* (Anacardiaceae). (© Coleen Mannheimer.)

FIGURE 4.3:
The wild camphor bush, *Tarchonanthus camphoratus* (Asteraceae). (© (Silke Rügheimer.)

Africa in the south. It has several common names, such as the Kalahari Christmas tree, sickle-bush, marabou-thorn and princess-earring. In Namibia, it is commonly called the *omutjete* among the Otjiherero-speaking people and ǀgoes among the Khoekhoegowab-speaking people of southern Namibia. It grows as a shrub with a height of 5–10 m. The leaves are compound and pinnate. The flowers are pinkish-white basally and yellow terminally (Banso & Adeyemo, 2007).

Searsia tenuinervis is a plant indigenous to Namibia, which belongs to the Anacardiaceae family and is commonly called the Kalahari currant. The San eat the sweet, round, brown berries of this plant, sometimes soaking them and eating them as porridge. Its leaves can also be crushed to treat bee-stings, implying that they have anti-inflammatory properties. The roots of this plant are used to treat coughs and diarrhoea.

FIGURE 4.4: The bitter bush, *Pechuel-loeschea leubnitziae* (Asteraceae). (© Coleen Mannheimer.)

Tarchonanthus camphoratus (wild camphor bush) has been used in traditional settings to treat ailments such as bronchitis and inflammation, as well as abdominal cramps and asthma (van Wyk, van Oudtshoorn, & Gericke, 1997). Apart from preparations of tinctures and infusions from leaves and twigs, which are either taken orally or chewed to produce a therapeutic effect, van Wyk et al. (1997) reported the traditional use of diaphoretic preparations for the treatment of abdominal complaints, headaches, toothache, asthma, bronchitis and inflammation.

Pechuel-loeschea leubnitziae is commonly known as bitter bush. It is a shrub that grows up to 2 m tall and has straight, grey leaves and purple-to-white flowers. It is ubiquitous in southern Africa; *Pechuel-loeschea leubnitziae* is the only species of this genus found in Namibia. The plant leaves and roots are used to treat colds, fevers, stomach ailments and skin diseases.

Plant collection and preparation

The leaves, roots or stems of plants were collected in Ohangwena, Oshikoto, Omaheke and Otjozondjupa regions of Namibia. A voucher specimen, which is simply a dried and preserved specimen of plant leaves, fruit, flowers or tubers, was prepared for each plant and sent to the National Botanical Research Institute (NBRI) in Windhoek for scientific identification. The harvested plant material was air dried for 2–3 weeks, and then ground to powder using a blender and a mortar and pestle to increase its surface area prior to preparation of the extract. The grinding process assists the solvent to penetrate to the cellular structure of the plant tissues, thereby helping to dissolve the secondary metabolites and increase the yields of extraction. Generally, the smaller the particle sizes, the more efficient the extraction (Osei-Akosah, 2010). The powdered plant material was subsequently macerated in various organic solvents to produce organic extracts; water was used to produce aqueous extracts.

Solvent extraction is the most common method of extracting compounds from plant materials. The type of solvent chosen depends on the type of compound to be extracted from the plant material. Water is a universal solvent used mostly by traditional healers as they have limited or no access to other solvents such as alcohols. Properties of a good solvent include ease of evaporation at low heat; low toxicity; absorption of the extract; preservative action; and inability to cause the extract to complex or dissociate (Das, Tiwari, & Shrivastava, 2010).

Extraction was followed by separation of the solution from plant debris using filtration. The solvent was then evaporated out of the solution using a rotary evaporator and subsequently left on a freeze dryer. The resulting crude extract was then used for all analyses to determine chemical composition and antimicrobial activity. It was dissolved in solvents to constitute extracts of varying concentrations.

Antimicrobial assay

Phytochemical tests were done to detect the presence of certain phytochemical parent groups, which may have antibacterial properties, using thin-layer chromatography (TLC), a simple technique to separate chemical compounds in the extract. Phytochemical screens were also used to detect the presence or absence of classes of antibacterial compounds. Crude extracts were qualitatively analysed for the presence of glycosides using the methods of Farnsworth (1966) and Njoku and Obi (2009). Terpenoids were detected using the protocols used by Egwaikhide, Okeniyi and Gimba (2007).

Human pathogenic bacteria, multi-resistant *Escherichia coli* ATCC 25922, *Staphylococcus aureus* ATCC 25923, *Enterobacter aerogenes* ATCC 13048, *Proteus vulgaris*, *Serratia marcescens*, *Salmonella typhi*, and the fungus, *Candida albicans*, were obtained from the Central Veterinary Laboratory of Namibia for the antimicrobial assay. The bacterial strains were used to inoculate freshly prepared nutrient broth from which streak plates on nutrient agar were prepared. Single colonies from the streak plates were then used to maintain cultures of the bacteria on nutrient-agar plates.

The 'well diffusion' method or the 'disc diffusion' method was used to test the plant extracts for antimicrobial activity. Agar plates were prepared for each bacterial strain as per the manufacturer's instructions and incubated for 24 hours to ensure no contamination had occurred. The plates were then inoculated with 100 μl of broth culture of the relevant bacteria, which was spread over the agar and allowed to dry. Water and dimethyl sulfoxide (DMSO) were used as negative controls and antibiotics, erythromycin and gentamycin, were used as positive controls. Assays were carried out in triplicate whereby in each plate designated for one concentration of any particular extract, three wells measuring 8 mm in diameter were made. The plates were left to sit for thirty minutes to allow the agar to absorb the extracts before being incubated at 37 °C. For the disc-diffusion method, three paper discs immersed in plant extract were placed on the surface of the inoculated petri dish.

Antimicrobial activity was recorded 24 hours after initial incubation and again 24 hours later (after two days). A transparent ruler was used to measure the diameters of the zones of inhibition in millimetres for all three triplicates.

RESULTS AND DISCUSSION

Dichrostachys cinerea

Phytochemical screening of the methanolic extract of *D. cinerea* leaves revealed the presence of four secondary metabolites – tannins, flavonoids, phenols and terpenoids (Table 4.4). The twig extract showed no flavonoids, but tested positive for the other three metabolites, although in lower quantities than in the leaves.

TABLE 4.4: Phytochemical constituents of leaves and twigs of *Dichrostachys cinerea*.

Constituent	Inference	
	Leaves	Twigs
Flavonoid	+	−
Tannin	+++	+
Phenol	+++	+
Terpenoid	+++	+

− = absent   + = present   +++ = abundant

TABLE 4.5: Inhibition of *P. vulgaris* by crude extracts of *Dichrostachys cinerea*.

Concentration of extracts (mg/mℓ)	Zones of inhibition (mm)*			
	Leaf extracts		Twig extracts	
	Methanol	Aqueous	Methanol	Aqueous
50	21.5	11.8	19.1	0.0
30	16.1	0.0	16.5	0.0
20	15.7	0.0	13.0	0.0
15	14.0	0.0	12.7	0.0
5	12.7	0.0	0.0	0.0

* mean of triplicates

TABLE 4.6: Inhibition of *S. marcescens* by crude extracts of *Dichrostachys cinerea*.

Concentration of extracts (mg/mℓ)	Zones of inhibition (mm)*			
	Leaf extracts		Twig extracts	
	Methanol	Aqueous	Methanol	Aqueous
50	17.7	0.0	15.8	0.0
30	15.4	0.0	14.0	0.0
20	13.8	0.0	13.0	0.0
15	13.3	0.0	11.8	0.0
5	11.5	0.0	0.0	0.0

* mean of triplicates

The antimicrobial activities of leaf and twig extracts of *D. cinerea* against two different pathogens – *Proteus vulgaris* and *Serratia marcescens* – are presented in Tables 4.5 and 4.6.

The highest concentrations (50 mg/mℓ) of aqueous extracts of the leaves showed a very narrow inhibition zone (11.8 mm) of *Proteus vulgaris*, whilst the methanol extract at the same concentration showed significant antimicrobial activity (21.5 mm) (Table 4.5). No inhibition of *P. vulgaris* was observed for the twig aqueous extracts, but methanol extraction showed antimicrobial activity. The methanol extracts of leaves and twigs were comparable in activity, although phytochemical analysis showed the leaf extract had more compounds.

From Table 4.6, methanol extracts of leaves and twigs of *D. cinerea* inhibited the growth of *Serratia marcescens* with zones ranging from 11.5 mm to 17.7 mm in size. The aqueous extracts did not show any inhibition of *S. marcescens*. Trends of antimicrobial activity of the extracts were similar to those for *P. vulgaris*. The increase in antibacterial effectiveness observed with increase in concentration of phytochemicals isolated in this study supports a concentration-dependent mode of action.

The methanol and aqueous extracts of *D. cinerea* did not manifest any zones of inhibition against the fungus, *Candida albicans*.

Phytochemical studies performed on *D. cinerea* extracts have revealed the presence of tannins, sterols and triterpenes, polyphenols and flavonoids as well as of cardiotonic heterosides, similar to results of Raissa, Souza, Kpahé, Konaté, and Datté (2011). Tannins exert antimicrobial activity by iron deprivation, hydrogen bonding or specific interactions with vital proteins, such as enzymes. Herbs that have tannins are astringent in nature and are used for treating intestinal disorders such as diarrhoea and dysentery. The activities of terpenes or terpenoids have been demonstrated against bacteria, fungi, viruses and protozoa (Khullar, 2010). Phenols and polyphenols present in plants are known to be toxic to microorganisms in the treatment of inflamed or ulcerated tissues, whilst flavonoids have been reported to have both antibacterial and antifungal activities (Patil & Gaikwad, 2011).

Traditional healers use water primarily to form their extracts, but plant extracts from organic solvents have been found to give a more consistent antimicrobial activity (Ncube et al., 2008). In this study, plant extractions with organic solvents provided stronger antibacterial activity than extraction with water. The high inhibitory potential of the methanol extracts might be due to the high solubility of phytoconstituents in this polar organic solvent (Patil & Gaikwad, 2011). This study demonstrated that the activity of the extracts depends on the solvent used, and that the leaf extracts of *D. cinerea* showed stronger antibacterial effects than the twigs. This indicates that the phytochemical constituents are more active in the leaves than in the twigs.

Searsia tenuinervis

A strong presence of flavonoids and terpenoids were detected in the roots and leaves of *S. tenuinervis*, respectively (Table 4.7). The antimicrobial activity of plants has been ascribed to the presence of several phytochemicals such as flavonoids and alkaloids (Edeoga, Okwu, & Mbaebie, 2005; Owoseni et al., 2010). The roots and bark of *S. tenuinervis* tested positive for five phytochemical constituents – alkaloids, flavonoids, saponins, tannins and terpenoids. No steroids were detected. The leaves also showed no saponins, but tested positive for the other four phytochemicals found in the roots and bark.

Tables 4.8 and 4.9, and Figure 4.5 show the effect of *S. tenuinervis* extracts on *Staphylococcus aureus*. Organic extracts of the leaves, bark and roots of *S. tenuinervis* showed inhibition of *S. aureus* at all concentrations tested (Table 4.8). Inhibition zones of 10.50–15.25 mm were obtained for the organic leaf extracts, while inhibition zones of 12.25–23.25 mm and 12.0–21.5 mm were observed from the activity of the bark and roots extracts, respectively, at concentrations of 1–20 mg/mℓ.

TABLE 4.7: Phytochemical constituents of the leaves, bark and roots of *Searsia tenuinervis*.

Constituent	Roots	Bark	Leaves
		Inference	
Alkaloid	+	+	+
Flavonoid	+++	++	++
Saponin	++	+	−
Steroid	−	−	−
Tannin	++	+	++
Terpenoid	+	+	+++

+++ = strongly positive   ++ = moderately positive   + = positive   − = not detected
Source: Dushimemaria et al. (2012)

TABLE 4.8: Average zones of inhibition of *S. aureus* by organic extracts of *Searsia tenuinervis*.

Concentration of extracts (mg/mℓ)	Leaf	Bark	Root
	Zones of inhibition (mm)		
20	15.25 ± 1.48	23.25 ± 4.87	21.50 ± 1.66
10	14.75 ± 0.83	17.75 ± 2.49	21.00 ± 0.71
5	12.00 ± 1.00	17.00 ± 1.22	18.00 ± 0.71
1	10.50 ± 0.87	12.25 ± 1.89	12.00 ± 0.82

Source: Dushimemaria et al. (2012)

Aqueous leaf extracts (20 mg/mℓ) prepared at 20 °C and 60 °C showed average inhibition zones of 16.5mm and 20.25 mm, respectively, against *S. aureus*, while aqueous root or bark extracts exhibited no antibacterial activity (Table 4.9). This suggests that the leaves of the plant have superior antibacterial compounds than the roots or bark. At concentrations less than 20 mg/mℓ, the bacterial colonies were observed to grow again, implying that the extract did not kill the bacteria at these concentrations, but was merely bacteriostatic.

Interestingly, aqueous preparations of the root are used traditionally, yet they showed poor activity. This is a cautionary example of how lab-based testing may be inconsistent with clinical use of plants, as some phytochemicals require the body to break them down before they are effective. This also underscores the importance of testing in live animals, not just in cell cultures.

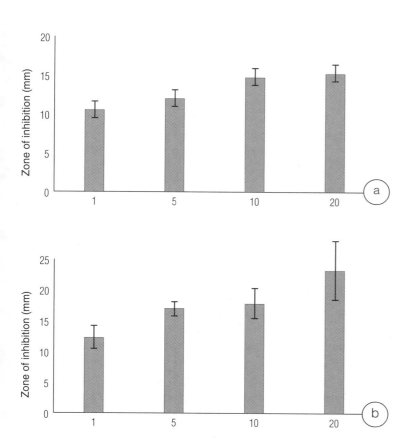

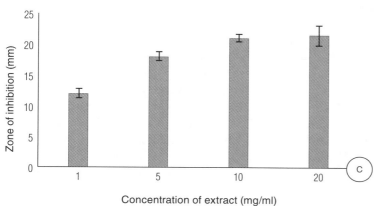

FIGURE 4.5:
Comparative zones of inhibition resulting from different concentrations of organic extracts of *Searsia tenuinervis* on *Staphylococcus aureus*: (a) leaf organic extract, (b) bark organic extract, (c) root organic extract. (From Dushimemaria, Mumbengegwi, du Preez, & Böck, 2012.)

TABLE 4.9: Average zones of inhibition of *S. aureus* by aqueous extracts of *Searsia tenuinervis*.

Concentration of extracts (mg/mℓ)	Inference					
	Leaf		Bark		Root	
	20 °C	60 °C	20 °C	60 °C	20 °C	60 °C
20	16.5 ± 2.52	20.25 ± 5.5	–	–	–	–
10	BS	BS	–	–	–	–
5	BS	BS	–	–	–	–
1	BS	BS	–	–	–	–

BS = bacteriostatic   – = no observed antibacterial activity
Source: Dushimemaria et al. (2012)

The antibacterial activity observed in this study was concentration dependent, as shown in Tables 4.8 and 4.9 and Figure 4.5. According to Adesokan, Akanji and Yakubu (2007), a dosage-dependent response of *S. aureus* to the aqueous extracts of *Enantia chlorantha* (a plant commonly used in traditional medicine elsewhere in Africa) was reported.

Extracts of *S. tenuinervis* have antibacterial activity against gram-positive bacteria, such as *S. aureus*. This activity might be due to the presence of phytochemicals, such as flavonoids, and confirms the use of the Kalahari currant for the treatment of gastrointestinal ailments. Neither organic nor aqueous extracts of *S. tenuinervis* had an effect on *Enterobacter aerogenes*, a gram-negative bacterium. Gram-negative bacteria are usually unsusceptible to both organic and aqueous extracts of plants, which is attributed to the structure of their cell walls, which is thick and impermeable, creating a barrier to the extracts. Inhibition zones of 22 mm on *S. aureus* and 18 mm on *E. aerogenes* from the antibiotic, gentamycin, in the control experiment were observed.

Tarchonanthus camphoratus

Qualitative phytochemical tests conducted on aqueous and organic extracts of *T. camphoratus* leaves, stems and bark showed the presence of terpenoids and glycosides in all of them (Table 4.10).

Glycosides and terpenoids are significant antibiotic compounds and have not previously been reported for *T. camphoratus*. Previous phytochemical testing done on plant extracts of *T. camphoratus* revealed the presence of tannins, saponins and reducing sugars (Mwangi & Achola, 1994), but not alkaloids, nor cardiac and anthraquinone glycosides. Various flavanones, such as luteolin, apigenin, nepetin and hispidulin, have also been identified from Egyptian collections, as well as a sesquiterpene lactone (parthenolide) and a quaternary alkaloid, tarchonanthine (Scott & Springfield, 2005). The volatile oil of the plant has a characteristic camphor-like

TABLE 4.10: Phytochemical properties of aqueous and organic extracts of leaves, stems and bark of *Tarchonanthus camphoratus*.

Phytochemical constituent	Aqueous extracts			Organic extracts		
	Leaves	**Stems**	**Bark**	**Leaves**	**Stems**	**Bark**
Terpenoid	+	+	+	+	+	+
Glycoside	+	+	+	+	+	+

+ = present
Source: Auala et al. (2012)

aroma, but the plant only contains a small amount of camphor, which is said to be responsible for its reported analgesic, decongestant, diaphoretic and analgesic effects (Bruneton, 1995). Glycosides form an important compound called aminoglycosides from which antibiotics such as streptomycin and gentamicin are made. Terpenoids are oxygen-containing derivatives of terpenes, many of which have been found to be effective against many types of bacteria. The presence of these compounds may be significant for antibiotic activity.

All aqueous extracts showed no antibacterial activity against *E. coli* ATCC 25922 and *S. aureus* ATCC25923, and a field strain of *S. typhi*. All leaf, stem and bark organic extracts, however, had varying levels of antimicrobial activity against all the three test organisms (Figures 4.6–4.8). Zones of inhibition were defined as bacteriostatic (partial inhibition of microbial growth) and antimicrobial (defined zones of growth inhibition). The organic leaves and bark extracts both exhibited bacteriostatic activity against the three test microorganisms while the organic stem extracts exhibited antimicrobial activity.

The organic leaf extracts (Figure 4.6) exhibited the highest inhibitory activity against all the three test organisms, with the most activity being observed against *S. typhi* at a concentration of 0.5 mg/mℓ (inhibition zone of 19.3 mm), then against *S. aureus* at 10 mg/mℓ (inhibition zone of 19.7 mm). Antimicrobial activity of the organic leaf extract against *E. coli* was not dependent on concentration (inhibition zones of 5.0–7.3 mm).

The organic stem extracts (Figure 4.7) showed the greatest potency against *S. typhi* at 0.5 mg/mℓ (inhibition zone of 17.3 mm). Activity against *S. aureus* was only observed at concentrations of 5 mg/mℓ and 10 mg/mℓ (inhibition zones of 6.0–7.7 mm), with no activity at lower concentrations. Antimicrobial activity of the organic stem extracts was not concentration dependent against *E. coli* (inhibition zones of 3.7–5.7 mm).

The organic bark extracts (Figure 4.8) showed the least antimicrobial activity with zones of inhibition of 9.3 mm for *S. typhi*; no activity against *S. aureus* at any concentration; and zones of exhibition of 4.7–7.0 mm for all concentrations against *E. coli*.

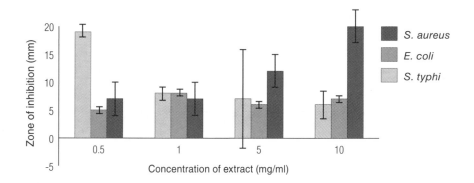

FIGURE 4.6: Mean antimicrobial activity of organic leaf extracts of *Tarchonanthus camphoratus*. (From Auala, Mumbengegwi, du Preez, & Böck, 2012.)

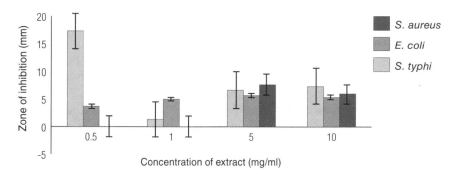

FIGURE 4.7: Mean antimicrobial activity of organic stem extracts of *Tarchonanthus camphoratus*. (From Auala et al., 2012.)

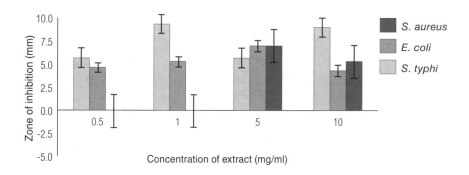

FIGURE 4.8: Mean antimicrobial activity of organic bark extracts of *Tarchonanthus camphoratus*. (From Auala et al., 2012.)

TABLE 4.11: Preliminary phytochemical screening of *Pechuel-loeschea leubnitziae* for compounds with known antimicrobial properties.

Phytochemical constituent	Inference		
	Leaves	Stems	Roots
Flavonoid	+	−	−
Tannin	−	−	−
Polyphenol	+	−	++
Anthraquinone	+++	−	−
Alkaloid	−	−	−
Saponin	+	+	++

+++ = strongly positive   ++ = moderately positive   + = positive   − = not detected
Source: Hedimbi et al. (2012)

The medicinal uses of the wild camphor bush are remarkably similar throughout its geographical range. Fresh or dried plant leaves and branches are usually crushed and burnt, and the smoke inhaled by the patient (Watt & Breyer-Brandwijk, 1962; Hutchings & van Staden, 1994). The ethnomedicinal preparation of *T. camphoratus*, which uses aqueous solvents such as water, was shown to be ineffective against all three pathogens in the well-diffusion assays in contrast to the organic extracts. This might have been due to the antimicrobial compounds not dissolving freely in the aqueous solvent during extraction. Extraction at higher temperatures or for a shorter period might have resulted in a greater yield of active compounds. The organic extracts may have shown more activity due to the increased solubility of the plant compounds in the methanol used to prepare them. The antimicrobial activities of the plant's organic leaf and bark extracts seemed to be more of a bacteriostatic nature against the test microorganisms (*S. typhi*, *E. coli* and *S. aureus*), whilst the activity of the organic stem extract appeared to be more of an antimicrobial nature.

The ethnomedicinal properties of *T. camphoratus* as an antibiotic were validated in this study and they may have been due to the presence of glycosides and terpenoids in the extracts. The use of this plant can be recommended as a natural antibiotic supplement to other drug treatments.

Pechuel-loeschea leubnitziae

Phytochemical tests detected the presence of anthraquinones, saponins, polyphenols and flavonoids in the leaves, roots and stems of *P. leubnitziae*.

No zones of inhibition were observed for the organic and aqueous extracts of the leaves, stems and roots of *P. leubnitziae* against *E. coli* and *C. albicans*. However, organic extracts of the roots exhibited activity against *S. aureus* (5.6–7.3 mm) at concentrations of 2.5–10.0 mg/mℓ, (Figure 4.9).

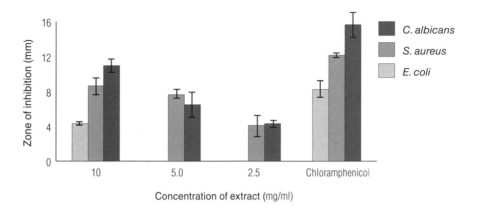

FIGURE 4.9: Mean antimicrobial activity of *P. leubnitziae* methanol root extracts. (From Hedimbi, Kaputjaza, Hans, Mumbengegwi, & Böck, 2012.)

Only *P. leubnitziae* methanol root extract showed antimicrobial activity against *S. aureus* even though antimicrobial classes of compounds – saponins, anthraquinones, flavonoids and polyphenols – which may be responsible for the observed activity, were detected in the different parts of the plant. Further studies using different solvents should be conducted on this plant.

CONCLUSION

Phytochemical analysis validated the ethnomedicinal use of four plant species as antibacterial and antifungal agents. All the extracts from these plants revealed the presence of at least one class of compounds that is associated with antimicrobial activity. Organic extracts showed more compounds, as well as greater quantities of the compounds, because of increased solubility of the compounds in the organic solvents compared to the aqueous solvents. A caveat to this conclusion is that the presence of a class of antimicrobial compound does not necessarily guarantee antimicrobial activity, although it is a good indicator.

Aqueous extracts prepared using water – the solvent most commonly used in ethnomedicinal preparations – showed lower activity than expected. This is probably because laboratory preparation of plants might not have followed the same method as that carried out in the ethnomedicinal setting. Furthermore, some plants might require the biological environment of the patient's body to become active; cell-based or animal studies might be more revealing. Interestingly, some plant parts, which are not used traditionally, appeared to have more activity than those used; this underlines the fact that a combination of science and indigenous knowledge can make the use of medicinal plant resources more effective.

Given the challenges posed by microbial infections especially in resource poor settings, this research shows the potential for antimicrobial medicinal plants to be a viable alternative treatment to provide primary healthcare needs. However, sustainability of this treatment option has to be ascertained. Either resource surveys should be conducted before promoting the use of these plants or, alternatively, collaboration with chemists could be pursued to synthesize versions of the active compounds of these plants. Drug discovery is an expensive enterprise with many leads being discarded during the development process with only one in 5,000 lead compounds successfully advancing through development and clinical trials to be approved for use. Medicinal plants have a better hit-to-miss ratio than synthetic compounds, but challenges related to the quantity of materials required for optimization and political issues surrounding access to the plants and benefit-sharing complicate matters.

Faster and more reliable methods of plant collection, bioassay screening, compound isolation, and compound development must be employed. Innovative strategies, such as the design of appropriate, clinically relevant, high-throughput bioassays and screening of extracts libraries, can make drug discovery from medicinal plants more competitive.

References

Adesokan, A. A., Akanji, M. A., & Yakubu, M. T. (2007). Antibacterial potentials of extract of *Enantia chlorantha* stem bark. *African Journal of Biotechnology*, 6(22), 2502-2505.

Adjogble, K. L., Lourd M., Njanpop-Lafourcade, B. M., Traoré, Y., Hlomaschi, A. F., Amegatse, K. A., Agbenoko, K., Sanou, O., Sita, K., Mueller, J. E., & Gessner, B. D. (2007). The epidemiology of *Neisseria meningitidis* meningitis in Togo during 2003–2005. *Vaccine*, 25(Suppl. 1), A47-A52.

Anburaja, V., Nandagopalan, V., & Marimuthu, C. (2011). Antimicrobial activities of *Hemionitis arifolia* (Hemionitidiaceae) ethanol leaf extract. *Journal of Research in Antimicrobials*. 1(1), 9-12.

Anon. (2012, 22 October). Africa: Infectious diseases account for 63 percent of deaths in the continent – WHO official. AngolaPress. Retrieved from http://allafrica.com/stories/201210230197.html

Arif, T., Bhosalea, J. D., Kumara, N., Mandala, T. K., Bendreb, R. S., Lavekara, G. S., & Dabura, R. (2009). Natural products – antifungal agents derived from plants. *Journal of Asian Natural Products Research*, *11*(7), 621-638.

Auala, J. R., Mumbengegwi, D. R., du Preez, C. I., & Böck, R. (2012). Evaluation of *Tarchonanthus camphoratus* plant extracts for antimicrobial activity against food-borne pathogens. *Journal of Research in Microbes*, *1*(2), 96-104.

Avila, M., Ojcius, D. M., & Yilmaz, O. (2009). The oral microbiota: Living with a permanent guest. *DNA and Cell Biology*, *28*(8), 405-411.

Azevedo, M. J., Prater, G. S., & Hayes, S. C. (2010). Human immunodeficiency virus and tuberculosis co-infections in Kenya: Environment, resources and culture. *International Journal of Sociology and Anthropology*, *2*(4), 55-65.

Banso, A., & Adeyemo, S. O. (2007). Evaluation of antibacterial properties of tannins isolated from *Dichrostachys cinerea*. *African Journal of Biotechnology*, *6*(15), 1785-1787.

Berkley, J. A., Lowe, B. S., Mwangi, I., Williams, T., Bauni, E., Mwarumba, S., Ngetsa, C., Slack, M., Njenga, S., Hart, C., Maitland, K., English, M., Marsh, K., & Scott, J. A. (2005). Bacteremia among children admitted to a rural hospital in Kenya. *New England Journal of Medicine*, *352*(1), 39-47.

Bessong, P. O., & Obi, C. L. (2006). Ethnopharmacology of human immunodeficiency virus in South Africa: A mini review. *African Journal of Biotechnology*, *5*(19), 1693-1699.

Bruneton, J. (1995). *Pharmacognosy, phytochemistry, medicinal plants*. Hampshire, England: Intercept.

Cai, L., Wei, G. X., van der Bijl, P., & Wu, C. D. (2000). Namibian chewing stick, *Diospyros lycioides*, contains antibacterial compounds against oral pathogens. *Journal of Agricultural and Food Chemistry*, *48*(3), 909-914.

CDC [Centers for Disease Control and Prevention]. (2011). CDC estimates of foodborne illness in the United States. Retrieved from www.cdc.gov/foodborne burden/2011-foodborne-estimates.html

Cheikhyoussef, A., Shapi, M., Matengu, K., & Mu Ashekele, H. (2011). Ethnobotanical study of indigenous knowledge on medicinal plant use by traditional healers in Oshikoto Region, Namibia. *Journal of Ethnobiology and Ethnomedicine*, *7*, 10. doi: 10.1186/1746-4269-7-10

Chinsembu, K. C. (2009). Model and experiences of initiating collaboration with traditional healers in validation of ethnomedicines for HIV/AIDS in Namibia. *Journal of Ethnobiology and Ethnomedicine*, *5*, 30. doi:10.1186/1746-4269-5-30

Chinsembu, K. C., & Hedimbi, M. (2010). An ethnobotanical survey of plants used to manage HIV/AIDS opportunistic infections in Katima Mulilo, Caprivi Region, Namibia. *Journal of Ethnobiology and Ethnomedicine*, *6*, 25. doi:10.1186/1746-4269-6-25

Coppi, A., Cabinian, M., Mirelman, D., & Sinnis, P. (2006). Antimalarial activity of allicin, a biologically active compound from garlic cloves. *Antimicrobial Agents and Chemotherapy, 50*(5), 1731-1737.

Cowan, M. M. (1999). Plant products as antimicrobial agents. *Clinical Microbiology Reviews, 12*(4), 564-582.

Das, K., Tiwari, R. S. K., & Shrivastava, D. K. (2010). Techniques for the evaluation of medicinal plant products as antimicrobial agents: Current methods and future trends. *Journal of Medicinal Plants Research, 4*(2), 104-111.

David, O. M., Famurewa, O., & Olawale, A. K. (2010). *In vitro* assessment of aqueous and ethanolic extracts of some Nigerian chewing sticks on bacteria associated with dental infections. *African Journal of Microbiology Research, 4*(19), 1949-1953.

Doughari, J. H., & Okafor, N. B. (2008). Antibacterial activity of *Senna siamea* leaf extracts on *Salmonella typhi*. *African Journal of Microbiology Research, 2*, 42-46.

Dushimemaria, F., Mumbengegwi, D. R., du Preez, I., & Böck, R. (2012). Qualitative phytochemical screening and *in vitro* antimicrobial effects of plant extracts of *Searsia tenuinervis*. *Journal of Research in Microbes, 1*, 088-095.

Edeoga, H. O., Okwu, D. E., & Mbaebie, B. O. (2005). Phytochemical constituents of some Nigerian medicinal plants. *African Journal of Biotechnology, 4*(7), 685-688.

Egwaikhide, P. A., Okeniyi, S. O., & Gimba, C. E. (2007). Screening for anti-microbial activity and phytochemical constituents of some Nigerian medicinal plants. *Advances in Biological Research, 1*(5-6), 155-158.

Farnsworth, N. (1966). Biological and phytochemical screening of plants. *Journal of Pharmaceutical Sciences, 55*(3), 225-276.

Gillespie, S. H., & Bamford, K. B. (2007). *Medical microbiology and infection at a glance* (3rd ed.). Massachusetts, USA: Blackwell Publishing Inc.

Govindappa, M., Kumar, A. N. V., & Santoyo, G. (2011). *Crotalaria pallida* extracts as a putative HIV-protease inhibitors. *Journal of Research in Biology, 1*(4), 285-291.

Hammer, K. A., Carson, C. F., & Riley, T. V. (1999). Antimicrobial activity of essential oils and other plant extracts. *Journal of Applied Microbiology, 86*(6), 985-990.

Hedimbi, M., Kaputjaza, D. K., Hans, R. H., Mumbengegwi, D. R., & Böck, R. A. (2012). Phytochemical analysis and antimicrobial screening of *Pechuel-loeschea leubnitziae* (Kuntze) O. Hoffm. (Asteraceae) crude extracts. *Journal of Research in Microbes, 1*(1), 39-43. Open access, Ficus Publishers.

Hesketh, T., & Zhu, W. X. (1997). Health in China. Traditional Chinese medicine: One country, two systems. *British Medical Journal, 315*(7100), 115-117.

Hutchings, A., & van Staden, J. (1994). Plants used for stress-related ailments in traditional Zulu, Xhosa and Sotho medicine, Part 1: Plants used for headaches. *Journal of Ethnopharmacology, 43*(2), 89–124.

Khullar, N. (2010). Antimicrobials from plants and their use in therapeutics and drug discovery. *Institute of Intergrative Omics and Applied Biotechnology Journal*, *1*(3), 31-37.

Ku, M. J., Dossin, F. M., Choi, Y., Moraes, C. B., Ryu, J., Song, R., & Freitas-Junior, L. H. (2011). Quantum dots: A new tool for anti-malarial drug assays. *Malaria Journal*, *10*, 118. doi:10.1186/1475-2875-10-118.

Mohammed, M. S. A. (2009). Traditional medicinal plants and malaria in Africa. In H. R. Juliani, J. E. Simon, & C.-T. Ho (Eds.), *African natural plant products: New discoveries and challenges in chemistry and quality* (Vol. 1021, pp. 1-595). Paper presented at the American Chemical Society Symposium, Washington, DC.

MoHSS [Ministry of Health and Social Services]. (2010). *Malaria Strategic Plan 2010–2016*. Windhoek, Namibia: Author.

Muhammad, S., & Lawal, M. T. (2010). Oral hygiene and the use of plants. *Scientific Research and Essays*, *5*(14), 1788-1795.

Mulholland, K. E., & Adegbola, R. A. (2005). Bacterial infections – a major cause of death among children in Africa. *New England Journal of Medicine*, *352*, 75-77.

Mwangi, J. W., & Achola, K. J. (1994). Volatile constituents of the essential oil of *Tarchonanthus camphoratus*. *Journal of Essential Oil Research*, *6*, 183-185.

Naidoo, A., & Patric, K. (2002). Cholera: A continuous epidemic in Africa. *Perspectives in Public Health*, *122*(2), 89-94. doi: 10.1177/146642400212200209

Ncube, N. S., Afolayan, A. J., & Okoh, A. I. (2008). Assessment techniques of antimicrobial properties of natural compounds of plant origin: Current methods and future trends. *African Journal of Biotechnology*, *7*(12), 1797-1806.

Ncube, B., Finnie, J. F., van Staden, J. (2010). Seasonal variation in antimicrobial and phytochemical properties of frequently used medicinal bulbous plants from South Africa. *South African Journal of Botany*, *77*(2), 387-396.

Njoku, O. V., & Obi, C. (2009). Phytochemical constituents of some selected medicinal plants. *African Journal of Pure and Applied Chemistry*, *3*(11), 228-233.

Ogunlana, O. O., Ogunlana, O. E., & Ademowo, O. G. (2009). Comparative *in vitro* assessment of the antiplasmodial activity of quinine-zinc complex and quinine sulphate. *Scientific Research and Essay*, *4*(3), 180-184.

Olajuyigbe, O. O., & Afolayan, A. J. (2012). Antimicrobial potency of the ethanolic crude bark extract of *Ziziphus mucronata* Willd. subsp. *mucronata* Willd. *African Journal of Pharmacy and Pharmacology*, *6*(10), 724-730.

Osei-Akosah, E. (2010). *Antimicrobial activity profile of the constituents of four Ghanaian aromatic medicinal plants* (Master's thesis, Kwame Nkrumah University of Science and Technology, Kumasi, Ghana). Retrieved from http://ir.knust.edu.gh/bitstream/123456789/420/1/Thesis%20one%20final.pdf

Owoseni, A. A., Abimbola, A., Ayanbamiji, T. A., Ajayi, Y. O., Yejide O., Ewegbenro., I. B., & Ikeoluwa B. (2010). Antimicrobial and phytochemical analysis of leaves and bark extracts from *Bridelia ferruginea*. *African Journal of Biotechnology*, *9*(7), 1031-1036.

Palombo, A. E. (2011). Traditional medicinal plant extracts and natural products with activity against oral bacteria: Potential application and treatment of oral diseases. *Evidence-Based Complementary and Alternative Medicine*, 2011, 1-15.

Patil, U. H., & Gaikwad, D. K. (2011). Phytochemical evaluation and bactericidal potential of *Terminalia arjuna* stem bark. *International Journal of Pharmaceutical Sciences & Research*, *2*(3), 614-619.

Raissa, R. R., Souza, A., Kpahé, F., Konaté, K., & Datté, J. Y. (2011). *Dichrostachys cinerea* (L.) Wight et Arn (Mimosaceae) hydro-alcoholic extract action on the contractility of tracheal smooth muscle isolated from guinea-pig. *Complementary and Alternative Medicine*, *11*, 23. doi:10.1186/1472-6882-11-23

Reddy, E. A., Shaw, A. V., & Crump, J. A. (2010). Community-acquired bloodstream infections in Africa: A systematic review and meta-analysis. *The Lancet Infectious Diseases*, *10*(6), 417-432.

Rosenthal, P. J. (2003). Antimalarial drug discovery: Old and new approaches. *Journal of Experimental Biology*, *206*, 3735-3744.

Sawhney, R. (2012). Drug resistance: A social perspective. *Journal of Research in Biology*, *2*(4), 370-376.

Scott, G., & Springfield, E. (2005). *Tarchonanthus camphoratus* Herba. Retrieved from www.plantzafrica.com/me dmonographs/tarchonanthcamp.pdf

Sigaúque, B., Roca, A., Mandomando, I., Morais, L., Quintó, L., Sacarlal, J., Macete, E., Nhamposa, T., Machevo, S., Aide, P., Bassat, Q., Bardají, A., Nhalungo, D., Soriano-Gabarró, M., Flannery, B., Menendez, C., Levine, M. M., & Alonso, P. L. (2009). Community-acquired bacteremia among children admitted to a rural hospital in Mozambique. *Pediatric Infectious Disease Journal*, *28*(2), 108-113.

Smith, A. M., Keddy, K. H., & de Wee, L. (2008). Characterization of cholera outbreak isolates from Namibia, December 2006 to February 2007. *Epidemiology and Infection*, *136*(9), 1207-1209.

USAID [United States Agency for International Development]. (2011). Saving lives: A global leader in fighting malaria. USAID: From the American People. Infectious diseases. Retrieved from http://ec.europa.eu/research/health/infectious-diseases/povertydiseases/malaria_er.html

Van Huyssteen, M. (2008). *Collaborative research with traditional African health practitioners of the Nelson Mandela Metropole; Antimicrobial, anticancer and anti-diabetic activities of five medicinal plants* (PhD thesis, Nelson Mandela Metropolitan University, Port Elizabeth, South Africa).

Van Wyk, B. E., van Oudtshoorn, B., & Gericke, N. (1997). *Medicinal plants of South Africa* (1st ed.) Pretoria, South Africa: Briza Publications.

Watt, J. M., & Breyer-Brandwijk, M. G. (1962). *The medicinal and poisonous plants of southern and eastern Africa* (2nd ed.). Edinburgh, Scotland: Livingstone.

WHO [World Health Organization]. (2003). *Traditional medicine.* Retrieved from http://www.who.int/mediacentre/factsheets/2003/fs134/en/

Yoda, T., Suzue, T., Hirao, T., Yoshioka, A., Jazek, J., Jimenes, E., Yanagi, T., Minematsu, K., Goto, K., Nmor, J. C., Tachibana, H., Rakue, Y., Sakano, N., & Miyatake, N. (2011). Asymptomatic intestinal protozoan infections among inhabitants in Mexico City, Mexico. *International Journal of Medicine and Medical Sciences, 3*(7): 223-226.

5

Indigenous knowledge and antimicrobial properties of plants used in ethnoveterinary medicine

Kazhila C. Chinsembu

INTRODUCTION

The use of chemical pesticides and pharmaceutical drugs to manage livestock pests and diseases is anathema to the environment and leads to the development of resistance. Most resource-poor farmers also face problems, such as inaccessibility, unaffordability and inappropriate use of chemical pesticides and drugs. Faced with these constraints, livestock farmers in Namibia and other African countries turn to indigenous knowledge as an alternative option and as a key to unlock the power of plants to control various vectors and diseases of livestock. Utilization of plant extracts as ethnoveterinary medicines (EVMs) is perhaps one of the most sustainable methods readily adaptable to rural livestock-farming communities. Plants identified as herbal remedies in the management of livestock diseases, especially those with antimicrobial and antiparasitic properties, present considerable potential for further scientific research which may lead to the discovery of new and safer drugs.

Although many rural communal farmers use plants to treat livestock diseases, the current status of information on the use of plants in EVM Namibia, and the biological activities and toxicities of this flora, is still inadequate. For example, a complete systematic ethnobotanical list has not yet been compiled, creating an urgent need to record EVM knowledge in Namibia. Work in this field could help increase livestock productivity through improved management of diseases and parasites. Improved livestock productivity will, in turn, spur many socioeconomic benefits, such as increased family incomes and wealth, secure livelihoods, and improved food security and nutrition.

By way of preamble, this chapter reviews important issues related to livestock farming and disease status, and beef production and marketing in Namibia, and defines EVM.

Livestock farming and disease status in Namibia

Namibia is the most arid country in sub-Saharan Africa. Only 2% of Namibia's land receives enough rainfall to grow crops. As a result of this climatic quandary, most of the farming activities in Namibia revolve around livestock farming. Up to 40% of Namibians are small-scale farmers that eke out a living through herding on marginal and fragile rural lands. Extensive small-stock farming is the main agricultural activity in areas that receive less than 200 mm of rain per annum, while large-stock farming is prominent in areas where average annual rainfall exceeds 300 mm. Mixed large- and small-stock farming is practised in areas where rainfall is 200–300 mm. In communal areas where subsistence farming practices are common, livestock provide a variety of benefits, for example, milk, meat and draft power. Livestock is also a symbol of local wealth and provides a medium of exchange when buying and selling, and a means for paying lobola and compensation.

Small-scale farmers living on marginal lands in communal areas own about 10% of all the sheep, 60% of the cattle and 65% of the goats in Namibia (NNFU, 2008). Livestock productivity is hampered by several infectious bacterial diseases, including black-quarter, diarrhoea, anthrax, botulism, brucellosis, tuberculosis, rabies, foot-and-mouth disease (FMD), hoof problems and pleuropneumonia. Other ailments are caused by parasitic worms and protozoa. Overall, animal diseases in Namibia are caused by pathogens, most of which are said to be emerging or re-emerging.

About 40% of all the cattle with densities of up to 10–44 head per square kilometre, are found in the northern communal areas, which are prone to FMD (NNFU, 2008). The veterinary cordon fence (VCF) divides the northern FMD-prone area from the southern FMD-free area. All animals north of the VCF undergo a 21-day quarantine period before slaughtering (NNFU, 2008). In order to improve the incomes and livelihoods of northern communal farmers, there are discussions to enable them to access markets by allowing the free movement of domestic animals from the north to Windhoek.

Beef production and marketing in Namibia

Beef production is the main activity in Namibia's agricultural sector, constituting approximately 85% of agricultural incomes and, on average, 10% of gross national product (NNFU, 2008). About 85% of Namibian beef is exported to the European

Union (EU) and South Africa. Namibia is fortunate to have three EU-approved beef-export abattoirs and two EU-approved small-stock abattoirs, as well as two South-African-approved beef and two South-African-approved small-stock abattoirs, available for international exports (NNFU, 2008). Namibia exports approximately 9,000 tonnes of beef to the EU, Norway and Switzerland, and approximately 12,000 tonnes of beef to South Africa, per year (NNFU, 2008).

Export-led livestock and meat marketing chains have to meet increasingly stringent standards and requirements set by importing countries. In recent years, the costs of national regulation and the requirements for export standards have been increased (NNFU, 2008). Consequently, Namibia has implemented a costly 'Farm Assured Namibian Meat Scheme' (FAN Meat), the first of its kind in Africa. This quality-assurance scheme covers aspects of animal health and welfare, farming practices and traceability of livestock (NNFU, 2008).

These stringent measures have coerced farmers to rely on the heavy use of chemicals for dipping against disease-transmitting vectors such as ticks and to apply higher dosages of drugs for the treatment of diseases and parasites. Sadly, only commercial farmers use chemicals for vector control and pharmaceutical drugs for treatment because small-scale farmers cannot afford the cost of these products. This means that livestock production in communal areas is still burdened by diseases that decimate the herds and threaten the livelihoods of small-scale farmers. On commercial farms, the heavy use of synthetic chemicals threatens human and environmental health.

According to the Food and Agriculture Organization (FAO), the inaccessibility of pharmaceutical drugs to treat diseases and infections causes losses of 30%–35% in the livestock breeding potential of many developing countries, where poor animal health remains the major constraint to breeding (FAO, 2002). In Namibia, the use of traditional herbs to treat parasites has been reported by Siegmund-Schultze, Lange, Schneiderat and Steinbach (2012). According to these authors, most communal farmers cannot afford pharmaceutical drugs. In most Namibian communities, herbal preparations used to treat human diseases are also used to treat sick animals.

Before the advent of pharmaceutical drugs, communal farmers were known to treat animal diseases with herbs and other indigenous medical practices. The costs, inaccessibility and other factors associated with the conventional veterinary system have contributed to the persistence of EVM (Confessor, Mendonça, Mourão, & Alves, 2009). Nevertheless, associated with environmental degradation, indigenous knowledge and culture, including practices aimed at treating livestock, have been lost through the decades (Hauser, Little, & Roberts, 1994). There is therefore an urgent need to document EVM knowledge to maintain this important cultural practice.

What is ethnoveterinary medicine?

Ethnoveterinary medicine – or EVM – is a term that denotes indigenous animal healthcare. It refers to the use of ethnobotanical remedies to prevent and control diseases, as well as people's knowledge, skills, methods, practices and beliefs about the care of their domestic animals (McCorkle, 1986). EVM includes the use of diagnostic procedures, animal husbandry practices, surgical methods and traditional veterinary theory. According to Mathias (2001), EVM is developed by farmers in fields and barns, rather than by scientists in laboratories and clinics. Therefore, it is less systematic and less formalized, and is usually transferred by word of mouth rather than in writing. EVM is now recognized as a distinct field of study especially after the publication of three important reviews by McCorkle (1986), Wanzala et al. (2005) and McGaw and Eloff (2008).

Recent research has addressed a broad range of topics within this field, including plant-based and non-plant-based preparations; folk categories of illness; efficacy of treatments; and zoopharmacognosy. EVM research is often undertaken as part of a community-based approach that serves to improve animal health and provide basic veterinary services in underserved areas (Mathias-Mundy & McCorkle, 1989). It can provide low-cost alternatives to allopathic drugs.

Ethnoveterinary practices are appealing to organic livestock farmers whose goal is to improve meat quality without chemical residues (Lans & Turner, 2011); organic livestock agriculture allows only a restricted number of synthetic chemical substances for pest control. Natural herbal products are also less likely to become environmental pollutants than synthetic chemical products (Lans & Turner, 2011); hence, EVM practices present a more environmentally friendly approach to animal healthcare. Lans and Tuner (2011) argued that increased use of ethnoveterinary plants for parasite control reduces antibiotic contamination of the soil; this may lessen or delay the onset of antimicrobial resistance in certain animal parasites.

EVM is usually not as fast working and potent as pharmaceutical drugs. EVM is also less suitable to control and treat epidemic and endemic infectious diseases such as FMD, rinderpest, haemorrhagic septicaemia, anthrax, black-quarter, rabies and acute life-threatening bacterial infections (Mathias, 2001). Yet, for common diseases and more chronic conditions, such as colds, skin diseases, worms, wounds, reproductive disorders, nutritional deficiencies and mild diarrhoea, EVM has much to offer and can be a cheaper and more readily available alternative than costly, imported pharmaceutical drugs. For some diseases, a combination of modern and local remedies and management practices might be preferable. Even with infectious diseases, ethnoveterinary treatments should not be dismissed outright because many drugs used in chemotherapy are based on chemical substances of plant origin, or on the semi-synthetic derivatives of such substances.

Ethnoveterinary practices and plants need to be validated before they can be widely promoted. Several levels of validation are possible: tapping the experience of local people, for example, by asking them to rank local treatments according to their perceived efficacy; searching the scientific literature for data on the botany, phytochemistry, and *in-vitro* and *in-vivo* efficacies of medicinal plants; conducting laboratory assays; carrying out clinical tests in experimental herds at research stations; and conducting experiments in selected animals kept by small-scale farmers (Mathias, 2001). Alternatively, farmers could conduct their own tests by monitoring their use of ethnoveterinary remedies in the field and studying its influence on production and economic parameters.

Mathias (2001) asserts that ethnoveterinary technologies can be the starting point for drug and technology development. Ideally, information obtained from local farmers should be used within the communities of its origin to ensure that they benefit from their own knowledge. Sometimes a selected ethnoveterinary remedy can be improved through pharmacological and clinical research. Scientific validation of EVM, standardization of dosages, and improved packaging and storage techniques are the exact forms of value-addition that can benefit the livestock farming community.

STATUS OF ETHNOVETERINARY MEDICINE IN SELECTED AFRICAN COUNTRIES

Knowledge of EVM on the African continent is being embraced within the biotechnological framework and scientific renaissance spearheaded by the New Partnership for Africa's Development (NEPAD). To understand the importance of EVM in Namibia, it is critical to follow the trends of EVM research in other African countries. Therefore, the status of EVM in selected African countries is presented below to provide additional perspective and to encourage Namibian scientists, farmers and indigenous knowledge practitioners to appreciate the value of EVM.

Botswana

Research by Madibela, Boitumelo and Letso (2000) illustrated that small-scale farmers in Botswana use a range of small hemiparasitic plants known as mistletoes as supplements to feed cattle, sheep and goats, which improves their nutrition, health and wellbeing. Goats fed *Viscum verrucosum* (mistletoe) leaves and stems had reduced counts of gastrointestinal parasite eggs (Madibela & Jansen, 2003). Condensed tannins extracted from *Tapinanthus oleifolius* (another mistletoe) and *Grewia flava* stimulated T-cell immune response in goats (Tibe, Pernthaner, Sutherland, Lesperance, & Harding, 2012). Recently, fresh samples of *Viscum rotundifolium*, *Ipomoea sinensis* and

G. flava completely inhibited the development of gastrointestinal parasites (Tibe, Sutherland, Lesperance, & Harding, 2013). These results suggest that extracts of some forage plants from Botswana have antiparasitic properties in livestock.

Côte d'Ivoire

Koné and Atindehou (2008) documented 44 plant species that are harvested for ethnoveterinary medicinal purposes by rural communities in northern Côte d'Ivoire. The most common plants used by farmers were *Cassia sieberiana*, *Khaya senegalensis*, *Diospyros mespiliformis*, *Sterculia setigera*, *Bridelia ferruginea*, *Guiera senegalensis*, *Opilia amantalea*, *Saba senegalensis* and *Vitellaria paradoxa*. These plant species were used to treat gastroenteritis and skin diseases. The same authors stated that the plants *Maytenus senegalensis*, *Mitragyna inermis*, *K. senegalensis*, *V. paradoxa* and *Anogeissus leiocarpus* were used to treat diarrhoea and intestinal worms. Anthelmintic activity was reported for *K. senegalensis*, *V. paradoxa* and *A. leiocarpus*. Farmers frequently use decoctions of *D. mespiliformis* to treat skin diseases and fever. This is understandable given that *D. mespiliformis* displays a broad antimicrobial spectrum and a potent antipyretic effect.

Ethiopia

Several studies have documented the ethnoveterinary use of plants in Ethiopia. In the Tigray Region in northern Ethiopia, plants such as *Achyranthes aspera*, *Ficus caria*, *Malvi parviflora*, *Vernonia* spp., *Calpurnia aurea*, *Nicotiana tabacum* and *Croton macrostachyus* have shown activity against isolates of bacteria that cause mastitis, wounds and gastrointestinal complications in cattle (Kalayou et al., 2012). Due to its antibacterial and antifungal effects, *F. caria* is traditionally applied as a treatment for diarrhoea, sores and conjunctivitis (Mesfin, Demissew, & Teklehaymanot, 2009).

Eguale, Tadesse and Giday (2011) observed that extracts of the plants *Leucas martinicensis*, *Leonotis ocymifolia*, *Senna occidentalis* and *Albizia schimperiana* inhibited egg hatching of the sheep helminthic parasite *Haemonchus contortus*. These medicinal plants showed significant and dose-dependent egg hatching inhibition. The extract of *Hedera helix* completely inhibited the hatching of *Haemonchus contortus* eggs (Eguale, Tilahun, Debella, Feleke, & Makkonen, 2007).

Abebe and Ayehu (1993) also claimed that the plant *Albizia anthelmintica* is used as an anthelmintic in both humans and animals. Extracts from the bark of *A. anthelmintica* reduced faecal egg counts by up to 100% in sheep infected with mixed gastrointestinal parasites in Kenya (Gathuma et al., 2004). The same plant was reported to be 95.5% effective against the trematode parasite *Fasciola gigantica* in goats (Koko, Galal, & Khalid, 2000). These authors also stated that the stem bark of another species, *Albizia gummifera*, had significant *in vitro* and *in vivo* anthelmintic activity against nematode parasites of sheep.

Kenya

In Kenya, Gakuubi and Wanzala (2012) documented plants and plant products traditionally used in livestock health management in Buuri District. According to these authors, the main routes of administration in the study area were oral, topical (dermal), through the eyes and directly to a fresh wound or cut. Correct dosage (as described by an ethnopractitioner) was an important aspect of ethnoveterinary medicine according to respondents because under dose was known to make the remedy ineffective, while overdose caused livestock poisoning and subsequent death.

Many respondents were of the opinion that the correct dosages for various ethnomedicines had been established through a lengthy period of trial and error. Among the factors that determined the frequency and dose of administration of the herbal remedies were livestock species, age, body weight, severity of illness and other conditions, such as pregnancy and lactation. Most of the plant species used in remedies were members of the family Fabaceae, followed by plants in the Solanaceae, Asteraceae and Euphorbiaceae families. Most herbal preparations were used to treat east coast fever, followed by anaplasmosis and diarrhoea, in that order. These are the most commonly encountered and perhaps most well-diagnosed diseases by traditional animal healthcare practitioners in Buuri District, Kenya.

Nigeria

Offiah et al. (2011) conducted an ethnobotanical survey of medicinal plants used to treat animals with diarrhoea in Plateau State, Nigeria. Medicinal plants believed to be effective in diarrhoea management were collected using the guided field-walk method for identification and authentication. About 83% of farmers acknowledged the use of plants from 25 families, mostly Fabaceae and Combretaceae, in diarrhoea management.

Adansonia digitata and *Khaya senegalensis* are the most commonly used plants in the management of diarrhoea in livestock. *Adansonia digitata* (baobab) is very common in the northern parts of Nigeria where it is also used to treat malaria and coughs. *Khaya senegalensis* (mahogany) is known to have anthelmintic properties (Ndjonka, Agyare, Luersen, Djafsia, Achukwi, Nukenine, Hensel, & Liebau, 2010), hence its use in the management of diarrhoea is justified.

Cucumis metuliferus and *Solanum dasyphyllum* are used as herbal remedies for diarrhoea in poultry. Incidentally, the fruits of the non-bitter *C. metuliferus* have worm-expellant activity and are also effective in the management of HIV/AIDS-related conditions in Plateau State. Plant formulations are often prepared by soaking the fresh or dried parts of the plants in water and the extract administered by drenching. Sometimes the plant materials are mixed with feed and/or potash to improve palatability.

TABLE 5.1: Plants used as ethnoveterinary medicines in South Africa

Family	Species	Condition/disease treated
Amaryllidaceae	*Boophone disticha* (L.f.) Herb.	red water and constipation in cattle
Anacardiaceae	*Protorhus longifolia* (Bernh.) Engl.	heart-water and diarrhoea in cows
	Searsia lancea (L.f.) F.A.Barkley	diarrhoea, gall sickness
Apocynaceae	*Acokanthera oppositifolia* (Lam.) Codd	heart-water in goats and sheep, red water in cattle, snakebites, anthrax, tapeworms, swollen limbs
	Strophanthus speciosus (Ward & Harv.) Reber	snakebites
	Sarcostemma viminale (L.) R. Br.	aids lactation in cows
Asparagaceae	*Asparagus suaveolens* Burch.	retained placenta in cows
	Asparagus virgatus Baker	anthelmintic for animals and humans
Asphodelaceae	*Aloe marlothii* A.Berger	Newcastle disease in chickens
	Bulbine alooides (L.) Willd.	red water in cattle
Asteraceae	*Brachylaena discolor* DC.	anthelmintic for calves, sheep and goats
	Schkuhria pinnata (Lam.) Kuntze ex Thell.	eye infections, pneumonia, diarrhoea, heart-water
	Senecio tamoides DC.	anthrax
Chenopodiaceae	*Exomis microphylla* (Thunb.) Aellen	endometritis and vaginitis
Combretaceae	*Combretum caffrum* (Eckl. & Zeyh.) Kuntze	conjunctivitis
	Combretum paniculatum Vent.	fertility problems
	Terminalia sericea Burch. ex DC.	wounds
Convolvulaceae	*Seddera suffruticosa* (Schinz) Hallier f.	fractures
Cornaceae	*Curtisia dentata* (Burm.f.) C.A.Sm.	heart-water in cows
Dryopteridaceae	*Dryopteris athamantica* (Kunze) Kuntze	retained placenta in cows
Ebenaceae	*Diospyros mespiliformis* Hochst. ex A.DC.	aids milk production
Euphorbiaceae	*Jatropha curcas* L.	drench for constipation in cattle and goats
Fabaceae	*Indigofera frutescens* L.f.	anthelmintic for animals and humans, especially roundworm
	Tephrosia macropoda (E.Mey.) Harv.	roots and seeds used for killing vermin on animals and humans
Gunneraceae	*Gunnera perpensa* L.	used to facilitate expulsion of afterbirth from animals and women
Hyacinthaceae	*Ledebouria revoluta* (L.f.) Jessop	Gall sickness in animals
Malvaceae	*Hibiscus microcarpus* Garcke	retained placenta, intestinal worms
Moraceae	*Ficus ingens* (Miq.) Miq.	administered to cows to increase milk production
Oleaceae	*Olea europaea* L.	leaves used for endometritis and vaginitis in cows, bark infusion for diarrhoea in goats, gall sickness in cattle, eye lotion for animals and humans

Family	Species	Condition/disease treated
Pedaliaceae	*Harpagophytum procumbens* (Burch.) DC.	retained placenta
Phytolaccaceae	*Phytolacca octandra* L.	lung-sickness in cattle
Rhamnaceae	*Ziziphus mucronata* Willd.	fertility enhancement, sores, burns
Strychnaceae	*Strychnos henningsii* Gilg	heart-water and diarrhoea in cattle
Thymelaeaceae	*Gnidia capitata* L.f.	heart-water in cows, anthrax
Tiliaceae	*Grewia flava* DC.	fertility enhancement
	Grewia occidentalis L.f.	Gall sickness in stock
Vitaceae	*Rhoicissus tomentosa* (Lam.) Wild & R.B.Drumm.	anthelmintic for calves
Zygophyllaceae	*Tribulus terrestris* L.	retained placenta

Adapted from McGaw and Eloff, 2008.

South Africa

In their extensive review of the literature, McGaw and Eloff (2008) detailed a total of approximately 202 South African plant species that are used as EVMs in South Africa. Ethnoveterinary plants are used to treat red water (babesiosis), heart-water, anaplasmosis, sweating sickness, diarrhoea, helminthic infections, conjunctivitis, anthrax, wounds, gall sickness, lung sickness, constipation, infertility, retained placenta, endometritis, vaginitis, snakebites, fractures, lack of lactation, and Newcastle disease (Table 5.1). Several plant remedies, including *Tephrosia* spp., are used to get rid of animal and human vermin, such as ticks.

Many publications in the literature also report on the antibacterial activity of many plants used as remedies for livestock diarrhoea, dysentery, wounds and coughs. For example, extracts of the plant *Ziziphus mucronata* (Rhamnaceae) showed high antibacterial activity (McGaw and Eloff, 2008). Laboratory assays such as these confirm indigenous claims about the efficacy of *Z. mucronata* leaves in treating bacterial infections in domestic animals. In assays using the free-living nematode *Caenorhabditis elegans*, many other plants including *Protasparagus virgatus* have shown anthelmintic activity.

Zambia

Although many peasant farmers in Zambia use local plants as sources of chemical extracts to control various animal pests and diseases, much of the research on EVM is unpublished, largely because of a lack of expertise to scientifically identify the plants (M. Syakalima, personal communication, July 10, 2013). Kaposhi, Mundia,

Mwangala, Banda and Mugoya (1994) reported that several plants are used to manage ticks and other ectoparasites of cattle. For example, *Acanthosicyos naudinianus* (known as *lungwatanga* in Lozi) is used for tick control; *Boscia salicifolia* (known as *nakabombwe* in Tonga) is used to control fleas and other insects; *Cassia abbreviata* (known as *mululwe* in Tonga) is an insect poison; *Maerua edulis* (*soozwe* or *choozwe* in Tonga) is used to kill many different types of ectoparasites, including ticks and fleas; and *Tephrosia vogelii* (known as *ububa* in Bemba) is used to kill ticks.

PLANTS USED AS ETHNOVETERINARY MEDICINES IN NAMIBIA

Indigenous knowledge of plants that are used to treat disease in domestic livestock, such as cattle, sheep, goats, donkeys and poultry, is quite widespread among farmers in the communal areas of Namibia. However, much of this knowledge about ethnoveterinary medicinal plants is just beginning to be documented. Chinsembu, Negumbo, Likando and Mbangu (2014) reported on the ethnobotanical studies of medicinal plants used to treat livestock diseases in the Oshikoto and Zambezi regions, Namibia (see Table 5.2). According to these authors (Chinsembu et al., 2014), skin rashes are managed using *Aloe angolensis*, *Salvadora persica*, *Friesodielsia obovata* and *Acanthosicyos naudinianus*. Diarrhoea is treated using the plants *Ziziphus mucronata*, *Acacia karroo* and *Solanum delagoense*. *Ximenia americana*, *Combretum imberbe* and *Geigeria pectidea* are used to relieve eye infections in cattle, goats and sheep. The use of these plants to treat eye infections may be attributable to their antimicrobial properties. It was reported that wounds were treated with *Orthanthera jasminiflora*, *Aloe zebrina* and *Baphia massaiensis*. Livestock owners use water extracts from the roots of *Capparis tomentosa* to improve appetite in cattle and goats. *Fockea angustifolia* roots are used to treat cattle suffering from anthrax. Alternatively, the beef of animals that die from anthrax is treated using water extracts from the roots of *F. angustifolia*.

Antibacterial properties of ethnoveterinary plants

Parts of the 16 plants (roots, stems, leaves) listed in Table 5.2 were collected so that they could be tested for antimicrobial properties. The plant parts were air-dried at room temperature and crushed into powder. A 2-g sample of the powdered material from each plant was macerated in 4 mℓ of 95% ethanol for two hours, and occasionally mixed using a vortex mixer. The extracts were filtered and solid particles were discarded.

Several bacterial test strains were used to test the properties of the extracts: *Shigella flexneri* (ATCC12022), *Nesseria meningitidis* (ATCC 35561), *Pseudomonas aeruginosa* (ATCC 9027), *Proteus vulgaris* (ATCC 3420), *Staphylococcus aureus*, *Legionella pneumophila* (isolated from Goreangab Dam in Windhoek), *Escherichia coli*, *Listeria monocytogenes*, and *Enterobacter aerogenes* (ATCC 1304). All the bacterial cultures were grown on nutrient agar at 37 °C for 24 hours.

Paper discs (6 mm diameter) were dipped in 1 mℓ of plant extract and placed on the surface of nutrient agar inoculated with the respective bacterium. An antibiotic Gentamycin® was used as a positive control and 60% ethanol was used as a negative control. The plates were then inverted, and incubated at 37 °C. After 24 hours, zones of inhibition were measured (mm). Although the bacterial strains do not represent livestock diseases, the assays showed that all 16 plants had antibacterial activities, which explains why these plants are used to treat bacterial infections such as diarrhoea, coughing, and eye and skin infections.

Comparing Namibian EVM plants with information from other studies

As is generally the case elsewhere, many plants used in the treatment of livestock diseases are also used to treat human diseases.

Our laboratory tests confirm that all the plants used as EVMs by livestock owners in Namibia have varying levels of antibacterial activity. *Ziziphus mucronata* (locally known as *omusheshete* or *mukekete*) is used by local farmers in northern Namibia to treat diarrhoea in cattle and goats. The antidiarrhoeal properties of *Z. mucronata* are supported by the moderate antibacterial activity of the plant extracts. The use of *Z. mucronata* as an EVM for diarrhoea in animals in Namibia is supported by accounts from Ethiopia where farmers use the same plant to treat mastitis, wounds and gastrointestinal complications in cattle (Kalayou et al., 2012).

Yirga (2010) reported that *Z. mucronata* has anti-dandruff and anthelmintic properties. In South Africa, *Z. mucronata* is used to treat livestock infertility, sores and burns (McGaw & Eloff, 2008). Semenya, Potgieter and Erasmus (2013) described Bapedi healers using *Z. mucronata* (known as *mokgalo* in Sepedi) to treat gonorrhoeal and chlamydial infections in humans. In Uganda, a related species, *Ziziphus mauritiana*, is used to treat livestock constipation (Gradé, Tabuti, & van Damme, 2009).

Villagers in the Omusati Region use *Aloe angolensis* to treat skin infections and coughs in cattle and goats. The *in vitro* antibacterial properties of *A. angolensis* support wide EVM applications of this plant species. Earlier reports in Owambo also found that *A. angolensis* is used to prevent bacterial infection of cuts and burns in humans (Rodin, 1985). The same authors documented that *Aloe asperifolia* was used in Namibia to treat donkeys after grazing on poisonous plants. Among the Topnaar people of Namibia, van den Eynden, Vernemmen and van Damme (1992) claimed that *A. asperifolia* is a treatment for arteriosclerosis.

In Botswana and Namibia, young fruits of *Orthanthera jasminiflora* are eaten fresh or cooked as a vegetable (Strohbach, 2000). Although *O. jasminiflora* is used to heal wounds, the plant is also known to treat diarrhoea, and to help expel placenta and assist the postpartum condition, generally; an infusion made by boiling leaves is cooled and

TABLE 5.2: Plant species used as ethnoveterinary medicines collected in Onayena in Oshikoto and Katima Mulilo in Zambezi, Namibia

Scientific name (family)	Voucher number	Local name	Frequency index	Collection place	Plant parts	Mode of preparation and ethnoveterinary uses
Acacia karroo Hayne (Fabaceae)	M012	*muboto*	75.0	Zambezi	leaves, roots	Roots and leaves are mixed together, crushed and soaked in water overnight. Water solution is drunk to treat diarrhoea in cattle and goats.
Acanthosicyos naudinianus (Sond.) C. Jeffrey (Cucurbitaceae)	M038	*umbwiti*	60.0	Zambezi	roots	Roots are crushed and directly rubbed into skin rashes of cattle and goats.
Aloe angolensis Baker (Asphodelaceae)	M009	*endombo*	81.8	Oshikoto	leaves	Crushed, fresh leaves are soaked in water and topically applied to treat skin infections (rashes) and falling hair; drenching to treat coughs.
Aloe zebrina Baker (Asphodelaceae)	M001	*icenka, licenka*	85.0	Zambezi	leaves	Crushed leaves are rubbed into the wounds of cattle and goats.
Baphia massaiensis Taub. subsp. obovata (Schinz) Brummitt (Fabaceae)	M046	*isunde*	70.0	Zambezi	leaves	Leaves are ground and directly rubbed into sores of cattle and goats.
Boscia albitrunca (Burch.) Gilg. & Gilg.-Ben. (Capparaceae)	M017	*omukuzi*	63.6	Oshikoto	leaves, roots	Fresh leaves and roots are crushed, mixed with water and filtered through a wire sieve. Extract is orally taken to treat lung and liver infections in cattle and goats.
Capparis tomentosa Lam. (Capparaceae)	M033	*mukanangwe*	40.0	Zambezi	roots	Roots are crushed and soaked in water overnight. Filtrate is drunk by sick animal to restore appetite.
Combretum imberbe Wawra (Combretaceae)	M030	*omukuku*	45.4	Oshikoto	leaves	Fresh leaves are crushed, soaked in water and rubbed into infected eyes of cattle and sheep.
Fockea angustifolia K.Schum. (Apocynaceae)	M035	*enongo*	36.4	Oshikoto	roots	Crushed roots are mixed with water and filtered. Extract is taken orally to treat cattle suffering from anthrax or to wash the carcass of animal that has died from anthrax.

Scientific name (family)	Voucher number	Local name	Frequency index	Collection place	Plant parts	Mode of preparation and ethnoveterinary uses
Friesodielsia obovata (Benth.) Verdc. (Annonaceae)	M040	*muchinga*	60.0	Zambezi	roots	Roots are crushed, soaked in water, and rubbed into sores or skin rashes of cattle and goats.
Geigeria pectidea (DC.) Harv. (Asteraceae)	M018	*ehindhi*	40.9	Oshikoto	leaves, stems, flowers	Fresh leaves, stems and flowers are crushed and soaked in water and filtered through cloth. Drops of extract are applied into eyes to treat conjunctivitis in cattle.
Orthanthera jasminiflora (Decne.) Schinz (Apocynaceae)	M021	*eshompwa*	77.3	Oshikoto	leaves, stems	Stems and leaves are crushed and soaked in water and topically applied to treat parasitic wounds in cattle and goats.
Salvadora persica L. (Salvadoraceae)	M028	*omunkwavau*	54.5	Oshikoto	bark, stems	Bark and stems are crushed, soaked in water and filtered through cloth. Topically applied to treat skin infections in goats.
Solanum delagoense Dunal (Solanaceae)	M024	*tulukiza, tulwa-tulwa*	35.0	Zambezi	fruits, roots	Crushed roots and fruits are mixed with water. The solution is drunk to treat diarrhoea and coughs in cattle.
Ximenia americana L. (Olacaceae)	M026	*oshipeke*	68.2	Oshikoto	leaves	Fresh leaves are crushed, soaked in water overnight, and filtered through cloth. Drops of extract are applied to treat eye infections in cattle, goats and sheep.
Ziziphus mucronata Willd. (Rhamnaceae)	M014	*omusheshete, mukekete*	50.0	Oshikoto	leaves	Ground, fresh leaves are soaked in water overnight and administered orally to treat diarrhoea in cattle and goats.

Adapted from Chinsembu et al., 2014.

dribbled into the ear to manage earache. It is also used as a uterine stimulant among the San of the Omaheke Region. Rodin (1985) explained that the Aakwanyama plant *O. jasminiflora* in or near their homesteads in order to invite good luck. When worn around the waist, *O. jasminiflora* is believed to prevent backache during hoeing.

Els (2000) reported that *Geigeria pectidea* (known as *vermeerbos* in Afrikaans) is eaten by small stock in Namibia. Although *Geigeria* species are moderately nutritious, *vermeersiekte* following ingestion of different *Geigeria* species is a major cause of poisoning in small stock in South Africa (Botha et al., 1997). Here in Namibia, the use of *G. pectidea* to treat eye infections could be attributable to antibacterial nature. A similar herb, *Geigeria aspera* (family Asteraceae), also known as *makgonatsohle* in South African Bapedi society, is used to alleviate HIV/AIDS symptoms in people (Semenya et al., 2013).

In Namibia, *Ximenia americana* is used to treat eye infections in cattle and goats. This finding is supported by many reports from West Africa where *X. americana* was reported as being frequently used to treat ailments such as throat infection, malaria and dysmenorrhoea in humans (Grønhaug et al., 2008). The use of *X. americana* for healing wounds was also described in Mali (Diallo et al., 2002). In Nigeria, *X. americana* has been used against malaria, leprotic ulcers and skin diseases (Ogunleye & Ibitoye, 2003). Other reports declared activity of *X. americana* against human schistosomiasis, fever, diarrhoea, ringworm, craw-craw and toothache (Burkill, 1997).

In a review of the medicinal uses of *Salvadora persica*, Halawany (2012) documented various studies where the aqueous extracts of *S. persica* had an inhibitory effect on the growth of *Candida albicans*, *Enterococcus faecalis*, *Streptococcus* spp. and *Staphylococcus aureus*. This may help explain why *S. persica* is used to treat skin infections in Namibian goats. In this study, the plants *G. pectidea*, *X. americana*, *Combretum imberbe* (known as *omukuku* in Oshiwambo) were used to treat eye infections in cattle and sheep. In many parts of Mozambique, leaves and roots of *C. imberbe* are macerated in water and administered orally as a treatment for stomachache in humans (Bruschi, Morganti, Mancini, & Signorini, 2011).

Symptoms of liver and lung infections in Namibian cattle and goats are alleviated by the oral administration of fresh leaf and root extracts of *Boscia albitrunca*. Again, this is not surprising given the antibacterial effects of this plant's extracts. In the Ohangwena Region, Hedimbi and Chinsembu (2012) reported that rubbing leaves of *B. albitrunca* into infected wounds and drinking a bark filtrate alleviates syphilis. Roots of *B. albitrunca* (known as *mohlophi* by Bapedi healers in South Africa) are used to treat HIV/AIDS-related symptoms (Semenya et al., 2013). In Mozambique, *B. albitrunca* (locally called *muvalavala* or *mupopu*) is a treatment for muscular pain and constipation (Bruschi et al., 2011).

In the Kongola area of Namibia, livestock farmers use the plant *Friesodielsia obovata* (locally known as *muchinga*) for treating animal sores and skin rashes. This ethnoveterinary usage of the plant is in agreement with our laboratory finding that *F. obovata* has good antibacterial activity. In Mozambique, roots of *F. obovata* are crushed in water and the filtered extract is taken orally to treat stomachache in humans (Bruschi et al., 2011). In other studies, phytochemical analysis of *F. obovata* (Annonaceae) indicated significant antiplasmodial, cytotoxicity and larvicidal activities (Joseph, Magadula, and Nkunya, 2007).

Livestock owners in Namibia use water extracts from the roots of *Capparis tomentosa* to treat jaundice-like symptoms and a lack of appetite in cattle and goats. The finding that *C. tomentosa* has antibacterial efficacy supports claims that the plant can treat jaundice-like symptoms and lack of appetite because these conditions could be the result of underlying bacterial infections. Ndhlala, Ncube, Okem, Mulaudzi and Staden (2013) reported that *C. tomentosa*, traditionally used as a treatment for infertility and impotency, also had antimicrobial and antioxidant properties. Teklehaymanot (2009) found that *C. tomentosa* powder mixed with water is taken orally as a treatment for 'buda evil eye', tonsillitis, sore throats, anthrax and trypanosomiasis in Ethiopia.

Namibian plant species in the genus *Solanum* are used to treat diarrhoea and coughs in cattle and goats. Ndhlala et al. (2013) documented that *Solanum incanum* contains steroid alkaloids that conferred antifungal and antibacterial properties. The presence of isothiocyanates makes *S. incanum* toxic. In Ethiopia, Teklehaymanot (2009) documented that fresh leaf juice of *S. incanum* is topically applied to heal wounds and external injuries, while crushed root juice is taken orally to alleviate stomachaches.

In Namibia, formulations from *Acacia karroo* leaves and roots are used to treat diarrhoea in cattle and goats. This indigenous veterinary knowledge of the plant is supported by the antibacterial properties of *A. karroo* shown in our laboratory assays. In their review of the use of *A. karroo* in smallholder beef production in southern Africa, Mapiye, Chimonyo, Marufu, and Dzama (2009) found that *A. karroo* leaves have moderate levels of detergent fibres. *Acacia karroo* has been reported to contain chemical substances that have anthelmintic properties. Steers fed with *A. karroo* leaves had lower nematode burdens compared to those fed on rangeland species only. Supplementing ruminants with *A. karroo* leaves reduces nematode burdens.

Therefore, Mapiye et al. (2009) recommended that *A. karroo* could be used as an affordable and accessible substitute to broad spectrum and toxic chemical nematicides. It may also play a vital role in controlling the escalating problem of anthelmintic resistance and alleviating consumer concerns about chemical residues in meat. Mapiye et al. (2009) stated that establishing dosage levels of *A. karroo* leaves required for optimum control of helminths could be worthwhile. Development of a commercial anthelmintic product based on *A. karroo* leaves deserves research priority. Such an effective, low-cost, safe and eco-friendly strategy for controlling helminths is of paramount importance to the livestock industry.

It has been reported that the fresh roots of some *Fockea* species, because of their diuretic properties, were applied to snakebites and stings to 'draw out the poison' (van Wyk, 2008). It is hypothesized that extracts from *F. angustifolia* roots help to remove anthrax toxins from infected animals and contaminated meat.

For example, Hedimbi and Chinsembu (2012) found that *Boscia albitrunca* alleviates syphilis while *Solanum delagoense* is used to treat coughs in humans. Hedimbi and Chinsembu (2012) also found that gonorrhoea is treated by formulations from several plants including *Combretum imberbe*, *Acanthosicyos naudinianus*, *Ziziphus mucronata* and *Ximenia caffra*. In southern Africa, *B. albitrunca* is used as a treatment for epilepsy (van der Walt and Riche, 1999). A cold fusion of the leaves of *B. albitrunca* heals inflamed eyes in cattle while an extract of the roots remedies haemorrhoids in humans (Coates Palgrave, 1983).

CONCLUSION

This chapter has attempted to place within the broader African context the need for Namibia to pursue EVM as a credible alternative to manage microbial diseases of livestock. The use of indigenous knowledge can contribute to the management of livestock diseases in rural Namibia by encouraging the use of plants to treat livestock diseases and conditions. Many plants currently used as EVMs in Namibia have shown antibacterial efficacy in the laboratory. Indigenous knowledge can therefore help pinpoint EVM plants with antibacterial efficacies. But there is an urgent need for more research to identify, evaluate and document local plants and their organic compounds for use in livestock diseases and vector control. This is because livestock owners with restricted access to classical veterinary healthcare services commonly use ethnomedicinal remedies to treat animal diseases. Future studies will determine the minimum inhibitory concentrations, biological activities and toxicities of plant extracts, and characterize the plants' chemical compounds.

ACKNOWLEDGMENTS

Augustine Mbangu, Selma Kangongo, Julia Negumbo, Mayumbo Likando, Elicie Naujoma and David Aiyambo are thanked for their efforts during data collection.

References

Abebe, D., & Ayehu, A. (1993). *Medicinal plants and enigmatic health practices of northern Ethiopia*. Addis Ababa, Ethiopia: Berhanena Selam Printing Enterprise.

Botha, C. J., Gous, T. A., Penrith, M. L., Naudé, T. W., Labuschagne, L., & Retief, E. (1997). Vermeersiekte caused by *Geigeria burkei* Harv. subsp. *burkei* var. *hirtella* Merxm. in the Northern Province of South Africa. *Journal of the South African Veterinary Association, 68*(3), 97-101.

Bruschi, P., Morganti, M., Mancini, M., & Signorini, M. A. (2011). Traditional healers and lay people: A qualitative and quantitative approach to local knowledge on medicinal plants in Muda (Mozambique). *Journal of Ethnopharmacology, 138*(2), 543-563.

Burkill, H. M. (1997). *The useful plants of tropical West Africa* (3rd ed., pp. 166-179). London: Royal Botanic Gardens, Kew.

Chinsembu, K. C., Negumbo, J., Likando, M., & Mbangu, A. (2014). An ethnobotanical study of medicinal plants used to treat livestock diseases in Onayena and Katima Mulilo, Namibia. *South African Journal of Botany, 94*, 101-107.

Coates Palgrave, K. (1983). *Trees of southern Africa* (2nd ed.). Cape Town, South Africa: Struik Publishers.

Confessor, M. V. A., Mendonça, L. E. T., Mourão, J. S., & Alves, R. R. N. (2009). Animals to heal animals: Ethnoveterinary practices in semiarid region, northeastern Brazil. *Journal of Ethnobiology and Ethnomedicine, 5*, 37. doi:10.1186/1746-4269-5-37

Diallo, D., Sogn, C., Samaké, F. B., Paulsen, B. S., Michaelsen, T. E., & Keita, A. (2002). Wound healing plants in Mali, the Bamako region: An ethnobotanical survey and complement fixation of water extracts from selected plants. *Pharmaceutical Biology, 40*(2), 117-128.

Eguale, T., Tadesse, D., & Giday, M. (2011). *In vitro* anthelmintic activity of crude extracts of five medicinal plants against egg-hatching and larval development of *Haemonchus contortus*. *Journal of Ethnopharmacology, 137*(1), 108-113. doi: 10.1016/j.jep.2011.04.063

Eguale, T., Tilahun, G., Debella, A., Feleke, A., & Makonnen, E. (2007). *In vitro* and *in vivo* anthelmintic activity of crude extracts of *Coriandrum sativum* against *Haemonchus contortus*. *Journal of Ethnopharmacology, 110*(3), 428-433.

Els, J. F. (2000). Diet selection of four free-ranging breeds of small stock. II. Species composition. *Agricola, 2000*, 36-38.

FAO [Food and Agriculture Organization of the United Nations]. (2002). *Genetics and animal health – Spotlight*. Rome, Italy: Author.

Gakuubi, M. M., & Wanzala, W. (2012). A survey of plants and plant products traditionally used in livestock health management in Buuri district, Meru County, Kenya. *Journal of Ethnobiology and Ethnomedicine, 8,* 39. doi:10.1186/1746-4269-8-39

Gathuma, J. M., Mbaria, J. M., Wanyama, J., Kaburia, H. F., Mpoke, L., & Mwangi, J. N. (2004). Efficacy of *Myrsine africana, Albizia anthelmintica* and *Hilderbrantia sepalosa* herbal remedies against mixed natural sheep helminthosis in Samburu district, Kenya. *Journal of Ethnopharmacology, 91*(1), 7-12.

Gradé, J. T., Tabuti, J. R., & van Damme, P. (2009). Ethnoveterinary knowledge in pastoral Karamoja, Uganda. *Journal of Ethnopharmacology, 122*(2), 273-293.

Grønhaug, T. E., Glæserud, S., Skogsrud, M., Ballo, N., Bah, S., Diallo, D., & Paulsen, B. S. (2008). Ethnopharmacological survey of six medicinal plants from Mali, West-Africa. *Journal of Ethnobiology and Ethnomedicine, 4,* 26. doi:10.1186/1746-4269-4-26

Hauser, G., Little, M., & Roberts, D. F. (1994). *Man, culture and biodiversity: Understanding interdependences.* Paris, France: International Union of Biological Sciences.

Halawany, H. S. (2012). A review of miswak (*Salvadora persica*) and its effect on various aspects of oral health. *Saudi Dental Journal, 24*(2), 63-69.

Hedimbi, M., & Chinsembu, K. C. (2012). Ethnomedicinal study of plants used to manage HIV/AIDS-related disease conditions in the Ohangwena Region, Namibia. *International Journal of Medicinal Plant Research, 1*(1), 004-011.

Joseph, C. C., Magadula, J. J., & Nkunya, M. H. (2007). A novel antiplasmodial 3', 5'-diformylchalcone and other constituents of *Friesodielsia obovata. Natural Product Research, 21*(11), 1009-1015.

Kalayou, S., Haileselassie, M., Gebre-Egziabher, G., Tiku'e T., Sahle, S., Taddele, M., & Ghezu, M. (2012). In-vitro antimicrobial activity of some ethnoveterinary medicinal plants traditionally used against mastitis, wound and gastrointestinal tract complication in Tigray Region, Ethiopia. *Asian Pacific Journal of Tropical Biomedicine, 2*(7), 516-522.

Kaposhi, C. K. M., Mundia, M. P., Mwangala, F. S., Banda, R., & Mugoya, C. (1994). Extraction and evaluation of active ingredients from selected Zambian plants with acaricidal and insecticidal properties. Proceedings from the first National Symposium in Zambia, Lusaka, 2–5 August, 1994. Retrieved from http://www.vaxteko.nu/html/sll/slu/rapport_vaxtsk_vetensk/RVX04/RVX04N.HTM

Koko, W. S., Galal, M., & Khalid, H. S. (2000). Fasciolicidal efficacy of *Albizia anthelmintica* and *Balanites aegyptiaca* compared with albendazole. *Journal of Ethnopharmacology, 71*(1-2), 247-252.

Koné, W. M., & Atindehou, K. (2008). Ethnobotanical inventory of medicinal plants used in traditional veterinary medicine in Northern Côte d'Ivoire (West Africa). *South African Journal of Botany, 74*(1), 76-84.

Lans, C., & Turner, N. (2011). Organic parasite control for poultry and rabbits in British Columbia, Canada. *Journal of Ethnobiology and Ethnomedicine, 7*, 21.

Madibela, O. R., Boitumelo, W. S., & Letso, M. (2000). Chemical composition and *in vitro* dry matter digestibility of four parasitic plants (*Tapinanthus lugardii, Erianthenum ngamicum, Viscum rotundifolium* and *Viscum verrucosum*) in Botswana. *Animal Feed Science and Technology, 84*(1-2), 97-106.

Madibela, O. R., & Jansen, K. (2003). The use of indigenous parasitic plant (*Viscum verrucosum*) in reducing faecal egg counts in female Tswana goats. *Livestock Research for Rural Development, 15*(9). Retrieved from http://www.lrrd.org/lrrd15/9/madi159.htm

Mapiye, C., Chimonyo, M., Marufu, M. C., & Dzama, K. (2009). Utility of *Acacia karroo* for beef production in Southern African smallholder farming systems: A review. *Animal Feed Science and Technology, 164*(3-4), 135-146.

Mathias, E. (2001). Introducing ethnoveterinary medicine. Retrieved from http://www.ethnovetweb.com/docs/whatisevm.pdf

Mathias-Mundy, E., & McCorkle, C. M. (1989). *Ethnoveterinary medicine: An annotated bibliography. Bibliographies in Technology and Social Change, No. 6.* Ames, USA: Iowa State University.

McCorkle, C. M. (1986). An introduction to ethnoveterinary research and development. *Journal of Ethnobiology, 6*(1), 129-149.

McGaw, L. J., & Eloff, J. N. (2008). Ethnoveterinary use of southern African plants and scientific evaluation of their medicinal use. *Journal of Ethnopharmacology, 119*(3), 559-574.

Mesfin, F., Demissew, S., & Teklehaymanot, T. (2009). An ethnobotanical study of medicinal plants in Wonago Woreda, SNNPR, Ethiopia. *Journal of Ethnobiology and Ethnomedicine 5*, 28. doi:10.1186/1746-4269-5-28

Ndhlala, A. R., Ncube, B., Okem, A., Mulaudzi, R. B., & Staden, J. V. (2013). Toxicology of some important medicinal plants in southern Africa. *Food and Chemical Toxicology, 62*, 609-621. doi: 10.1016/j.fct.2013.09.027

Ndjonka, D., Agyare, C., Luersen, K., Djafsia, B., Achukwi, D., Nukenine, E. N., Hensel, A., & Liebau, E. (2011). *In vitro* activity of Cameroonian and Ghanian medicinal plants on parasitic (*Onchocerca ochengi*) and free-living (*Caenorhabditis elegans*) nematodes. *Journal of Helminthology, 85*(03), 304-312.

NNFU [Namibia National Farmers Union]. (2008). *Livestock marketing in Namibia.* Windhoek, Namibia: Author.

Offiah, N. V., Makama, S., Elisha, I. L., Makoshi, M. S., Gotep, J. G., Dawurung, C. J., ... Shamaki, D. (2011). Ethnobotanical survey of medicinal plants used in the treatment of animal diarrhoea in Plateau State, Nigeria. *BMC Veterinary Research, 7*:36. doi:10.1186/1746-6148-7-36

Ogunleye, D. S., & Ibitoye, S. F. (2003). Studies of antimicrobial activity and chemical constituents of *Ximenia americana*. *Tropical Journal of Pharmaceutical Research, 2*(2), 239-241.

Rodin, R. J. (1985). *The ethnobotany of the Kwanyama Ovambos*. Kansas, USA: Allen Press, Inc.

Semenya, S. S., Potgieter, M. J., & Erasmus, L. J. C. (2013). Exotic and indigenous problem plants species used, by the Bapedi, to treat sexually transmitted infections in Limpopo Province, South Africa. *African Health Sciences, 13*(2), 320-326.

Siegmund-Schultze, M., Lange, F., Schneiderat, U., & Steinbach, J. (2012). Performance, management and objectives of cattle farming on communal ranges in Namibia. *Journal of Arid Environments, 80*, 65-73.

Strohbach, B. J. (2000). Vegetation degradation trends in the northern Oshikoto Region: II. The *Colophospermum mopane* shrublands. *Dinteria, 26*, 63-75.

Teklehaymanot, T. (2009). Ethnobotanical study of knowledge and medicinal plants use by the people in Dek Island in Ethiopia. *Journal of Ethnopharmacology, 124*, 69-78.

Tibe, O., Pernthaner, A., Sutherland, I., Lesperance, L., & Harding, D. (2012). Condensed tannins from Botswanan forage plants are effective priming agents of T cells in ruminants. *Veterinary Immunology and Immunopathology, 146*(3-4), 237-244.

Tibe, O., Sutherland, I.A., Lesperance, L. & Harding, D.R.K. (2013). The effect of purified condensed tannins of forage plants from Botswana on the free-living stages of gastrointestinal nematode parasites of livestock. *Veterinary Parasitology, 197*(1-2), 160-167. doi:10.1016/j.vetpar.2013.07.004

Van Damme, P., van den Eynden, V. (2000). Succulent and xerophytic plants used by the Topnaar of Namibia. *Haseltonia, 7*, 53-62.

Van den Eynden, V., Vernemmen, P., & van Damme, P. (1992). *The ethnobotany of the Topnaar*. Gent, Belgium: University of Gent.

Van der Walt, P., & le Riche, E. L. (1999). *The Kalahari and its plants*. Pretoria, South Africa: Author.

Von Koenen, E. (2001). *Medicinal, poisonous and edible plants in Namibia*. Windhoek & Göttingen, Namibia & Germany: Klaus Hess Publishers.

Van Wyk, B.-E. (2008). A review of Khoi-San and Cape Dutch medical ethnobotany. *Journal of Ethnopharmacology, 119*(3), 331-341.

Wanzala, W., Zessin, K. H., Kyule, N. M., Baumann, M. P. O., Mathias, E., & Hasanali, A. (2005). Ethnoveterinary medicine: A critical review of its evolution, perception, understanding and the way forward. *Livestock Research for Rural Development, 17*(11), 1-31.

Yirga, G. (2010). Assessment of traditional medicinal plants in Endrta District, South-eastern Tigray, Northern Ethiopia. *African Journal of Plant Science, 4*(7), 255-260.

6

School learners' knowledge and views of traditional medicinal plant use in two regions in Namibia

Choshi Darius Kasanda & Hileni Magano Kapenda

INTRODUCTION

Local knowledge about natural resources that may be of use to communities, including medicinal plants, is becoming increasingly important globally. This knowledge is important for the participation of indigenous peoples in the conservation and maintenance of indigenous forests (Gazzaneo, de Lucena, & de Albuquerque, 2005) in addition to the frequent use of these resources in the treatment of common ailments and diseases.

Knowledge about the use of local fauna and flora, nowadays, is minimal. To ensure the preservation of indigenous knowledge, this state of affairs needs to be rectified. In fact, Teklehaymanot, Giday, Medhin and Mekonnen (2007, p. 272) note that 'traditional knowledge is rapidly eroding', hence, there is real danger that if something is not urgently done, this knowledge might be lost for good. This is due to the fact that often indigenous knowledge is passed on from older to younger generations orally, and is not documented. According to Kambizi and Afolayan (2006), it is essential to make an effort to avoid the loss of this important knowledge in order to conserve medicinal plants, especially in rural communities. There is an increasing advocacy for the integration of indigenous knowledge into mainstream science curricula.

School can play an important role in ensuring this knowledge is not lost. The school is thus seen as a conduit through which this knowledge could be passed from one generation to the next. One way of doing this is to integrate indigenous knowledge systems (IKS) into the mainstream science curriculum in our schools so that it is taught formally (Onwu & Mosimege, 2004).

This chapter presents research findings from a study of the views and knowledge of junior-high-school learners in the Omusati and Oshana regions of Namibia on the use of medicinal plants and how such knowledge could be integrated into the school science curriculum. The study addressed the following research questions: What views do junior-high-school learners have on the use of traditional medicinal plants for the treatment of common ailments? What knowledge do they have of traditional medicinal plants used for treatment of common ailments? How do they think such knowledge should be integrated into the science curriculum?

BACKGROUND

The study of African medicinal plants has not been documented as fully as Indian and Chinese treatments, although more than 5,000 plants are known to be used for medicinal purposes on the African continent (Taylor, Rabe, McGaw, Jäger, & van Staden, 2001). However, in recent years, several studies have been conducted on traditional medicinal plants in relation to their knowledge and use (Teklehaymanot et al., 2007); the impact of their use on conservation (Kambizi & Afolayan, 2006); scientific validation of their efficacy (Taylor et al., 2001; Chinsembu & Hedimbi, 2010; Cheikhyoussef, Shapi, Matengu, & Mu Ashekele, 2011), as well as the integration of indigenous knowledge into African school science curricula (Mpofu, Vhurumuku, Kapenda, Kasanda, & Dudu, 2011).

According to Teklehaymanot et al. (2007), Ethiopia has about 800 species of plants that are used in the traditional healthcare system to treat nearly 300 mental and physical disorders. Teklehaymanot and colleagues carried out a study around the Debre Libanos Monastery (Ethiopia), which involved 250 villagers, 13 monks and three nuns. They used semi-structured questionnaires to interview the participants on the 'knowledge and use of medicinal plants' in their area. Their results showed that the villagers had knowledge on traditional medicines, especially on the use of plants that were used to treat diseases characterized by fevers, headaches and sweating; *Herpes labialis* (cold sores); muscle spasms or *mich*; intestinal illnesses and parasites; problems related to rabies; and unidentified swellings and cancers. Unfortunately, the monks and nuns refused to give information on the known medicinal plants and their uses, although they were perceived to be resourceful informants.

According to Taylor et al. (2001), there is an increasingly pressing demand to develop new effective drugs. Hence, traditionally used medicinal plants are receiving the attention of pharmaceutical and scientific communities. Taylor et al. (2001, p. 32) carried out an intensive study to scientifically validate the use of some of the traditional medicinal plants in South Africa. One of the main findings was that, 'While anti-bacterial screening results ascribe a certain degree of pharmacological relevance to medicinal usage, a large percentage of the plants are used because of their traditional or spiritual significance and availability in the environment.'

However, Taylor et al. (2001) suggested that their work could be extended in cooperation with natural-product chemists in order to identify the bioactive compounds in medicinal plants as a starting point for further pharmacological studies. In Namibia, Chinsembu (2009) conducted a similar study on the validation of ethnomedicines used for HIV/AIDS in Namibia. Chinsembu noted that one of the barriers was that traditional remedies have neither been rigorously evaluated nor properly standardized and they are poorly prepared, packaged and preserved. He proposed a five-step model that could be used as a preliminary, but important, prerequisite to identify candidate plants for scientific testing in Namibia (see Chapter 1). These two studies indicate a dire need for the scientific validation of traditional medicinal plants.

Scientific validation of traditional medicinal plants is crucial because in many developing countries they form a significant component of primary healthcare (Kambizi & Afolayan, 2006). Many inhabitants tend to consult traditional healers first, or try traditional medicines, before going to the hospital. Indeed, approximately 70–80% of the world's population relies chiefly on traditional herbs or medicines to meet their primary healthcare needs (Hamilton, 2003). According to Taylor et al. (2001, p. 23), 'A large proportion of developing countries use traditional medicine alone, or in combination with Western drugs, to treat a wide variety of ailments.'

In Namibia, the use of medicinal plants to treat bilharzia and other diseases using plants has been reported (Hoareau & da Silva, 1999; Mills, Cooper, Seely, & Kanfer, 2005). Cheikhyoussef et al. (2011) reported that the majority of people in the Oshikoto Region in Namibia are still dependent on medicinal plants, at least for the cure of some common ailments, such as colds, coughs, fever, headaches, poisonous bites, skin diseases and tooth infections. Chinsembu and Hedimbi (2010) found that 72 species of plants from 28 families are used to manage opportunistic infections of HIV/AIDS in Katima Mulilo, Zambezi Region (Namibia). They further reported that these plants were used to treat conditions such as herpes zoster, diarrhoea, malaria, coughs, tuberculosis and meningitis. Moreover, van der Walt, Mossanda, Jivan, Swart and Bezuidenhout (2005) concluded that in order to enhance consumer resistance to diseases, indigenous African food plants probably possess phytochemicals that could counteract the damaging effects of harmful dietary substances.

Given the importance of traditional medicinal plants, there is a need to ensure that health personnel including medical doctors accept the use of them. 'Pure' scientific research on traditional medicinal plants has focused on validating their use (Taylor et al., 2001), rather than on their healing efficacies, which is important for those dependent on them.

For science educators, the interest is in how such knowledge can be captured and conveyed to a rural schoolchild in a manner that is interesting and sensible. Vhurumuku and Mokeleche (2009) identify the need for science-education researchers to look into ways in which indigenous knowledge can be integrated into mainstream science education. Accordingly, in this chapter, we explore learners' knowledge and views on traditional medicinal plant use and their views on the integration of indigenous knowledge into the school science curriculum in Namibia.

METHODOLOGY

Two schools in two regions of Namibia, Omusati and Oshana, were selected to take part in the study. Entry into the two schools was negotiated through the Director of Education in each of the regions. For ethical reasons, the names of the two schools will be referred to as A and B (see appendices, pages 152 to 156). A total of 85 junior-high-school learners (43 males and 42 females) in Ongwediva and Outapi constituencies – in Oshana and Omusati regions, respectively – comprised the sample. The researchers first administered a questionnaire to find out learners' knowledge and their use of traditional medicinal plants. Second, an identified traditional healer taught the learners the different local medicinal plants that were used in treating the identified common ailments. After the intervention by the traditional healer, the learners completed the same questionnaire. For the purposes of this chapter, the responses from the two groups, A and B were lumped together (except in the appendices). In many cases, the total number of responses exceeds the total number of students in the sample; this is because some of the students gave more than one answer.

The questionnaire with closed and open-ended questions comprised three sections: Section A sought the participants' biographical information; Section B sought the learners' knowledge of traditional medicinal plants that are used in the treatment of stomachaches, fever, headaches, wounds and HIV/AIDS in their immediate environment. Section C sought the learners' views on the possible integration of indigenous knowledge on medicinal plants in the school science curriculum. It should be pointed out that not all the questions were answered by all the learners. In some cases, they skipped one question and answered the next. Four focus group discussions led by the researchers were held with six to eight learners in each group. Several learners expressed interest in being part of the focus group discussions. It should be noted that the learners' knowledge of traditional medicinal plants was not verified with the traditional healer(s) due to the fact that Appendices 6.1 and 6.2

indicate the origin of the learners' knowledge of the traditional medicinal plants to cure the above indicated ailments. Further, the results presented in this chapter are part of a larger study in which the role of the traditional healer has been reported upon (Kapenda & Kasanda, 2013).

The questionnaire was first piloted with 58 Grade-9 learners at one school that did not take part in the main study. Items that were not clear were revised to ensure clarity. In addition, focus group discussions during the pilot study helped the researchers improve their questioning technique for this study.

Descriptive statistics, graphs and content analysis were used to analyse the data. The learners' responses have been edited to ensure clarity.

RESULTS

The information collected through the questionnaire and focus group discussions are given in this section of this chapter.

Age and sex of respondents

The ages of the 85 junior-high-school learners ranged from 14 to 24 years. The mean age of the group was 16.8 years with 59 (69%) of the learners between the ages of 14 and 17 years (see Figure 6.1).

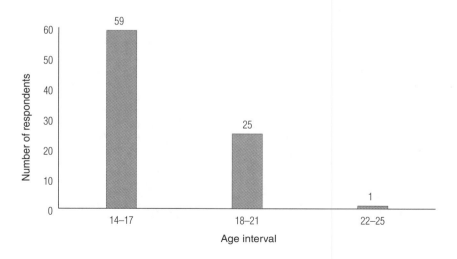

FIGURE 6.1: Ages of the respondents.

TABLE 6.1: Names of traditional medicinal plants used to treat five common ailments and diseases identified by female and male learners in Omusati and Oshana regions.

Ailment	Plant name	Females	Plant name	Males
Stomachache	baobab (roots of small tree)	1	*endombo* (aloe)	1
	iizimba (*Pechuel-loeschea* sp.)	7	guava (leaves)	3
	mopane (*Colophospermum mopane*)	4	*iizimba* (*Pechuel-loeschea* sp.)	3
	ombundjambundja (*Sesamum* sp.)	1	jackal berry	1
	omidhi (roots) *dhomugolo*	2	mopane (*Colophospermum mopane*)	5
	omungaalipi (*Eucalyptus* sp.)	2	*omushe* (*Grewia* sp.)	2
	oshipeke (*Ximenia* sp.)	1	*omukonati* (*Lophiocarpus tenuissimus*)	1
	sub-total	**18**	**sub-total**	**16**
Fever	*iizimba* (*Pechuel-loeschea* sp.)	5	*iizimba* (*Pechuel-loeschea* sp.)	5
	lemon plant	1	mopane (*Colophospermum mopane*)	1
	marula (*Sclerocarya birrea*)	2	*omungaalipi* (*Eucalyptus* sp.)	2
	omungaalipi (*Eucalyptus* sp.)	10		
	sub-total	**18**	**sub-total**	**8**
Headache	baobab (*Adansonia digitata*)	1	*etse lyakuku* (*Acrotome* sp.)	1
	etse lyakuku (*Acrotome* sp.)	1	garlic plant	1
	herbs (unspecified)	3	*gecorbasy* (jackal berry; *Diospyros mespiliformis*)	1
	iizimba (*Pechuel-loeschea* sp.)	7	*iizimba* (*Pechuel-loeschea* sp.)	1
	marula (*Sclerocarya birrea*)	1	*omungaalipi* (*Eucalyptus* sp.)	4
	mopane (*Colophospermum mopane*) bark	5	*sandamaria*	1
	omungaalipi (*Eucalyptus* sp.)	3		
	omwiidhi (grass)	1		
	palm tree	1		
	sub-total	**23**	**sub-total**	**9**
Wounds	*Aloe* sp.	12	*endobo* (*Aloe* sp.)	7
	marula (*Sclerocarya birrea*)	1	*eevia*	2
	mopane (*Colophospermum mopane*)	2	*okalyoipute* (*Corchorus tridens*)	3
	okalyoipute (*Corchorus tridens*)	4	*omazimba* (*Pechuel-loeschea* sp.)	1
	omupya (*Elaeodendron transvaalense*)	1	*omungaalipi* (*Eucalyptus* sp.)	1
	ongonya	1		
	onguma	1		
	sub-total	**22**	**sub-total**	**14**
HIV/AIDS	*Aloe* sp.	2		
	omatumbula (Kalahari truffle)	2		
	sub-total	**4**	**sub-total**	**0**
Total		**85**		**47**

Knowledge of traditional medicinal plants used for common ailments

In order to assess the learners' knowledge and disposition towards the use of traditional medicinal plants to cure ('cure' was the term used in the study) common ailments, they were asked to indicate the use of these medicines for stomachaches, fever, headaches, wounds and HIV/AIDS. Specifically, the learners were asked (1) to provide the names (in their mother tongue; where possible, scientific names are provided) of medicinal plants used to treat each ailment and disease; (2) to indicate which part of the plant was used; (3) how the medicine was prepared; and (4) from where they gained this knowledge.

Table 6.1 shows the variety of medicinal plants used in healing the five common ailments and diseases covered in this study. It was found that the learners gave a maximum of 12 different plants for the treatment of stomachaches, followed by ten for both wounds and headaches and a minimum of two for the treatment of HIV/AIDS. Information on how they were used to cure the identified common ailments and diseases is given in Appendices 6.1 and 6.2. Even though the learners were required to provide names of the traditional medicinal plants in their mother tongue, some learners opted for the English names. Perhaps they did not know the mother tongue names.

It is clear from the long list and variety of names of traditional medicinal plants provided by the learners that they were aware of medicinal plants that could be used to cure particular common ailments. All the learners indicated the names of the plants they knew would cure some of the common ailments. It was found that not all the learners were able to provide such information for the five indicated common ailments. This, in our view, is an indication that the learners have been exposed to indigenous knowledge related to the use of medicinal plants to treat these five common ailments. It should also be pointed out that the female learners tended to provide more names of the medicinal plants for curing the named common ailments than the male learners (56% against 44%).

Respondents' sources of knowledge on the use of medicinal plants

All the respondents were asked to indicate the source(s) of their information on traditional medicines. If young people have access to the source of the information on medicinal plants, its future would be guaranteed. Table 6.2 presents the sources of knowledge on traditional medicines to treat common ailments as indicated by the learners.

It is clear from Table 6.2 that grandparents are the most common source of knowledge on traditional medicines (31%). The common practice of children growing up with grandparents (both male and female) in Namibia might have contributed to the grandparents being the main source of this knowledge.

TABLE 6.2: Learners' sources of indigenous knowledge on medicinal plants.

Source	Stomach-ache	Fever	Headache	Wound	HIV/AIDS	Total
			Ailment			
Parents	7	2	5	4	–	18
Grandparents	14	6	7	3	–	30
Family members	1	–	–	–	–	1
Teachers	1	–	1	–	–	2
Self	4	4	6	5	–	19
Other learners	–	2	–	–	–	2
Others	10	3	5	4	–	22
Culture	–	1	1	–	–	2
Total	**37**	**18**	**25**	**16**		**96***

* Total exceeds the total number of respondents because some learners gave more than one answer.

TABLE 6.3: Numbers of respondents indicating that they had consulted a traditional healer for a medical problem.

Respondents	Yes	No	Total
Male	8	33	41
Female	11	27	38
Total	**19**	**60**	**79**

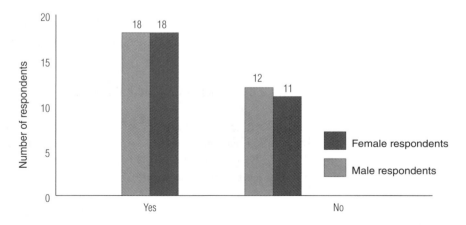

FIGURE 6.2: Numbers of male and female respondents with a family member that had visited a traditional healer.

TABLE 6.4: Numbers of respondents indicating that a family member had been healed upon consulting a traditional healer.

Respondents	Yes	No	Total
Male	23	10	33
Female	24	7	31
Total	**47**	**17**	**64**

Learners' views regarding use of traditional medicinal plants

Table 6.3 shows the numbers of learners that had consulted a traditional healer at some time. The majority of the 79 learners who answered the question indicated that they had never visited a traditional healer (76%), while 19 (24%) of these learners said that they had.

Figure 6.2 shows the number of the respondents who said that their family member(s) had consulted a traditional healer. Of the 85 learners, 59 (69%) answered the question. The majority of these respondents (36; 61%) indicated that one or more of their family member(s) had consulted a traditional healer. Only 23 (39%) of the respondents to that question indicated that none of their family member(s) had consulted a traditional healer.

When asked whether a family member had been healed on consulting a traditional healer, 47 (73%) of the respondents to that question indicated that the family member was healed after taking the prescribed traditional medicine (Table 6.4). This was also illustrated by the following quotations from the participants, which have been edited, but the original meaning is maintained:

'She was not able to do anything, but when she went to the traditional healer and stayed there for a week she became better.'

'He was very sick, close to death, but the traditional healer managed to heal him and he is now completely recovered.'

The quotes above seem to suggest that the actual healing of a close relative appears to have been an indication of the effectiveness and healing power of traditional medicines used by the traditional healers. In these examples, it is clear that the respondents believed that the traditional healers cured complex conditions in addition to the stomachache, fever, headache and wounds presented by their clients. The science teachers could use such contextual instances to teach indigenous knowledge of medicinal plants.

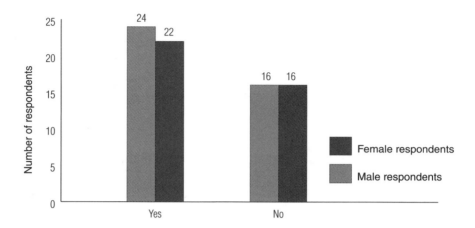

FIGURE 6.3: Numbers of learners for and against the integration of indigenous knowledge in the science curriculum.

Integration of traditional medicines in the science curriculum

In this study, learners were asked whether they thought indigenous knowledge should be included in their school science curriculum and, if so, how this should be done. The majority of learners (46) were of the view that traditional medicines should form part of the science curriculum (Figure 6.3).

Some of the reasons advanced for wanting knowledge on traditional medicines integrated into the science curriculum were:

'So that I can use the traditional medicines.'

'So that we can treat and cure ourselves.'

'To not throw away our tradition.'

'Because we want to know the different types of traditional medicine and their uses …'

About 42% of the learners who responded to the question did not agree to the inclusion of traditional medicine knowledge as part of the science curriculum. Some reasons given included:

'I don't think they are real, and I don't believe in them.'

'They are not controlled by anyone.'

'Not all traditional healers are to be trusted.'

As can be seen from the responses above, some of the reasons given by the learners for inclusion of indigenous knowledge on medicinal plants in the science curriculum were for personal growth – to know more about traditional medicines, the workings of the traditional healer and the use of traditional medicines in healing common ailments and other diseases.

TABLE 6.5: Learners' preferences on how indigenous knowledge on traditional medicines should be taught at school.

Means of transferring knowledge to learners	Number of respondents		
	Male	Female	Total
Taught by traditional healer	19	18	37
Teacher demonstrates	24	24	48
Both teacher and traditional healer teach together	14	19	33
I don't want to learn about traditional medicines	14	14	28
Total	**71**	**75**	**146**

* Total number exceeds the total number of respondents because some learners gave more than one answer.

Mode of integration

It is important to ensure that an appropriate mode and agent of presenting indigenous knowledge on traditional medicinal plants is used in the classroom if it is to be accepted by the learners. Table 6.5 shows learners' preferences on how indigenous knowledge should be presented in the classroom.

The responses shown in Table 6.5 show that the majority of the participating junior-high-school learners favoured the teacher demonstrating the use of traditional medicines to the class. This preference was followed by the option of the traditional healer teaching (26%). Possibly the reason for preferring the classroom teacher to teach the indigenous knowledge of medicinal plants could be the learners' familiarity with the teacher.

As indicated earlier, some learners did not seem to trust the traditional healers as much as they trusted their teacher to provide the appropriate information on medicinal plants, or Western-trained medical doctors to treat the different diseases. This was brought into sharp focus by one learner who said: 'Because not all of traditional healers are ... to be trusted ...'.

The learners that indicated that they would like to have the traditional healer teach the use of traditional medicinal plants to them, had this to say:

'Yes, traditional healers must be available at each school and they must be paid for their work.'

'I want lessons from a traditional healer to be provided.'

'We want the traditional healer to come and teach us.'

'To learn how traditional healers work, and how they can improve our health.'

'Yes. It is better for a traditional healer to come to class and teach us his/ her skills.'

Information on what the study participants would like to learn of traditional healing practices was sought. Specifically, if the practices and uses of traditional medicinal plants were integrated into the school science syllabus, what content would they actually like to learn about? The learners were asked to indicate the extent to which they would like to learn more about healing each of the five common ailments using traditional means by selecting: (1) strongly disagree; (2) disagree; (3) I don't know; (4) agree; and (5) strongly agree. Figure 6.4 shows their responses.

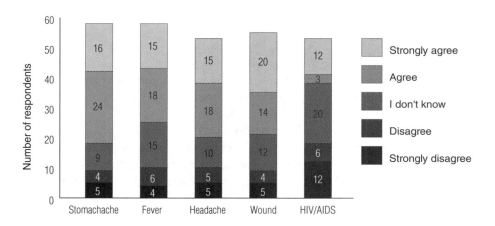

FIGURE 6.4: Learners' consensus on gaining more knowledge on traditional treatments for common ailments.

DISCUSSION

Perceptions about an event, object or person(s) are important in accepting or rejecting something or someone (Woolfolk, 2010). In this study the researchers sought to find out the learners' views regarding the use of traditional medicinal plants in their communities.

It is interesting that female learners in this study know more about the uses of traditional medicinal plants for common ailments and diseases than male learners. It is assumed that this finding is probably due to the female learners' closer interactions with their parents and grandparents who are usually the repository of traditional medicinal plant knowledge in the community.

Figure 6.2 shows a low number of respondents whose family member(s) had consulted a traditional healer. The low numbers are due to the fact that the question seemed to be personal and sensitive because it asked them to indicate whether they have consulted a traditional healer. Some of the health problems that led the family members to consult the traditional healer include the four common ailments (stomachache, fever, headache and wounds), as well as malaria, 'eye problem', 'okwa hala okushiwa oyinima mbino tayi vulu okuyeludha omuntu' (he/she wants to know things which help to cure a person), among others. This gives an idea of the variety of health problems that traditional healers treated in the communities, often being the first port of call for the sick. Table 6.4 shows the high number of respondents whose family members were healed upon consulting a traditional healer. The discrepancy in the number of respondents who indicated that their family members had visited the traditional healer and the number of respondents indicating that a family member had been healed upon consulting a traditional healer is due to the fact that some learners skipped the first question but answered the follow-up question.

It is interesting to note that even though they had relatives who had consulted and seen the effectiveness of the traditional medicines through the healing of their relative(s) (Table 6.4), the majority of the learners viewed the traditional healers with distrust and indicated that they had never consulted them for any health-related problem. Unfortunately, it is not possible to verify the truthfulness of their response to this question in this study.

The results also indicate that more than half of the learners in this study were of the view that traditional medicine practice should form part of the science curriculum. This revelation does not come as a surprise. In fact, Nakata (2002) mentions that there has been a push in the past decade by educators and researchers to integrate indigenous perspectives across the curriculum, in order to make it more inclusive. Nakata believes that the inclusion of indigenous knowledge in formal education promotes the visibility of it and helps to raise self-esteem and interest in schooling. This view is also supported by Diwu and Ogunniyi (2011) from their study in which learners that were exposed to lessons on IKS in science classes showed much enthusiasm for this content.

If we deliberate on the diverse interpretation and understanding of indigenous knowledge, teachers should consider that using different approaches to include it in formal education, as suggested by Nakata (2002), is a complex issue. In fact, Aikenhead (2001) is of the view that most of our science curricula seem to attempt to enculturate students into the value systems of Western science and it seems that they generally reject the assimilation of their culture into Western science in spite of the latter having a major global influence on their lives. Hence, Aikenhead (2001) proposed a cross-cultural approach to science teaching and to achieve this, science teachers need to play the role of a tour guide because Western science has its own culture. Ogunniyi (2011) is of the view that, border-crossing 'a learning experience brought about by relating one worldview to another', becomes an essential tool in this process of integrating indigenous knowledge into the school science curriculum.

However, Nakata (2002) also cautions against the inclusion of indigenous knowledge into the school curriculum. He notes that in too many instances indigenous knowledge inclusion does little to orient students to the Western knowledge context. Diwu and Ogunniyi (2011) suggest that it is crucial that science and IKS should not be dichotomized and seen as separate knowledge but should rather be harnessed through the process of 'dialogical argumentation'. Hewson (2011), on the other hand, notes that the harmonization process of the two world-views can be achieved by understanding the epistemological differences between them, which will provide important guidance on how to integrate indigenous knowledge into a conventional Western science curriculum. Hewson (2011, p. 47) therefore, recommends that in the integration process, 'teachers need to create conceptual bridges from students' prior knowledge to new knowledge.'

Some learners in this study, however, did not seem to trust the traditional healers as much as they trusted the Western-trained medical doctor. It seems the perceived 'deceiving practices' of some traditional healers tainted the practices of genuine traditional healers and contributed to the negative perception of their practice and themselves as health providers. Our participants were not the only ones to indicate negative perceptions of some traditional healers. Chinsembu (2009) warned of traditional healers that were 'charlatans' and stated that some officials in north-eastern Namibia were also sceptical about traditional medicine practices, especially as the work of traditional healers is not watched by a professional body. Therefore, there is need for educational programmes to change the mind-set of those with negative perceptions of IKS.

School learners' knowledge and views of traditional medicine 149

CONCLUSION AND IMPLICATIONS FOR THE SCIENCE CURRICULUM

Based on the study results, it can be concluded that the participating junior-high-school learners in the Omusati and Oshana regions knew the names of some traditional medicinal plants used in their communities. They also knew from personal experiences which medicinal plants were used to treat a particular common ailment. Further, the study showed that female learners were more knowledgeable about medicinal plant use than male learners. We can also conclude that there seems to be some agreement among the participating learners in this study, that indigenous knowledge should be integrated into the science curriculum.

The other implication for teaching that should be emphasized here is the issue of assessment. Classroom assessment procedures will be crucial when one integrates indigenous knowledge into the school science curriculum. Traditional methods of assessment need to be replaced by relevant and authentic assessment methods that fit the integration processes. For example, Aikenhead (2001) suggests that portfolios promote student autonomy because they reflect the cultural context of learning. Therefore, science teachers should be encouraged to use alternative methods of assessment that will enhance and promote learners' understanding from their cultural perspectives.

This study recommends that the integration of IKS related to medicinal plants into the school science education curriculum in Namibia should be seriously considered. This would be a beginning for both learners and teachers in starting to appreciate the importance and uses of indigenous knowledge in their lives. Furthermore, both teachers and learners would start to appreciate the important role that IKS plays in the lives of our people who might not have easy access to the hospital services or Western-trained doctors.

ACKNOWLEDGMENTS

Silke Rügheimer and her colleagues David Aiyambo, Hendrina Hasheela and Leevi Nanyeni are gratefully acknowledged for their help in determining the plants referred to in the questionnaires by their local names.

References

Aikenhead, G. (2001). Integrating Western and Aboriginal sciences: Cross-cultural science teaching. *Research in Science Education, 31*(3), 337-355.

Cheikhyoussef, A., Shapi, M., Matengu, K., & Mu Ashekele, H. (2011). Ethnobotanical study of indigenous knowledge on medicinal plant use by traditional healers in Oshikoto Region, Namibia. *Journal of Ethnobiology and Ethnomedicine, 7,* 10. doi: 10.1186/1746-4269-7-10

Chinsembu, K. C. (2009). Model and experiences of initiating collaboration with traditional healers in validation of ethnomedicines for HIV/AIDS in Namibia. *Journal of Ethnobiology and Ethnomedicine, 5,* 30. doi:10.1186/1746-4269-5-30

Chinsembu, K. C., & Hedimbi, M. (2010). An ethnobotanical survey of plants used to manage HIV/AIDS opportunistic infections in Katima Mulilo, Caprivi region, Namibia. *Journal of Ethnobiology and Ethnomedicine, 6,* 25. doi:10.1186/1746-4269-6-25

Diwu, C. T., & Ogunniyi, M. B. (2011). Realising a science and indigenous knowledge systems curriculum: A case study of a dialogical argumentation-based teaching approach. In M. B. Ogunniyi & S. K. Kwofie (Eds), *Proceedings of the 3rd International Conference on the Integration of Science and Indigenous Knowledge Systems* (pp. 93-108). Cape Town, South Africa: University of the Western Cape.

Gazzaneo, L., de Lucena, R., & de Albuquerque, U. (2005). Knowledge and use of medicinal plants by local specialists in a region of Atlantic forest in the state of Pernambuco (Northeastern Brazil). *Journal of Ethnobiology and Ethnomedicine, 1,* 9. doi: 10.1186/1746-4269-1-9

Hamilton, A. C. (2003). Medicinal plants, conservation and livelihoods. *Biodiversity and Conservation, 13*(8), 1477-1517.

Hewson, M. G. (2011). The education of Africa's children: IKS and traditional healers. In M. B. Ogunniyi and S. K. Kwofie (Eds), *Proceedings of the 3rd International Conference on the Integration of Science and Indigenous Knowledge Systems* (pp. 46-57). Cape Town, South Africa: University of the Western Cape.

Hoareau, L., & da Silva, E. J. (1999). Medicinal plants: A re-emerging health aid. *Electronic Journal of Biotechnology, 2*(2), 56-70.

Kambizi, L., & Afolayan, A. J. (2006). Indigenous knowledge and its impact on medicinal plant conservation in Guruve, Zimbabwe. *Indilinga: African Journal of Indigenous Knowledge Systems, 5*(1), 26-31.

Kapenda, H. M., & Kasanda, C. D. (2013). Teachers' vews and perceptions on the use of traditional medicinal plants in the treatment of common ailments and diseases in the Oshana region, Namibia. In M. Oginniyi (Ed.). *Harnessing indigenous knowledge for sustainable development. Proceedings of the 4th International Conference of the Science and Indigenous Knowledge Systems (IKS) Project/South African-Mozambican Collaboration Research Programme* (pp. 246-251). Cape Town, South Africa: UWC.

Mills, E. J., Cooper, C., Seely, D., & Kanfer, I. (2005). African herbal medicines in the treatment of HIV: *Hypoxis* and *Sutherlandia*. An overview of evidence and pharmacology. *Nutrition Journal, 4,* 19-24.

Mpofu, V., Vhurumuku, E., Kapenda, H. M., Kasanda, C., & Dudu, W. (2011). A comparative study of student teachers' perceptions of traditional medicine and its integration into science curriculum. In M. B. Ogunniyi and S. K. Kwofie (Eds), *Proceedings of the 3rd International Conference on Science and Indigenous Knowledge Systems* (pp. 79-92). Cape Town, South Africa: University of the Western Cape.

Nakata, M. (2002). Indigenous knowledge and the cultural interface: Underlying issues at the intersection of knowledge and information systems. *International Federation of Library Associations and Institutions (IFLA) Journal, 28*(5-6), 281-291.

Ogunniyi, M. B. (2011). Science and indigenous knowledge in the melting pot: Prospects and challenges. In M. B. Ogunniyi and S. K. Kwofie (Eds), *Proceedings of the 3rd International Conference on the Integration of Science and Indigenous Knowledge Systems* (pp. 2-31). Cape Town, South Africa: University of the Western Cape.

Onwu, G., & Mosimege, M. (2004). Indigenous knowledge systems and science and technology education: A dialogue. *African Journal of Research in Mathematics, Science and Technology Education, 8*(1), 1-13.

Taylor, J. L. S., Rabe, T., McGaw, L. J., Jäger, A. K., & van Staden, J. (2001). Towards scientific validation of traditional medicinal plants. *Plant Growth Regulation, 34,* 23-37.

Teklehaymanot, T., Giday, M., Medhin, G., & Mekonnen, Y. (2007). Knowledge and use of medicinal plants by people around Debre Liabnos monastery in Ethiopia. *Journal of Ethnopharmacology, 111*(2), 271-283.

Van der Walt, A. M., Mossanda, K. S. A., Jivan, S. D., Swart, W. J., & Bezuidenhout, C. C. (2005). Indigenous African food plants: Vehicles of diseases or sources of protection? *Indilinga: African Journal of Indigenous Knowledge Systems, 4*(1), 270-279.

Vhurumuku, E., & Mokeleche, M. (2009). The nature of science and indigenous knowledge systems in South Africa, 2000–2007: A critical review of the research in science education. *African Journal of Research in Mathematics, Science and Technology Education, Special Issue 2009,* 96-114.

Woolfolk, A. (2010). *Educational psychology* (11th ed.). Upper Saddle River, New Jersey, USA: Pearson.

Appendix 6.1: Information on the use of medicinal plants to treat various ailments gathered from participants at School A, Outapi Constituency, Omusati Region.

Plant name	Part used	How it is used	How participant knows about its use
Stomachache (e.g. acidity, ulcers, general problems)			
herbs (unspecified)	stems	Put in boiling water and drink.	I used to hear it from people.
omusati (mopane tree; *Colophospermum mopane*)	leaves	Pound the leaves and put in water and drink; or put the leaves in water and drink; or you chew it until it becomes small pieces.	Because it kills acid in stomach, especially in human body.
omazimba (bitter bush)	roots	Pound the roots and put in water and drink.	
mopane (*Colophospermum mopane*)	leaves	For example, if you have diarrhoea, you will chew the leaves and swallow that saliva.	People they just try. Old people they come up with that idea.
omukonati	stems	They are pounded and put in the cup with water.	We used it sometimes.
omukwa (baobab tree – the small one; *Adansonia digitata*)	roots	Boil the roots and allow to cool; then do suppository (insert from behind to clean the stomach).	I was told by my mother.
omukwaava (guava)	leaves	Chew the leaves and suck water then swallow.	I have been told by my grandpa to do so.
okampingo	roots	Put the roots in boiled water; allow to cool and drink.	
omugolo (yellow-wood; *Terminalia sericea*)	leaves	Boil the leaves, filter them and drink them.	
okampingo	roots	You take the root, remove the outer layer, dry the root and pound it. Put in boiled water and drink.	When I was sick in the stomach and my grandmother gave it to me to drink, then I got better.
mahangu (pearl millet)	seeds	You pound the grain and the meal; you put in water and start to drink.	I was told by my grandmother.
onyanga (onion)	leaves	You eat the leaves.	I was sick in my stomach one day and I tried to use it and I got cured.
omuheli	roots	Boiling with water and you may drink that water.	My parents told me that in the old times they used it if they were sick in stomach.
omazimba (bitter bush)	leaves	Burn them and inhale the smoke; or you pound the leaves, put in water and drink; or moisten them and put on tray, then roast them and inhale the smoke.	I was told by grandmothers.
	bark	Put on hot coal and inhale the smoke.	

Plant name	Part used	How it is used	How participant knows about its use
omungaalipi (eucalyptus)	leaves	Pounding them and put in water; to use to them for flu and cough if needed; boil the leaves and inhale the steam under the blanket or sniff the leaves; or chew the leaves to ease the pain; pound the leaves and put in water to cure yourself.	
moringa (Moringa ovalifolia)	leaves	You put those leaves in the pot.	
omugolo (yellow-wood; Terminalia sericea)	stem	Chew	
omuhama	leaves	Used for chewing by person who is sick.	I do not know for this.
Headache			
omulunga (palm tree)	leaves	Put a bandage on your forehead.	From our grandmother.
etselyakuku (Acrotome sp.)	leaves	Burn the leaves and inhale smoke; or burn leaves and inhale smoke.	
okamulonde	leaves	Put the leaves on a plate then the gases that get out, you breathe in.	I tried it and I got better.
omusati (mopane tree; Colophospermum mopane)	bark	Chew the bark, put it on a cloth and put it near the ears.	I saw it done by one of grandmothers.
ombidhi (Cleome gynandra)	leaves	You put them in water then you put the pot on the fire.	Because I see my grandmother doing it.
moringa (Moringa ovalifolia)	leaves	Pound them and boil them in water. Cover yourself with a blanket and inhale steam.	
omupopo (Albizia anthelmintica)	leaves	Boil the leaves.	
omusati (mopane tree; Colophospermum mopane)	leave	Pound the leaves and boil them; then inhale the steam.	
olwiivike	leaves	Pound the leaves, boil in water and wash your head.	From my parents.
omazimba (bitter bush)	leaves and branches	Put on hot coals and inhale the smoke.	
Wounds			
okalyaipute	seeds	Crush the seeds until they become powder; put the powder on the wound; or pound the leaves and mix with body lotion and put it on the wound.	I used to do it. I was told by my grandmother.
	leaves	Tie and then put on the wound; they are pounded and they are put on the wounds.	I was told by my parent.
ongonya	all parts	Put on coal and when cold put on the wound.	
	fruits	You roast them and put the ashes on the wound.	

continues

Appendix 6.1 continued

Plant name	Part used	How it is used	How participant knows about its use
okashilakonoka	leaves and stem	You put it on hot coal.	
iizimba (bitter bush)	leaves	Put in water and place them on the wound.	From my mother.
omupopo	leaves	Boil.	
endombo (*Aloe* sp.)	leaves	Put the sap on the wound.	Used by the community.
omungaalipi (eucalyptus)	leave	Chew or grind and put a smaller amount on the wound.	
omupya	leaves	Pound the leaves; mix with water and put on the wound.	
HIV/AIDS			
endombo (*Aloe* sp.)	roots	Drink water from the roots of aloe plant.	

Appendix 6.2: Information on the use of medicinal plants to treat various ailments gathered from participants from School B in Ongwediva Constituency, Oshana Region.

Plant name	Part of plant used	How it is used	How did you know about its uses as a medicine
Stomachache (e.g. acidity, ulcers and general problems)			
omushe	roots	Put it in cup of water and drink or chew and swallow; or put it in cup of water and drink or chew and swallow; or chew it and swallow the saliva.	I was told by my grandparents.
etama (tomato plant)	leaves	You pound it and then you chew and swallow the saliva and you peel out leaves.	I learned it from it from my grandmother.
omusati (mopane; *Colophospermum mopane*)	leaves	Chew it; or you take the leaves and dry them so that you make them fine and boil them in a pot with fire; or by pounding the leaves and boil in water.	Through parents; through my grandmother.
	stem	You have to cut pieces of mopane stem and put it in water.	From family members.
iizimba (bitter bush)	leaves	You crush and put in water and insert from behind (in the anus); or apply it by chewing leaves and swallowing the saliva.	From my family members; parents; granny; mom.
Jackal-berry (*Diospyros mespiliformis*)	fruit	By chewing it and swallowing it.	I was told by my grandmother.
ombundjambundja	leaves	It is pounded in a small cup with a stick, then you put water in the cup and then you start to drink it.	I have been told by my grandmother.
omukwaava (guava)	leaves	You take a cup with water and put leaves in.	
oshipeke	leaves	Chew it.	From family members.
omungaalipi (eucalyptus)	leaves	Chew the leaves.	We were told by family members.
omungaalipi (eucalyptus)	leaves	Pound them and put the leaves in the hot water and inhale the steam; or eat the leaves.	My grandmother told me; by my friend.
Fever			
iizimba (bitter bush)	leaves	Pound them, put in boiled water and inhale the steam.	Told by my mother; I also saw many people use it.
omugongo (marula; *Sclerocarya birrea*)	water from roots	Boiling the water.	
omugongo (marula; *Sclerocarya birrea*) imema	stem	Chewing a piece of the stem.	

continues

Appendix 6.2 continued

Plant name	Part of plant used	How it is used	How did you know about its uses as a medicine
omugongo (marula; *Sclerocarya birrea*)	leaves	You boiled the leaves in water then cover your head with a blanket and inhale the steam.	From my fellow learners.
lemon plant	leaves	Chew the leaves and swallow saliva.	I saw a person using it.
iizimba (bitter bush)	leaves	You put them in a tin together with water and put it on the fire for them to boil and then put in your nose.	I have been told by my grandmother.
omusati (mopane; *Colophospermum mopane*)	leaves	You burn the leaves and sniff the smoke.	I was told by my grandmother.
omungaalipi (eucalyptus)	leaves	Put them in hot water and cover your body and inhale steam; or you boil the water, put the leaves in then start drinking; or you smash the leaves and chew them.	I heard it from my teacher when I was in Grade 5; from my forefathers; I have been told by my grandmother; I tried it; I was told by my grandma.

Headache

iizimba (bitter bush)	roots	You just chew them and swallow with the water.	It was used by our forefathers.
iizimba (bitter bush)	leaves	Put them on charcoal with fire and use a blanket to inhale the smoke.	I was told by grandmother.
omugongo (marula; *Sclerocarya birrea*)	fruit	Drink the juice.	I was told by grandparents.
omusati (mopane; *Colophospermum mopane*)	roots	By boiling them in water; or chew and swallow the juice; or just eat the roots.	My grandmother told me about it; my stepmother told me.
omugongo (marula; *Sclerocarya birrea*)	stem	You must put the water coming from the stem to the wound.	I heard it from my father.

Wounds

endombo (*Aloe* sp.)	leaves	You have to cut the leaves in pieces and dry them; when they are dry, pound them until they are fine and mix them with water and put it on the wound; or put a drop of juice on a wound.	From grandmother.
endombo (*Aloe* sp.)	stem	Pound it and mix them with water.	
omusati (mopane; *Colophospermum mopane*)	dry leaves	Take the leaves and dry them and put them on the wound.	
omupya	stem	Melt the stem and smear it on.	By grandma.
omatumbula	roots	Eat them.	I got information from someone.

HIV/AIDS

endombo (*Aloe* sp.)	leaves	Drink the juice.	I heard it.

7

Namibian leafy vegetables: From traditional to scientific knowledge, current status and applications

Lynatte F. Mushabati, Gladys K. Kahaka & Ahmad Cheikhyoussef

INTRODUCTION

For centuries, our forefathers traditionally used vegetables that grow naturally in the wild. Many enjoyed a relish prepared with traditional vegetables. Moreover, they used these vegetables to treat a number of ailments. This is our African heritage – our Namibian leafy vegetables. These vegetables fall under a broad category that has come to be termed as leafy vegetables (LVs) or African leafy vegetables (ALVs). In this chapter, all Namibian leafy vegetables will be referred to as ALVs and NLVs interchangeably.

According to Rubaihayo (1995), ALVs are considered traditional vegetables for at least three reasons:

1. ALVs are easily found and harvested in their natural habitat.
2. The majority of ALVs have been consumed for many generations, reflecting their importance in local culture.
3. ALVs contribute significantly to the food security of rural and urban populations in many African countries. They are nutritional, having high levels of vitamins and minerals.

Leafy vegetables have been part of the staple diet in many Namibian households for years. Furthermore, traditional healers and the elderly have prescribed NLVs for the treatment of a wide variety of ailments ranging from digestive complaints to urinary tract infections, and used to aid the birthing process. Sadly, we see a growing trend of NLVs only being used in rural settings. This might be because most NLVs grow

FIGURE 7.1: Exotic and African leafy vegetables being sold at a traditional market. (© L. F. Mushabati.)

in the wild. However, younger generations are under the impression that NLVs are foods consumed only by poor or old-fashioned individuals, while modern and advantaged individuals consume exotic vegetables, such as spinach and broccoli (van Rensburg, Vorster, van Zijl, & Venter, 2007).

This chapter has been dedicated towards demonstrating that five NLVs have phytochemical properties that can be beneficial to human health on nutritional and non-nutritional levels and, as such, should not be considered inferior. It is hoped that the value of these vegetables will thus be much more appreciated. NLVs could potentially boost the income of many households. As these NLVs have been used for medicinal purposes for many years, validating their medicinal potential might make their use as alternatives to Western medicines more appealing. The five NLVs at the centre of discussion in this chapter are *Cleome gynandra* (known as *sishungwa* in siLozi and as *ombowayozondu* in Otjiherero, Figure 7.2), *Amaranthus hybridus* (*tepe* in siLozi, *omboga* in Oshindonga), *Amaranthus dinteri* (*libowa* in siLozi, |*horob* in Khoekhoegowab), *Hibiscus sabdariffa* (*sindambi* in siLozi) and *Corchorus tridens* (*delele* in siLozi). English names for plants, such as cat's whiskers, pigweed or wild jute, might not be familiar to local audiences, so traditional names, such as *omboga*, *sindambi*, *mutete*, |*horob* and *ombowayozondu*, which are better known, are used here.

FIGURE 7.2: African leafy vegetable *Cleome gynandra*, locally known as *shisungwa* in siLozi and *ombowayozondu* in Otjiherero, is popular in Namibia. (© Silke Rügheimer.)

TRADITIONAL KNOWLEDGE ON INDIGENOUS LEAFY VEGETABLES

Indigenous knowledge is defined as a unique and traditional knowledge to a given culture or society and communities, particularly in non-literate societies that, by and large, rely on local technologies for its transmission. In most instances, it is undocumented and is therefore at risk of being lost to future generations (Raseroka, 2008). Indigenous knowledge is found in both rural and urban communities and deals with issues concerning the survival of people in the community, food security, and the protection and use of the local environment (Dweba & Mearns, 2011). Indigenous knowledge covers a range of subjects from agriculture and social welfare, to peace building and conflict resolution, as well as medicine and food technology (Odora Hoppers, 2005).

Like many other types of indigenous knowledge systems, knowledge about traditional vegetables is vanishing and this situation warrants immediate action to retain or regain it (Adebooye & Opabode, 2004). This can then be passed on to future generations instead of it fading into history.

CURRENT KNOWLEDGE ON INDIGENOUS LEAFY VEGETABLES

Considering the potential that NLVs have, as well as the threat of losing this vital heritage, very little research and documentation has been done to date. There are inadequate scientific databases (germplasms and gene banks) to counter the rate of loss of knowledge on NLVs. Economic, political and social factors continue to put a lot of pressure on the use of NLVs. Changes in climate and environmental degradation, such as bush encroachment, which could potentially wipe out large areas of habitat of these plants also adversely influence the survival of NLVs. As some of these ALVs are endemic to Namibia, we could be facing the potential extinction of many plant species (Adebooye & Opabode, 2004). One way to counter these threats is to create seed banks. In Namibia, institutions such as the National Botanical Research Institute (NBRI) and the Centre for Research Information Action in Africa Southern African Development and Consulting (CRIAA SA-DC) have already started to establish seed banks of hundreds of plant species.

Recent studies show that considerable interest in replacing synthetic antioxidants with natural ones from plants is growing. Many ALVs have been proven to be of a nutritionally high value, however, few publications have documented the phytochemical profiles and biological activities of these plants. Public awareness of their benefits may help elevate the status of NLVs, and thereby encourage the sustainable harvesting and cultivation of them, and increase their marketing. This in turn, may result in food security and an increased income for people whose livelihoods depend heavily on NLVs (Kolberg, 2001).

SCIENTIFIC KNOWLEDGE ON AFRICAN LEAFY VEGETABLES

Nutritional value

A number of studies have been carried out on the nutritional aspect of many ALVs and these studies indicate that most of them have a high concentration of proteins and essential minerals. *Corchorus tridens*, for example, exhibited calcium (10 mg/g), iron (400 µg/g), and magnesium (4 mg/g) among other minerals (Freiberger et al., 1998). In addition, *C. tridens* contains proteins that make up to 25% of its dry weight (Freiberger et al., 1998).

Cleome gynandra is rich in vitamins A and C – 1,200 µg and 40 µg, respectively, in each 100 g portion of edible fresh weight. These figures are relatively high since the daily recommended dietary intake for an adult is 800 µg of vitamin A and 40 mg of vitamin C. Minerals such as calcium and iron can also be found in the same edible portions in amounts of 200 mg and 2.7 mg, respectively (Uusiku, Oelofse, Duodu, Bester, & Faber, 2010). The *Amaranthus* spp. are also a source of vitamin

A (7 mg/100g), vitamin C (120 mg/100g), calcium (500 mg/100g) and proteins (4 g/100g) (Kolberg, 2001).

ALVs such as the leaves and pods of cowpeas (*Vigna unguiculata*), African nightshade (*Solanum scabrum* and *S. villosum*), spider plant (*Cleome* spp.), African eggplant (*Solanum aethiopicum, S. anguivi* and *S. macrocarpon*) and moringa (*Moringa oleifera*) have been reported to be rich in micronutrients and other health-related phytochemical antioxidants (Yang & Keding, 2009).

The functional compounds of ALVs such as antibiotics, probiotics and prebiotics can restore the balance of beneficial decomposing bacteria in the digestive tract (Erasto, Bojase-Moleta, & Majinda, 2004; Afari-Sefa, Tenkouano, Ojiewo, Keatinge, & Hughes, 2012). Increased consumption of diets rich in micronutrients and antioxidants are strongly recommended to supplement medicinal therapy in fighting HIV/AIDS (Friis, 2006). ALVs contribute significantly to the food security of rural and urban populations in many African countries because of their high nutritional value (vitamins A, B and C, proteins, and minerals such as iron, calcium, phosphorus, iodine and fluorine).

Phytochemical profile

Phytochemicals are chemicals exclusively produced by plants that have non-nutritional benefits to the body in terms of promoting a healthy immune system (Cheikhyoussef et al., 2010). ALVs have been tested for a number of phytochemical classes. Phytochemicals are first extracted from the plant materials using a solvent of choice that can range from polar to non-polar depending on the phytochemical class that is being extracted. The screening process is then carried out by exposing the plant extract to phytochemical testing reagents under specific conditions. The presence of the specific phytochemical being tested for is indicated by a change in colour. The intensity of the colour gives an idea of the approximate amount of that specific phytochemical present in the plant extract (Cheikhyoussef et al., 2010).

NLVs *Amaranthus dinteri, A. hybridus, Cleome gynandra, Corchorus tridens* and *Hibiscus sabdariffa* demonstrate the presence of cardiac glycosides, terpenoids, steroids, flavonoids and saponins. Extracts of *A. dinteri, C. gynandra* and *C. tridens* contain the highest amounts of flavonoids, saponins and cardiac glycosides, respectively. *Cleome gynandra, H. sabdariffa,* and *A. dinteri* show almost equal quantities of terpenoids. All five NLVs' extracts exhibit high levels of steroids.

Why is this information significant? Flavonoids have antimicrobial activities that inhibit specific enzymes, and antioxidant activities that aid in scavenging free radicals. This makes them invaluable in the prevention of cancers (Havsteen, 2002). Flavonoids are referred to as 'nature's biological response modifiers' because of their inherent ability to modify the body's reaction to allergies, viruses and carcinogens (Aiyelaagbe & Osamudiamen, 2009). Saponins have antifungal and antiviral activities, which can boost the body's defence system (George, Zohar, Harinder, & Klaus, 2002). Also, saponins can be used in managing hypercholesterolaemia, hyperglycaemia and weight loss, and as antioxidant, anticancer and anti-inflammatory agents (Aiyelaagbe & Osamudiamen, 2009). Cardiac glycosides, as their name suggests, can be useful in the treatment of heart conditions. They are known to work by inhibiting the sodium–potassium pump. They are used in the treatment of congestive heart failure and cardiac arrhythmia. They are also used to strengthen a weakened heart and allow it to function more efficiently, though the dosage must be controlled carefully, since the therapeutic dose is close to the toxic dose (Denwick, 2002). Steroids are an important class of phytochemicals and are routinely used in medicine because of their profound biological activities (Denwick, 2002) and their relationship with sex hormones (Okwu, 2001).

BIOLOGICAL ACTIVITY

Antioxidant activity

Antioxidants are molecules that prevent other molecules from being oxidised by free radicals. They accomplish this by reacting with the free radicals. Free radicals are chemical compounds that have one unpaired electron. They become stable by extracting electrons from other molecules. Many reactions that take place in the body produce free radicals. This can lead to oxidative stress, as a result of these radicals reacting with important molecules such as DNA. Diseases such as cancer and neurodegenerative diseases have been linked to the activity of free radicals in the body (Chanda & Dave, 2009).

Examples of antioxidants include vitamins (A, C and E), carotenes, xanthophylls, tannins and thiols. The total phenolic content of plant extracts was determined using the Folin–Ciocalteu assay (Singleton and Rossi, 1965). Table 7.1 shows that NLVs have antioxidant activities, especially in fresh and dry, methanol extracts, but even after five months of storage. This indicates NLVs' potentials as antioxidant agents and makes them invaluable in a diet, especially of those whose health is compromised and those at risk of disease such as cancer.

The radical-scavenging activities of plant extracts were tested using 1,1-diphenyl-2-picrylhydrazyl (DPPH). Gallic acid was used as a positive control. The DPPH radical-scavenging activity of plant extracts was determined using the spectrophotometric method of Brand-Williams, Cuvelier and Berset (1995). The chloroform and diethyl ether extracts of *H. sabdariffa* gave the highest absorbance values compared to the other ALV extracts tested. The water and ethanol extracts of *C. gynandra* and *C. tridens* showed the lowest absorbance.

TABLE 7.1: Spectrophotometric readings indicating total phenolic content of a number of extracts of NLVs.

Sample		Total phenolic content					
		Extraction solvent[1]					
Status	NLV	Water	Ethanol	Methanol	Hexane	Diethyl ether	Chloroform
Fresh	C. gynandra	2.962	0.467	4.051	ND	ND	ND
	H. sabdariffa	4.615	1.442	11.080	ND	ND	ND
	A. dinteri	ND	0.359	ND	ND	ND	ND
	A. hybridus	3.029	1.087	12.310	1.336	0.776	1.464
Dry	C. gynandra	2.748	0.406	2.642	0.497	ND	0.761
	H. sabdariffa	3.765	1.686	8.668	ND	0.898	1.305
	C. tridens	0.785	0.518	7.465	0.129	0.158	0.838

[1] The values given here are the means of three readings. Gallic acid, the positive control, had an average value of 3.640.

ND = 'not done' (because there was not enough plant material to carry out the required tests).

Antimicrobial activity

The inhibitory effects of ALV extracts on microorganisms can be determined by using the disc diffusion method (van Vuuren, 2008) whereby indicator strains of bacteria and fungi are incubated in the presence of the ALVs extracts for 24 and 48 hours, respectively. The area around the disc that shows no growth is the so-called zone of inhibition (Kossah, Hao, & Wei, 2011).

All five vegetable extracts exhibited strong inhibition to *Escherichia coli* and *Candida albicans*. The water and ethanol extracts of *C. gynandra* showed the greatest inhibitory effect on *E. coli* (6-mm and 7-mm zone of inhibition, respectively). The ethanol extract of *C. tridens* gave a 6-mm zone of inhibition on *Staphylococcus aureus*. The water extract of *A. dinteri* and ethanol extract of *C. gynandra* inhibited *Shigella flexneri* (7-mm and 6-mm zone of inhibition, respectively). *Escherichia coli* is a usual suspect in food poisoning and *C. albicans* is responsible for many opportunistic infections of the mouth and genitals. The ethanol extract of *A. dinteri* showed a 9-mm zone of inhibition towards pathogenic *C. albicans*. The ethanol extracts of *C. gynandra* gave a 6-mm zone of inhibition towards *Saccharomyces cerevisiae*.

These results are noteworthy as some of the extracts had been stored in a fridge for more than four months and still showed antimicrobial activity. This demonstrates their potentials as antimicrobial agents towards bacteria that cause food spoilage. Water extracts of all tested ALVs showed less inhibition of the indicator strains compared to the organic solvent extracts.

These findings of the antimicrobial activities of ALVs are important for the development of health-promoting, functional foods and in food preservation (Puupponen-Pimiä et al., 2001).

CONSERVATION AND DOMESTICATION

With regard to the destruction of the natural habitat of the ALVs, issues such as bush encroachment need to be addressed. Activities are required to increase awareness and build the capacity of local harvesters on sustainable methods, such as harvesting only the leaves instead of uprooting whole plants. Cultivation of the ALVs at a household level can also be encouraged (Kolberg, 2001). ALV production is profitable and has the potential of offering employment and income-generating opportunities through increased commercialization of ALVs in local markets (Weinberger & Lumpkin, 2007; Afari-Sefa et al., 2012).

The use of plant biotechnology in the conservation of ALVs should also be encouraged, especially germplasm conservation, which would ensure the preservation of the genome of these NLVs. Biotechnology, however, offers a wide range of opportunities for ALV conservation and can help address the many unanswered research questions that currently limit efforts towards exploiting the nutritional and production potentials of NLVs. Recently, biotechnology has become more computationally intensive (bioinformatics), which has significant potential in the identification of useful genes, leading to the development of new gene products, drugs and diagnostics.

IMPORTANCE AND APPLICATION

National agenda, such as food insecurity, can be addressed by motivating local communities to increase their cultivation and consumption of indigenous and traditional, dark green, leafy vegetables (IPGRI, 2002). However, more information about the nutrient content of NLVs is required before these traditional vegetables can be recommended as a contributing ingredient to improved diets (Schönfeldt & Pretorius, 2011). Future food and nutritional security policies, and agricultural development aid policies should emphasize the integration of intervention efforts to increase the production and consumption of health-promoting vegetables to help address the chronic and emerging problems of malnutrition (Schönfeldt & Pretorius, 2011). Many of these ALVs could be transformed into food-grade supplements, which can be integrated into many other food products to increase their nutritional value and biological activities. They can be introduced to national school feeding programmes, and to children with malnutrition and patients with special nutritional requirements, such as those with HIV/AIDS. Furthermore, the antioxidative and antimicrobial activities of plant extracts have formed the basis of many applications, including raw and processed food preservation, pharmaceutical and alternative medicine development, and natural therapies (Lis-Balchin & Deans, 1997).

CONCLUSION

The ALVs that have been dealt with in this chapter demonstrate antimicrobial and antioxidant activities, as expected. Yet this is just the tip of the iceberg. ALVs have potential that is yet to be discovered. In fact, with the current knowledge that exists, databases are necessary to keep track of the research being carried out on NLVs. Conservation techniques are imperative in combating the destruction of ALV habitats and enlightening the nation as to their importance as part of our history and heritage. Education programmes are necessary to inform the local public about the nutritional benefits of these plants. It is evident that indeed the ALVs have both nutritional and non-nutritional values that can be used to benefit the economy and diet of both rural and urban Namibians. Moreover, with further research we can determine better methods of extending the shelf life of ALVs and how to reap the benefits of their pharmaceutical properties.

ACKNOWLEDGMENTS

The authors would like to thank the Multidisciplinary Research Centre, the Department of Chemistry and Biochemistry, and the Directorate of Research, Science and Technology (DRST) of the Ministry of Education (now named the National Commission on Research, Science and Technology (NCRST)), for the financial support to conduct the analytical research on the ALVs presented in this chapter.

References

Adebooye, O. C., & Opabode, J. T. (2004). Status of conservation of the indigenous leaf vegetables and fruits of Africa. *African Journal of Biotechnology*, 3(12), 700-705.

Afari-Sefa, V., Tenkouano, A., Ojiewo, C. O., Keatinge, J. D. H., & Hughes, J. d'A. (2012). Vegetable breeding in Africa: Constraints, complexity and contributions toward achieving food and nutritional security. *Food Security*, 4(1), 115-127.

Aiyelaagbe, O. O., & Osamudiamen, P. M. (2009). Phytochemical screening for active compounds in *Mangifera indica* leaves from Ibadan, Oyo State. *Plant Sciences Research, 2*(1), 11-13.

Brand-Williams, W., Cuvelier, M. E., & Berset, C. (1995). Use of free radical method to evaluate antioxidant activity. *Lebensmittel-Wissenschaft & Technologie, 28*(1), 25-30.

Chanda, S., & Dave, R. (2009). *In vitro* models for antioxidant activity evaluation and some medicinal plants possessing antioxidant properties: An overview. *African Journal of Microbiology Research, 3*(13), 981-996.

Cheikhyoussef, A., Naomab, E., Potgieter, S., Kahaka, G., Raidron, C., & Mu Ashekele, H. (2010). Phytochemical properties of a Namibian indigenous plant; Eembe (*Berchemia discolor*). *Proceedings of the 1st National Research Symposium*, 15–17 September 2010, Windhoek, Namibia, pp. 313-321.

Denwick, P. M. (2002). *Natural products: A biosynthetic approach* (2nd ed.). London, England: John Wiley and Sons Ltd.

Dweba, T. P., & Mearns, M. A. (2011). Conserving indigenous knowledge as the key to the current and future use of traditional vegetables. *International Journal of Information Management, 31*(6), 564-571.

Erasto, P., Bojase-Moleta, G. A., & Majinda, R. R. T. (2004). Antimicrobial and antioxidant flavonoids from the root wood of *Bolusanthus speciosus*. *Phytochemistry, 65*(7), 875-880.

Freiberger, C. E., Vanderjagt, D. J., Pastuszyn, A., Glew, R. S., Mounkaila, G., Millson, M., & Glew, R. H. (1998). Nutrient content of the edible leaves of seven wild plants from Niger. *Plant foods for Human Nutrition, 53*(1), 57-69.

Friis, H. (2006). Micronutrient interventions and HIV infection: A review of current evidence. *Tropical Medicine & International Health, 11*(12), 1849-1857.

George, F., Zohar, K., Harinder, P. S. M., & Klaus, B. (2002). The biological action of saponins in animal systems: A review. *British Journal of Nutrition, 88*(6), 587-605.

Havsteen, B. H. (2002). The biochemistry and medical significance of the flavonoids. *Pharmacology & Therapeutics, 96*(2-3), 67-202. Retrieved from http://www.ncbi.nlm.nih.gov/pubmed/12453566

IPGRI [International Plant Genetic Resources Institute]. (2002). *Neglected and underutilized plant species: Strategic action plan of the International Plant Genetic Resources Institute*. Rome, Italy: Author. Retrieved from http://www.bioversityinternational.org/fileadmin/_migrated/uploads/tx_news/Neglected_and_underutilized_plant_species_837.pdf

Kolberg, H. H. (2001). Indigenous Namibian leafy vegetables: A literature survey and project proposal. *Agricola, 2001*, 54-60.

Kossah, R., Hao, Z., & Wei, C. (2011). Antimicrobial and antioxidant activities of Chinese sumac (*Rhus typhina* L.) fruit extract. *Food Control, 22*(1), 128-132.

Lis-Balchin, M., & Deans, S. G. (1997). Bioactivity of selected plant essential oils against *Listeria monocytogenes*. *Journal of Applied Bacteriology, 82*, 759-762.

Qdora Hoppers, C. A. (2005). *Culture, indigenous knowledge and development: The role of the university* (Occasional Paper No. 5, CEPD). Braamfontein, South Africa: Centre for Education Policy Development. Retrieved from http://www.cepd.org.za/files/pictures/CEPD_Occasional_paper5_Culture_Indigenous_Knowledge_and_Development.pdf

Okwu, D. E. (2001). Evaluation of the chemical composition of indigenous spices and flavouring agents. *Global Journal of Pure & Applied Sciences, 7*(3), 455-459.

Puupponen-Pimiä, R., Nohynek, L., Meier, C., Kähkönen, M., Heinonen, M., Hopia, A., & Oksman-Caldentey, K.-M. (2001). Antimicrobial properties of phenolic compounds from berries. *Journal of Applied Microbiology, 90*(4), 494-507.

Raseroka, K. (2008). Information transformation Africa: Indigenous knowledge – securing space in the knowledge society. *The International Information & Library Review. 40*(4), 243-250. doi:10.1016/j.iilr.2008.09.001

Rubaihayo, E. B. (1995). Conservation and use of traditional vegetables in Uganda. In L.Guarino (Ed.) *Proceedings of the IPGRI International Workshop on Traditional Vegetables in Africa: Options for Conservation and Use* (pp.104-116), 29–31 August. Nairobi, Kenya: IPGRI.

Schönfeldt, H. C., & Pretorius, B. (2011). The nutrient content of five traditional South African dark green leafy vegetables: A preliminary study. *Journal of Food Composition & Analysis, 24*(8), 1141-1146.

Singleton, V. L., & Rossi, J. A. (1965). Colorimetry of total phenolics with phosphomolybdic-phosphotungstic acid reagents. *American Journal of Enology and Viticulture, 16*(3), 144-158.

Uusiku, N. P., Oelofse, A., Duodu, K. G., Bester, M. J., & Faber, M. (2010). Nutritional value of leafy vegetables of sub-Saharan Africa and their potential contribution to human health: A review. *Journal of Food Composition & Analysis, 23*, 499-509.

Van Rensburg, J. W., Vorster, I. H. J., van Zijl, J. J. B., & Venter, L. S. (2007). Conservation of African leafy vegetables in South Africa. *African Journal of Food, Agriculture, Nutrition & Development, 7*(4), 10-13.

Van Vuuren, S. F. (2008). Antimicrobial activity of South African medicinal plants. *Journal of Ethnopharmacology, 119*(3), 462-472.

Weinberger, K., & Lumpkin, T. A. (2007). Diversification into horticulture and poverty reduction: A research agenda. *World Development, 35*(8), 1464-1480.

Yang, R. Y., & Keding, G. B. (2009). Nutritional contribution of important African vegetables. In C. M. Shackleton, M. W. Pasquini, & A. W. Drescher (Eds.), *African indigenous vegetables in urban agriculture* (p. 298). London, England: Earthscan.

8

Traditionally fermented milk products

Lusia Heita & Ahmad Cheikhyoussef

INTRODUCTION

Fermented milk is one of the foods that are highly respected and form a part of the daily intake in Namibia. There are many types of fermented milk in Namibia, which have different preparation methods. Milk fermentation assists in preserving the milk by generating organic acids (e.g., lactic and acetic acids) and antimicrobial compounds (e.g., bacteriocins), as well as flavour compounds (e.g., acetaldehyde) and other metabolites (e.g., exopolysaccharides) that contribute to the product's organoleptic properties. Fermented milk provides special therapeutic and prophylactic properties against many diseases, symptoms and health problems.

This chapter outlines the types of traditionally fermented milks produced in Namibia – *omashikwa*, *mashini ghakushika* and *mabisi* – their modes of fermentation and physicochemical properties, and the dominant microflora in them. The health and social benefits of these fermented milk products are also discussed.

Traditional, African fermented milk

Traditionally fermented milk has a long history in Africa and its production relies on the indigenous knowledge of the population. The history of fermented milks is often described in terms of a sequence of two generations of products (Steinkraus, 2002). In the first generation of producing fermented milk products (800 bc to ad 1900), the microflora were not defined and differed from village to village. This first generation was followed from about 1910 by a second generation of fermented milks in which the microflora was defined and the fermentation process was controlled (Chandan, & Shah, 2013). Generally, fermentation processes are believed to have been developed by women over the years, in order to preserve food for times of shortage, and also to introduce desirable flavours into food (Rolle & Satin, 2002). The oldest references highlight the fact that the earliest fermented milks have existed for more than 3,000 years and doubtless date right back to the original domestication of dairy animals (Jashbhai & Baboo, 2003). The recipes and fermentation processes have been handed down from generation to generation, sometimes changing and giving rise to a new type of fermented milk.

There is an enormous diversity of names dedicated to these traditionally fermented milks throughout the world: they are all words used to describe a taste, texture or a specific acidity created through skill and specific strains. In the early years of milk fermentation, milk was simply allowed to ferment by its normal microbiota, but the process was not completely understood. Cultures were maintained by inoculating fresh milk with fermented milk (Kerr & McHale, 2001).

Traditional fermentation is a form of food processing where microbes, such as lactic acid bacteria (LAB), are used to preserve perishable food products. It is a form of food preservation technology. Over the years, it became part of the cultural and traditional norm in indigenous communities in most developing countries, especially in Africa. People came to prefer the fermented products to the unfermented foods. These products are an important constituent to the local diet and provide vital elements for growth, good health and an appreciated flavour. Traditional fermentations take place as a result of the activity of the natural flora present in the food or added from the surroundings. A widely known type of fermented milk is yoghurt, which is consumed throughout the world. Similar popularity has made fermented foods one of the main dietary components of the developing world.

Traditionally fermented milk is defined by Abdelbasset and Djamila (2008) as a dairy product obtained by the spontaneous fermentation of milk, which may have been made from products obtained from milk, with or without any modification of their composition, through the appropriate processes of microorganisms, which result in lowering the pH, with or without coagulation.

Fermentation

Fermentation is a cheap and energy-efficient way of preserving perishable raw materials; it is accessible and affordable to most people. However, to the microbiologist, the term 'fermentation' describes a form of energy-yielding microbial metabolism in which an organic substrate, usually a carbohydrate, is incompletely oxidized with an organic carbohydrate acting as the electron acceptor (Farhad, Kailasapathy, & Tamang, 2010). This definition means that processes involving ethanol production by yeasts or organic acid production by LAB are considered fermentations.

The microbiology of fermentation was first studied by Louis Pasteur in the 1850s and 1860s. He demonstrated that living cells caused fermentation (Ali, 2011). During fermentation, LAB and other microorganisms in the milk convert lactose into lactic acid, which in turn reduces the pH below the isoelectric point of most milk proteins. This causes coagulum or curd of gel-like uniformity to form, which results in the change of texture and sour flavour of the milk. This fermentation process increases the shelf life of the product, as well as adding to the taste and improving the digestibility of milk. Fermentation also improves the nutritional value of milk by, for example, releasing free amino acids or synthesizing vitamins (Kailasapathy, 2008).

TYPES OF TRADITIONALLY FERMENTED MILKS IN NAMIBIA

Each and every community has a distinct fermented milk product that symbolizes its heritage and the sociocultural aspects of its ethnicity. *Omashikwa, mashini ghakushika, mabisi* and *omaere* are some of the traditionally fermented milk products that are found in Namibia. Milk prepared by different communities is unique and distinct due to their geographical location, environmental factors, food preferences and the availability of natural ingredients. The processing method and the microbes that are involved in these types of milk products also differ. The technology and the processing methods to produce them depend on the indigenous knowledge of the community members, which is passed on orally from generation to generation. Little has been done in terms of their microbiological analysis. Only one study by Bille, Buys and Taylor (2007) has looked at the technological and sensory aspects of *omashikwa*.

Omashikwa

Omashikwa is the traditionally fermented buttermilk produced by local Aawambo farmers of the northern regions of Namibia (Oshana, Ohangwena, Oshikoto and Omusati). It is consumed as a refreshing drink and as a condiment for other foods, such as gruel or thick porridge made from maize or pearl millet (*omahangu* flour). *Omashikwa* is common during the rainy season, when there is enough food for the cattle.

Before milking in the morning, the cows are let out of the kraal to feed for about an hour to acquire energy. Milking is mostly done by men using an *eholo* – a bucket made from wood (Figure 8.1). The *omashikwa* is prepared by placing the milk in an *ohupa* (a gourd or calabash) or plastic container to which the roots of the *Boscia albitrunca* tree (locally known as *omunkuzi*) are added; it is allowed to ferment for two to three days at ambient temperatures, usually 30–37 °C. The root is believed to add flavour to the product, increase the rate of milk fermentation and help in churning the fermented milk (Bille et al., 2007). After fermentation, milk is churned by shaking the calabash for two to three hours until butter granules accumulate on top of the sour milk; then the roots are removed. The butter is then removed using a wire mesh or just one's hands. The butter granules are then washed using

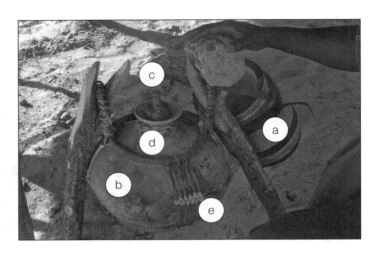

FIGURE 8.1:
(a) The calabash (*ohupa*) used to churn fermented milk; (b) the wooden bucket (*eholo*) used for milking; (c) the cap (*ekumbo*); (d) *oshedi* (lid holder) and (e) the woven calabash handles (*omalimango*). (© L. Heita.)

clean, cold, water to remove excess milk. The churned *omashikwa* is usually kept in plastic containers with or without lids, depending on the availability of utensils in the house. *Omashikwa* has a unique effervescent acid taste with a rooty flavour, and ropy appearance; the whey slowly separates off the curd when left undisturbed for some time (Bille, Ozuuko, & Ngwira, 2002).

The *eholo* is a traditional container used for milking (Figure 8.1b), which is carved from the *omboo* tree (*Vangueria infausta*). This tree is used because the wood does not crack when it is dry. The *eholo* is usually made during the rainy season because that is the time the tree is full of water and is softer. During the rainy season, most houses in northern Namibia usually grow *iitila* (gourd species) around the house, which are used to make the *ohupa* (Figure 8.1a), a traditional calabash that is made from a family of gourds well known in Oshikwanyama as *iitila oshikola* (gourd). Women are responsible for finding the big *oshikola* (big gourds) after the rainy season, that are suitable for making the *ohupa*. An opening at the top of the *oshikola* is made and all the seeds removed. Then the women weave around the opening of the calabash a bowl-shaped *oshedi* (Figure 8.1d) from palm leaves or string from outer root layers or strands of green bark (*omufuva*) of the *omwoolo* tree (*Terminalia sericea*). The *oshedi* holds the carved wooden calabash cap (*ekumbo*) in place (Figure 8.1c). Thereafter, the men weave handles from the outer layers (*omufuva*) of the *omushendje* tree (*Combretum zeyheri*) onto the calabash making the handles (*omalimango*; Figure 8.1e).

Mashini ghakushika

In the Kavango regions of Namibia, fermented milk is also common; here, it is called *mashini ghakushika*, which means 'churned milk'. The Aawambo and the Kavango people have similar ways of processing their traditionally fermented milk. *Mashini*

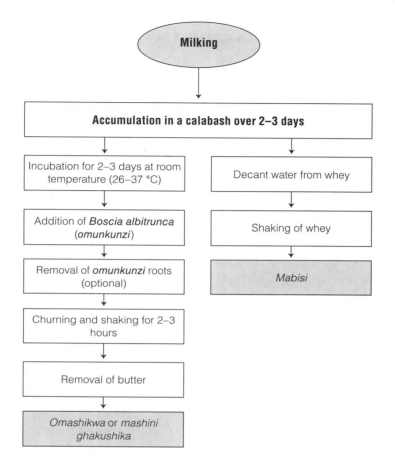

FIGURE 8.2: The household processes used to produce *omashikwa*, *mashini ghakushika* and *mabisi* from the northern and north-eastern regions of Namibia.

ghakushika is also prepared by collecting milk in a calabash and adding the roots of *omunkunzi* (*Boscia albitrunca*) or *mfughu* (*Sansevieria aethiopica*).

Masanza or *mabisi*

Masanza or *mabisi* is the fermented milk produced in Zambezi Region of north-eastern Namibia. This product is made by allowing milk to ferment in a calabash for two to three days until the whey is separated from the curd. The whey is then decanted, and the curd shaken until it is smooth. The fat is not removed.

The processes for the household preparation of the three above-mentioned fermented milk products are shown in Figure 8.2.

THE NUTRITIONAL VALUE OF NAMIBIAN FERMENTED MILK

The nutritional compositions of yoghurt and fermented milks are based on that of cow's milk from which they are made. Many factors influence the composition and nutritional quality of the milk: breed, region, season, time of milking and, of course, food intake. According to Branca and Rossi (2002), fermented milks are nutritionally enhanced to unfermented milk. A number of additional health benefits are attributed to the consumption of fermented milks, including: enhanced bioavailability of iron and calcium, as well as an excellent source of protein and phosphorus; control of undesirable pathogens in the gastrointestinal tract; improved immune response; enhanced lactose digestion; detoxification action; control of serum cholesterol; and lowering the blood pressure in hypertensive individuals (Panesar, 2011).

From a dietary point of view, fermented milk products in Namibia, such as *omashikwa*, *mabisi*, *omaere* and *mashini ghakushika*, are far more valuable than fresh milk. *Omashikwa* is broadly composed of 89.8% moisture and 10.2% total solids, with a pH of 3.25 and no whey separation (Bille et al., 2002). Of the solids, 1.6% is fat, while the remaining 8.6% of solids-not-fat is made up of 3.28% crude protein, 0.76% ash and 4.56% lactose (see Table 8.1). To date, no nutritional values are available for *mabisi*, *omaere* and *mashini ghakushika*.

Ghandi (2006) found that during the fermentation process, the composition of the minerals remains unchanged, while those of proteins, carbohydrates, vitamins and to some extent fat constituents change, which are responsible for the enhanced physiological effects of fermented milk products. Dietary and therapeutic qualities of sour milk products are determined by microorganisms and substances formed as a result of biochemical processes accompanying milk fermentation, such as lactic acid, alcohol, carbon dioxide, antibiotics and vitamins.

TABLE 8.1: Percentage composition of *omashikwa*

Components	Percentage (%)
Crude protein	3.28
Lactose	4.56
Ash	0.76
Solids-not-fat	8.60
Fat	1.60
Total solids	10.20
Moisture	89.80

Source: Bille et al. (2007)

MICROBIOLOGY OF NAMIBIAN FERMENTED MILK

Fermentation process

Fermentations can basically be performed either spontaneously by backslopping, or by adding starter cultures. Spontaneous, traditional fermentation of milk is caused by the natural microflora present in the milk, which consists of different species and strains of LAB and the associated growth of yeasts in minor proportions.

Lactic acid bacteria (LAB)

Lactic acid bacteria – or LAB – are a group of gram-positive bacteria from the genera *Bifidobacterium, Lactobacillus, Lactococcus, Leuconostoc, Pediococcus* and *Streptococcus* (Rattanachaikunsopon & Phumkhachorn, 2010). The general description of the bacteria included in this group is that they are gram-positive, non-spore-forming cocci or rods, which produce lactic acid as the major end product through the fermentation of carbohydrates. LAB are used in the production of fermented milk because they can produce several compounds that contribute to taste, smell, colour and texture of the milk product.

LAB are divided into two main groups based on the end products they form during the fermentation of glucose. Homofermentative LAB, such as *Pediococcus* spp., *Streptococcus* spp., *Lactococcus* spp. and some *Lactobacillus* spp. produce lactase or lactic acid as the major or sole end product of glucose fermentation (see Figure 8.3a). The second group – heterofermentative LAB – ferment glucose with lactic acid, ethanol or acetic acid, and carbon dioxide (CO_2) as by-products (Figure 8.3b). Testing for heterofermentative fermentation generally involves the detection of gas (CO_2). With the exception of certain fermented milk products, heterofermentative LAB are hardly ever used as dairy starter cultures. Heterofermentative LAB include *Leuconostoc* spp. (gram-positive cocci) and gram-positive rods, such as *Lactobacillus brevis, L. fermentum* and *L. reuteri*.

Traditional milks are fermented using traditional utensils towards which the environment and hygiene is not considered, hence, specific microorganisms are introduced that are responsible for the rich, full and unique flavours found in traditionally fermented milk. These cannot easily be imitated by modern dairy starter cultures.

In Namibia, traditionally fermented milk is mostly found in rural areas and open markets. The market for this type of milk is relatively narrow; it is sold in recycled plastic containers, which do not display any information on the milk product. Furthermore, it is not stored in a fridge or freezer. Therefore, most people who are conscious of health standards shy away from buying it. Fermented milk products

FIGURE 8.3:
Equations showing
(a) homolactic
fermentation and
(b) heterolactic
fermentation.

(a) $C_6H_{12}O_6 \rightarrow 2CH_3CHOH \cdot COOH$
glucose → 2 moles of lactic acid

(b) $C_6H_{12}O_6 \rightarrow CH_3CHOH \cdot COOH + C_2H_5OH + CO_2$
glucose → lactate + ethanol + carbon dioxide

are, however, part of the daily diet of small children in villages, who are better nourished than urban children.

There are four main species of LAB found in Namibian traditionally fermented milk, the cultures of each having their own characteristic shapes and appearance (Figure 8.4). The dominant species belong to the genus *Lactobacillus* (Figure 8.5) making up 42% of the microflora. According to Akabanda, Owusu-Kwarteng, Glover and Tano-Debrah (2010), the microflora present in milk depends on the climatic conditions of the area where the milk was collected. Thus, traditionally fermented milk from regions with a cold climate was found to contain mesophilic bacteria, such as

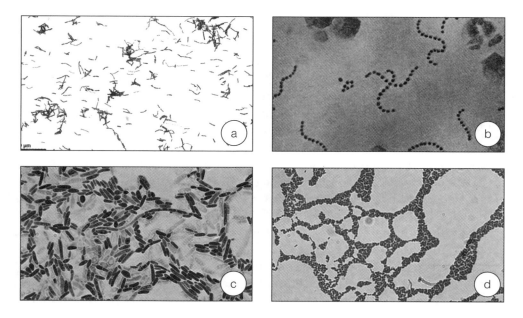

FIGURE 8.4: Lactic acid bacterial species found in Namibian traditionally fermented milk products come from four genera, (a) *Lactobacillus*, (b) *Streptococcus*, (c) *Bacillus* and (d) *Lactococcus*.

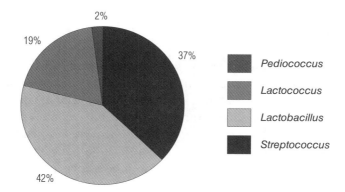

2%

19%

37%

42%

Pediococcus

Lactococcus

Lactobacillus

Streptococcus

FIGURE 8.5: The proportions of dominant microflora of traditionally fermented milk products (*omashikwa, mabisi* and *mashini ghakushika*) in Namibia.

Lactococcus spp. and *Leuconostoc* spp., whilst thermophilic bacteria, such as *Lactobacillus* spp. and *Streptococcus* spp., prevailed in regions with hot, subtropical or tropical climates.

PHYSICOCHEMICAL PROPERTIES OF NAMIBIAN FERMENTED MILK

pH

The acidity or alkalinity of a solution is described by its pH. It is actually a measure of the concentration of hydrogen ions in solution; a low pH indicates acidic conditions and a high pH indicates basic (alkaline) conditions. Fermented foods are normally considered to be safe against food-borne pathogens because of their low pH. The pH in lactic-acid fermented foods is usually reduced to less than 4, which is usually sufficient to suppress the growth of most food-borne pathogens (Gadaga, Nyanga, & Mutukumira, 2004).

The average pH of traditionally fermented milk from the five northern regions studied ranged between 3.54 (Oshana) to 3.77 (Zambezi) (Figure 8.6). The root of the shepherd's tree (*omunkunzi*; *Boscia albitrunca*) has a significant lowering effect on the pH of fermented milk (Bille, 2013). Samet-Bali, Ayadi and Attia (2012) reported that low pH had an effect on cell growth, lactose utilization and lactic acid production. The process of producing *mabisi* does not involve the addition of any natural product, also no churning of the butter, which could explain why *mabisi* (produced in Zambezi) has a higher pH than the two other types of fermented milk produced in the other regions.

Titratable acidity

Titratable acidity is a measure of freshness and bacterial activity in milk. A number of organic acids are known to occur in fermented milk, including lactic, citric, orotic, sialic, benzoic and sorbic, amongst others. Organic acids are produced as end products, which create an acidic environment that is unfavourable for the growth of many pathogenic and spoilage microorganisms. The predominant organic acid in raw milk is citric acid (Urbienė & Leskauskaitė, 2006). The levels and types of organic acids produced during the fermentation process depend on the species of microorganisms, culture composition, growth conditions, fermentation environment and the state of raw materials (Rattanachaikunsopon & Phukhachorn, 2010).

The concentration of acetic acid within the three types of fermented milk collected from various sample sites was found to be 0.022–0.130% in *omashikwa*, 0.484–0.956% in *mabisi* and 0.037–0.040% in *mashini ghakushika* (Figure 8.7a). Meanwhile the concentration of lactic acid was found to be 0.015–0.048% in *omashikwa*, 0.015–0.026% in *mabisi* and 0.194–0.592% in *mashini ghakushika* (Figure 8.7b). The samples from Zambezi region (*mabisi*) were found to have the highest acetic acid concentrations, in comparison to samples from other regions (Figure 8.8). Lactic acid concentrations were found to be highest (up to 1.4%) in *mashini ghakushika* samples from the Kavango regions (Figure 8.9). The ratio of lactic acid to acetic acid in the samples varied from 1:2 to 1:1.

Antimicrobial compounds of LAB

LAB are able to produce a variety of compounds, which contribute to the flavour, colour, texture and consistency of fermented milk. They also inhibit the growth and activity of other microorganisms. LAB can therefore be used as protective cultures to improve the microbial safety of foods by inhibiting pathogens such as *Staphylococcus aureus*, *Salmonella* spp. and *Listeria monocytogenes*; they also play an important role in the preservation of fermented foods, by inhibiting spoilage bacteria, such as *Pseudomonas* spp. (Mobolaji & Wuraola, 2011). The primary antimicrobial effect exerted by LAB is through the production of lactic acid and reduction of pH (Khay, Castro, Bernárdez, Senhaji, & Idaomar, 2011). In addition, LAB produce various antimicrobial compounds that can be classified as low-molecular-mass compounds, such as hydrogen peroxide (H_2O_2), carbon dioxide (CO_2), diacetyl (butane-2,3-dione or butanedione), uncharacterized compounds, and high-molecular-mass compounds, such as bacteriocins (Ammor, Tauveron, Dufour, & Chevallier, 2006). See Figure 8.10.

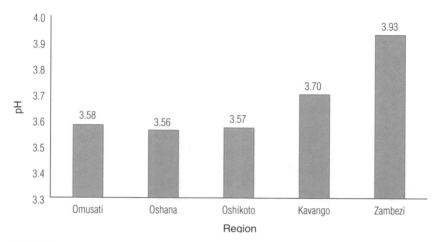

FIGURE 8.6: Average pH of fermented milk products from Omusati, Oshana, Oshikoto, Kavango West and East and Zambezi regions.

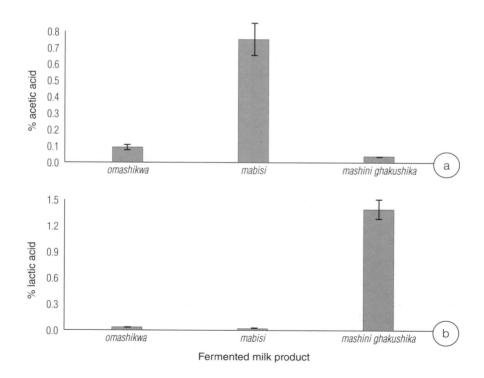

FIGURE 8.7: The percentage of (a) acetic acid and (b) lactic acid in three traditionally fermented milk products in Namibia.

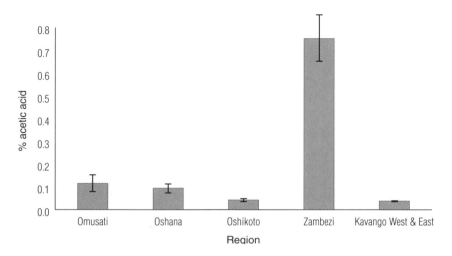

FIGURE 8.8: Percentage of acetic acid in traditionally fermented milk samples from different villages in Omusati, Oshana, Oshikoto, Kavango West and East, and Zambezi regions of Namibia.

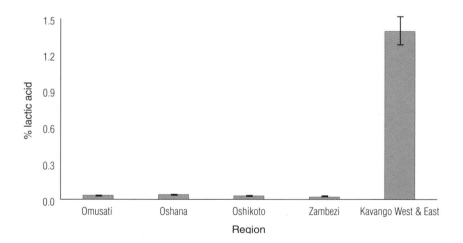

FIGURE 8.9: Percentage of lactic acid in traditionally fermented milk samples from different regions in Omusati, Oshana, Oshikoto, Kavango West and East, and Zambezi regions of Namibia.

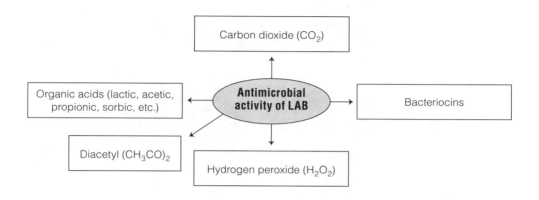

FIGURE 8.10: The primary antimicrobial compounds of lactic acid bacteria.

SOCIOECONOMIC AND HEALTH BENEFITS OF NAMIBIAN FERMENTED MILK

Socioeconomic values

Locally fermented foods, especially milk products have a role to play in developing economies in Namibia. It enables citizens with few resources to transform and succeed, which will assist in eliminating or reducing poverty, ignorance and disease, so that the nation can live in dignity. Fermented milk products play a significant socioeconomic role in Namibia.

Food security

Locally fermented milk products promote and improve milk processing and preservation at all levels, which are essential components of Namibia's Vision 2030 to achieve national food security. If adequately developed into an industrial scale, Namibia's fermentation technology also has the potential of helping to meet the country's food needs. Fermented milk is widely consumed by most marginalized and vulnerable groups in Namibia, especially those living in rural areas, being eaten with soft porridge by children and *pap* (a stiff porridge) by elders.

Provision of employment opportunities

Apart from the nutritional properties of fermented milk products, the production of them provides occupations for women and youth who sell them at open markets.

FIGURE 8.11:
Traditionally
fermented milk for
sale at an open
market in Omuthiya,
Oshikoto Region.
(© L. Heita.)

Due to increases in living costs, and limited employment opportunities in the formal sector, more people are running their own businesses. In the near future, fermented milk products could provide more job opportunities as a result of upcoming research in indigenous knowledge in Namibia. Small-scale markets in rural areas can help reduce rural–urban migration and its associated social problems. In addition, the availability of fermented milk products reduces the dependency of rural and urban populations on food imports, and provides producers and sellers with a source of income (Figure 8.11).

Poverty alleviation

Fermented milk is highly nutritious and forms a significant component of the diets of people in rural areas. It is eaten with *pap* or given to small children with a soft porridge. This contributes to a balanced diet and helps to combat malnutrition and alleviate poverty in Namibia. Fermented milks serve as food supplements as well. For example, *omashikwa* can be eaten as a relish. In addition, cattle herders occasionally eat a meal called *olumbololo*, which is a mixture of *omahangu* flour and fermented milk, because they do not usually have time to cook.

Health benefits of fermented milk

The health benefits of milk and fermented milk products have been known since age-old times. Drinking milk provides extensive nutritional value to children, as well as to adults and the elderly. Fermented milk products, however, contain live cultures, which can help restore the correct balance of intestinal flora, boost the immune system, prevent gastrointestinal infections, aid digestion and help to ease other health disorders in addition to their nutritional value (Ebringer, Ferenčík, & Krajčovič, 2008). Fermented milks also have beneficial physiological properties, they:

1. Balance intestinal pH balance and improve gastric emptying
2. Alleviate constipation
3. Assist in the digestion of lactose and alleviate lactose intolerance
4. Lower serum cholesterol
5. Have antiallergenic properties.

The availability of calcium is also increased after fermented milk ingestion. Not all fermented milks are equally beneficial – their health benefits depend on the species and strain of the bacteria used.

OTHER TYPES OF MILK PRODUCTS IN NAMIBIA

Traditional butter (*omagadhi gongombe*)

It is not only fermented milk products that are produced, but others too. The Aawambo also make butter, which is commonly used for cooking. It is known as *omagadhi gongombe* by the Oshindonga-speaking people and *omaadi eengobe* by Oshikwanyama-speaking people. The butter is semi-solid and golden-yellow in colour. It is not really found in urban areas, but common in rural areas. This traditional butter is valued socially by the Aawambo and usually served to visitors to symbolize their importance.

Apart from being used as a food, the uncooked butter (*ongudi*) is used in traditional rituals, such as weddings. The night before the wedding, the bride's body is smeared with the *ongudi* (lard), which is usually mixed with *oshide*, the pink powder made from *Omuuva* tree (*Pterocarpus angolensis*) which serves as a symbol of good luck and blessing to the bride so that she may own many cattle in the future.

Omagadhi gongombe is a by-product of the process to make *omashikwa*. The butter granules that collect on top of the fermented buttermilk are removed and washed. They are then boiled in a pot until the foam disappears and the oil turns a golden-yellow or brown colour with dark brown sediment. The oil is left to stand in the pot while the sediment settles. Before it hardens, the oil is decanted and sometimes filtered using cloth into clean plastic containers or laminated tins for storage in order to prevent tampering or contamination. *Omagadhi gongombe* is characterized by its short shelf life, high moisture and sediment contents, and rancid and oxidized flavours.

CONCLUSION

Traditionally fermented milk in Namibia is a highly nutritious food product that forms an important part of the diet of many rural people. The household processing methods to produce fermented milks differ slightly, which has a significant effect on the taste, texture and quality of the final product. The pH decreased over the fermentation period, from 6.5 on the first day of fermentation to 3.54 over four days (Oshana Region). There was no significant difference ($p<0.05$) in the pH values between the three types of fermented milk preparations. The concentration of acetic acid was found to be 0.022–0.130% in *omashikwa*, 0.484–0.956% in *mabisi* and 0.037–0.040% in *mashini ghakushika*. Lactic acid was found to be 0.015–0.048% in *omashikwa*, 0.015–0.026% in *mabisi* and 0.194–0.592% in *mashini ghakushika*. They are able to produce a variety of compounds, which contribute to the flavour, colour, texture and consistency of these fermented milk products. These LAB strains should be tested for their biotechnological properties and microbial interactions. This will enable product development and innovation for dairy products in Namibia.

ACKNOWLEDGMENTS

This research project is fully funded by the Directorate of Research, Science and Technology (DRST) of the Ministry of Education (now called National Commission on Research Science and Technology (NCRST)). The authors would also like to thank the Multidisciplinary Research Centre for financial support.

References

Abdelbasset, M., & Djamila, K. (2008). Antimicrobial activity of autochthonous lactic acid bacteria isolated from Algerian traditional fermented milk 'Raïb'. *African Journal of Biotechnology*, 7(16), 2908-2914.

Akabanda, F., Owusu-Kwarteng, J., Glover, R. L. K., & Tano-Debrah, K. (2010). Microbiological characteristics of Ghanaian traditional fermented milk product, *nunu*. *Nature and Science*, 8(9), 178-187.

Ali, A. A. (2011). Isolation and Identification of lactic acid bacteria isolated from traditional drinking yoghurt in Khartoum State, Sudan. *Current Research in Bacteriology*, 4(1), 16-22.

Ammor, S., Tauveron, G., Dufour, E., & Chevallier, I. (2006). Antibacterial activity of lactic acid bacteria against spoilage and pathogenic bacteria isolated from the same meat small-scale facility: 1–Screening and characterization of the antibacterial compounds. *Food Control, 17*(6), 454-461.

Bille, P. G. 2013. Effect of *Boscia Albitrunca (Omukunzi)* Root on the Bacteriology and Viscosity of Omashikwa, Traditional Fermented Buttermilk from Namibia. *African Journal of Food, Agriculture, Nutrition and Development. Vol 13*(4), 7927.

Bille, P. G., Buys, E., & Taylor J. R. N. (2007). Technology and properties of traditional fermented buttermilk (*omashikwa*) processed with plant roots (*Boscia albitrunca – omunkunzi*) by small-holder communal farmers in northern Namibia. *International Journal of Food Science & Technology, 43*(5), 620-624.

Bille, P. G., Ozuuko, A. T. R., & Ngwira, T. (2002). Sensory properties of traditionally fermented buttermilk (*omashikwa*) processed in Namibia. *The Journal of Food Technology in Africa, 7*(2), 52-54.

Branca, F., & Rossi, L. (2002). The role of fermented milk in complementary feeding of young children: Lessons from transition countries. *European Journal of Clinical Nutrition, 56*(4), 16-20.

Carr, F. J., Chill, D., & Maida, N. (2002). The lactic acid bacteria: A literature survey. *Critical Reviews in Microbiology, 28*(4), 281-370.

Chandan, R. C., & Shah, N. P. (2013). Functional foods and disease prevention. In R. C. Chandan, C. H. White, A. Kilara, & Y. H. Hui (Eds.), *Manufacturing yoghurt and fermented milks* (pp. 311-326). Oxford, United Kingdom: Wiley Blackwell.

Ebringer, L., Ferenčík, K., & Krajčovič, J. (2008). Beneficial health effects of milk and fermented dairy products – Review. *Folia Microbiology, 53*(5), 378-394.

Farhad, M., Kailasapathy, K., & Tamang, J. P. (2010). Health aspects of fermented foods. In J. P. Tamang, & K. Kailasapathy (Eds.), *Fermented foods and beverages of the world* (pp. 391-414). New York, USA: CRC Press.

Gadaga, T. H., Nyanga, L. K., & Mutukumira, A. N. (2004). The occurrence, growth and control of pathogens in African fermented foods. *African Journal Food, Agriculture, Nutrition and Development, 4*(1). Retrieved from http://bioline.org.br/request?nd04009

Gandhi, D. N. (2006). Food and industrial microbiology: Microbiology of fermented dairy products. Retrieved from http://nsdl.niscair.res.in/jspui/bitstream/123456789/117/1/dairymicrobiology.pdf

Jashbhai, B. P., & Baboo, M. N. (2003). The history of fermented food. In E. R. Farnworth (Ed.), *Handbook of fermented functional foods* (pp. 1-24). New York, USA: CRC Press.

Kailasapathy, K. (2008). Chemical composition, physical and functional properties of milk and milk ingredients. In R. C. Chandan, A. Kilara, & N. Shah (Eds.), *Dairy processing and quality assurance* (pp. 75-103). Ames, Iowa, USA: Wiley Blackwell.

Kerr, T. J., & McHale, B. B. (2001). *Applications in general microbiology: A laboratory manual.* Winston-Salem, USA: Hunter Textbooks.

Khay, E. O., Castro, L. M. P., Bernárdez, P. F., Senhaji, N. S., & Idaomar, M. (2011). Growth of *Enterococcus durans* E204 producing bacteriocin-like substance in MRS broth: Description of the growth and quantification of the bacteriocin-like substance. *African Journal of Biotechnology, 11*(3), 659-665.

Panesar, P. S. (2011). Fermented dairy products: Starter cultures and potential nutritional benefits. *Food and Nutrition Sciences, 2*(1), 47-51.

Rattanachaikunsopon, P., & Phumkhachorn, P. (2010). Lactic acid bacteria: Their antimicrobial compounds and their uses in food production. *Annals of Biological Research, 1*(4), 218-228.

Rolle, R., & Satin, M. (2002). Basic requirements for the transfer of fermentation technologies to developing countries. *International Journal of Food Microbiology, 75*(3), 181-187.

Samet-Bali, O., Ayadi, M. A., & Attia, H. (2012). Development of fermented milk 'Leben' made from spontaneous fermented cow's milk. *African Journal of Biotechnology, 11*(7), 1829-1837.

Steinkraus, K. H. (2002) Fermentations in world food processing. *Comprehensive Reviews in Food Science Food Safety, 1*(1), 23-32.

Urbienė, S., & Leskauskaitė, D. (2006). Formation of some organic acids during fermentation of milk. *Polish Journal of Food and Nutrition Sciences, 15/56*(3), 277-281.

9

Oshikundu: An indigenous fermented beverage

Werner Embashu, Ahmad Cheikhyoussef & Gladys Kahaka

INTRODUCTION

Oshikundu is a common beverage in Oshana, Omusati, Ohangwena, Oshikoto and Kavango West and East regions of Namibia. As in many parts of Africa, cereal foods and beverages form part of the daily diet in these regions. Cereal beverages, such as *oshikundu*, undergo fermentation, which is a natural process that has been used for many years as an economical form of food preservation. Fermentation kills harmful microorganisms and prolongs the shelf life of basic foodstuffs; it also enhances the nutritional value and organoleptic quality of them, as it does to their quality and stability.

Oshikundu fermentation is dominated by lactic acid bacteria (LAB). The use of LAB offers many advantages, such as increasing food palatability and improving the quality of foods and beverages. Using starter cultures has led to the large-scale production of fermented cereal beverages in many parts of the world. However, the inconsistency of the organoleptic properties of *oshikundu* remains a challenge in household processing technology. Consumer choice is greatly influenced by the sensory attributes of *oshikundu*, such as its aroma and taste. Furthermore, the brewing technology depends on backslopping of an unknown starter culture, preventing the successful production of it on a large scale. Commercializing the production of *oshikundu* would guarantee the use of local traditional resources, help preserve local culture, create jobs and ultimately help reduce poverty (Mu Ashekele, Embashu, & Cheikhyoussef, 2012). In addition, applying biotechnology to the brewing process and improving the quality of starter cultures is very important to which several approaches could then be applied, such as genetic manipulation, biofortification and biocatalysis.

Cereal foods and beverages

Cereal-based fermented foods and beverages have become of interest to researchers in recent years, especially the indigenous fermented products. Cereals are the most important staple sources of energy in the world, more especially in Africa and India (Adebayo, Otunola, & Ajao, 2010). These cereals can supply sufficient quantities of quality carbohydrates, fats, proteins, fibre and minerals such as calcium, iron, zinc, copper and manganese (Hulse, Laing, & Pearson, 1980; Adebayo et al., 2010; Hui et al., 2012). However, cereal-based diets, as they are in most African countries, are high in carbohydrates, but deficient in vitamins and protein.

Millet tops the list of the common staple cereal foods in Africa, with pearl millet (*Pennisetum glaucum*) and maize (*Zea mays*) being the most common in Namibia. Pearl millet has also been shown to have several therapeutic uses, such as inhibiting cancer, controlling blood pressure, and treating severe constipation and stomach ulcers, and it is antiallergenic (Nambiar, Sareen, Daniel, & Gallego, 2012). In Namibia, half of the population consumes pearl millet mainly as porridge, which is rich in unsaturated fatty acids (Nantanga, Seetharaman, de Kock, & Taylor, 2008). Products from millet are greatly influenced by people's taste and cultural preferences (Adebayo et al., 2010). These products significantly enhance human nutrition and health (Musaiger, Ahmed, & Rao, 2000).

Diversity of cereal-based beverages in Namibia

Namibia has a bewildering variety of cereal-based beverages as a result of cultural diversification. The manufacturing processes of these beverages vary depending on the availability of raw materials, beverage group, ingredients used and, most importantly, cultural diversity (Hui et al., 2012). There are alcoholic and non-alcoholic beverages, but all are brewed from cereal grains such as maize, *mahangu* and sorghum.

Foods and beverages uniquely identify the different cultures in Namibia, and become trademarks. In the southern regions of Namibia, you commonly find *mahau*, a maize-based fermented beverage. In the north and north-east you find *otombo*, *omalovu giilya* (sorghum beer), *epwaka*, *okatokele*, *efau*, *omagongo*, *ombike*, *chikontini*, *chinyungela* and *munati*. Some of the beverages from different cultures are similar, if not the same; only the names differ with different languages and slight differences in preparation techniques.

Oshikundu history

Oshikundu (Figure 9.1) is an *Oshiwambo* word derived from *oshikundifa*, which literally means, 'greetings' in Oshikwanyama. *Oshikundu* is served to greet guests during social visits, before conversation begins to break the ice. It is a non-alcoholic

FIGURE 9.1:
Oshikundu beverage.
(© Werner Embashu.)

beverage brewed in northern and north-eastern Namibia using water, pearl millet bran, pearl millet meal (locally known as *omahangu*) and sorghum (*Sorghum bicolor*) malt. *Oshikundu* is brown in colour with a slightly viscous consistency. It is mostly associated with the Aawambo people in the Omusati, Oshana, Ohangwena and Oshikoto regions, but is also occasionally brewed by the people of the Kavango West and East regions.

Food fermentations

Africa has an almost bewildering variety of traditionally fermented foods and beverages. Fermented foods and beverages are defined as those products that have been subjected to the effects of microorganisms or enzymes to cause desirable biochemical changes (Blandino, Al-Aseeri, Pandiella, Cantero, & Webb, 2003). Fermentation is one of the oldest and most economical forms of food preservation in the world (Blandino et al., 2003; Chelule, Mbongwa, Carries, & Gqaleni, 2010; Rhee, Lee, & Lee, 2011). Traditionally fermented products are characterized by LAB, yeasts, moulds and, to some extent, *Bacillus* spp. (Sanni, 1993; Blandino et al., 2003; Jespersen, 2003; Vieira-Dolodé et al., 2007). Although fermentation generally improves shelf life, nutritional values, food safety and organoleptic quality, product quality and stability are variable because the technology relies on backslopping and spontaneous fermentations (Mukisa et al., 2012).

Fermentation is classified as alcoholic, acidic or alkaline (Hui et al., 2012). Alcoholic fermentation produces ethanol and carbon dioxide as the main product from sugar metabolism carried out by yeast – beer, for example; acidic fermentation results in the production of acid (and pH reduction) from sugar metabolism, such as lactic acid by LAB; alkaline fermentation involves ammonia production from amino acid deamination, which increases pH (Blandino et al., 2003; Hui et al., 2012).

Fermentation can be also classified as either natural or controlled (Pfeiler & Klaenhammer, 2007). A natural fermentation is carried out by the microflora naturally present in the product at harvest. The product is often first treated with salt, for example, to limit the growth of undesirable microorganisms, but allow desirable microorganisms to grow. Most plant fermentations, such as sauerkraut production, are natural fermentations. In a controlled fermentation, the product is first treated to eliminate or control the natural microflora and then a starter culture is added to carry out the process. Historically, this was accomplished by inoculating fresh material with a portion of the fermented product, a technique known as backslopping. Many fermented dairy products such as yogurt are produced through controlled fermentation.

Fermentation plays a number of roles in the processing of foods and beverages (Steinkraus, 1994; Kohajdová & Karovičová, 2007):

1. It enhances the human diet through development of a wide diversity of flavours, aromas and textures.
2. It plays a role in preserving substantial amounts of food through lactic acid, alcoholic, acetic acid and alkaline fermentations.
3. It enriches food substances biologically with proteins, essential amino acids, essential fatty acids and vitamins.
4. It is also involved in the detoxification of foods and beverages.
5. It decreases cooking time and fuel requirements.

Flavour is one of the sensory attributes that is transformed by fermentation. During cereal fermentation, several compounds are formed that contribute to a complex blend of flavours (Table 9.1). For example, diacetyl, acetic acid and butyric acids make fermented cereal-based products more appetizing (Kohajdová & Karovičová, 2007).

Carbohydrates, proteins, lipids, organic acids, amino acids, phenol compounds and glycosides are transformed into non-volatile and volatile flavour compounds that affect taste and aroma and enhance beverage acceptability (Hui et al., 2012). Hence, flavour diversification is an emerging trend because of consumer demand for novel and diverse flavours. These flavour compounds have a profound impact on a range of other sensory attributes such as sweetness (e.g., mannitol), sourness (e.g., lactic acid), savouriness or umami (e.g., L-glutamic acid), bitterness (e.g., hydrophobic peptides), fruitiness (ester) and sulphurous notes (volatile sulphur compound) (Hui et al., 2012).

Lactic acid bacteria

Lactic acid bacteria (LAB) are a large group of closely related bacteria that are gram-positive, catalase-negative, non-sporing rods or cocci that utilize carbohydrates and have similar properties in lactic acid production, which is an end product of

TABLE 9.1: Compounds formed during cereal fermentation.

Organic acids	Alcohols	Aldehydes and ketones	Carbonyl compounds
acetic	amyl alcohol	acetaldehyde	furfural
benzylic	2,3-butandieol	acetoin	glyoxal
butyric	ethanol	acetone	hydroxymethyl furfural
n-butyric	isoamyl alcohol	butanone	methional
capric	isobutanol	diacetyl	3-methyl butanal
caproic	β-phenylethyl alcohol	formaldehyde	2-methyl butanal
caprylic	n-propanol	n-hexaldehyde	
crotonic		isobutryaldehyde	
formic		isovaleraldehyde	
hepatonic		2-methyl butanol	
hydrocinnamic		methyl ethyl ketone	
isoburyic		propionaldehyde	
isocaprilic		n-valderaldehyde	
isovaleric			
itaconic			
lactic			
lauric			
mevulinic			
myristic			
palmitic			
pleagronic			
propionic			
pyruvic			
succinic			
valeric			

Adapted from Campbell-Platt (1994).

fermentation (Blandino et al., 2003; Chelule et al., 2010). Examples of LAB genera involved in cereal fermentation are shown in Table 9.2 (McKay & Baldwin, 1990; Oberman & Libudzisk, 1996; Šušković, Kos, Matošić, & Marić, 1997; Blandino et al., 2003).

Lactic acid fermentation is widely applied in tropical climates as a low-cost method for enhancing food quality, safety and shelf life (Nout & Sarkar, 1999). Some of the main reasons for this fermentation practice – using LAB – are to increase food palatability and improve the quality of food by increasing the availability of proteins and vitamins. Furthermore, LAB confer preservative, detoxifying and antimicrobial effects on food (Chelule et al., 2010; Rhee et al., 2011). The antimicrobial effects are due to acid action in the bacterial cytoplasmatic membrane, which interferes with normal cell physiology (Blandino et al., 2003). Consequently, this contributes

TABLE 9.2: Characteristics of genera of lactic acid bacteria (LAB) involved in cereal fermentation.

Genus	Cell form	Catalase production	Gram stain reaction
Aerococcus	cocci	−	+
Bifidobacterium	branched rods	−	+
Carnobacterium	cocci	−	+
Enterococcus	cocci	−	+
Lactobacillus	rods	−	+
Lactococcus	cocci	−	+
Lactosphaera	cocci	−	+
Leuconostoc	spheres in chains (cocci)	−	+
Oenococcus	cocci	−	+
Pediococcus	spheres in tetrads (cocci)	−	+
Sporolactobacillus	rods	−	+
Streptococcus	spheres in chains (cocci)	−	+
Vagococcus	cocci	−	+
Weissella	cocci	−	+

− = negative   + = positive

Adapted from McKay and Baldwin (1990), Oberman and Libudzisk (1996), Šušković et al. (1997) and Blandino et al. (2003).

towards increased nutritional value, shelf life, acceptability and most importantly food safety.

Beverages are often prepared in unsterile conditions, and the resulting microbial community composition will be of a mixed nature (Nout & Sarkar, 1999). LAB are often the dominant organisms in addition to yeasts, which are present in considerable numbers (Vogel et al., 1999). Lactic acid fermentation occurs during the preparation of foods and beverages made from raw plant and animal material (Nout & Sarkar, 1999). LAB are most likely to be responsible for the fermentation of *oshikundu* from its cereal base, and for conferring some of its organoleptic properties.

OSHIKUNDU

Household processing methods

The traditional art of *oshikundu* brewing is passed on orally from generation to generation; no formal channels of instruction are followed in this knowledge transfer.

Omahangu and sorghum grains are stored in *omashisha* (large storage baskets) (Figure 9.2a), crafted from the mopane tree (*Colophospermum mopane*). *Omahangu*

FIGURE 9.2: (a) *Omashisha* baskets for storing *omahangu*; (b) pounding *omahangu* grain using a traditional pestle and mortar; (c) *omahangu* meal in *oshimbale*; (d) sorghum malt in *oshimbale*. (© Werner Embashu.)

seeds are decorticated using a traditional pestle and mortar to remove the husks (Figure 9.2b). The bran is separated from the grain by sieving. The grains are then soaked in water (steeping) for 4–24 hours before being ground into flour or meal using a traditional pestle and mortar or by mechanical crushing. The sorghum seeds are covered under sandy soil, which is occasionally sprinkled with water from the hand until the seeds start to germinate (a process known as malting). During malting, enzymes such as amylase are produced, which hydrolyze the starch in the seeds to sugar (Dewar & Taylor, 1999). The sand is then sieved from the grains, which are ground into a meal using a traditional pestle and mortar. The *omahangu* and malted sorghum meals are sundried before they are stored in a traditional clay pot (*oluyo*) or basket woven from the makalani palm (*Hyphaene petersiana*), known as *oshimbale* (Figures 9.2c and d).

It is usually the women and girls in the households who brew the *oshikundu*. It involves a few steps (Figure 9.3). Boiled water is mixed with *omahangu* meal and the thick mixture is left to cool to about room temperature, before the malted sorghum meal is added. This step is regarded as the crucial step in determining the flavour of *oshikundu*. Addition of malted sorghum meal to the mixture while it is hot, gives a tasteless *oshikundu*. Malted sorghum also plays an important role in the fermentation of *oshikundu*. The malting process produces enzymes, such as amylase,

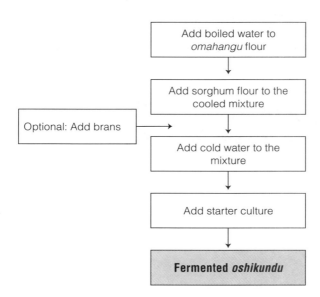

FIGURE 9.3: A flow chart outlining the traditional process for making *oshikundu*. This was compiled after gathering information through a questionnaire distributed to a number of households in different regions in Namibia.

which hydrolyze the grain's starch to sugar (glucose and maltose) thus freeing sugars for LAB to metabolize and produce the fermented *oshikundu* (Taylor, 2004).

Bran (if available) is added to the *omahangu* and sorghum mixture, which gives *oshikundu* a rich brown colour. Cold water is then added to dilute the wort. Backslopping follows, which is the addition of previously fermented *oshikundu* and usually the sediment that settles at the bottom. The mixture is covered and left to ferment for up to eight hours into *oshikundu*.

Socioeconomic value

Oshikundu is an important beverage that serves many purposes. It is a home beverage that is given to both the elderly and children. In many villages in northern Namibia, it is common practice for children to take *oshikundu* to school every day, forming part of their daily diet. It is also served during social visits and other social gatherings. A household that does not offer *oshikundu* to its guests is perceived to be unwelcoming and, in some cases, such a household may be assumed to be poverty stricken. *Oshikundu* is also fed to orphaned livestock – kids and calves – a popular practice among the Aawambo. *Oshikundu* is an important beverage drunk during work in the fields and work done in the household. In towns, women sell *oshikundu* providing a source of income to their households. It is easy and economical to brew in terms of raw materials, since many grow *omahangu* and sorghum in their fields.

Physicochemical properties

Titratable acidity and pH has a particular impact on food and beverage quality (Sadler & Murphy, 2010). Total acidity is the measurement of total acid concentration. Inorganic acids, such as phosphoric and carbonic acids, play an important role in food and beverage acidulation. The organic acids present in foods and beverages influence the flavour (tartness), colour (through anthocyanin and other pH-influenced pigments) and microbial stability (via inherent pH-sensitive characteristics of organisms), and maintain quality (arising from varying chemical sensitivities of food components to pH) (Sadler & Murphy, 2010).

Nielson's (1998) method was used to determine the titratable acidity and pH of *oshikundu*. The pH of *oshikundu* tested from various villages in northern Namibia was found to range from 3.14 to 3.56 (Figure 9.4). At such low pH, pathogenic bacteria such as *Salmonella typhimurium* are destroyed (Dewar & Taylor, 1999). This makes *oshikundu* an important beverage in rural areas, because it is not likely to contain potentially harmful bacteria. Hence, few cases (if any) of food poisoning from *oshikundu* are reported. Despite its safety, it is worth noting that not all people have access to clean water to use in the brewing process.

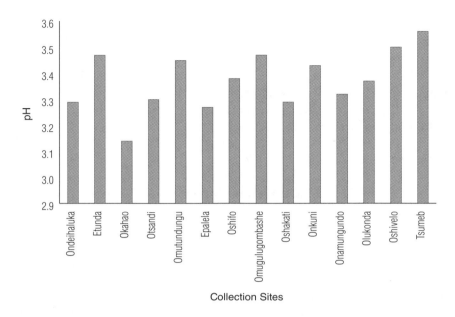

FIGURE 9.4: The pH of *oshikundu* samples from different villages in Oshana, Oshikoto, Ohangwena and Omusati regions.

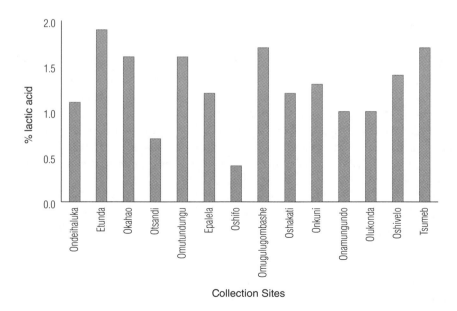

FIGURE 9.5: Percentage lactic acid of *oshikundu* samples from different villages in Oshana, Oshikoto, Ohangwena and Omusati regions.

Lactic acid concentration of these samples of *oshikundu* ranged from 0.44% to 1.93% (Figure 9.5) and acetic acid concentration ranged from 0.009% to 0.040% (Figure 9.6). Lactic acid was found to be high in comparison to acetic acid, due to the domination of LAB during *oshikundu* fermentation. The acidity may be attributable to a variety of bacterial species in the fermentation of *oshikundu*, which have not yet been scientifically characterized.

Nutritional value and chemical composition

African beverages are not known only to quench thirst, but are also known for their nutritional contribution to humans' diets. This is brought about by the complex micro- and macronutrients required by the human body. Cereal foods and beverages, including *oshikundu*, are the most important sources of dietary proteins, carbohydrates, minerals and fibre (Blandino et al., 2003; Kohajdová & Karovičová, 2007).

Oshikundu is very moist (96% water), which is consistent with the amount of water used in brewing. Water is an important component of daily intake and forms part of the diet. Not all people, especially adults, drink adequate amounts of water. *Oshikundu* can serve as a source of water. Total solids were found to be 3.9%. With such a low proportion, one expects *oshikundu* to have a low concentration of minerals based on

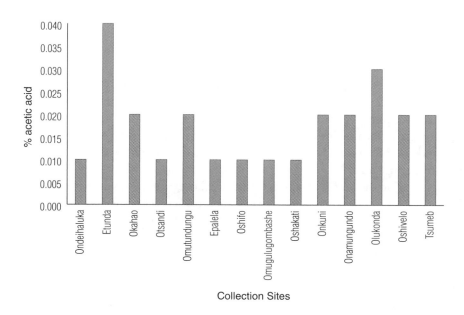

FIGURE 9.6: Percentage acetic acid of *oshikundu* samples from different villages in Oshana, Oshikoto, Ohangwena and Omusati regions.

total solids, which needs further investigation. The high water content might be one of the major factors contributing to the short shelf life of *oshikundu* and the growth of microorganisms despite being a fermented beverage. High moisture (water) content is the preferred breeding environment for most non-beneficial bacteria, especially water-borne pathogens; however, the low pH and fermentation of *oshikundu* might have played a role in its safety.

The ash content of *oshikundu* was found to be low (0.08%). The importance of ash analysis is that it gives an idea of the amount of minerals present in *oshikundu*. It thus further indicates that a low concentration of individual minerals is likely. Mineral content is important when quality grading edible products (AOAC, 1990).

Protein content was found to be 0.16 mg/mℓ. *Oshikundu* is therefore a good source of protein, which is derived from the *mahangu* and sorghum flour as the main ingredients, and probably also from the fermentation process. Protein is a major source of energy and essential amino acids, which our body cannot synthesize, so are only available through the food we eat. In addition, proteins contribute to a desirable appearance in food texture and stability.

The content of fibre in *oshikundu* was found to be 0.02%, which is very low considering cereal grain is an important source of fibre. Adequate consumption of dietary fibre protects against colon cancer, keeps blood lipids within the normal range, and reduces the risk of obesity, hypertension and cardiovascular disease (BeMiller, 2010). In addition, certain types of fibre can slow glucose absorption and reduce insulin secretion in diabetics and probably in non-diabetics as well (BeMiller, 2010).

Starter cultures of *oshikundu*

Starter cultures are acid-producing microorganisms that are used in the production of dairy products such as buttermilk, cheese, sour cream and yogurt. Although they are genetically diverse, common characteristics of these microorganisms include being gram-positive, non-motile and non-spore forming (Adams & Nicolaides, 1997). Each product requires its own starter culture and these contain different mixtures of organisms.

The application of a defined starter culture to beverage processing aims to select and improve the microorganisms used to enhance aroma, taste, shelf life, texture and nutritional values. According to Cogan and Accolas (1996), starter cultures usually consist of a cultivation medium, such as grains, seeds or nutrient liquids that have been well colonized by the microorganisms used for fermentation. In non-dairy fields of food and beverage fermentation, the development of starter cultures is increasingly advancing.

Oshikundu brewing technology, as for any other African cereal-based beverage, relies on backslopping. Although the brewing technology of *oshikundu* has been perfected at the household level, inconsistency in organoleptic properties remains a challenge. Aroma, taste and texture are the main sensory characteristics that influence consumer choice. These factors hinder the large-scale commercial processing of *oshikundu* (Sanni, 1993). The presence of unspecified microorganisms in *oshikundu* complicates the control of the fermentation process and results in products of variable quality. Hence, a defined starter culture approach should be developed to standardize fermentations, and ensure consistency in the quality and organoleptic properties of *oshikundu* (Sanni, 1993).

Role of biotechnology in improving *oshikundu*

The application of biotechnology to food and beverage production has been in practice for centuries. It has been used to create new and improved products through fermentation and food additives (Achi, 2005). Advancements in the application of food biotechnology have increased food security in many developing countries. The indigenous processing method of *oshikundu* needs to be transformed into a new and better technology that integrates improved process control, optimization, yields, safety, efficiency and standardized quality of the end product without losing the desired taste and its nutritional attributes.

The addition of biocatalysts (enzymes) in fermentation results in the conversion of raw materials into products much faster than they would otherwise occur. This will not only make the production of fermented products (*oshikundu*) faster, but will also improve the yield (quantity). This will increase the production of *oshikundu* at a large scale, which is required for commercialization. Addition of a biocatalyst to sorghum would ensure the production of a controlled amount of enzyme amylase, which in turn would improve control over the process and consistence of organoleptic properties in *oshikundu*.

Genetic engineering is an alternative technique that can be applied in the production of the raw materials. Through the isolation of a single gene in a precise, controlled and expedient manner, the gene code for specific desirable traits can be derived from virtually any living organism, such as a plant, animal, microbe or virus. The selection of specific genes in *omahangu* and sorghum grains for resistance to diseases and drought will improve their yields, quality and nutritional values as the starting materials for *oshikundu* production.

The nutritional value of *oshikundu* can be improved through biofortification. Cereal-based fermented foods and beverages are composed of various antinutrient factors, such as polyphenols, phytic acid, trypsin inhibitors and lectin. These are reduced through the fermentation process, but could be inhibited further through genetic modification. In addition, biofortification can also be applied to produce more beneficial microorganisms in *oshikundu*. Such genetic manipulation of the microflora could manifest desired characteristics, such as improved flavour and prolonged shelf life, in *oshikundu*. Such technology not only ensures the quality of *oshikundu*, but adds value to the product.

Probiotics could also be introduced into *oshikundu* through biotechnology. Probiotics are live microorganisms that, when administrated in adequate amounts, confer a health benefit on the host (Fuller & Gibson, 1997). They form a defence against the colonization of pathogenic microorganisms by competing for absorption to mucous and epithelial cells and, in certain cases, through the production of hydrogen peroxide and bacteriocins (Velraeds, van de Belt-Gritter, van der Mei, Reid, & Busscher, 1998). Introducing probiotics to *oshikundu* will also provide wider benefits of enhancing its safety and nutritional value, and prolonging its shelf life.

CONCLUSION

Oshikundu has been brewed in Namibia for many years and is an important daily beverage in Aawambo households. It has significant nutritional value that improves human health. Fermentation is the driving force behind the indigenous art of *oshikundu* brewing. Development of a defined starter culture will address the main challenge of inconsistency regarding its organoleptic properties. *Oshikundu*'s combination of physicochemical properties, such as pH and lactic acid content, have a profound effect on the final product's chemical stability and shelf life. Applying new biotechnologies could improve the indigenous methodology of brewing *oshikundu*. For example, the introduction of probiotic microflora can increase the palatability and improve the quality of *oshikundu*. Nevertheless, more scientific knowledge is still needed for us to clearly understand *oshikundu* biochemistry and microbiology to optimize the product and possibly its commercialization.

ACKNOWLEDGMENTS

This research project was fully funded by the Directorate of Research, Science and Technology (DRST; since, renamed National Commission on Research, Science and Technology (NCRST)) of the Ministry of Education. The authors would like to thank the Multidisciplinary Research Centre (MRC) and the Department of Chemistry and Biochemistry of the University of Namibia (UNAM) for their assistance and support.

References

Achi, O. K. (2005). The potential for upgrading traditional fermented foods through biotechnology. *African Journal of Biotechnology*, *4*(5), 375-380.

Adams, M. R., & Nicolaides, L. (1997). Review of sensitivity of different food-borne pathogens to fermentation. *Food Control*, *8*(5/6), 227-239.

Adebayo, G. B., Otunola, G. A., & Ajao, T. A. (2010). Physicochemical, microbiological and sensory characteristics of Kunu prepared from millet, maize and Guinea corn and stored at selected temperature. *Advanced Journal of Food Science and Technology*, *2*(1), 41-46.

AOAC [Association of Analytical Chemists]. (1990). *Official methods of analysis of AOAC International* (4th ed.) (pp. 73-74). Washington DC, USA: Author. 1, 73-74.

BeMiller, J. N. (2010). Chapter 10 : Carbohydrate analysis. In S. S. Nielsen (Ed.), *Food Analysis* (4th ed.) (pp. 147-177). New York, USA: Springer.

Blandino, A., Al-Aseeri, M. E., Pandiella, S. S., Cantero, D., & Webb, C. (2003). Cereal-based fermented foods and beverages. *Food Research International*, *36*, 527-543. doi:10.1016/S0963-9969(03)00009-7

Campbell-Platt, G. (1994). Fermented foods: A world perspective. *Food Research International*, *27*, 253-257.

Chelule, P. K., Mbongwa, H. P., Carries, S., & Gqaleni, N. (2010). Lactic acid fermentation improves the quality of amahewu, a traditional South African maize-based porridge. *Food Chemistry*, *122*(3), 656-661.

Cogan, M. T., & Accolas, J. P. (1996). *Dairy starter cultures*. Canada: Wiley-VCH, Inc.

Dewar, J., & Taylor, R. N. (1999). Beverages from sorghum and millet. In: R. K.Robinson, C. A. Batt, & P. D. Patel, (Eds). *Encyclopaedia of Food Microbiology*. *Vol. 3* (pp. 759-767). San Diego, USA: Academic Press.

Fuller, R., & Gibson, G. R. (1997). Modification of intestinal microflora using probiotics and prebiotics. *Scandinavian Journal of Gastroenterology*, *32*, 28-31.

Hui, Y. H., Evranus, E. Ö., López, F. N. A., Fan, L., Hansen, Å. S., Flores, M. E. J., ... Zhou, W. (Eds.) (2012). *Handbook of plant-based fermented food and beverage technology*. New York, USA: CRC Press.

Hulse, J. H., Laing, E. M., & Pearson O. E. (1980). *Sorghum composition and nutritive value*. London, UK: Academic Press.

Jespersen, L. (2003). Occurrence and taxonomic characteristics of strains of *Saccharomyces cerevisiae* predominant in African indigenous fermented food and beverage. *FEMS Yeast Research*, *3*(2),191-200.

Kohajdová, Z., & Karovičová, J. (2007). Fermentation of cereals for specific purpose. *Journal of Food and Nutrition Research*, *46*(2), 51-57.

McKay, L. L., & Baldwin, K. A. (1990). Application of biotechnology: Present and future improvements in lactic acid bacteria. *FEMS Microbiology Reviews*, *87*(1-2), 3-14.

Mu Ashekele, H., Embashu, W., & Cheikhyoussef, A. (2012). Indigenous knowledge system best practise from Namibia: The case of *Oshikundu* processing methods. *Trends in Applied Science*, *7*(11), 913-921.

Mukisa, I. M., Porcellato, D., Byaruhanga, Y. B., Muyanja, C. M. B. K., Rudi, K., Langsrud, T., & Narvhus, J. A. (2012). The dominant microbial community associated with fermentation of *Obushera* (sorghum and millet beverages) determined by culture-dependent and culture-independent methods. *International Journal of Food Microbiology*, *160*(1), 1-10.

Musaiger, A. O., Ahmed, A., & Rao, M. V, (2000). Nutritional value of traditional sweets consumed in the Arab Gulf Countries. *International Journal of Food Science and Nutrition*, *51*, 403-408.

Nambiar, V. S., Sareen, N., Daniel, M., & Gallego, E. B. (2012). Flavonoids and phenolic acids from pearl millet (*Pennisetum glaucum*) based foods and their functional implications. *Functional Foods in Health and Disease*, *2*(7), 251-264.

Nantanga, K. K. M., Seetharaman, K., de Kock, H. L., & Taylor, J. R. N. (2008). Thermal treatments to partially pre-cook and improve the shelf-life of whole pearl millet flour. *Journal of the Science of Food and Agriculture*, *88*, 1892-1899.

Nielsen, S. S. (1998). *Food analysis laboratory manual* (2nd edition). New York, USA: Springer Science Business Media, LLC.

Nout, M. J., & Sarkar, P. K. (1999). Lactic acid food formation in tropical climates. *Antonie van Leeuwenhoek*, *7*, 395-401.

Oberman, H., & Libudzisk, Z. (1996). Fermented milks. In J. B. Woods (Ed.), *Microbiology of fermented foods* (pp 308-350). London, UK: Blackie Academic.

Pfeiler, E. A. & Klaenhammer, T. R. (2007). The genomics of lactic acid bacteria. *Trends in Microbiology*, *15*(12), 546-553.

Rhee, S. J., Lee, J. E., & Lee, C. H, (2011). Importance of lactic acid bacteria in Asian fermented foods. *Microbial Cell Factories*, *10*(Suppl. 1), S5. doi:10.1186/1475-2859-10-S1-S5

Sadler, G. D., & Murphy, P. A. (2010). Chapter 13: pH and titratable acidity. In: Nielsen, S. S. (Ed.), *Food Analysis*, (4th Edition) (pp. 219-238). New York, USA: Springer.

Sanni, A. L. (1993). The need for process optimization of African fermented foods and beverages. *International Journal of Food Microbiology*, *18*, 85-95.

Steinkraus, K. H. (1994). Nutritional significance of fermented foods. *Food Research International*, *27*(3), 259-267.

Šušković, J., Kos, B., Matošić, S., & Marić, V. (1997). Probiotic properties of *Lactobacillus plantarum* L4. *Food Technology and Biotechnology*, *35*(2), 107-112.

Taylor, J. R. N. (2004). Millet. In C. W. Wrigley, H. Corke, & C. Walkers (Eds.), *Encyclopedia of Grain Science, Vol. 2*, (pp. 253-261). Oxford, UK: Elsevier Academic Press.

Velraeds, M., van de Belt-Gritter, B., van der Mei, H., Reid, G., & Busscher, H. (1998). Interference in initial adhesion of uropathogenic bacteria and yeast and silicone rubber by *Lactobacillus acidophilus* biosurfactant. *Journal of Medical Microbiology*, *47*(12), 1081-1085.

Vieira-Dolodé, G., Jespersen, L., Hounhouigan, J., Moller, P. L., Nago, C. M., & Jakobsen, M. (2007). Lactic acid bacteria and yeasts associated with gowé production from sorghum in Benin. *Journal of Applied Microbiology*, *103*, 342-349.

Vogel, R. F., Knorr, R., Müller, M. R. A., Steudel, U., Gänzle, M. G., & Ehrmann, M. A. (1999). Non-dairy lactic fermentations: The cereal world. *Antonie van Leeuwenhoek*, *76*(1-4), 403-411.

10

Harvesting and consumption of the giant African bullfrog, a delicacy in northern Namibia

Daniel O. Okeyo, Lineekela Kandjengo & Martha M. Kashea

INTRODUCTION

Namibia covers an area of approximately 800,000 square kilometres and has a human population of about 2.1 million. This gives an average density of about 2.6 people per square kilometre. Most of the people of Namibia belong to one of five main ethnic groups of African origin: the Aawambo, Ovaherero, Kavango, Caprivian, and Damara and Nama peoples.

The diet of ethnic Namibians comprises a variety of foods such as millet, sorghum, maize, sweet potatoes, groundnuts and fruits. Millet and maize are staple foods. Fruits are mainly wild and indigenous. Staple foods in northern Namibia are generally accompanied with indigenous vegetables, beef, lamb, mutton or fish. Giant African bullfrogs – locally known as *efuma* (sing.) or *omafuma* (pl.) – form a delicacy, especially during the rainy season (Figure 10.1). The Aawambo are not alone in appreciating these frogs (*Pyxicephalus adspersus*) as a delicacy. Reports exist of others also eating it within Namibia as well as elsewhere in southern Africa. For example, the Nsenga people in the eastern Luangwa Valley (Eastern Province, Zambia) also consume whole bullfrogs, which they locally call *kanyama kaliye fupa* – the animal without bones.

The giant African bullfrog is distributed widely throughout southern and eastern Africa (Figure 10.2) and found in areas of Namibia, Angola, Botswana, South Africa, Zimbabwe, Zambia, Mozambique, Malawi, Tanzania and Kenya (Channing, 1991; Conradie, Branch, Braack, & Manson, 2010; IUCN, 2011). It is reported to occur in the central and northern areas of Namibia (Channing 1991; Griffin, 1997) and is found in considerable numbers on the northern plains, especially during the early rain season.

FIGURE 10.1:
The giant African
bullfrog, *Pyxicephalus
adspersus*. (© Graham
Alexander.)

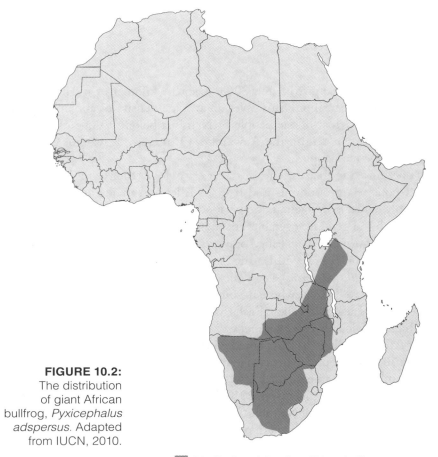

FIGURE 10.2:
The distribution
of giant African
bullfrog, *Pyxicephalus
adspersus*. Adapted
from IUCN, 2010.

Distribution of the giant African bullfrog

The frogs begin their lives as eggs, which are laid in the shallow waters of *oshanas* (shallow, seasonal, interconnected water channels found in central northern Namibia) as well as in ponds, pools, swamps and streams or rivers with slow-moving water. The eggs hatch into tadpoles and after a month or so, they metamorphose into froglets. During the rainy season, the frogs appear in various sizes: the sub-juveniles and the juveniles are locally known as *ukadhinahanya* (small ones) and the adults as *namuhogelela* (big ones). The frogs take about eight years to reach sexual maturity (Yetman, Mokonoto & Ferguson, 2012) and if they are not killed by predators, such as snakes or humans, they can live in close proximity to water or in aestivation (Loveridge & Withers, 1981; Yetman & Ferguson, 2011), to a ripe age of about forty years (Yetman et al., 2012). It is understood that they aestivate for much of the year and come to the surface after the first rains to breed.

The aim of this study was to record background information about the human consumption of frogs in localities of northern Namibia. Although it is clear that giant African bullfrogs are a delicacy and contribute to the pet trade industry, published information for setting up policies on their sustainable use and conservation is still scarce (IUCN, 2010). Here we compare harvesting and consumption practices of community members at different sites in northern Namibia, and how they prevent and treat the harmful side effects of eating frogs. We also discuss similarities in local practices in different areas and conclude by highlighting information gaps and recommending areas for future research.

MATERIALS AND METHODS

This study is based on interviews with local people, coupled with direct observations with the most recent in November 2011. We interviewed people about the consumption of the giant African bullfrog (*Pyxicephalus adspersus*), in three localities of central northern Namibia (Oshakati–Ongwediva, Okahao and Okambebe–Okalongo). The Oshakati–Ongwediva and Okahao groups represented areas with urban influence, which are accessible along tarmac roads. The Okambebe–Okalongo group represented areas with little urban influence and are only accessible along gravel roads; interviews were conducted at a number of villages located between these two villages. All information was openly recorded on a questionnaire with the consent of the interviewees. In each locality, two groups of people were independently interviewed.

Study sites

Oshakati–Ongwediva

Oshakati and Ongwediva are two main commercial centres in Oshana Region in northern Namibia, which merge geographically. Oshakati (17°46'51.44"S, 15°41'56.85"E) and Ongwediva (17°47'29.15"S, 15°46'28.87"E) lie in an area where three tarred highways (C45, C46 and C41) meet. The following facilities are found there: an agricultural research centre (the Rural Development Centre), inland fisheries research station and agricultural showground, open-air markets, shopping malls, banks, tourist resorts, a hospital and nurses' training college and two university campuses.

Okahao

Okahao (17°53'13.36"S, 15°4'9.72"E) in the Omusati Region lies on a tarmac highway (C41) about 45 km west of Oshakati. It is the traditional home to two of Namibia's respected leaders – the King of the Ongandjera and Namibia's Founding President. Okahao has a post office, some small shops and a hospital.

Okambebe–Okalongo

Okambebe (17°28'39.39"S, 15°34'30.85"E) in the Ohangwena Region and Okalongo (17°26'36.76"S, 15°19'47.75"E) in the Omusati Region are villages with little urban influence. They are only accessible along gravel roads. Both are located close to the border between Namibia and Angola, and were the most northerly study areas. Services available in the Okambebe–Okalongo areas include open-air markets, which offer cross-border exchange of goods, small schools, clinics and traditional healers.

Questionnaires

Questionnaires used in the study specified comparative questions concerning the giant African bullfrog and practices related to the use of it as a delicacy: emergence from aestivation; harvesting; preparation; cooking methods; eating hierarchies; preservation; and propagation. We also investigated the acquisition, prevention and treatment of a harmful condition that occurs as a result of eating the frogs.

RESULTS

Emergence from aestivation

In the Oshakati–Ongwediva area, frogs of different sizes emerge immediately after rainfall; they begin calling (croaking) two to three weeks after this. When breeding begins, large males mount and position themselves on top of smaller females in order to fertilize the eggs with their sperm. After pairing, a couple occupies the shallow areas of pools. The differences between males and females or juveniles and adults are not very distinct to most local people.

In Okahao, frogs also emerge after the first rainfall of the season. They start calling while jumping around after the second rainfall. Frogs of different colours and sizes are found – some are yellow-green on the back, some have yellow bellies with green backs; and some are small and blackish in colour. Amongst the small blackish frogs is one kind usually found in peoples' residences. We found that the small, blackish frogs were considered females (containing eggs), while the large, yellow-bellied, green-backed frogs (containing lots of fat, but no eggs) were considered males.

In Okambebe–Okalongo, frogs emerge in October and in December or January with the first rainfalls of the early (October) and main rain seasons (December or January). They are seen moving from the deep areas of the *oshanas* to occupy the shallows. The frogs were reported to call and breed after the third rainfall of the season.

Harvesting

In Oshakati–Ongwediva, the first calling of the frogs triggers the start of the local harvesting season – it begins the following morning. Torches are used to collect frogs at night as well. The frogs move towards light, perhaps to catch the plentiful insects that are attracted to the light, especially during the rainy season. Historically, wood of the *omuhongo* tree (*Spirostachys africana*) was burnt and used as torches or candles were lit; battery-powered torches have since replaced the use of these.

The frogs are usually so abundant in the early morning after rain that people manage to catch them with their bare hands. Collected frogs are tied together using strips of bark from mopane trees (*Colophospermum mopane*) or strips of fronds from palm trees. Individual frogs form part of a woven network of upside-down-facing frogs, tied together at the hip region, to which the collector drags along adding more as he goes (Figure 10.3).

Large frogs are known to fight back; their tricuspid teeth can cause painful lacerations to the collector's fingers. A common technique used to release the grip of the frog's mouth on the fingers is simply by poking the frog in the nostrils with a piece of dried grass or a twig, which causes the frog to open its mouth – it can otherwise do a lot of damage to the finger. It is not clear whether males, females or

FIGURE 10.3:
A collector with a
healthy harvest of
frogs tied together with
strips of palm fronds.
(© John Mendelsohn.)

juvenile frogs are all harvested; what is clear is that amongst the harvest, the large frogs are selected to keep and the small ones are released back to the wild – an indigenous conservation practice!

In Okahao, it was said that long ago, frogs were easier to catch than in recent times. The giant African bullfrogs did not run away from humans as quickly as they do nowadays. There is a saying, which goes, 'frogs of nowadays come from the university' – implying that they are educated and know when to run, especially from human collectors, to safety. The intensive labour involved in catching frogs has resulted in their buying price increasing and so only a few people now eat them.

Harvesting takes place at the second rainfall in Okahao, when frogs become more active around the water. The collector waits until the frogs come out of the water, when he/she chases and catches them using their bare hands. Harvesting also takes place at night, when torches are used. There is speculation that the light produced by the torches blinds the frog, thus allowing the collector easy access and catch! Large frogs are also actively harvested here while small frogs are released back to the wild helping to conserve the species.

In Okambebe–Okalongo, frogs are harvested for food after the third rainfall. Collection is also done using bare hands. Long ago, strips from palm leaves and the bark of mopane trees were used in tying harvested frogs together, but today frogs are collected in bags (sacks made from synthetic Manila hemp – similar to those used to contain cross-border grain exchanges). Children might catch and keep small frogs, however, only large frogs are kept for food usually. The locals do not concern themselves with differentiating the sexes of the frogs, although they speculate that small frogs could be females and large ones males. Eggs are not seen when the frogs are harvested, which could indicate that collection (after the third rainfall) takes place after breeding. It is unclear when exactly the frogs breed.

Preparation for cooking

In the Oshakati–Ongwediva area, the frogs are cut open from under the lower jaw (mandible) to the vent. The intestines and all viscera, except fat, are removed as waste. The tongue and the upper jaw and palate and accessories (which are golden in colour), are considered inedible and are removed from the buccal area. In some homesteads this 'waste' is offered to chickens or dogs to eat. Some people prefer the fat to be removed and cooked separately, while others cook the frogs together with the fat. To be finally ready for cooking, the inside and outside of the frog is rinsed clean with water.

In Okahao, they remove the frog's guts and internal viscera, as well as the ganglions lying in front of the vertebral column. The tongue is also removed – a touch of oil (from frog fat) to the fingers aid in the easy removal of the tongue. The fat is removed and prepared separately.

In the Okambebe–Okalongo area, a similar gutting procedure is followed to that described for Oshakati–Ongwediva, and the fat is either separated from or left on the frog.

Cooking methods

In the Oshakati–Ongwediva area, frogs are cooked in a similar way to fish. Pieces of bark from the stalks of maize (*Zea mays*) and *mahangu* (pearl millet, *Pennisetum glaucum*), or twigs from other edible and medicinal plants (such as *omuhongo* and mopane trees), are laid on the base of the cooking pot, which, indigenously, is made from clay. The bark or twigs prevent the frog skin or meat from sticking to the bottom of the pot and peeling off. It is believed that *omuhongo* has the additional advantages of preventing *oshiketaketa*, a harmful side effect of eating frogs that have been harvested too early (see below). The frogs are piled on top of the lining and a little water is then poured into the pot and boiled for approximately two hours, or until the water has completely evaporated. The amount of water and boiling time varies, depending on the choice of the individual cooks and whether soup is preferred or not. Salt is added to taste during boiling – it is commonly added when boiling foods in Africa.

Frying or spicing the frogs, which some people do today, was historically unheard of. There is a belief that, if spiced, the frogs will look strange, which is linked to the saying – 'ino tulange ondungu' – 'Please, don't spice me'. Ondungu is a local name for chilli. Perhaps spicing the frogs makes the food less appetizing and appealing. Locals prefer frog meat that retains its texture and shape during cooking – i.e. eyes open, fingers and toes stretched.

In Okahao, cooking pots are also lined with pieces of bark from mahangu stalks, to prevent the frog meat from sticking to the bottom. This has been common practice in Okahao since long ago. Once the frogs are in the pot, some water, oil and salt are added. Frog meat is usually spiced in Okahao, cooking it no differently from any other meat – fish, chicken or beef.

In the Okambebe–Okalongo area, the cooking pot is lined with pieces of sticks gathered from edible plants; sometimes the frogs are cooked without laying sticks at the bottom of cooking pots. Water and spices are added. Stirring is discouraged to avoid breaking the frog meat into small pieces. It is not advised to fry frog meat.

Preparation of frog fat for cooking

In the Oshakati–Ongwediva area, some homes prefer cooking frog fat separately to the rest of the meat. When this is done, fat is removed from the frog and a little water is added to the pot in which the fat is cooked, which is said to start fat dissolution. Some salt might be added to the cooking fat. When melted, the 'oil' is poured over the previously cooked frog meat before it is eaten. There is no explanation why some people prefer cooking frog fat separately to the meat.

In Okahao, the elders melt frog fat into 'oil'. The oil is used as an ointment to 'unblock' children's ears after adding some 'unknown' substance to the melting fat. Frog fat is not used in homes of Christians; it is thrown away. It is not clear why Christians in Okahao communities have this practice.

In the Okambebe–Okalongo area, a similar procedure to that described for Oshakati–Ongwediva above is followed.

Eating the frog meat

In the Oshakati–Ongwediva area, meat from the giant African bullfrog is eaten in a similar manner to fish. The frog meat is served with oshifima (a thick porridge made from *mahangu* meal, in absence of which maize meal could also be used) or eaten on its own. The frog skin is also eaten. Cooked frog meat easily separates from the bones (much more easily than from boiled fish or chicken). The bones are not usually eaten.

In Okahao, frog meat is eaten in a similar way as other meats, such as chicken or beef. It might be served with *oshifima*. As in Oshakati–Ongwediva, the bones are not eaten; people claim that they are tasteless. Only large frogs with a yellow belly and green back (thought to be males), are eaten, while the small, black frogs (thought to be females) are not. Frogs' eggs are also not eaten, also not the tongue – elders get furious when the tongue is offered with the food – or the ganglions near the spinal cord, even when cooked with the frog meat.

In Okambebe–Okalongo, frog is eaten in a similar way to other meals.

Eating hierarchies in traditional homesteads

In the Oshakati–Ongwediva area, all family members eat frog meat when it is in plenty. In some homes, however, when there is not enough meat to go around, only elders (especially the heads of families, usually men) eat the delicacy. The culture of reserving frog meat for men is an antagonistic issue in the society (especially between men and women), and it also varies from family to family.

Typically in Okahao homesteads some family members eat frog meat and others do not. This depends on availability of frogs, and the size of the cooking pot and whether it can accommodate enough frogs for everyone; the larger the pot, the greater the number of people that will eat.

Historically in Okambebe–Okalongo, people started eating frogs during long droughts and famine. Today, everybody in the household eats frog meat. When in abundance, leftover meat is kept for meals the following day.

Preservation of frog meat

In Oshakati–Ongwediva communities, the excess from a catch of frogs that cannot be cooked and eaten that day are sun-dried. This avoids spoilage and allows the frogs to be stored for extended periods. After eviscerating the inner parts and fat of the frogs, they are tied and hung up on rope lines (similar to a clothesline). The dried meat is left hanging on the line and only removed just before they are cooked. Apparently the dried meat spoils quickly once removed from the sun. The procedures for cooking and eating dried frog meat are similar to those followed for fresh frog meat (described above). In recent times, frogs are also frozen fresh or dry in households that have electricity.

Frog meat is also preserved in Okahao by drying in the sun on lines, roofs or wooden racks. The dried frog meat is also prepared for eating in a similar manner to fresh frog meat. Twigs for lining the pot, however, are not required when cooking dried meat, as it does not stick to the bottom of the pot.

In Okambebe–Okalongo communities, frogs are also sun-dried on lines when there is surplus. Fresh frogs spoil quickly, just as fish would. Again, no twigs are required to line the pot when cooking dried frogs. Unlike communities of Oshakati–Ongwediva and Okahao, some people here crush and fry the bones of dried frogs.

Harmful side effects

Eating bullfrogs can have harmful side effects. It is commonly believed that if *ukadhinahanya* (juvenile frogs) are eaten – or frogs that are harvested before they first call – people become ill from a condition locally known as *oshiketaketa*. The symptoms are rather similar to those of bilharzia (schistosomiasis) caused by a fluke, which is co-hosted by a freshwater snail. The symptoms of *oshiketaketa* are acute inflammation and pain when passing urine (dysuria), and blood (and sometimes fragments of the membrane lining of the urethra) in the urine. The condition is thought to cause temporary kidney failure. It affects males and females of all age groups.

Interviewees at all the study sites reported on *oshiketaketa*. They also all provided information on how to avoid it and/or treat the condition should it occur. The indigenous knowledge and technologies that they use are applied in similar ways with slight differences between the various communities interviewed (Table 10.1).

Generally, to prevent the *oshiketaketa* condition from occurring, frogs should not be harvested too early – either when they are too young or before the mature frogs start calling. In addition, cooking them with pieces of wood from specific trees will help prevent the condition. Treatments are aimed at relieving the pain that *oshiketaketa* causes; many seek help at their local clinic or hospital.

Propagation and marketing

Frog meat provides an important source of protein during the wet season and is considered a delicacy in this area of Namibia. Propagating and marketing the giant African bullfrog could make it available throughout the year, become an economic concern and relieve the pressure on wild frog populations.

Interviewees in Oshakati–Ongwediva welcomed the idea of propagating the bullfrog saying that propagation would make the delicacy available throughout the year. Technicians at the Department of Fisheries (Ministry of Fisheries and Marine Resources, Ongwediva) demonstrated their trials of propagating frogs in round, galvanized fish tanks. Fresh frogs are readily sold at open markets. Frogs go 'like hot cake[s]' at the market at the price of N$1.00 each – 'now you see it, now you don't,' as the popular product is quickly bought up.

TABLE 10.1: Acquisition, prevention and treatment of the *oshiketaketa* condition reported by communities at three sites in northern Namibia.

Oshakati–Ongwediva	Okahao	Okambebe–Oshikango
Acquisition		
People who harvest and feed on frogs before croaking time become ill. It is therefore advised not to eat immature frogs.	People, who harvest and feed on frogs when the animals first emerge from aestivation, become ill. They are also affected after eating immature frogs.	People who catch and eat frogs before croaking or before the third rainfall get into trouble.
Prevention		
'Prevention is better than cure,' when it comes to *oshiketaketa*. Those who opt to harvest and feed on the meat of immature frogs can prevent the *oshiketaketa* condition by using dry wood from the *omuhongo* (*Spirostachys africana*) tree as pot liners when cooking the frog meat. Although apparently fool proof, no one could explain how this 'trick' works.	The only prevention practice known was to avoid eating the frog before they make noises (call or croak).	Two types of trees – *omuuva* (*Pterocarpus angolensis*) and *oshipeke* (*Ximenia caffra*) – are used to prevent *oshiketaketa*. Two small pieces from either one of these trees are used to line the pot while cooking the meat. (Interestingly, the *omuhongo* tree found in the Oshakati–Ongwediva area is not known here.) A second way to prevent the condition is by cutting off the tips of the frog's toes prior to cooking. It is not yet clear how either of these methods work.
Treatment		
A piece from a broken indigenous clay pot is placed over charcoal until red-hot; the 'patient' then kneels within close proximity to the hot piece of clay and urinates on it. The hot steam hits the bottom areas and private parts of the patient, relieving the pain, immediately. A metallic hoe can be used in place of clay shards. Without treatment, the pain lasts longer, with the patient only recovering after some time. Could it be a kind of chemotherapeutic, heat shock, which perhaps disperses the poison from the kidneys?	People who become ill seek treatment at the local clinic, where they are prescribed medication. The medicine, however, does not seem to work effectively. The pain disappears eventually.	Treatment is sought at the hospital (e.g. Okalongo Hospital).

People in Okahao also welcome the idea of propagating bullfrogs. They believe that through propagation, they will be able to protect their own frog populations from outsiders. Furthermore, it was suggested that the people who live close to Etunda – a floodplain with seasonal, slow-moving water on the western side of the Cuvelai drainage system, could use this area for frog propagation.

In Okambebe–Okalongo frog propagation is already taking place. One individual collects young frogs from the *oshanas* near Oshakati and transports them to Okambebe village, where he raises them to adulthood in his 'lined' dam until they are large enough to eat and sell – he is passionate about this practice. Frogs from Okambebe–Oshikango are sold at the Oshakati market at N$1.00 per frog (any size).

DISCUSSION

There are a number of similarities in the way people from different communities in northern Namibia (Oshakati–Ongwediva, Okahao and Okambebe–Okalongo) harvest and eat bullfrogs. The frogs first emerge from aestivation after the initial October or December–January rains, then croak and breed. Frogs are harvested for food; normally, large frogs are collected. In preparation for cooking, frogs are gutted of intestines and internal organs, parts and accessories. The upper palate and tongue are also removed. The rest of the frog parts are edible. Frog fat is either removed from or left on the frog. Fat is cooked either together with frog meat or separately; if cooked separately, the fat is added to the meat before eating. The main method for cooking fresh frog meat is by boiling in a little, salted water. The cooking pot is lined with twigs from edible plant material in order to prevent frog skin from sticking to the bottom. When in surplus, frogs are sun-dried. Eating frogs before croaking and breeding (when they first emerge from aestivation) causes inflammation of the urethra and a burning sensation when passing urine, or some kind of temporary kidney failure. Harvesting the frogs only once they begin calling prevents this condition.

People in northern Namibia interviewed during the study support the idea for propagating bullfrogs. This would give them the right to ownership and protection over their frog populations, and would reduce pressure on the wild populations. There is evidence in recent literature which points towards a decline in amphibians (e.g. Kusrini & Alford, 2008; Alford, 2010). Propagation attempts were reported from Ongwediva and Okambebe; demonstration sites are required to encourage more propagation activities.

According to Walls (1995), caring for an adult bullfrog is simple requiring few resources. The animals require a terrarium with a moisture-holding substrate (such as potting soil or moss), a shallow water bowl, and a lamp or florescent lighting, for 10–12 hours a day (Yetman et al., 2012). Full spectrum lighting, however, is not required. It is recommended that the terrarium is well covered and locked, to keep out predators and to prevent the frogs from escaping. The cage should be kept at 26.6–30.0 °C in the day and 23.8 °C at night (Walls, 1995). The keeper should avoid putting anything else in the cage with the bullfrogs – including rocks that will fit in their mouths, plastic objects, and other creatures; they will all end up as dinner. Plants placed at a distance are fine, for they enhance the environment.

Recommendations for future research

There are a number of practices around the harvesting and preparation of *omafuma* in northern Namibia. Some of these seem important in avoiding *oshiketaketa*, the potentially harmful side effect of eating bullfrogs. Research into this would improve our understanding of what causes it, how to treat it and the mechanisms behind the 'folk wisdom' currently practised to prevent and treat the condition.

In addition, research into the natural history, physiology, biochemistry and ecology of the giant African bullfrog (*Pyxicephalus adspersus*) would provide valuable information to guide the sustainable harvesting and propagation of them. Assessment of the traditional use and importance of this species is critical for its effective regional protection and conservation.

Information gaps should be addressed through scientific research and collaborative investigation with community members. Future collaboration is envisaged to engage in multidisciplinary research relevant to the giant African bullfrog, its use and conservation. For example, botanical research should analyse the chemical composition and compounds of the species, whose branches are used to line the cooking pots, and which apparently prevent people from developing the *oshiketaketa* side effects of eating the frogs. Zoological research could give insight into why the tongue of the frog and surrounding parts are inedible (toxic to human consumption). Could the buccal areas be infested by oral fungi or bacteria as suggested by Fellers, Green and Longcore (2001)? Finally, research should look into how harvesting and other anthropogenic effects, and natural changes, such as global warming (Alford, Bradfield, & Richards, 2007) and climate change (Cary & Alexander, 2003), influence the conservation of the herein mentioned trees and the frogs.

ACKNOWLEDGMENTS

We are grateful to our informants – Johanna Mukwanambwa Nghitaunapo (Okambebe–Okalongo), the late Kuku Helvi Gwakondombolo and Auma Mijiro (Okahao) and Philip Nekondo (Oshakati–Ongwediva) – who kindly guided our teams and who devoted time to discuss the subject with us. We warmly thank the students of the Department of Zoology (UNAM) who showed dedication and teamwork during the various stages of the study. We appreciate the assistance of staff at the Rural Development Centre and the Inland Fisheries Station (Ongwediva), UNAM and the National Museums of Namibia (Windhoek) in the identification of frogs and in various other ways and the partial funding and help in kind from these institutions, as well as the University of Fort Hare (South Africa).

References

Alford, R. A. 2010. Declines and the global status of amphibians. In D. W. Sparling (Ed.). *Ecotoxicology of amphibians and reptiles* (2nd ed.) (pp. 13-45). Pensacola, USA: SETAC Press.

Alford, R. A., Bradfield, K. S., & Richards S. I. (2007). Global warming and amphibian losses. *Nature, 447*(7144), E3-E4.

Carey, C., & Alexander, M. A. (2003). Climate change and amphibian decline: Is there a link? *Diversity and Distributions, 9*, 111-121.

Channing, A. (1991). An illustrated key to the frogs of Namibia. *Madoqua, 17*(2), 227-232.

Conradie, W., Branch, W. R., Braack, H., & Manson, M. (2010). Notes on the diet of recently metamorphosed giant African bullfrogs (Anura: Pyxicephalidae: *Pyxicephalus adspersus*) and growth increase during the first nine months in a semi-natural habitat. *Herpetology Notes, 3*, 215-219.

Fellers, G. M., Green, D. E., & Longcore, J. E. (2001). Oral chytridiomycosis in the mountain yellow-legged frog (*Rana mucosa*). *Copeia, 4*, 945-953.

Griffin, M. (1997). *Checklist and provisional national conservation status of amphibians, reptiles and mammals known or expected to occur in Namibia: Biodiversity inventory.* Unpublished manuscript. Ministry of Environment and Tourism, Windhoek, Namibia.

IUCN [International Union for Conservation of Nature]. (2010). *IUCN Red List of Threatened Species (Version 2010.1):* Pyxicephalus adspersus *(an online reference).* Retrieved from http://www.iucnredlist.org/details/58535/0

IUCN [International Union for Conservation of Nature]. (2011). *IUCN Red List of Threatened Species (species range map):* Pyxicephalus adspersus *(an online reference).* Retrieved from http://maps.iucnredlist.org/map.html?id=58535

Kusrini, M. D., &. Alford, R. A. (2008). Frogs for human consumption. In S. N. Stuart, M. Hoffman, J. S. Chanson, N. A. Cox, R. J. Berridge, P. Ramani, & B. F. Young (Eds.). *Threatened amphibians of the world* (p. 28). Barcelona, Spain: Lynx Edicions for IUCN (Gland, Switzerland) and Conservation International (Arlington, USA).

Loveridge, J. P., & Withers, P. C. (1981). Metabolism and water balance of active and cocooned African bullfrog *Pyxicephalus adspersus. Physiological Zoology, 54*, 203-214.

Walls, J. G. (1995). *Fantastic frogs.* Neptune City, New Jersey, USA: TFH Publications.

Yetman, C. A., & Ferguson, J. W. H. (2011). Spawning and non-breeding activity of adult giant bullfrogs (*Pyxicephalus adspersus*). *African Journal of Herpetology, 60*(1), 13-29.

Yetman, C. A., Mokonoto, P. J., & Ferguson, W. H. (2012). Conservation implications of the age/size distribution of Giant Bullfrogs (*Pyxicephalus adspersus*) at three peri-urban breeding sites. *The Herpetological Journal, 22*(1), 23-32.

11

Indigenous knowledge used in the management of human–wildlife conflict along the borders of the Etosha National Park

Selma M. Lendelvo, Margaret N. Angula & John Kazgeba E. Mfune

INTRODUCTION

Humans and wildlife in Africa have coexisted for millennia, but conflicts between them have become common phenomena (Shemwetta & Kideghesho, 2000). Worldwide, borders between humans and wild spaces have become blurred, particularly those surrounding protected areas. As a result, wildlife frequently moves out of protected areas and enters nearby human settlements (Ogra, 2008). In addition, the frequency of human–wildlife conflicts (HWCs) in these areas has grown in recent decades, largely because of the increase in human population, the expansion of human activities and changes in wildlife management systems (Graham, Beckerman, & Thirgood, 2005).

In this chapter, we describe how commercial and communal farmers who live along the borders of Etosha National Park (ENP) use their indigenous knowledge in dealing with HWC. We interviewed 48 farmers from cattle posts in the communal areas north of ENP and 51 commercial farmers on private land south of ENP through a semi-structured questionnaire. The majority of farmers indicated that they have techniques and strategies to protect their livestock, crops, families and property from being harmed by problem wildlife. Understanding the indigenous knowledge that farmers have to deal with HWC is important for improving wildlife management systems in Namibia.

General background

Although humans and wildlife have coexisted for millennia, there has been a great shift in the human–wildlife relationship due to implementation of different conservation approaches. Protected areas are a 'cornerstone of conservation', playing a vital role in saving wildlife populations from regional or range-wide extinction (Treves, 2008), but for those living in close proximity to them, they have become a burden as human–wildlife interactions have turned into serious conflicts. The expansion of protected areas, coupled with the increase in human population, has exacerbated the conflicting interests between parks and neighbouring communities (Milenković, 2008). Contradictions between wildlife conservation and local interests have become a concern in which wildlife and humans increasingly compete for space and resources (Madden, 2004). Frequently, wildlife conservation initiatives suffer, the economic and social wellbeing of local people is impaired and local support for conservation declines (Nepal & Weber, 1995). Today, HWC has become a serious impediment to the conservation and management of protected areas in most developing countries. For example, predators increasingly turn to livestock for food, a behaviour that is not acceptable to and not tolerated by farmers (Naughton-Treves, Holland, & Brandon, 2005; Milenković, 2008; Thomassen, Linnell, & Skogen, 2011).

Human–wildlife coevolution and cultural tolerance to wildlife in many African societies, including Namibia, have led to traditional land-based practices, beliefs and knowledge, which are necessary for the sustainable use of natural resources and for environmental conservation (Madden, 2004). Indigenous knowledge is typically derived from people who have interacted with the environment and wildlife for decades (Gilchrist, Mallory, & Merkel, 2005). It has the potential to provide insight for the conservation of biodiversity (Menzies, 2006). It is globally recognized that indigenous ecological knowledge is one of the most important sources of information to complement western scientific approaches to resource management (Gilchrist et al., 2005). The dynamics of indigenous ecological knowledge are also linked to wider social and economic processes. Indigenous people and local communities have a wealth of knowledge not only of traditional medicines, ecological processes, and conservation and management of biodiversity, but also in managing HWC.

Here, we document the knowledge that local farmers use in making decisions on HWC around ENP. We describe strategies that local farmers in this area have developed to reduce and prevent conflicts, and their knowledge of predators and other wildlife that cause problems.

Human–wildlife conflict

'Human–wildlife conflict occurs when the needs and behaviour of wildlife impact negatively on the goals of humans or when the goals of humans negatively impact the needs of wildlife. These conflicts may result when wildlife damage crops, injure or kill domestic animals including livestock, or when they threaten or kill people.' (Madden, 2004).

According to Madden (2004), the world's conservationists have identified three main reasons for HWC escalating around protected areas:

1. Local people perceive that the needs or values of wildlife are given priority over their own needs;
2. Local institutions and people are not adequately empowered to deal with the conflict; and
3. Protected area authorities fail to address the needs of the local people or to work with them in addressing HWC adequately.

In general, HWC may also increase if human use of wildlife habitats expand, or environmental changes emanating from climate change drive some sensitive and vulnerable species into areas with more people (Treves, 2008).

HWC occurs throughout Namibia on communal and freehold land, and it involves a variety of wildlife species. Although HWC incidents in Namibia are highest in wildlife-rich regions, such as Kunene Region in the north-west and Zambezi Region in the north-east (Jones & Barnes, 2006), they are also high along the borders of protected areas, such as Etosha and Bwabwata national parks. Farmers that neighbour protected areas are more vulnerable to problems that arise from wildlife (Patterson, Kasiki, Selempo, & Rays, 2004; Shrestha, 2007). As human pressure increases in rural areas, people are progressively moving into 'wild lands' where more predators are likely to live. Movements of livestock and wildlife across the boundaries of protected areas increase the risk of encounters; and most of the protected areas have weak fences (Chardonnet et al., 2010). There has been a rapid increase in the number of livestock and cattle posts close to the northern ENP fence (Mfune, Mosimane, Hamukuaja, & Angula, 2005), which has contributed to escalating numbers of conflicts along this border.

Rural Namibians are particularly vulnerable to HWC because of their high dependence on agriculture and natural resources. Local livelihoods depend on a combination of livestock farming, crop production and the use of natural resources. The different wildlife management systems in Namibia – such as proclaimed protected areas, conservancies on communal and freehold lands and commercial wildlife farming – have different forms of HWC associated with them. The type of land use adjacent to a protected area also influences the extent of HWC. For example, predators are unwelcome intruders onto livestock farms adjacent to protected areas (Matson, Goldizen, & Jarman, 2004; Schiess-Meier, Ramsauer, Gabanapelo, & König, 2007). Fewer conflicts occur further away from the borders of protected areas.

In 1996, the Namibian Government promulgated the Nature Conservation Amendment Act (based on the Nature Conservation Ordinance of 1975), which includes procedures to manage wildlife in protected areas. In addition, the National Policy on Human–Wildlife Conflict Management was developed and implemented by the Ministry of Environment and Tourism (MET) in 2009 to manage HWC in farming areas outside of protected areas. The HWC policy stipulates strategic approaches and procedures to deal with conflicts that arise from wildlife. These approaches encourage establishment of concessions and adoption of compatible land uses, such as wildlife and tourism, on lands adjacent to national parks. The MET, through this policy, implements joint HWC management and mitigation plans together with local communities, and provides technical support in carrying them out (GRN, 2009). Large mammals, such as elephant and lion, contribute to most of the HWC outside protected areas damaging crop fields and local infrastructure, and endangering livestock as well as human lives (Jones & Barnes, 2006). Specific procedures have been developed by MET for target predators and problem animals, such as lion and elephant, to improve the effectivity of HWC management. However, local farmers' knowledge and management practices also contribute in addressing HWC and are described in this chapter.

Indigenous ecological knowledge

Over the years, local farmers have accumulated knowledge on how to manage HWC. Indigenous ecological knowledge (IEK) is defined as 'a cumulative body of knowledge, practice, and belief, evolving by adaptive processes and handed down through generations by cultural transmission' (Berkes, Colding, & Folke, 2000). It also encompasses the relationship of living beings (including humans) with one another and with their environment. Similarly, Menzies (2006) defined IEK as a 'body of information on the interconnected elements of natural environments taught from generation to generation'. In general, therefore, IEK involves the transfer of knowledge that is ever growing and dynamic, and is mainly informed by traditional or customary lifestyles and environmental changes. Mauro and Hardison (2000) cited the need for preserving traditional knowledge because of its intellectual and economic values in production development.

Globally, IEK is recognized for its potential instrumental value to science and conservation (Sitati & Ipara, 2012). Therefore, recognizing the importance of IEK means recognizing the in-depth know-how that local people have about their immediate environments and the manner in which they make decisions on how to use and manage natural environments. An understanding of local farmers' prior knowledge is essential to managing HWC. Linking HWC and IEK is, however, very rare in the literature and there is a need to understand the connections between the two in the Namibian context.

OVERVIEW OF THE COMMUNITIES AROUND ENP

Brief history of ENP

ENP is one of the oldest and largest national parks in Namibia and a major biodiversity hotspot. It provides home and protection to a wide variety of wildlife species (Mendelsohn, el Obeid, & Roberts, 2000). The park was initially proclaimed the Etosha Game Reserve in 1907, based on Ordinance 88 of 1907 of the German colonial administration in Namibia. ENP is bordered by freehold land along the southern and south-eastern boundaries, while along the northern, western and north-eastern boundaries, it is bordered by communal land (Berry, 1997; Botha, 2005). The Aawambo, Hai‖om and Ovaherero people occupied the northern part of the Etosha Pan while the southern part was occupied by white settlers (Berry, 1997; Botha, 2000; Dieckmann, 2007). Historically, the Etosha Game Reserve was first under private ownership of farms and trading rights, which lapsed in 1935. This was later followed by a system that made provision for emergency grazing rights to farmers in the neighbourhood of the reserve. For example, farmers were allowed to graze their cattle in Etosha Game Reserve during the serious drought experienced in the early 1960s (Berry, 1997).

Etosha Game Reserve then received the status of a national park in 1967 by an Act of Parliament of the Republic of South Africa. In 1970, a new boundary for the park was demarcated based on the Odendaal Plan for South West Africa. ENP was thereby reduced from 93,240 km² to its present size of 22,270 km², in order to separate wildlife protection from farming activities. The largest portion of the ENP fence was erected only after these latest demarcations and boundary definitions were completed. Fencing between the farming areas and ENP was undertaken from 1955 to 1960. In 1961, a 2.6-m-high, game-proof fence was first erected along the southern boundary of ENP after an outbreak of foot-and-mouth disease in wildlife species such as kudu. This fence was reinforced with a 1.5-m-high wire mesh that was entrenched into the ground to prevent the movement of smaller species and those that could dig their way out, such as warthog. By 1973, ENP was completely fenced off with a normal (1.2-m-high, small-stock) fence, which did not prevent many species, such as warthog, lion and elephant, from escaping from the park. In later years, an electric fence was erected in areas where predators and other smaller

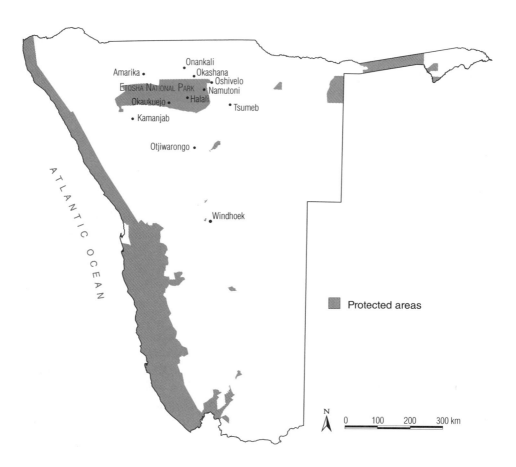

FIGURE 11.1: The present boundary of Etosha National Park.

animals frequently escaped from the park while an elephant-proof fence was erected along the north-eastern boundaries of ENP (Berry, 1997; Botha, 2005).

A wildlife census in 1926 was one of the first game count exercises to provide a list of wildlife species, especially mammals, that were present in the reserve and the surrounding areas. Mammals that were recorded included spotted and brown hyena, lion, elephant, leopard, cheetah, wild dog, warthog, caracal and black rhino. This census focused on the area around Etosha Pan and the northern neighbouring region, which was known as 'Owamboland' at that time (Berry, 1997). It was noted that most of these mammal species were found both inside the present ENP while others also roamed outside ENP. The 1998 aerial survey of wildlife reported similar species as those found in the 1926 census, although some species such as wild dog were not detected in the park (Mendelsohn et al., 2000). Furthermore, the 1998 aerial survey showed that the wildlife species were predominantly confined to the ENP and not found in the central northern area of Namibia as they had been in 1926 when wildlife was roaming freely and before the ENP fence was erected. However, a few species – such as hyena, lion and elephant – were found outside ENP, particularly in the northern, western and southern areas beyond the park, which were common migration routes for most wildlife (Mendelsohn et al., 2000).

Aerial censuses are now carried out on a regular basis. Although census methods have changed over the years, there has been a considerable change in the populations of wildlife in and outside ENP. As an example, Table 11.1 below shows that predators such as lion and hyena were recorded in the 1926 census and in 2012.

Although ENP is inhabited by large numbers and a variety of ungulates and predators, this chapter focuses more on predators and large mammals that are classified as problem animals, such as lion and elephant, because they are the main species involved in conflicts with communities surrounding ENP. Studies have shown that the fence around ENP is not completely 'animal proof' and some animals are still able to move out of the park onto neighbouring farmlands where they interact with humans and cause conflicts (Mendelsohn et al., 2000; Mfune et al., 2005).

TABLE 11.1: Numbers of some problem animal species recorded in and around Etosha, 1926 and 2012.

| Species | 2012[1] | 1926[2] | |
	Etosha National Park	Etosha Pan	Owamboland
Spotted hyena	650	4,000	300
Lion	410–505	200	10

Note: As different census methods were used in 1926 and 2012, and the boundaries and areas differed, the numbers given in this table are not directly comparable.
[1] Source: MET data.
[2] Source: Berry (1997).

Historical background of the focus communities

Namibia has a unique history of human settlement and social grouping. In this section, we describe the situation of farmers that live north of and south of ENP, as recorded during the study in 2010.

Farmers along the southern boundary of ENP

The area south of ENP consists of privately owned, commercial farmlands. Historically, these farms were occupied by what Botha (2000) called '[W]hite settlers'. White settlers started to occupy the land as early as 1900 during German colonial rule. By 1913, about 1,587 White settlers occupied 1,331 farms in Namibia.

White farmers have therefore interacted with wildlife for a long time and accumulated knowledge about their natural environment along the southern boundary of ENP. The descendants of the White settlers along the southern borders of ENP are predominantly livestock farmers, although some have now ventured into game farming and tourism. Most game farms are closest to the border with ENP since livestock farming in this area results in heavy losses due to predation. However, at the dawn of Namibia's independence, some native or Black Namibian farmers acquired some of the farms along the southern boundary of ENP through the land reform programme.

The historical interaction of White settlers and wildlife along ENP is well narrated by Botha (2005). Before the 1950s, most farmers were poor and were dependent on hunting of wildlife species towards their livelihoods. The human population census of 1946 indicated that only 8% of farmers on freehold land had an annual income of £1,000, an amount that was considered the minimum to meet obligations at that time. The high dependency of farmers on wildlife resources exerted great pressure on the management of ENP. The areas south of ENP were then set apart for farming during the 1950s. However, the Nature Conservation Ordinance of 1967 enabled freehold farmers to hunt, sell, capture and relocate wildlife according to their own economic interests. By 1968, freehold farmers had legal rights to consumptively and otherwise utilize wildlife on their farms. Landowners were encouraged to pool their land and financial resources and make available large units on which integrated management practices could be carried out. Although access to these rights created positive attitudes towards wildlife, conflicts between the farmers and wildlife continued.

Farmers along the northern boundary of ENP

The areas north of ENP are primarily communal land, mainly inhabited by the Aawambo. The Aawambo farm a combination of crops and livestock. Crop fields are, generally, not found along the park boundaries, but further away from ENP. The area well known to the Aawambo as Okashana, served as a buffer zone between the park and local communities and has provided habitat for a wide range of wildlife species (Mendelsohn et al., 2000).

Today, however, due to increasing pressure of population and expanding settlements further north, many farmers have established cattle posts for their livestock within this former buffer zone. Cattle posts have mushroomed along the northern border of the park. Although around the 1920s, wildlife was abundant in 'Owamboland' and comparable to that in the Etosha Pan area (Berry, 1997), resident large mammals are now virtually extinct in the central northern communal areas, including the area north of the ENP boundary.

The establishment of conservancies on communal lands started after the enactment of the Nature Conservation Amendment Act of 1996. A conservancy is a local, membership-based entity established at community level under the community-based natural resource management programme (CBNRM) in Namibia. The programme's aim is to actively engage farmers on communal lands in the conservation of wildlife resources while deriving economic benefits from those resources (NACSO, 2004). This programme presented a conservation opportunity to expand the distribution and range of wildlife species outside protected areas (Murphy, Vaughan, Katjiua, Mulonga, & Long, 2004; Paterson et al., 2008). However, areas that communities earmarked for wildlife conservation are the same areas that were also targeted for cattle posts.

Namibian pastoralists, including those north of ENP, have developed management systems to cope with large fluctuations in the availability of grazing resources. Local farmers north of ENP track the grazing resources base and move their animals according to the availability of grazing areas, capitalizing on good years in order to survive the drought years (Nangula, 2001). Transhumance, or seasonal cattle movement, is the regular movement of herds in order to exploit the seasonal availability of pastures and is one of the key elements of indigenous range management. The temporary locations are referred to as *oohambo* in Oshindonga, meaning cattle posts. Cattle posts are in most cases set up in wild areas without permanent human settlements. These areas, also known as *okuti* or wild lands, are isolated and are within the home range of a wide variety of wildlife.

Socio-economic background of the interviewed farmers

During the study, we interviewed 51 commercial farmers from the Kamanjab and Outjo constituencies of Kunene Region. In the communal areas, 48 owners or herders at cattle posts were interviewed in the Oshikoto, Oshana and Omusati regions along the northern border of ENP. The field study was undertaken in February 2010. The majority of respondents (78%) in the southern freehold farmlands were farm owners, while at cattle posts respondents were both livestock owners (45%) and livestock herders (44%). The remaining 11% of the respondents comprised relatives of farm owners and temporal caretakers. Most of the owners interviewed at the cattle posts and on freehold land were pensioners (above the age of 60 years). These elderly farmers are the custodians of indigenous knowledge that has been generated over the years as they have interacted with wildlife on their farms and in the livestock grazing areas.

Farmers that were interviewed were predominantly livestock farmers (small stock and large stock). Only 14% of the farmers in the freehold areas indicated farming with game and this was mainly on farms directly bordering ENP. Analysis of the data collected showed that the household income of farmers on freehold land was higher than that for farmers at the cattle posts (Table 11.2). The temporary nature of most cattle posts has probably contributed to lower incomes, unlike south of ENP

TABLE 11.2: Household income of farmers along the northern and southern borders of ENP.

Monthly income (N$)	Northern cattle posts		Southern freehold farms	
	Frequency	%	Frequency	%
Less than 1,000	35	74	18	35
1,001–2,000	3	6	5	10
2,001–3,000	4	8	3	6
3,001–4,000	1	2	2	4
4,001–10,000	2	4	5	10
10,001 and more	0	0	10	20
Not indicated	3	6	8	15
Total	**48**	**100**	**51**	**100**

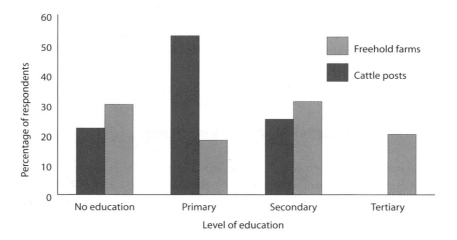

FIGURE 11.2: Levels of education of respondents at the cattle posts and on freehold farms along the borders of ENP.

where there are well-established, commercial farmers in the livestock farming and game business.

The study showed that most farmers that were interviewed on freehold land had attained higher levels of education (secondary and tertiary) compared to local farmers (Figure 11.2). However, there was a notable 31% who possessed no formal education. More than half of respondents at the cattle posts (53%) had attained at least primary education. The education level of farmers and herders is an important component for the management of HWC, although it does not hinder the application of traditional knowledge.

Levels of household income and education attainments influence the type of HWC management approaches, practices and options, and the extent to which households might cope with losses of livestock, crops and even property due to problem animals. Poorer households are likely to depend on traditional methods of preventing wildlife from raiding their livestock, unlike commercial farmers who may use more modern methods.

INDIGENOUS KNOWLEDGE ON MANAGEMENT OF HWC

HWC is not a new phenomenon around ENP, but rather historical. In the past, White farmers south of ENP depended heavily on wildlife for their direct livelihoods (Botha, 2005), suggesting that they hunted game for household consumption or traded dried game meat (biltong) with each other. However, as farmers became more established in livestock farming, they became less tolerant of species that threatened their livestock. Botha (2005) reiterates that in 1961, farmers were permitted to kill species such as jackal, hyena, caracal, leopard and wild dog because these killed their livestock. In addition, large numbers of lion and other problem animals that threatened livestock were also killed. Farmers did not only have conflict with predators, but also with ungulates that competed for scarce grazing resources and carried diseases that threatened livestock, for example foot-and-mouth disease (Botha, 2005). Botha (2005) reported that more than 6,000 jackals were killed in the 1960s. In 1982, farmers along the southern border of the park killed 79 lions (Mendelsohn et al., 2000). The numbers of lion killed along the northern borders of ENP between 1992 and 2004 ranged from 2–10 lions annually, the highest being in 2000 (MET, 2005).

Similarly, wildlife species such as the black rhino, elephant, lion, caracal, warthog, cheetah, leopard, wild dog and brown and spotted hyena roamed communal areas north of ENP in the 1920s (Berry, 1997). However, as human population numbers and settlements increased, wildlife has moved away from areas near the ENP fence or was eventually killed. There are many human–wildlife tales among the Aawambo people that indicate the long historical relationship between these people and the wildlife (see the box below).

Although ENP aims to protect wildlife by confining them within the fenced area of the park, some species of wildlife still escape into the areas bordering it. For example, some villages, for example Onanke village in Oshikoto Region and Akunya village in Omusati Region, suffer because elephant move out of ENP and destroy their crops and infrastructure such as water installations, and also threaten human lives (Mendelsohn et al., 2000; NACSO, 2014).

The relationship of farmers and wildlife at cattle posts: An interview with Tate Neifo of Onankali village, 2010

'The success of preventing or managing wildlife conflicts at cattle posts is dependent on three factors. Firstly, it is the preparation of the journey to the cattle posts. Women are expected to send off the team to the cattle posts with a meal, known as *onguta*, and the attitude and manner in which this *onguta* is prepared, determines how successful the journey to the cattle posts will be. Secondly, it is the importance of totem groups and the belief within those groups. Different totem groups have different beliefs and traditional means to protect them against wildlife attack[s]. For example, there was a cattle post where even if their livestock get lost in the wild, they always found the livestock. According to the culture, I cannot go and ask the secrets of such success at not losing livestock so that I also don't lose livestock or always find my livestock after they have been lost in the wild. Thirdly, it is the livestock herding skills that are imparted to every young man, who will herd and look after livestock at the cattle posts, through orientation. This orientation is mainly carried out by experienced elderly men in the household or family. Traditionally, people among the Aawambo do not share where their success lies. The Aawambo people are today distinct not so much by the language groups but through the totems.'

According to Peter, Codella and Eid (2007), 'A totem is an animal, plant, or natural object (or representation of an object) that serves as the emblem of a clan or family among a tribal or traditional people. A totem represents a mystical or ritual bond of unity within the group.'

Identifying the predators in their areas

Farmers from both communal and freehold farms are aware that different species of wildlife roam their lands (Table 11.3). In the case of problem animals, the farmers at cattle posts mainly mentioned lion, hyena, jackal and elephant. The problem animals that are often spotted by farmers on freehold farms include hyena, jackal, lion and cheetah. Farmers indicated that there are three ways to identify problem animals in their areas:

1. **Spoor of wildlife:** Farmers indicated that 'wild cats', e.g. lion, leopard and caracal, were the most problematic animals; they are not easily noticed because they hide in the thick bush. Schiess-Meier et al. (2007) reported that lions live in prides and are rarely found on human-altered land, but rather confine themselves to protected areas and move out to raid livestock once in a while. As a result, farmers rely on their knowledge of lion spoor in order to detect their presence. Stander (1998), for example, relied on the broad ecological knowledge and in-depth

TABLE 11.3: Proportion of respondents with the knowledge to identify problem animals, February 2010.

Problem animal	Communal farmers (%)	Commercial farmers (%)
Lion	30	14
Hyena	26	25
Jackal	17	23
Elephant	15	3
Rhino	5	0
Caracal	5	7
Leopard	2	6
Cheetah	0	13
Do not know	0	9

understanding of the Ju|'hoansi San of animal spoor, when he used spoor to estimate the number of large carnivores in the Tsumkwe area.

2. **Calls of problem animals:** Farmers also use their knowledge of the different vocal sounds of predators to detect and identify them in their surroundings. For example, the sounds made by hyena at night are distinct from the roar of lions.

3. **Sight of animals:** Although farmers do not commonly encounter most predators, they use their knowledge of the physical appearance of animals in order to identify problem animals.

Farmers' understanding of the seasonal movements of problem predators

Having an understanding of seasonal movement patterns of predators and other problem animals is necessary for farmers to manage HWC. Most of these wildlife species move from ENP into communal and freehold areas bordering the park during different seasons. According to the farmers, some predators move out of the national park to catch prey. Farmers suggest that predators such as lion perhaps find it easier to catch and eat a cow that does not run away than to chase after a springbok or zebra that will run away very fast and escape predation.

The wet season in this area of Namibia is from January to May, while the dry season is from June to December (Trinkel, 2013). Farmers had two main views on these seasons and predator behaviour. Commercial farmers indicated that during the wet season, when there is thick vegetation, predators leave the park because it becomes difficult for them to catch natural prey, even though there is plenty of prey, especially ungulates, due to availability of adequate grazing during this time. Furthermore, some animals such as lion, which give birth to their young during the wet season, tend to raid livestock in order to obtain adequate food to have sufficient energy and nutrients to lactate and feed their young. It is no surprise therefore that Trinkel (2013) reported that a high number of adult females are destroyed on farmland during breeding in the wet season when they raid livestock. As Trinkel (2013) states, these high losses of lionesses may adversely affect the lion's social structure inside ENP.

Communal farmers, however, indicated that predator attacks increase during the dry season when their livestock have to travel long distances in search of food. These farmers also mentioned that they graze their livestock closer to ENP during the dry season because the vegetation is better and more readily available. This sentiment is supported by Arnord (2001) who reported high losses of livestock to predators in Kunene Region during the dry season due to the long distances that livestock move from the farmers' homesteads in search of grazing pastures, often close to ENP. The vulnerability of livestock to predators during the dry season is associated with less-dense vegetation, which makes the livestock more visible, and the lack of herding when the livestock move far away from cattle posts. Furthermore, the abundance of wildlife prey decreases during the dry season (Stander, 2010; Trinkel, 2013), which increases the vulnerability of livestock grazing close to ENP to predation.

Farmers' identification of the predators

Fifty per cent (50%) of freehold and communal farmers singled out jackal as the most dominant predator responsible for small-stock losses on their farms (Figure 11.3). A study in Kunene Region similarly revealed that the black-backed jackal was the greatest and most constant threat to livestock (Arnord, 2001). In the present study,

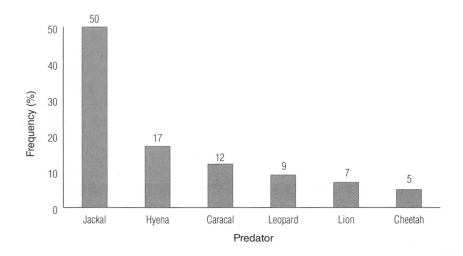

FIGURE 11.3: Frequency, indicated by interviewed farmers, that various predators were responsible for killing small stock on their farms north and south of the ENP boundary.

farmers mentioned hyena and caracal as the second and third most problematic animals, respectively, that kill their small stock (i.e. sheep and goats).

The study revealed slight variations in the perceptions of freehold and communal farmers regarding predators that were most problematic regarding large stock (cattle and donkeys) (Figure 11.4). The majority of communal farmers (60%) at cattle posts pointed to lion as the major killer of their large stock, while only 30% mentioned hyena (Figure 11.4). Freehold farmers ranked hyena (31%) and lion (28%) to be about twice as problematic to their large stock as leopard (12%).

Both freehold and communal farmers indicated that they are able to identify predators responsible for killing their livestock. They investigate the incidents at the site where it happened and the surrounding areas. Firstly, the farmer inspects the livestock carcass to identify claw and bite marks of the predator that might have killed the livestock. This is usually helpful in identifying the species and type of predator that killed their livestock. Predators have characteristic ways in which they kill and eat their prey. Secondly, the farmer inspects the surrounding area for spoor and the vegetation to detect the presence of predators. This assists in narrowing down the species of predator and is used to provide an accurate identification. Finally, the farmer follows the spoor to ascertain whether the predator is still in the vicinity and can be spotted, or might lead to the site along the ENP fence where the predator escaped.

This process is aided by the knowledge and understanding of the farmers of the external physical characteristics of each animal species, the predators' unique species-specific spoor and calls to provide a more accurate identification. In most cases, strategies which farmers develop are dictated by their experience of how

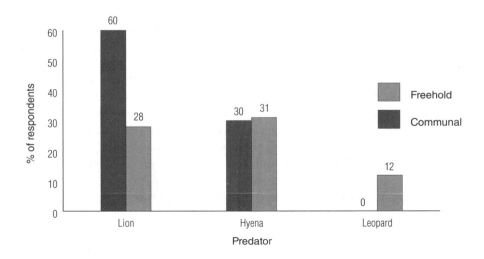

FIGURE 11.4: Frequency that respondents on freehold and communal farms stated the three main predators as responsible for killing large stock north and south of the ENP boundaries.

predators kill their livestock. For example, cattle-post farmers have learnt that lions do not usually kill livestock in the presence of humans. Hence farmers sometimes use fire and noise to scare off suspected lions. In addition, respondents in the study area stated that each predator has a characteristic and unique way in which they kill their prey. Farmers use this knowledge to identify the predator from the remains of the livestock. The knowledge of both freehold and communal farmers about bite and claw marks corresponds with identification of predators specified in Schumann's guide to integrated livestock and predator management (Schumann, 2004). The bite marks of a lion indicate a more powerful attack because of their strong jaws and canines. A hyena attack is very messy, with intestines and skin strewn or eaten. The jackal bites at the back of the legs and on the udder. Caracal claw marks are usually visible on the hindquarters. Furthermore, farmers are aware that jackal and hyena mostly attack small stock, whereas lion can kill large stock. Jackal is also associated with killing newborn kid goats in the veld.

Farmers' local knowledge to prevent conflicts with predators

The HWC that communities along the boundary of ENP have experienced over a long period of time has contributed to the development of methods or practices to prevent, reduce or mitigate it. Farmers erect kraals and fences, herd and kraal livestock, maintain fences and create buffer zones to prevent, reduce or mitigate against livestock losses.

The three most commonly used mitigation strategies to reduce HWC at cattle posts along the northern border of ENP include scaring off wildlife, and kraaling livestock at dusk and herding them during the day. Farmers at cattle posts in communal areas might graze their livestock close to or away from the cattle posts, while freehold farmers predominantly graze their livestock inside their (fenced) farms (Table 11.4). Farmers stated that they are aware that those grazing livestock away from cattle posts are more likely to come into conflict with predators than those who graze close to them. However, the pasture around the cattle posts is not always in good condition, so they venture further away from them.

Communal farmers erect strong kraals to help prevent predators from killing livestock. The structure and materials used to erect kraals, locally known as *iigunda*, at cattle posts have evolved over time in response to escalating HWC in the area (Figure 11.5). In the past, it was sufficient to erect kraals using thorny bush to make a hedge. These hedged kraals, however, became ineffective with increasing predator attacks. Livestock, especially cattle and goats, panic and react wildly when a predator comes near the kraal and some even jump or break out of it. With time, most farmers started erecting kraals that were made from poles only, but even these were not very effective. This has led most farmers to erect kraals that are made from wooden poles reinforced with chicken mesh wire to prevent predators entering the kraal or livestock from breaking out of the kraal (Figure 11.5).

FIGURE 11.5: Fences, similar to this one, built from sturdy timber poles and supported by barbed wire are used to construct kraals at cattle posts along the northern borders of ENP to prevent livestock losses to predators. (© John Mendelsohn.)

TABLE 11.4: Frequency of areas used by farmers to graze their livestock, 2010.

Area where livestock grazed	Communal farmers (%)	Commercial farmers (%)
Inside the farm	0	98[1]
Around cattle posts	48	0
Away from settlements and cattle posts	52	0

[1] 2% of commercial farmers did not indicate where they grazed their livestock.

Herding, or *okulitha*, is an old traditional practice of the Aawambo that continues to play an important role in protecting livestock from wildlife attacks along the borders of ENP.

Making noise by beating drums, singing or occasionally shooting in the air is used to scare off wildlife. Dogs, which bark when predators are close, and making fire, are also used to keep wildlife away (Table 11.5). However, MET discourages people from keeping dogs close to ENP, especially in areas where elephants move. One farmer supported MET on this saying, 'Elephants do not tolerate dogs. Dogs are a nuisance to them and they can destroy anything, including humans, because of dogs.' Although this may be the case, work by non-government organizations, such as the Cheetah Conservation Fund (CCF), have shown that keeping certain breeds of dogs that are trained to guard livestock may contribute to reducing losses of livestock to predators.

According to one cattle-post farmer, making noises such as beating drums and singing has been used traditionally to indicate human presence in the wilderness. Similar practices are used in Nepal to scare off or deter raiding wildlife (Shrestha, 2007). Making large fires around kraals is another strategy used to scare wildlife away from cattle posts. Firewood from *Dichrostachys cinerea*, or *onyege*, is preferred

TABLE 11.5: The four most-common mechanisms used by farmers bordering ENP to manage HWC.

Management action	Communal farmers %	Commercial farmers %
Scare-off wildlife	39	
Collect and kraal livestock	25	
Herd livestock	17	
Patrol farm camps and ENP fence	12	11
Trap, poison or kill predators		37
Maintain fences		20
Move to different grazing lands		8
No mechanism mentioned	7	24

and most commonly used at cattle posts to light fires because it burns through the night. According to one cattle-post farmer, 'the wood of this species is like oil; it makes strong fires and can even flame higher when it is raining.' At some cattle posts, herders or cattle owners occasionally shoot in the air to scare off predators. Some elderly farmers use shotguns, *omushasho*, which were acquired during World War II.

In contrast to communal farmers along the northern boundary of ENP, commercial farmers along the southern boundary mainly use four important traditional strategies to deal with HWC (Table 11.5). They patrol and maintain camp fences, rotate their livestock herds from one camp to the next, and trap, poison or kill predators. In addition to these practices, both communal and freehold farmers also patrol and fix sections of ENP fence that are broken. A strong fence reduces and deters predators from entering their farms. Commercial farmers practice rotational farming rather than transhumance. The movement of livestock between camps enables pastures to regenerate and recover from grazing and also reduces livestock losses to predators. The southern boundary fence of the ENP has sections that are game proof, with the fence at a height of 2.3 m (in contrast to a small-stock fence, which is 1.2 m high). Game-proof fencing is very expensive to maintain and, as a result, farmers suffer great livestock losses. While farmers in the communal areas only scare wildlife away by shooting, commercial farmers actually kill problem animals on their farms. Almost 50% of interviewed cattle-post farmers were in possession of a firearm while only 34% freehold farmers had guns.

In addition to physical fences, commercial and cattle-post farmers also create buffer areas or zones between their livestock farming areas and the ENP. Most herders north of the ENP graze their livestock a certain distance away from the park boundary to reduce conflicts with wildlife. Similarly, farmers on the southern boundary of ENP subdivide their farms into camps, allocating the camps that border directly onto the park to game farming. The game areas act as a buffer to the livestock, reducing losses to predation.

Although farmers use different mitigation strategies against HWC, most farmers (77%) north and south of the park are not sure if these methods are effective at all. This suggests that despite the different traditional methods farmers apply, HWC still happens.

CONCLUSION

Human–wildlife conflict (HWC) is not a new phenomenon around ENP, but has a long and rich history. Farmers from both northern and southern boundaries of ENP reported that there are different species of wild animals, including predators, that roam into their communities and on to farmlands. Problem animals commonly spotted in communal and commercial farms include lion, hyena, jackal and elephant. Farmers have a rich knowledge of problem animals that are involved in HWC. They demonstrate knowledge of wildlife behaviours, physical appearances, calls and spoors that is beneficial in understanding HWC and the problem animals involved.

In this chapter, we have reported that local farmers are aware of and continue to experience impacts caused by different predators and that they are able to identify predators from livestock wounds and other means. Farmers along ENP boundaries mitigate and manage HWC by applying traditional methods that create barriers to predators, and scare them away. Local farmers also ensure survival of their livestock by guarding and herding livestock. Although livestock and human numbers along the boundaries of ENP are increasing, especially in the north, farmers continue to maintain distance as a buffer between the park and their livestock as they have traditionally done, thus minimizing prey–predator incidents.

This study concludes that livestock farmers around ENP hold important indigenous knowledge and that this wealth of knowledge is important in the continuing efforts, by MET, its managers of this protected area and local communities, in the struggle to address and manage HWC. Such indigenous ecological knowledge is not only important to consider in future revisions of the HWC policy and strategy, but once documented, will serve as knowledge that can be shared, tested and applied along the boundaries of other protected areas where similar HWC exists.

References

Arnord, M. B. (2001). *Predators in the Kunene Region: An overview of problem animals and prospects.* Windhoek, Namibia: WILD Projects Working Paper, No. 6, Ministry of Environment and Tourism.

Berkes, F., Colding, J., & Folke, C. (2000). Rediscovery of traditional ecological knowledge as adaptive management. *Ecological Applications 10*(5), 1251-1262.

Berry, H. (1997). Historical review of the Etosha Region and its subsequent administration as a national park. *Madoqua*, *20*(1), 3-12.

Botha, C. (2000). The politics of land resettlement in Namibia, 1890–1960. *South African Historical Journal*, *42*, 232-276.

Botha, C. (2005). People and the environment in colonial Namibia. *South African Historical Journal*, *52*, 170-190.

Chardonnet, P., Soto, B., Fritz, H., Crosmary, W., Drouet-Hoguet, N., Mesochina, P., Pellerin, M., Mallon D., Bakker, L., Boulet, H., & Lamarque, F. (2010). *Managing the conflicts between people and lion: Review and insights from the literature and field experience*. Rome, Italy: Wildlife Management Working Paper, 13, Food and Agriculture Organization of the United Nations.

Dieckmann, U. (2007). *Hai//Om in the Etosha National Park: A history of colonial settlement, ethnicity and nature conservation*. Basel, Switzerland: Basler Afrika Bibliographien.

Gilchrist, H. G., Mallory, M. L., & Merkel, F. (2005). Can local ecological knowledge contribute to wildlife management? Case studies of migratory birds. *Ecology and Society*, *10*(1), 20.

Graham, K., Beckerman, A. P., & Thirgood, S. (2005). Human–predator–prey conflicts: Ecological correlates, prey losses and patterns of management. *Biological Conservation*, *122*(2), 159-171.

GRN [Republic of Namibia]. (2009). *National policy on human wildlife conflict management*. Windhoek, Namibia: Ministry of Environment and Tourism.

Jones, B. T. B., & Barnes, J. I. (2006). *Human–wildlife conflict study: Namibian case study*. Windhoek, Namibia: Design and Development Services.

Madden, F. (2004). Creating coexistence between humans and wildlife: Global perspectives on local efforts to address human–wildlife conflict. *Human Dimensions of Wildlife*, *9*, 247-257.

Matson, T. K., Goldizen, A. W., & Jarman, P. J. (2004). Factors affecting the success of translocations of the black-faced impala in Namibia. *Biological Conservation*, *116*(3), 359-365.

Mauro, F., & Hardison, P. D. (2000). Traditional knowledge of indigenous and local communities: International debate and policy initiatives. *Ecological Applications*, *10*, 1263-1269.

Mendelsohn, J. M., el Obeid, S., & Roberts, C. S. (2000). *A profile of north-central Namibia*. Windhoek, Namibia: Gamsberg Macmillan.

Menzies, C. (2006). *Traditional ecological knowledge and natural resource management*. Lincoln, Nebraska, USA: University of Nebraska Press.

MET [Ministry of Environment and Tourism]. (2005). *Proceedings of the national workshop on human–wildlife conflict management in Namibia, Safari Hotel, Windhoek, 16–17 March, 2005*. Windhoek, Namibia: Author.

Mfune, J. K., Mosimane, A., Hamukuaja, H., & Angula, M. (2005). *A preliminary survey of human–wildlife conflict along the northern borders of Etosha National Park*. Windhoek, Namibia: Ministry of Environment and Tourism.

Milenković, M. (2008). Large carnivores as added value – economic, biological and cultural aspects. In R. G. Potts, & K. Hecker, (Eds.), *Coexistence of large carnivores and humans: Threat or benefit? Proceedings of the International Symposium preceding the 54th CIC General Assembly, 1 May 2007, Belgrade, Serbia, 2007* (pp. 1-4). Budakeszi, Hungary: International Council for Game and Wildlife Conservation. Retrieved from http://www1.nina.no/lcie_new/pdf/634991314059237563_CIC_Full_Proceedings.pdf

Murphy, C., Vaughan, C., Katjiua, J., Mulonga, S., & Long, S. A. (2004). The cost of living with wildlife. In S. A. Long, (Ed.) *Livelihoods and CBNRM in Namibia: Findings of the WILD Project. Final technical report of the Wildlife Integration for Livelihoods Diversification Project (WILD)*. Windhoek, Namibia: Ministry of Environment and Tourism.

NACSO [Namibian Association of CBNRM Support Organisations]. (2004). *Namibia's communal conservancies: A review of progress and challenges*. Windhoek, Namibia: Author.

NACSO [Namibian Association of CBNRM Support Organisations]. (2014). *Community conservation in Namibia: A review of communal conservancies, community forests and other CBNRM initiatives*. Windhoek, Namibia: Author.

Nangula, S. (2001). *Effects of artificial water points on communal rangelands in the Uuvudhiya Constituency, North-Central Namibia*, (Master's thesis, Norwegian University of Life Sciences, Norway).

Naughton-Treves, L., Holland, M. B., & Brandon, K. (2005). The role of protected areas in conserving biodiversity and sustaining local livelihoods. *Annual Review of Environment and Resources, 30*, 219-252.

Nepal, S. K., & Weber, K. W. (1995). Prospects for coexistence: Wildlife and local people. *Ambio, 24*(4), 238-245.

Ogra, M. V. (2008). Human–wildlife conflict and gender in protected area borderlands: A case study of costs, perceptions, and vulnerabilities from Uttarakhand (Uttaranchal), India. *Geoforum, 39*, 1408-1422.

Paterson, B., Stuart-Hill, G., Underhill, L. G., Dunne, T. T., Schinzel, B., Brown, C., Beytell, B., Demas, F., Lindeque, M., Tagg, J., & Weaver, C. (2008). A fuzzy decision support tool for wildlife translocations into communal conservation in Namibia. *Environmental Modelling & Software, 23*, 521-534.

Patterson, B. D., Kasiki, S. M., Selempo, E., & Kays, R. W. (2004). Livestock predation by lions (*Panthera leo*) and other carnivores on ranches neighbouring Tsavo National Parks, Kenya. *Biological Conservation 119*, 507-16.

Peter, M., Codella, G. S., & Eid, Y. (2007). 'Totem'. In Cutler J. Cleveland (Ed.), *Encyclopedia of Earth*. Washington DC, USA: Environmental Information Coalition, National Council for Science and the Environment.

Schiess-Meier, M., Ramsauer. S., Gabanapelo, T., & König, B. (2007). Livestock predation – insights from problem animal control registers in Botswana. *Journal of Wildlife Management, 71*(4), 1267-1274.

Schumann, M. (2004). *Guide to integrated livestock and predator management*. Windhoek, Namibia: CCF/RISE, Cheetah Conservation Fund.

Shemwetta, D. T. K., & Kideghesho, J. R. (Eds.). (2000). *Human–wildlife conflicts in Tanzania: What research and extension could offer to conflict resolution? Proceedings of the 1st University Wide Conference, 5th – 7th April, Volume 3* (pp. 559-568). Institute of Continuing Education (ICE), SUA.

Shrestha, R. (2007). *A case study on human–wildlife conflicts in Nepal* (pp.1-62). Gland, Switzerland: Species Program, WWF International.

Sitati, N. W., & Ipara, H. (2012). Indigenous ecological knowledge of a human–elephant interaction in Transmara District, Kenya: Implications for research and management. *Advances in Anthropology, 2*(3), 107-111. doi: 10.4236/aa.2012.23012

Stander, F. (1998). Spoor counts as indices of large carnivore populations: The relationship between spoor frequency and true density and sampling effort. *Journal of Applied Ecology, 35*, 378-385.

Stander P. (2010). The impact of male-biased mortality on the population structure of desert-adapted lion in Namibia. *Research Report 2010, Desert Lion Conservation*. Retrieved from http://www.desertlion.info/reports/dlion2010.pdf

Thomassen, J., Linnell, J., & Skogen, K. (2011). *Wildlife-human interactions: From conflict to coexistence in sustainable landscapes, final report from a joint Indo-Norwegian project, 2007–2011*. Trondheim, Norway: Norwegian Institute for Nature Research (NINA).

Treves, A. (2008). The human dimensions of conflicts with wildlife around protected area. In M. J. Manfredo, J. J. Vaske, P. J. Brown, D. J. Decker, & E. A. Duke (Eds.), *Wildlife and society: The science of human dimensions* (pp. 214-228). Washington, USA: Island Press.

Trinkel, M. (2013). Climate variability, human wildlife conflict and population dynamics of lions *Panthera leo. Naturwissenschaften, 100*(4), 345-53.

12

Understanding indigenous coping strategies of the Basubiya on the flooded plains of the Zambezi River

Nchindo Richardson Mbukusa

> '*Umvuvu kaliwanikilwa feela mumuzuka musenamenzi mwadubwana*'
> – It isn't easy to find a hippo on dry lands where there is no water for wallowing and swimming –
> (Chief Kisco Liswani III of the Basubiya Tribal Authority)

INTRODUCTION

The Basubiya – or Bekuhane as they are also known – are often described as a riverine group of people (BNA, n.d.; Gibbons, 1904; Encyclopaedia Britannica, 1911; Shamukuni, 1972; Mainga, 1973; Mubitana, 1975; Tlou & Campbell, 1984; Likando, 1989; Masule, 1995; Larson, 2001; Gumbo, 2002; Ramsay, 2002; Manning, 2011; Ndana, 2011; Mabuta, Masule, & Tembwe, 2013). It is no wonder that Chief Kisco Liswani III warned that they would rather perish in the water than find themselves wandering in the drier areas away from the rivers and all that they would offer them. The Basubiya of the flooded plains of the Zambezi Region liken themselves to hippos and other amphibious animals. They feel that staying away from river waters 'deculturalizes' them. It is difficult to imagine the Basubiya outside this environment (Shamukuni, 1972; Masule, 1995; Gumbo, 2002; Samunzala, 2003; Ndana, 2011). In the face of possible relocation at times when water volumes increase, they might remark rhetorically, '*ho zwisa inswi mu meenzi mpohonachi ihala*?' – 'If you take a fish out of water, can it survive?'

From history immemorial, the Bekuhane (used interchangeably with Basubiya in this chapter) have lived along the Upper Zambezi River and its Chobe–Linyanti tributaries in southern Africa. The waters of these rivers flow and feed into each

FIGURE 12.1:
The Basubiya of the Zambezi floodplains liken themselves to the hippopotamus, which needs the river to survive. (© George Sanzila.)

other depending on where the rain has fallen and which is flowing more strongly. Seasonally, they flood the wedge of low-lying plains between them to variable levels. The Bekuhane's economic activities centre mainly on these surface waters of the Zambezi–Chobe basin. They have been reported to be agriculturalists that cultivate crops along rivers while also keeping livestock (Shamukuni, 1972; Tlou & Campbell, 1984; Masule, 1995; Olson, 1996; Ramsay, 2002; Ndana, 2011; Mabuta et. al., 2013). In the past, they would only be found on drier lands when they were besieged by their enemies, but would return to wetlands when opportunities availed themselves (Olson, 1996). Their environment comprises perennial rivers, lakes, depressions, rapids, marshes, slightly elevated areas, swamps and floodplains, which support a variety of aquatic plants, birdlife, fish and wildlife.

A good number of the Bekuhane still live on land that is always surrounded by water, although a few live permanently on drier land. The group that is on the drier land also have land on the floodplains as they initially lived there, and return from time to time. All the Basubiya groups prefer deep river channels of the mighty Zambezi River, which support a number of good-eating bream fish (cichlids from the genera *Serranochromis*, *Sargochromis* and *Oreochromis*). There are many types of fruits and plants that the Bekuhane eat, which grow in and around the river. They spend much of their time in and on the water – much like the hippos they identify with.

Although much work has been done by international and local researchers and practitioners on coping strategies in flooded areas (Lupala, 2002; Sakijege, Lupala, & Sheuya, 2012; Wisner, Blaikie, Cannon, & Davis, 2004; Parry, Canziani, Palutikof, van der Linden, & Hanson, 2007), no one has recently explored what it is about the rise and fall of the Zambezi River that gratifies the people of the Zambezi floodplains. In this chapter, the results of qualitative research through in-depth, face-to-face and focused group interviews with the Basubiya, and the insight these provided, are discussed. This chapter contributes to the indigenous knowledge of flood management.

Fifty adult Basubiya (39 males, 11 females) of 70 years and older, living on the floodplains of Zambezi Region in Namibia, voluntarily participated in this study. The majority had no formal education. Through narration, various themes were discussed, such as how they know when the floods will reach them; the joy these bring and the destruction they cause; how the waters are traversed; what foods the floods offer; and how they cope during the floods. The main purpose of this chapter is to help us understand what keeps the Basubiya on the floodplains by examining three pillars of the Basubiya's indigenous knowledge, namely:

1. How the Basubiya know the size of the flood that surrounds them;
2. What makes them enjoy the time of flooding; and
3. How they cope during the floods.

THE ZAMBEZI FLOODPLAINS

Namibia is well known for its vast contrasting landscapes, and the Zambezi Region is no exception. Zambezi Region boasts the Zambezi River in the north and the Kwando–Mashi–Linyanti–Chobe rivers system in the west and south. These rivers meet in the north-east where the region abuts Zimbabwe. At certain times of the year the Zambezi Region is more swampy and riverine in the areas around the villages of Isize, Malindi, Schuckmannsburg, Nantungu, Itomba, Nsundwa, Mpukano, Ikaba, Muzii, Impalila, Kasika, Mbalasinte, Ivilivinzi, Lusese, Kabbe, Masikili, Ioma, Mutikila, Ibbu and Mahundu (see Figure 12.2).

The large body of water that often covers the eastern floodplains around March and April, perhaps more than anything else, sets the Zambezi Region apart from the

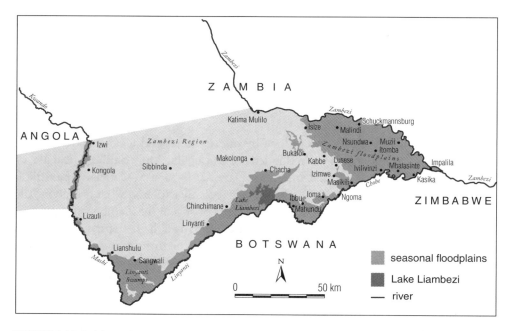

FIGURE 12.2: Map of eastern Zambezi Region showing the area and some villages prone to flooding. Adapted from Mendelsohn, Jarvis, Roberts, & Robertson (2002).

rest of Namibia. The catchment area for the Zambezi River, which feeds the eastern floodplains, is in Zambia, while the catchment for the Kwando–Mashi–Linyanti–Chobe system is in Angola (Aust, 2009). The Zambezi River floodplains start just east of Katima Mulilo and extend about 90 km to Impalila Island (the eastern-most tip of Namibia bordering on Zambia, Botswana and Zimbabwe). When the river is full, the river overflows its banks into small, interconnecting rivers that, as the water rises, then flood large areas of low-lying plains of eastern Zambezi Region, sometimes all the way to its southern border.

The beautiful wetlands created by this seasonal flooding teem with fish, birdlife, diverse vegetation and abundant wildlife in many areas (Sparg, 2007). These Zambezi floodplains have been seasonally inundated since time immemorial. The most-recent and most-devastating floods were experienced in 2004, 2007, 2009 and 2010. In these years, some of the lodges and residential houses along the Zambezi River were heavily flooded. Islands that usually serve as higher, dry grounds were totally immersed in water. The local fishermen's camps were destroyed. Low-lying schools and villages were flooded.

Dangers of the floods

Floods present numerous dangers to life including possible drownings, exposure to bacteria and pollutants, and threats from wildlife transported by floodwaters (Reacher et al., 2004; Makhanya, Tumbare, & Makurira, 2012). During the floods locals come into closer contact with crocodiles, snakes and hippos. Thousands of flood-affected villagers in the Zambezi Region also endure the seasonal headache of malaria-bearing mosquitos. Floods also submerge fields reducing local agricultural production. Livestock are put at risk when grazing areas become flooded, as they can drown. Losses of human life and livestock have been recorded over the past years (Maseheka, 2011). In addition, schools are closed, flooded or isolated from educational services provided by the government. In some cases, schools use temporary shelters, but the interruption of classes has always affected learners and teachers in the flooded areas.

Generally, floods displace people from their homes, which place burdens on governments. In the case of Namibia, people resettled during floods require temporary shelters and 'receive bags of maize meal, boxes of tinned fish, cooking oil, tents, blankets, mosquito nets and other items' (Sibeene, 2007). The Integrated Regional Information Networks reported that 'the government has done an excellent job in putting all their resources together to respond to the floods in Zambezi. They are using choppers and boats to deliver food [to flood-affected people]' (IRIN, 2003). Clinics and schools get their supplies by boat or helicopter during times of flood (Nalisa, 2003).

Move or stay?

The fact that people think rationally drives them to make choices in life. This way of making decisions is founded in rational choice theory (RCT). RCT attempts to explain all conforming and deviant social phenomena in terms of how self-interested individuals make choices under the influence of their preferences. It treats social exchange in a similar way to economic exchange in which all parties try to maximize their advantage or gain, and minimize their disadvantage or loss (Browning, Halcli, & Webster, 2000).

RCT premises that (1) human beings base their behaviour on thought processes that use logical, objective and systematic methods coupled with experience in reaching a conclusion or solving a problem; (2) they act rationally when making choices; and (3) their choices are aimed at optimizing their pleasure or profit (Business Dictionary, n.d.). The concept has applications in economics, marketing, criminology and international relations. Furthermore, it has higher applications in the decision of whether to move or stay on the flooded plains by the Bekuhane people.

There are many questions that are asked by the Bekuhane on why they should be relocated to drier lands when they have always lived in close association with the floodwaters. They question how they will live on higher, drier lands, and whether they will still have opportunities to catch fish, harvest plants and eat the foods their ancestors ate. They consider it part of their culture to live in wetlands. This situation has created conflict between the Bekuhane and the Government of Namibia, as the government's view is that the floods pose threats to human life and wellbeing.

Since fatalities due to the floods were incurred in post-independent Namibia, the government has insisted that people living on the floodplains should move to higher grounds permanently, or at least during the times they are flooded.

'Government is formulating logistics to permanently relocate, to higher ground, thousands of people who are displaced by floods in the Zambezi every year. The planned long-term solution could also save millions of dollars of government and donor money, which is spent on relocating and feeding people who are displaced by floods.' (Malumo, 2008).

Government officials considered the disastrous consequences of flooding as self-inflicted because many people ignored the government's early warnings to move to higher grounds. The local government had identified four higher-ground, temporary relocation sites – Lusese, Schuckmannsburg, Kabbe and Impalila. The areas identified as the most affected by floods were Muzii, Mpukano, Ikaba, Ivilivinzi, Malindi, Masikili, Nsundwa, Ioma, Mahundu and Nankutwe (DREF, 2007).

Brief history of floods in the region

The Basubiya have a long history of the flooded areas. Traditional history around the floods on the Zambezi floodplains is passed from generation to generation. The most serious floods that the elders still relive are those that occurred in 1948, 1952 and 1958. Great stories around these flood times have been told and are cherished by the elders of the entire Zambezi Region. Records of rainfall and the levels of the Zambezi River show how rainfall influences river level and flooding of the eastern Zambezi plains (Figure 12.3).

The levels of the Zambezi River measured close to, or above, 8 m in 1969, 1978 and 2009 (Figure 12.3). At such levels, volumes of water flooded the plains in the region. When rainfall of 800–900 mm is recorded in Zambezi Region, there is a higher expectation of floods. Experience has shown that river levels between 4 m and 8 m do greater damage to the infrastructure. The Basubiya of the Zambezi floodplains have lived with these floods for generations and learnt to cope with them and use them to their advantage. They show a high degree of preparedness, and have few recorded fatalities.

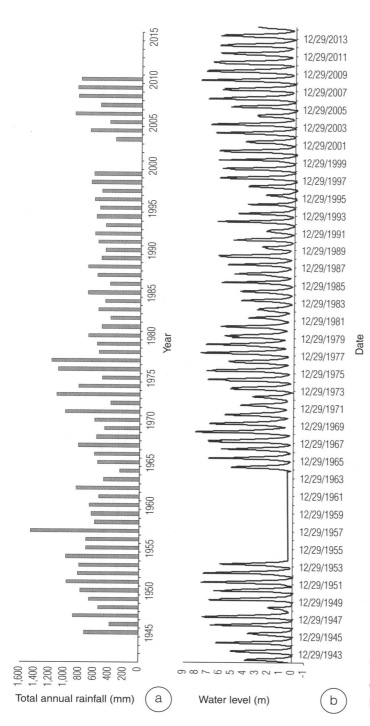

FIGURE 12.3:
(a) Total annual rainfall at Katima Mulilo, calculated from September of the previous year to August of the reported year, 1945–2010, adapted from Mendelsohn, Jarvis, Roberts and Robertson (2002) and Bosch (2011), and (b) the mean daily water levels of the Zambezi River at Katima Mulilo, 1942–2014 (courtesy of Hydrology Division, Ministry of Agriculture, Water and Forestry, Namibia, 2015).

UNDERSTANDING THE BASUBIYA'S ATTITUDE

Understanding how the Bekuhane of the Zambezi floodplains know when a flood is coming, to what extent it will disrupt their lives (and bring them peace), and how they deal with it and not fear it, contributes to the knowledge of flood management. Such understanding would help the present generation appreciate the indigenous knowledge and skills practised by the older generations.

Data collection

A qualitative research approach was used to investigate the case of the Bekuhane. Qualitative research seeks to explore a phenomenon or experience in order to discover and describe its general nature or, depending on the researcher's topic and goals, to build or test theories of human behaviour, opinion, motives or attitudes through observation or dialogue in a manner that places emphasis on the nuances and implicit meanings of the subjects' actions or words (Patton, 1990; Creswell, 2003; McMillan & Schumacher, 2006).

From a population of about 9,000 people affected by the flood in 2009 (GRN, 2009), 50 adults voluntarily participated in this study. The majority of the participants were male (78%), ranging between 60 and 90 years of age or older; about 90% of them had no formal education. Participants shared their experiences and knowledge of the floods through discussion in small groups of 6–12 people.

Semi-structured interviews guided the process for gathering information from these key informants, supported by field notes (Kvale, 1996). The researcher started with general questions, moved to specific questions and then returned to a set of more general questions. This funnel approach (from general to specific) engaged the interest of participants quickly, whereas very specific questions at the beginning might have led to a discussion that would become too focused and narrow.

Focus group discussions were held over four seasons (2006–2009) during flood migration (March and April) to gather the data. Such discussions created 'a social environment in which group members are stimulated by one another's perceptions and ideas...' which helped the researcher 'increase the quality and richness of data through a more efficient strategy than one-on-one interviewing' (McMillan & Schumacher, 2006). Group interviews are often used simply as a quick and convenient way to collect data from several people simultaneously, however, focus group discussions purposely use group interaction as part of the method. This means that instead of the researcher asking each person to respond to a question in turn, group members are encouraged to converse with each other – asking questions, exchanging anecdotes and commenting on each other's experiences and points of view. The method is particularly useful for exploring people's knowledge and experiences and can be used to examine not only what people think, but also how they think and why they think that way. It is an effective technique for exploring the attitudes and needs of respondents (McBrien, Felizardo, Orr, & Raymond, 2008).

PEOPLE'S VOICES AND IMPLICATIONS

The focus of this section is to share the memories of the floods in 1948 and 1958, as these were cited most often as being the greatest floods in recent years. In 1948 and 1958, the area now known as Zambezi Region was almost entirely covered by floodwaters, except the higher grounds, but that still:

> 'never made us move to higher grounds. We know that flood will subside when it opens out at Ngoma Bridge. Ngoma is like a funnel with higher volume of water from one side to the other. It is a pendulum-like situation. Remember that we would have higher floods in the *chaana* [(floodplains)] while *Bulwizi* [(Barotseland)] is subsiding. This is what would happen when Ngoma, Mutikitila, Ioma, Ibbu and Mahundu valleys flooded.'

There was plenty fish then. Properties and possessions were destroyed, but people managed to recover very well. Some of the land that was dry for a long time became ready for agriculture. 'We [did] not have these things that you use these days for watering. We [were] dependent solely on floodwater to irrigate our crops.'

Knowledge about the looming flood

There were several signs that helped the people of the Zambezi floodplains assess what the flood would hold for them. The ancestors 'taught us strategies that we should never forget.' The first sign was where the weaver and other birds that nest along the rivers nested.

> 'When we see that the nests of birds that are built on the reeds or twigs of shrubs ... above the level of the Zambezi River or its tributaries, we begin to estimate the level of the water that is coming. The higher the nest is built on the reed, the higher the body of the water. The lower the nest, the lower the level of the water that is coming.'

The lesser-masked weaver (*Ploceus intermedius*), for example, has always stood the test of floods on the Zambezi plains (Figure 12.4). The height of the weavers' nests has always served as a good indication of the coming flood level and has not failed the Basubiya in the prediction of flood levels yet.

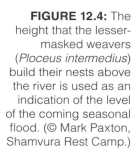

FIGURE 12.4: The height that the lesser-masked weavers (*Ploceus intermedius*) build their nests above the river is used as an indication of the level of the coming seasonal flood. (© Mark Paxton, Shamvura Rest Camp.)

Secondly, 'we have also known that when we see the earliest floods hitting Botswana in the south, and returning to the plains with higher volume and speed, there is trouble. If the volume and speed [of water] is seen continuing around January and February, we should begin to prepare ourselves for greater volumes of water.'

Floods breaking in January, earlier than the expected time of mid-March, also serve as an alert for greater floods that year.

Thirdly, *isunda lya mukwame* (the 'male wave' of the Zambezi River) is lower than the 'female wave' because the latter has *vana ni luhasi* (all the children with it), which makes it higher. When all this is seen, people should immediately know where the hills are. A 'female wave' is higher and flows faster than the normal 'male' wave. It feeds tributaries quicker than the ordinary wave. The 'male wave' is slower and might not go as far as a 'female wave'.

Lastly, 'when we sometimes see *ifulu* [(froth in the water)], we know that it is brought by fighting … tides or waves – that is a warning of higher tides. We also begin to move to higher grounds.'

Sometimes, interviewees knew by comparing the level of the water with those in the past floods, especially around February of each year. Floods are most likely in the month of March; March is known among the people of the floodplains as *Liatamanyi*, meaning 'the abundance of water as streams and rivers open up'. April is known as *Lungu* by the Basubiya, which is derived from *kuungumana* (the flood will subside for a while).

'If the flood is [only] approaching us during this month [April], we know that there will be little or no flood even [though] it could still spread around – *ku kandauka* – in May (*Kandao*). We know that the month of May is meant for *kuteya miono* [and] *mafula* (trapping fish with different types of fish traps) and many more. It is time for fish.'

FIGURE 12.5:
Catching fish using *miyono* fish traps on the Zambezi. (© BCW van der Waal, NNF/WWF/MFMR Fisheries Project, 2015.)

The people living on the floodplains prepared and readied themselves for fish when this time came. This time was thought of as 'payback time', as the fish ate their crops and thereafter the people would eat the fish, in return, when the tributaries were subsiding. This was the time of laying different types of fishing traps such as *miyono* (Figure 12.5) in the local language (the basket) and other different types.

Joy of being surrounded by the flood

It is important to know how the Basubiya regard flood times.

'It is generally a time of plenty for all. The local folks and especially *vasakasila* [(fishermen)] generally have two homes. They all live on and fish from river banks during the higher levels of water and once the water subsides the people return to their permanent homes on higher ground, where they keep their cattle and cultivate their crops.'

The interviewees insisted that more water always brought more fish, although it also destroyed their crops. One vicissitude they recalled that was associated with floods was the abundance of crocodiles, snakes and hippos, which were a worry. But, still, this seemed nothing compared to what they got in return when the floods subsided – fish.

Why then did the Basubiya not go to higher grounds? They gave a number of reasons. Firstly, they recalled that they had higher and drier areas that they could rely on. For example, they had trusted places, such as the Mukoche Highlands at Nantungu, which always served as their safe haven. All the people from areas neighbouring Nantungu came to Muchoke with their animals – all could fit there with ease. Of course, 'We were not as many as we are today. There were fewer schools around us and our animals were fewer too,' an old man reported. The higher grounds stretched from Muwuluka to Itomba, which, 'Up to this day, these areas have not been fully covered by any of the floods that have come our way. We are still able to keep a [large] number of animals on the hills.' The only difference is that the skill to graze animals in the water has disappeared with time.

With pressure from politicians, everyone in these areas has been, each year, encouraged to move their animals to higher grounds before the flood arrives. This, however, opens gaps in the lives of those living in the affected areas. People are encouraged by government to leave their homes earlier – even if the river level is as low as 4 m on the Zambezi. The locals perceive this as a forced activity because they do not like leaving the floodplains. They feel the government is working against their culture. The interviewees have experienced that anything below a six-metre level is manageable to them, even with the greater numbers of cattle of recent times.

Activities during the flood

A question was posed to find out where people grazed their cattle when the floodplains were covered by water. 'We knew where the sweetest grass for our animals was, even if it was underwater. Sweet grass, then, did not go down completely, it floated with water.' One male interviewee continued from the other, 'Our cattle would graze in the water guarded by us using *maato* [(dugouts)] around them.' See Figure 12.6.

Figure 12.7 shows a crocodile from the Zambezi River basking. The crocodile is one type of animal that can kill people or their livestock when they cross or fetch water from the rivers. But during the time that animals grazed in the flooded areas, 'there were no *ingwena* [(crocodiles)] because they [did] not like our presence.'

> 'We would hit the *vuwato* [(dugout)] each time and the crocodiles would know that we were around.'

How did the Basubiya know whether their cows had grazed enough?

> 'Cows talk when the grass is sweet, you will hear the sounds they make and these tell us that they are enjoying [it]. You need to be acquainted with this kind of life around the cows. A novice would not know and might force the cows to stay around them the whole day. When a cow is satisfied it leaves for the land.'

People who tended cattle grazing in floodwaters did not sleep in the *vuwato*.

FIGURE 12.6:
Dugouts are the
Basubiya's lifeline
during times of
flooding. (© George
Sanzila.)

FIGURE 12.7:
Crocodiles pose a
greater risk to the
Basubiya during
floods. (© George
Sanzila.)

'We would not sleep as we are used to the exercise. Dying in water is an accident. *Vantu veChaana* [(people of the floodplains)] do not just die in water. They have skills acquired from childhood, which they have kept on learning from [one] flood season to the other. It is easier for a *muuntu weChaana* [(person of the floodplain)] to die when in a boat than *muvuwato* [(in the canoe)].'

Did this way of life about cows not attract diseases?

'What are you talking about? There were no diseases during our time ... [as] what we see today. Diseases are only seen now when animals are being inoculated or vaccinated against diseases. It is your medicines that bring diseases around our animals. Their bodies are now used to the vaccines to an extent that they cannot fight diseases on their own as in our days.'

One very old man insisted that, 'We like being surrounded by water. There were fewer diseases ... [affecting] people and animals in our time. We see ticks today when cattle vaccinations are abundant.'

In addition, questions were raised about what should be done with schools during times of flooding. Most respondents said that schools were few at that time; learners were also few. They felt that it is only this that makes parents move to drier and higher grounds in modern times. However, they also felt that schools, such as Nantungu and Itomba (combined schools), could have the land around them raised in order to keep parents and their children safe from water. They thought that it would be cheaper (in terms of time for learning, feeding the learners away from their parents and supplying clothing to their children) to do this than ferrying people to places that are new to them.

Coping strategies during and after the flood

During floods *ingalani* (mats of sticks and soft grass) served as beds. They are also constructed outside for drying and storing fish. The *ingalani* were made from *mavaala* (*Searsia quartiniana*), a type of tree common on the floodplains. The *mavaala* grows in low-lying streams, in shallow water and on the dry banks of the streams. Sticks were cut either before – in anticipation of higher floods – or during the flood to construct the mattresses. The *mavaala* also grew quite commonly on the floodplains and the dried sticks could be used for firewood, and the timber for constructing houses, *malapa* (enclosures), and the yokes and sleighs for draught animals. The wood was also used for the handles of hoes and axes. The other tree that was trusted for constructing shelters was *mutoya* (*Searsia ciliata*).

During flood times, the dugouts meant everything to the local people. They used the dugout primarily for transport. They also used the dugouts on dry land – dragged by draught animals – to transport harvested grains from the fields to their homes, and to carry the sick from their homes to the nearest clinic. Hunting wildlife, such as situtunga and cane rats, could be conducted from a canoe. During the flood, cooking was also done in the canoes.

'We keep dry sand at the end of the canoe. We make fire from there and do our cooking if we are on a long journey. We rarely need maize meal during that time as we catch more fish and use it either dry or fresh'.

Today, dugout canoes are used more often than motorized boats to take tourists out to view animals from the waters in Zambezi Region.

FIGURE 12.8:
Dugouts are an important form of transport in the region. (© George Sanzila.)

The Basubiya enjoy different types of foods that grow along the rivers and streams. There are *isoto* (water lily pods) that grow in the water. Several delicacies are made from *isoto*. *Isuzwe* (a type of water lily) is dried and milled. 'We make porridge from the water lily flour and even make *mu'nende* (bread-like food) from the same flour.' *Isoto* is prepared just like *mahangu*. It is abundant between May and August each year, but in perennial rivers the water lilies can bear rhizomes and pods all year round.

After July (the coolest month), *intaanga* (different types of pumpkins) begin to germinate on the wet plains. Ploughing also starts at this time. The chilly winter months of June and July are easily dealt with as, 'we raise fire above *intaanga* so that they do not die from cold.' Thereafter, pumpkins are gradually replaced by *indongo* (groundnuts), *mundale* (maize) and *mahila* (sorghum). Sorghum harvests are used to brew beer, which is shared by the adults in the villages. This beer is not as intoxicating as modern ones and was drunk for pleasure, especially after the hard work in the village was done.

Between the pumpkins, *indulweti* and *iteepe* (leafy vegetables similar to spinach) grew, 'that give us a change of diet from fish. It is natural and maybe only God sends the seeds for it to grow.' The leaves of these indigenous vegetables are cooked whole. After boiling the leaves, one squeezes the water from the leaves. The water is served as tea and the cooked leaves are eaten. After drinking it, one will not feel hungry for the rest of the day. Sometimes it is served with cooked fish. 'We miss *indulweti* because it has disappeared … [through the] ages.'

Following the leafy vegetables, the pumpkins ripen. *Namundalangwe*, *maposi* and other pumpkins used to play a crucial role as food. *Matila* (related to the *La Granata* melon) and *maposi* were cooked and eaten without adding anything to them. They were 'sweet and helped us change diets.'

FIGURE 12.9: A dam is built across the river using sticks, which drives the fish into the *miyono* nets. (© BCW van der Waal, NNF/WWF/MFMR Fisheries Project, 2015.)

The pumpkin seeds are roasted, pounded and cooked as a delicacy, known as *ibwantuko*. Sometimes dried fish is also added to *ibwantuko* and 'fingers are licked one by one' as the 'seasoning is beyond human taste'. 'There were no tomatoes, onion and potatoes as additives to these soups,' in the past. *Indongo* made from dried peanuts is prepared in a similar manner as *ibwantuko*. An old lady commented that 'hunger was an issue … for the lazy, but such people were few.' During the day, especially after weeding and removing fish from the nets, *namunywa* (watermelon) is served, which acts as 'clean water and food at the same time.'

While the floods are subsiding, different types of fish can be caught. Nets, traps and snares are used. The popular method is *miyono*, which is a trap of interwoven sticks and grass. A bridge-like dam of other sticks and grass would be built across a stream, which drove the fish into the trap (see Figures 12.5 and 12.9). The children enjoyed using another type of trap, *ishundundo*, which is set collaboratively. Two or more children drag the trap at its ends, while a third child drags it in the middle to catch all the fish. This method worked well for catching fingerlings, such as *imbaala* (*Brycinus* and *Barbus* spp.), and other little types of fish such as *siluvango* (*Schilbe intermedius*), *chingongi* (*Synodontis nigromaculatus*) amongst many.

Despite the fact that the local people were not aware of the nutritional value of fish, they knew which type of fish was good for breakfast, lunch and supper. The fat of the fish was used as cooking oil and the eggs provided an extra delicacy as a soup thickener. Some of the fish, such as *unjuli* (*Hydrocynus vittatus*, commonly known as tigerfish) and *inembele* (*Petrocephalus* spp., commonly known as Churchill types), are cooked without removing the scales. The scales add to the flavour of the fish. 'We are sure that these are the foods that made us live longer than your generation. Deadly diseases were not as [common] as we hear [of] them today,' an old man close to 90 years said.

Different types of water tubers and rhizomes, such as *masiko, ino* and *inkuma*, are also cooked and served with fish or meat. *Ino* can be eaten raw as they are not as sour as *inkuma*, but add flavour to a mix of fish or meat when cooked. The tubers and rhizomes do not need any form of flour for preparation or when served.

From the accounts of the interviewees, the rich variety of foods provided the Basubiya with nutrients that kept them strong and healthy during and after the floods. Clinics were not easily accessible and adults treated some ailments with preparations of the naturally occurring plants on the floodplains. Some of the foods also served as medicines indirectly.

CONCLUSION AND RECOMMENDATIONS

The Bekuhane people have lived along rivers and on the floodplains for many decades. They have lived with the natural wet–dry flood pattern for a long time – and become dependent on the variety of resources it offers. They stayed on the flooded plains, seeing these plains as their natural habitat. They have made their livelihoods on the floodplains; these are difficult to do away with. They have cultivated the land with ease and joy. Leaving the floodplains would be leaving their culture. There are no dugouts or the activities associated with these on drier lands. The river and all the natural resources that are endowed by it will be missed. The plants that protected them from disease will also be missed. The absence of these could negatively affect their wellbeing. The indigenous knowledge and skills that were passed down from their ancestors would be lost. They need them, as they feel associated with the floodplains and all that is in them. Their culture of living within water makes them who they are. They identify with the rivers and the seasonal floods that come with them.

Flood management and coping strategies need further study in the Zambezi flooded plains. There is an urgent need for the Government of Namibia to study and understand the situation of the people of the floodplains of the Zambezi Region. There is a lot that could be learnt through consultation with the elders of the Bekuhane. Their reasons for not migrating to drier lands during times of floods could add tremendous knowledge on coping in seasonally flooded areas in general. Some of the foods that they use and value from the floodplains could also contribute to understanding the nutritional and medicinal values of these foods. These people may not live for long on pieces of land that are far away from water. Through consultation, government will be able to provide assistance with greater care and planning to support and complement the culture of the Bekuhane.

Such a study should include the younger generations, as well, to find out whether they still want to stay on the floodplains or seek more modern lifestyles on the drier lands. There is a possibility that most Basubiya that are still living on the floodplains will, at some time, move to drier lands. The coming generations might not like to live on the floodplains, especially when it is flooding and their modes of transport cannot reach their ancestral places. The gradual move of the Basubiya away from the floodplains will have an impact on their cultural activities associated with the river and floodplains. Their knowledge and skills could be lost and they might lose connection with their ancestral stories and culture in general.

References

Aust, P. W. (2009). *The ecology, conservation and management of Nile crocodiles* Crocodylus niloticus *in a human dominated landscape* (PhD thesis, Imperial College London, London, United Kingdom). Retrieved from http://www.the-eis.com/data/literature/Crocodiles%20in%20NE%20Namibia%20Patrick%20Aust%20Thesis%202009.pdf

BNA [Botswana National Archives]. (n.d.). File S. 349/1-2. Gaborone, Botswana: Botswana Government.

Bosch, N. (2011). *The level of the Zambezi at Katima Mulilo.* Retrieved from http://www.caprivi.biz/flooding.html

Browning, G., Halcli, A., & Webster, F. (Eds.). (2000). *Understanding contemporary society: Theories of the present.* London, UK: Sage Publications.

Business Dictionary. (n.d.) *BusinessDictionary.com.* Retrieved from http://www.businessdictionary.com/definition/rational-choice-theory-RCT.html

Creswell, J. W. (2003). *Research design: Qualitative, quantitative and mixed methods approaches* (2nd ed.). Thousand Oaks, USA: Sage Publications.

DREF [International Federation of the Red Cross and Red Crescent Societies]. (2007). *Namibia: Caprivi floods. Operations update, Appeal No. MDRNA003, Update No. 2, 23 April to 20 June, 2007.* Retrieved from http://www.ifrc.org/docs/appeals/07/MDRNA00302.pdf

Encyclopaedia Britannica. (1911). *The Encyclopaedia Britannica: A dictionary of arts, sciences, literature and general information.* Retrieved from http://chestofbooks.com/reference/Encycopedia-Britannica-1/Bantu-Language-Classifcation-Part3.html

Gibbons, M. St. (1904). *Africa from South to North through Marotseland.* New York, USA: The Caxton Press.

GRN (Government of the Republic of Namibia). (2009). *Post-disaster needs assessment: Floods 2009.* Windhoek, Namibia: Author. Retrieved from http://www.gfdrr.org/sites/gfdrr.org/files/documents/Namibia_PDNA_2009.pdf

Gumbo, G. B. (2002). *The political economy of development in the Chobe peasants, fishermen, and tourists, 1960–1995* (Master's Thesis, University of Botswana, Gaborone). Accessed from http://archive.lib.msu.edu/DMC/African%20Journals/pdfs/PULA/pula016002/pula016002008.pdf

IRIN [Humanitarian News and Analysis] Africa. (2003, 2 June). *Namibia: WFP to assist Caprivi flood victims.* Retrieved from allafrica.com/stories/200306020819.html

Kvale, S. (1996) *Interviews: An introduction to qualitative research interviewing.* London, UK: Sage Publications.

Larson, T. J. (2001). *The Hambukushu rainmakers of the Okavango, Botswana.* USA: Writers Club Press. Retrieved from http://armo20swell.acknowledgmentpdf.org/download/the-hambukushu-rainmakers-of-the-okavango_bxzcfgh.pdf

Likando, E. S. (1989). *The Caprivi: A historical perspective.* (Unpublished manuscript.)

Lupala, J. M. (2002). *Urban types in rapidly urbanising cities: Analysis of formal and informal settlements in Dar es Salaam, Tanzania* (Doctoral thesis, KTH Royal Institute of Technology, Stockholm). Retrieved from http://www.diva-portal.org/smash/get/diva2:9224/FULLTEXT01.pdf

Mabuta, K. D., Masule, N. W., & Tembwe, J. T. (2013). *Basubiya or Bekuhane: Socioeconomic and political history of the Basubiya or Bekuhane from (1440 to 2012).* (Unpublished manuscript.)

Mainga, M. (1973). *Bulozi under Luyana kings: Political evolution and state formation in pre-colonial Zambia.* London, UK: Longman.

Makhanya, S., Tumbare , M., & Makurira, H. (2012). *Floods and droughts in the middle Zambezi River basin: Causes, occurrence, frequency.* Saarbrücken, Germany: LAP LAMBERT Academic Publishing.

Malumo, R. (2008, April 10). Amathila hears Katima aches for development. *New Era.* Accessed from http://www.newera.com.na/2008/04/10/amathila-hears-katima-aches-for-development/

Manning, I. P. A. (2011). *Wildlife conservation in Zambia and the landsafe customary commons* (PhD thesis, University of Pretoria, Pretoria, South Africa). Retrieved from http://repository.up.ac.za/bitstream/handle/2263/25570/Complete.pdf?sequence=5

Maseheka. (2011). *Flooding in the Caprivi Region: Villages on the outskirts of Katima Mulilo.* Retrieved from http://en.wikipedia.org/wiki/User:Maseheka/Flooding_in_the_Caprivi_region:_villages_in_the_outskirts_of_Katima_Mulilo

Masule, L. M. (1995). *Origins and history of the Bekuhane of Iteenge (Basubiya or Bekuhane) from 1595 to 1995.* (Unpublished).

McBrien, S., Felizardo, G. R., Orr, D. G., & Raymond, M. J. (2008). Using focus groups to revise an educational booklet for people living with methicillin-resistant *Staphylococcus Aureus* (MRSA). *Health Promotion Practice, 9*(1), 19-28.

McMillan, J. H., & Schumacher, S. (2006). *Research in education: Evidence-based inquiry* (6th ed.). New York, USA: Allyn and Bacon.

Mendelsohn, J., Jarvis, A., Roberts, C., & Robertson, T. (2002). *Atlas of Namibia: A portrait of the land and its people.* Cape Town, South Africa: David Philip Publishers.

Mubitana, K. (1975). The traditional history and ethnography. In D.W. Phillipson (Ed.), *Moasi-oa-Tunya: A handbook to the Victoria Falls region* (pp. 59-72). Rhodesia: Longman Group Ltd.

Nalisa, R. (2003). Environment Namibia: Villagers grapple with the worst floods in 21 years. Retrieved from http://www.ipsnews.net/2003/05/environment-namibia-villagers-grapple-with-the-worst-floods-in-21-years/

Ndana, N. (2011). *The indigenous praise poetry of the Veekuhane: Culture, memory and history.* Cape Town, South Africa: CASAS.

Olson, J. S. (1996). *The peoples of Africa: An ethnohistorical dictionary.* Westport, USA: Greenwood Press.

Parry, M. L., Canziani, O. F., Palutikof, J. P., van der Linden, P. J., & Hanson, C. E. (Eds.). (2007). *Climate change 2007: Impacts, adaptation and vulnerability. Contribution of Working Group II to the Fourth Assessment Report of the Intergovernmental Panel on Climate Change.* Cambridge, UK: Cambridge University Press and IPCC.

Patton, M. Q. (1990). *Qualitative evaluation and research methods* (2nd ed.). London, UK: Sage.

Ramsay, J. (2002, February 1 & 22). The Bekuhane or Basubiya or Bekuhane. *Botswana Daily News.*

Ramsay, J., Morton, B., & Mgadla, P. (1996). *Building a Nation: A history of Botswana from 1800 to 1910.* Gaborone, Botswana: Longman.

Reacher, M., McKenzie, K., Lane, C., Nichols, T., Kedge, I., Iversen, A., Hepple, P., Walter, T., Laxton, C., & Simpson, J. (2004). Health impact of flooding in Lewes: A comparison of reported gastrointestinal and other illness and mental health in flooded and non-flooded households. *Communicable Disease and Public Health, 7*(1), 39-46.

Sakijege, T., Lupala, J., & Sheuya, S. (2012). Flooding, flood risks and coping strategies in urban informal residential areas: The case of Keko Machungwa, Dar es Salaam, Tanzania. *Journal of Disaster Risk Studies, 4*(1). http://dx.doi.org/10.4102/jamba.v4i1.46

Samunzala, S. C. (2003). *The social aspects of the life of the Basubiya or Bekuhane of Chobe, 1928–1991* (Bachelor of Arts Thesis, University of Botswana, Gaborone, Botswana).

Shamukuni, D. M. (1972). The Basubiya. *Botswana Notes and Records, 4*, 161-184.

Sibeene, P. (2007). Thousands still displaced by floods. *New Era*. Retrieved from http://www.*m.reliefweb.int/report/240343*

Sparg, V. (2007, May 28). Flooded Caprivi: A wonderful travel experience. *Allgemeine Zeitung*. Retrieved from http://www.az.com.na/tourismus/english-articles/flooded-caprivi-a-wonderful-travel-experience.19978.php

Tlou, T., & Campbell, A. (1984). *History of Botswana*. Gaborone, Botswana: Macmillan.

Wisner, B., Blaikie, P., Cannon, T., & Davis, I. (2004). *At risk: Natural hazards, people's vulnerability and disasters* (2nd ed.). London, UK: Routledge, Taylor and Francis Group.

13

Indigenous knowledge and climate change in rural Namibia: A gendered approach

Nguza Siyambango, Alex T. Kanyimba & Pempelani Mufune†

INTRODUCTION

Since 1972, robust literature about the need for men and women to respond to the impacts of climate change has emerged. The international response to climate change is embodied in the United Nations Framework Convention on Climate Change (UNFCCC). The UNFCCC that was adopted at the United Nations Conference on Environment and Development (UNCED) in 1992 has been in force since 1994. The ultimate objective of the UNFCCC is to:

> '... achieve stabilization of greenhouse gas concentrations in the atmosphere at a level that would prevent dangerous human-induced interference with the climate system within a timeframe sufficient to allow ecosystems to adapt naturally to climate change, to ensure that food production is not threatened and to enable economic development to proceed in a sustainable manner.' (UNFCCC cited in Kyoto 2, 2008.)

The strategies envisaged by both scientists and politicians are based on the combination of adaptation, mitigation and use of indigenous knowledge (MET, 2011a, 2011b & 2011c). Mitigation, adaption and integration of indigenous knowledge require both men and women to participate equally in decisions pertaining to adjusting ecological, social or economic systems in response to observed climate change, and a process of curtailing greenhouse gas emissions and other anthropogenic interventions. However, traditional configuration of gender roles means that women and men have multiple responsibilities in the home, at the workplace and in the community. These traditional demands, however, leave women with less time for active participation in the decision-making processes that impact their lives, environment and aspirations (Lambrou & Piana, 2006).

The aim of this chapter is to present perspectives on gender, climate change and indigenous knowledge in rural Namibia. The research had three objectives. The first objective is to explore the gender–climate-change nexus and examine the relevance of indigenous knowledge regarding this. The significance of indigenous knowledge in climate change is the subject of increasing attention in rural Namibia. Namibian Government policy emphasizes the importance of identifying and applying indigenous approaches to challenges facing the nation (GRN, 2004, p. 122). Therefore, reflection on indigenous knowledge is essential to address climate change, which is considered one of the challenges in rural Namibia (Reid, Sahlén, MacGregor, & Stage, 2007). The second objective is to highlight areas of vulnerability to climate change, which indigenous knowledge will be relevant towards addressing in rural Namibia. Lastly, this research suggests a mechanism to make indigenous knowledge explicit in rural Namibia.

The chapter is structured as follows. Firstly, we explain the context of the study by elucidating the Namibian economy and potential impacts of climate change. This section concludes with the explanation of our observations pertaining to the opinion of the Namibian rural public on climate change effects. In the second section, we explore the role of indigenous knowledge in the climate change and gender nexus. The gender and climate change framework is presented to simplify women's and men's differential access to natural resources. As the dichotomy between climate change and gender becomes clear, we elaborate the significance of indigenous knowledge in rural Namibia. This is followed by gender-disaggregated vulnerability to climate change in areas of flooding and drought; firewood and forestry; subsistence agriculture; and health. Finally, we present recommendations to empower women when responding to gender-disaggregated climate change vulnerability and suggest a mechanism to make indigenous knowledge explicit in rural Namibia.

NAMIBIAN BACKGROUND

Economy

The Namibian economy relies heavily on natural resources, many of which are climate sensitive. Agriculture, fisheries and mining, which account for 24% of the GDP, form the pillar of the country's economy (MET, 2011a). About 61% of Namibia's population lives in rural areas and depends on agriculture for a subsistence livelihood (Kuvare, Maharero, & Kamupingene, 2008). The Climate Change Vulnerability Assessment Report (Angula, Siyambango, & Conteh, 2012) revealed that although economic decisions are made in consultation with women, men have the power to overrule their decisions because the man is regarded as the head of the household, who should assume responsibility for key decisions regarding agricultural production, response to floods and droughts and harvesting of forest products, including firewood. Men are thus placed in the role of protecting the properties of their families. This lopsided responsibility also asserts men's roles in managing and controlling resources in agriculture and fisheries, and other ways of making income.

Climate change

Namibian climate is characteristically highly variable and the global effects of climate change increase this local variability (MET, 2011a). Recent historical trends of climate in Namibia reveal a consistent increase in daily maximum temperatures (Dirkx, Hager, Tadross, Bethune, & Curtis, 2008). Climate change also affects rainfall distribution – more heavy rainfall events interspersed with dry periods – more droughts, rising sea levels and increasing numbers of hot days and heat waves (Scholes & Biggs, 2004; MET, 2011b; MET, 2011c). Climate change will cause increased aridity due to the combined effects of variable rainfall and increased evaporation (30%) by 2020 (Dirkx et al., 2008).

In our observation, the opinion of the public on climate change effects in rural Namibia is divided along three lines of individual's perceptions. The first is the belief that the abandonment of cultural and traditional practices and rituals is responsible for changes in rainfall intensity and the occurrence of drought. This perception is held by those who call for the revival of indigenous knowledge to address the climate change crisis in rural Namibia. Secondly, others perceive that the changes in climate are a precursor to doomsday or the so-called end of the world. Those with reverence towards Christianity hold this perception. Thirdly, some individuals, especially those with relations to individuals with a science background, believe that anthropogenic effects are causes of climate change.

INDIGENOUS KNOWLEDGE IN THE CLIMATE CHANGE AND GENDER NEXUS

The impacts of climate change are connected to the different roles that women, men, girls and boys play in a society (Wamukonya & Rukato, 2001). Thus, men, women, youths and children are vulnerable in different ways to climate change. In rural areas of many developing countries, women execute climate-sensitive tasks, such as securing food, water, and fuelwood for cooking, while men are responsible for livestock, and land and forestry management. Women are exposed to risks related to climate change owing to existing gender roles (Aguilar, 2009). For example, in the 1991 cyclone disaster that killed 140,000 people in Bangladesh, 90% of the victims

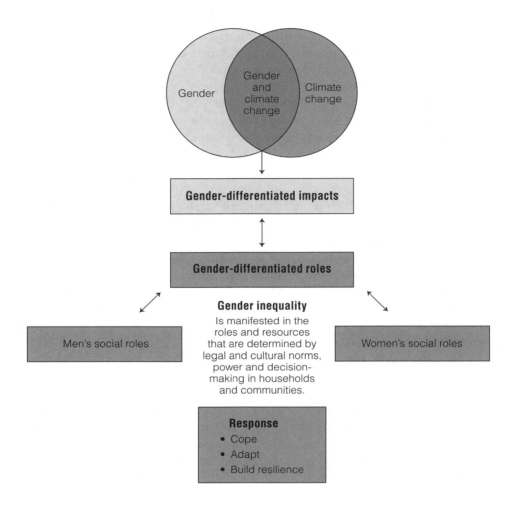

FIGURE 13.1: Gender and climate change framework. (Source: Babugura, 2010.)

were women (Aguilar, 2009). Women and children are 14 times more likely to die than men from natural disasters (Röhr, 2009). The World Health Organization (WHO) argues that health risks resulting from differences in gender roles will be exacerbated by climate change (WHO, 2010).

Men and women in rural Namibia experience climate challenges differently because of their differing roles in the management of resources. Nelson (2010) asserts that the main reason for the gender-differentiated climate change impact is the widespread existence of entrenched gender inequalities. 'Because women do different work, they have differential access to resources and have different priorities in their lives in most societies,' (Glazebrook, 2011, p. 762). The recognition of differentiated vulnerability to climate change between men and women has led to the discourse on the gender dimensions of climate change. These are conditioned by social, legal and cultural norms, power and decision-making in communities and households. The socially constructed gender roles downgrade women to tasks such as food preparation, child rearing and following instructions of their male counterparts. Men engage in income-generating activities, provide direction and make big and bold decisions in their communities and households. These norms are also extended to the use of natural resources and access to ecosystem services, such as recreation and food production. This scenario is further simplified in Figure 13.1.

The climate change and gender nexus warrants the need for indigenous knowledge. Several reasons that highlight the need to include indigenous knowledge in adapting to climate change can be cited. Firstly, indigenous knowledge is complementary to science-based knowledge. Science-based knowledge, however, tends to overuse and simplify complex ecological systems, resulting in a series of problems associated with climate change. Indigenous knowledge is the main asset many rural people have to invest in their struggle for survival, to produce food and shelter or to control their lives amidst a changing climate. It is the basis for local-level decisions on agriculture, management of resources, food preparation and even education in many rural communities in Namibia. Secondly, indigenous knowledge has the capacity to empower vulnerable and disadvantaged groups to take action and control their own destiny, instead of relying on external help (Gadgil, Berkes, & Folke, 1993; Johannes, 2010). Finally, it is important to note that some cultures possess a traditional conservation ethic, which has been eroded by external influences, while others perceive little or no relationship with the environment (Johannes, 1978). Gadgil et al. (1993) argue that it is the nomadic hunter-gatherers who are not tied to any specific resources who gain little or no traditional conservation ethic. The sedentary, horticultural or subsistence agricultural societies are likely to have accumulated a series of historical observations relevant to climate change. The majority of Namibian rural society is sedentary with ties to subsistence agriculture and is presumed to have accumulated such pertinent historical observations. For this reason, and with hindsight, a knowledge of traditional and local conservation ethics in rural Namibia is required to adequately mitigate and adapt to the effects of climate change.

Indigenous knowledge is herein understood to be local knowledge that forms the bedrock for a community to make decisions on issues related to food security, floods and droughts, forestry and firewood, gender relations, and natural resource management. It refers to the body of knowledge developed outside academic institutions, embedded in culture and unique to a given group of people (Hunter, 2005). Indigenous knowledge is usually tacit knowledge, which is stored in people's individual and collective memories and guarded jealously (Lodhi & Mikulecky, 2010, p. 94). Because indigenous knowledge is seen as knowledge that is implied and understood and not obviously stated, this chapter seeks to make indigenous knowledge more explicit, by suggesting mechanisms for codifying and transmitting it in non-formal and formal institutions, especially indigenous knowledge which is useful to climate change adaptation.

GENDER-DISAGGREGATED VULNERABILITY TO CLIMATE CHANGE

This section highlights some areas of climate change vulnerability, which could be redressed by integrating indigenous knowledge in adaptation in rural Namibia.

Floods and drought

Namibia's extremely variable climate regularly leads to seasonal flooding in some of the country's regions. Among the severely affected regions include Omusati, Oshana, Oshikoto and Ohangwena in the central northern parts of the country, as well as Zambezi and Kavango in the north-east. Floods in the central-northern regions are related to the extensive network of oshanas. Every four years, on average, the oshanas flood (*efundja*) as a result of heavy rainfalls locally or from Angolan highlands (Dirkx et al., 2008; Gremlowski, 2010). The seasonal rising of the Okavango and the Zambezi rivers causes flooding in the Kavango and Zambezi regions.

The Namibian Office of the Prime Minister estimated that the 2009 floods affected 677,542 people. During these floods 54,581 people were displaced, 105 died and the remaining people were relocated to higher grounds (GRN, 2010). Agricultural damage was notable. The crop fields of 24,754 farmers (an area of 53,208 ha) were damaged. It was estimated that 70–80% of crop production was lost that season. Furthermore, about 3,669 subsistence farmers lost their grain stocks and it was also estimated that farmers lost about 10,393 livestock. In addition, about 328 schools were flooded, affecting about 93,700 learners. Nearly 1,066 small business enterprises were negatively affected. In the health sector three hospitals, 29 clinics and 73 outreach services were cut off. On the whole, the Namibian Government estimated that the 2009 floods cost the country N$1.7 billion (1% of GDP) (OPM, 2009; Gremlowski, 2010).

According to Kuvare et al. (2008), the droughts of 1992/93, 1996/97, 2000/01 and 2003/04 exposed the vulnerability of Namibia's food security and water resource base to climatic extremes. In particular, droughts lead to crop failure and food shortages in many rural communities. As a consequence, many women and female-headed households become poorer. Furthermore, drought forces women and girls to travel longer distances to fetch water (Angula et al., 2012). Water scarcity also limits the development of small-scale projects. In situations where there is severe water scarcity, men travel long distances with donkey carts to fetch water for livestock and domestic use; they also move their livestock to areas less affected by climate change (Angula et al., 2012).

Drought is about shortage of water and this is where indigenous traditional knowledge can be brought to bear with regard to location, collection and storage of water; management of water, including irrigation; water conservation; forest management; and agricultural practices. In this regard the Kunene River Awareness Kit (n.d.) points out that:

'The Himba living in the Lower Kunene provide a good example of traditional water and land use knowledge. They traditionally move with their livestock, sometimes covering long distances to where there is pasture, and make use of a variety of surface and groundwater sources, each for a different purpose. *Orohawe* (springs) and *ondjombo* (hand-dug wells) may be used for people, whereas *oruua* (shallow wells) are used for livestock. Furthermore the livestock are often separated and oxen, cows and goats are watered at different water sources. Water is only used for drinking, stock watering and cooking, while washing water consumption is reduced by protecting the bodies with a layer of ochre and butter fat. These traditional ways of managing water and land resources, whereby livestock is moved across large areas between different water sources, is very important in keeping grazing areas productive, preventing land degradation and reducing the pressure on water points. Land and water resources are given a chance to 'rest and recover' and are not over-used in one place.'

In the event of intense drought, indigenous knowledge would be used in the harvesting of wild fruits and vegetables, and hunting for bushmeat in many African rural communities (Egeru, 2012).

Forestry and firewood

Namibian households are highly dependent for livelihoods, including energy needs, on what are fast becoming degraded forest resources (Palmer & MacGregor, 2008). Palmer and MacGregor (2008, p. 6) found that in the central northern regions of Namibia there is a:

'... high local dependence on forest resources for cooking, heating and building materials. On average, a household uses almost 12,000 kg of wood for energy and shelter annually, split between fuelwood and poles. The average per capita consumption of fuelwood is 913 kg, ranging from 144 kg in Oshana to 1,202 kg in Ohangwena. With annual harvests in fuelwood and poles exceeding the physically suitable annual yield, there appears to an over-harvesting of forest resources in Oshana.'

In Namibia, the tasks of collecting firewood are often split among the children, but carried mainly by girls (Ruiz-Caseres, 2007). Women and girls travel long distances to fetch firewood. Furthermore, shortages of fuelwood during floods affect cooking and heating in households (Angula et al., 2012). The accepted custom is that girls should learn these roles from their mothers. It is noted here that there has also been the development of transport services in fuelwood harvesting and men are increasingly involved in this business (Erkkilä & Siiskonen, 1992). With higher collection times, Namibian households increase their labour allocation to fuelwood collection more than by reducing energy consumption (Palmer & MacGregor, 2008). Fuelwood demand among rural households in Namibia is inelastic because it does not go down in response to the amount of time needed to collect it.

Subsistence agriculture

Namibian agriculture comprises livestock and crop production at commercial and subsistence levels. The contribution of the subsistence agricultural sector to Namibia's economy has been declining (MAWF, 2009). The contribution of livestock agriculture from the subsistence sector to total agricultural output decreased from 20.4% in 2000 to 1.3% in 2007. Similarly, subsistence sector crop production decreased from 5.3% to 4.6% during the same period. In 2007, the value of subsistence sector output only amounted to N$174.3 million, having been N$709.4 million in 2000 (MAWF, 2009). This decrease in output shows that subsistence agriculture is among the sectors most vulnerable to climate change.

In Namibia, women are responsible for most aspects of subsistence crop production, such as weeding, threshing and harvesting. The customary rules dictate and allocate these responsibilities to women. Accordingly, the woman's place is the homestead where these activities and functions are carried out. The traditional role of men is to till the land with a single-furrow plough. This is done with the help of their sons. Secondly, boys also have the responsibility of looking after the family's cattle and goats.

This scenario exacerbates the condition of poverty for rural women. For example, Terry (2009) argues that women have limited access and rights to resources and are also side-lined in many decisions. The author further explains that men participate in livestock production, especially in the northern, central-northern, coastal and southern regions of Namibia, which is economically profitable. However, experience shows that men will also be more greatly affected by losses of livestock due to lack of grazing induced by climate change.

According to Gebresenbet and Kefale (2012), traditional coping mechanisms for extreme conditions associated with droughts include migration, herd diversification, restocking and local alliances. These actions minimize losses or facilitate recovery during and after drought events. The Ovahimba of the Kunene Region in Namibia follow similar strategies. Bollig (2009) found that during drought years, migration and knowledge of these pastoralists on where to take cattle is important for minimizing their loss of cattle. Thus, in an interview, Chief Kapika stated, 'cattle was moved' to the Kunene River, to a place called Kehorouua. Livestock is also moved to the big mountain of Okuhama or the Omavanda Mountains 'where the grass never finishes'. The mountain has a cave with water that is easily accessed by cattle, which climb the mountain from many sides. During drought years, people were dependent on palm nuts for food, which was occasionally supplemented with meat from slaughtering a sheep or goat or, even more occasionally, a cow.

The traditional agricultural sector, including subsistence, dry-land cropping, will suffer more from climate change than other sectors (Reid et al., 2007). Climate change models predict a 40% reduction in subsistence agricultural productivity and a 50% reduction in livestock farm productivity. Such reductions will have serious implications for food security and livelihoods (Nelson, 2010, p. 8).

Dieckmann, Odendaal, Tarr and Schreij (2013, p. 101) argue that the Topnaar and Hai‖om communities still possess extensive traditional knowledge on the management of natural resources in their areas. These communities should be encouraged to treasure this knowledge because it is likely to be valuable in adapting to climate change (Dieckmann et al., 2013, p. 97). In particular, Dieckmann et al. (2013) point to the fact that the Hai‖om divide the year into three seasons – *sore gamas* (hot season), ‖*hao gamab* (rainy season) and *sao gamas* (winter, 'the cold months, [when] food is little') – with different wild food species available in each. Some edible plants can be harvested in more than one season; others grow at the end of one season, but mature in another season.

The Hai‖om know certain plants in their areas that can be useful for preserving foods. For instance the roots of the shepherd's tree (*Boscia albitrunca*) can be used to preserve meat. In addition, the dried roots are used to make tea and the bark is boiled and the decoction drunk to cure colds and soothe toothache and stomachache (Dieckmann et al., 2013, p. 98). They also identified a grass (*mi-e*) previously harvested to produce meal for porridge, as well as *!gub* from Etosha used to make flour for bread (Dieckmann et al., 2013, p. 98). In a drought-induced food scarcity this knowledge can be invaluable.

Health

Increased flooding and rising temperatures associated with climate change are likely to lead to an increased incidence of water- and vector-borne diseases. Malaria flourishes in warm, humid environments, making air temperature and rainfall the two most important natural factors that influence where it will strike and how quickly it is likely to spread (Ermert, Fink, Morse, & Paeth, 2011). With rising temperatures associated with climate change, mosquitos could expand their geographic range causing a higher and more widespread incidence of malaria. 'Increased floods in … northern Namibia could facilitate the breeding of malaria carriers in formerly arid areas and could cause disease in the predominantly farming communities' (Kuvare et al., 2008, p. 60). Climate change would also contribute to the expansion of endemic malaria and bilharzia (schistosomiasis) throughout the regions of the northern rivers and floodplains (Byers, 1997). In the Kwando area, 90–95% of the population suffers from bilharzia, and some children die from the disease. Furthermore, poor drainage in human settlements provides habitats for breeding mosquitoes and increases exposure to contaminated water leading to increased incidences of water- and vector-borne diseases (Costello et al., 2009).

The contamination of water resources as a result of increasing human pressure and closer contact between humans and animals is very likely. Contamination by human and animal faecal matter leads to diarrhoea, cholera, fever and related illnesses. This is partly confirmed by the Ministry of Environment and Tourism (MET, 2011a), which predicts that poor sanitary conditions due to increased flooding in some areas, as well as malnutrition due to reduced crop yields and reduced livestock productivity, will increase child mortality.

Heat stress could trigger meningitis and other high-temperature-related illnesses (Angula, 2010; Babugura, 2010). North-eastern and central Namibia would be especially vulnerable (Angula et al., 2012; von Oertzen, 2009).

Because women are the main caregivers of the children and the sick in rural Namibia, it is expected that they will be severely affected by malaria and other diseases induced by climate change.

Human–wildlife conflict

Human–wildlife conflict refers to the interaction between human beings and wild animals, and the negative consequences that result as they compete for resources and habitat (Dickman, 2010). Conflict between humans and wildlife often results as human populations expand into areas that were hitherto used by wildlife bringing them into closer contact. As climate change intensifies these conflicts might be exacerbated. There are many incidences of human–elephant conflict in Zambezi Region, to the extent that the MET argues that such conflict can seriously threaten the long-term conservation of elephant and other wild animals (Moore, 2009).

Both humans and wildlife are constantly threatened when they live in close contact and compete for resources. It is important to sensitize communities that this threat could increase and that both men and women should use their indigenous knowledge in efforts to reduce human–wildlife conflict in rural Namibia.

CRITICAL ISSUES AND RECOMMENDATIONS

There are three critical issues regarding gender and climate change in rural Namibia:

1. In rural Namibia, women are disproportionately affected by climate change. Men and women adapt to climatic events – droughts, water shortages and floods – in different ways.
2. Women have, over the years, developed knowledge and skills that can contribute to an effective and sustainable response to climate change.
3. Government policies dealing with climate change should therefore take account of gender-based vulnerabilities and knowledge.

One purpose of this study was to stimulate debate and action on gender-disaggregated response to climate change vulnerability in rural Namibia. The information in this chapter indicates that responsibilities between men and women are disaggregated along gender lines. Given Namibia's gender division, it is important to use these existing gender-disaggregated lines of responsibility to mitigate or adapt to potential climate change disasters in rural Namibia.

However, the role of women in the process needs to be elevated to management and decision-making levels. For example, when flood disaster strikes, men can play a major role in the construction of elevated latrines to avoid contamination of drinking water during floods (Gremlowski, 2010). At the same time, women should the take the lead in freshwater management, sanitation issues and waste disposal. In addition, women should also be regarded as crucial to mitigating fast-degrading forest resources on which livelihoods depend because gender division connects them more closely to these resources. Ways in which this can be achieved is by practising energy efficiency in households, using renewable energy, and through afforestation and reforestation activities (UNDP, 2009).

In our view, women can potentially contribute towards mitigation measures but, more often than not, they are not recognized when planning mitigation measures and strategies, which require action at community level. It is therefore necessary that strategies and action plans include women in the management of forests, drainage channels and healthcare service delivery for flood-affected people.

This chapter seeks to suggest a mechanism to make indigenous knowledge explicit in rural Namibia. The first step in integrating gender-responsive indigenous knowledge in rural Namibia is to identify a resource to which it could be applied (Hunter, 2005). In rural Namibia communities with indigenous knowledge have close ties with the land because it is a resource for their livelihoods, and the physical setting for the practice of their culture and application of rituals and social conventions. Land, as a resource, is threatened by climate change through frequent floods and droughts and the degradation of forests and firewood. Indigenous knowledge can reverse this trend through research on and revival of practices, rituals and social conventions. It is recommended that indigenous knowledge around certain subjects should be given priority – rainmaking, cultivation of food crops, medicinal plants, spirituality and forest preservation, and human–wildlife conflict. In addition, institutional structures should be put in place to codify and promote this indigenous knowledge.

Rainmaking

Namibian rural communities should be mobilized to re-introduce the practice of praying for and making rain fall. It is important to learn from the study by Murimbika (cited in Huffman, 2008, p. 2035), who explained the ideology that was associated with agriculture and rainmaking during drought periods in Zimbabwe. Accordingly, chiefs would send a black goat to their professed rainmakers, instructing the rainmakers to replenish their rain medicines and to repair their work areas.

Overall, chiefs controlled the process, but unless they had specific training, they were not usually rainmakers. Various people assisted the specialists. For example, during menstruation, young girls spread rain medicines on the fields. Later, headmen and other men of high standing would carry burning cattle dung from the capital to their homes in the belief that the smoke would call the clouds to all corners of the chiefdom. According to Huffman (2008, p. 2035) the 'normal rainmaking system appears to work most of the time. But when normal rituals and medicines consistently fail, and droughts persist, rainmakers climbed special hills to pull the rain down.'

It is important to encourage communities to re-introduce similar practices in rural Namibia to test the impact that such rituals might have in present-day conditions.

Cultivating food crops

The practice of cultivating maize and *mahangu* (pearl millet) around wetlands, rivers and areas of receding floods needs to be revived in rural Namibia. According to Adams (1993, p. 212), 'Wetland areas have an important place in the economy of many African countries. This can include direct production of surplus food or other commodities or simply providing sound and sustainable incomes in both good and bad years for fairly large numbers of people.' The wetlands, rivers and flood-recession areas could sustain the maize and *mahangu* that grow there. One example to learn from is the Niger Inland Delta in West Africa.

In the Niger Inland Delta, *décrue* (post rainy season) sorghum is planted on the receding flood in January, often with other crops such as cassava and groundnuts. Sorghum is sometimes transplanted from raised beds so that the growing plants can make good use of the moisture of the retreating floodwater in the soils. Rice is planted during the rains of July and August, which grows with the rising floodwaters and is harvested as the floods recede between December and February (Adams, 1993, p. 213).

Moreover, in the adaptation to drought conditions in rural Namibia, it is important to consider early maturing and drought-resistant varieties of maize and *mahangu*, especially. It is also important to use indigenous knowledge to enhance practices, similar to the one described above, in rural Kavango and Zambezi where wetlands and floodplains are found.

Medicinal plants

Wild plants that have a medicinal value need to be researched to help in the cure of malaria, bilharzia and other diseases that are likely to be more prevalent with climate change. A study by Dan, Mchombu and Mosimane (2010) identified various herbal remedies common to the San of Namibia. These include ‖*ganab* (*Acacia erioloba*) and *tima*, which were used for treating malaria. Others remedies identified include roots of *aruba* (*Albizia anthelmintica*) and *edada* or ǂ*aroba* (*Ziziphus mucronata*) used for treating stomachache. The *naruba*, ‖*gam*, ‖*gambe* (genus *Cucumis*) and *tima* are used to treat headaches by boiling the roots and drinking the infusion. The herbal remedy used to treat coughs is identified as |*gomme* (*Ricinodendron rautanenii*) and |hasa (*Combretum imberbe*) (Dan et al., 2010). (See also Chapters 2 and 4 in this volume).

Another study by Chinsembu and Hedimbi (2010) found that in Zambezi Region Combretaceae, *Anacardiaceae*, *Mimosaceae* and *Ebenaceae* were the most predominant plant families used in ethnomedicines for AIDS-related conditions. Although the active chemical compounds of the surveyed plants (and their modes of action) were largely unknown, Chinsembu and Hedimbi (2010) argued that it is plausible that the plant families contain bioactive secondary metabolites that work against AIDS-related infections. (See also Chapter 1, this volume).

Chinsembu, Hedimbi and Mukaru (2011) claim that in Kavango Region, 48 plant species from 22 families are known to treat several ailments including malaria, diarrhoea, sexually transmitted infections and tuberculosis. It is recommended that traditional herbalists in other parts of rural Namibia be consulted in order to explore other herbal remedies and establish medicinal values. This is important not only for conservation and restoration of valuable plants, but also to make them available for use by households and communities threatened by the geographic expansion of diseases resulting from climate change.

Spirituality and forest preservation

The spiritual dimension of forest preservation should be acknowledged in order to reverse deforestation and promote biological diversity. It is important to learn from an existing example in Kenya. Githitho (2003, p. 27) describes that the sacred Kaya

Forests situated on the coastal plains and hills of Kenya, are residual patches (from 10–200 ha in size) of once-extensive, diverse, lowland forest of East Africa and are home to more than half of Kenya's rare plant species. Additionally, 'the Kayas would seem to owe their existence to the beliefs, culture, and history of the nine coastal Mijikenda ethnic groups. These are: the Giriama, Digo, Duruma, Rabai, Kauma, Ribe, Jibana, Kambe, and Chonyi,' (Githitho, 2003, p. 27).

As can be seen in the above assertion, forest preservation because of its spiritual dimension can enhance and protect biological diversity. This practice does not only attract biological diversity connected to those forests, but is also a mechanism to offset greenhouse gas emissions.

Human–wildlife conflict

There is need to apply indigenous knowledge to minimize human–wildlife conflict. A study by Moore (2009) found that there exists among the Khwe people of Zambezi Region, indigenous traditional knowledge that assists rural people living in elephant range to avoid confrontation with elephants. According to Moore (2009, p. 334), 'such knowledge would enhance the government's current policy of utilization based approaches to elephant management which assist in mitigating human–elephant conflict where conservancies have been established.'

Moore (2009) documents extensive indigenous knowledge of the Khwe regarding elephants' behaviour, sounds and signs that elephants make when they interact with human beings. If people understand sounds and signs elephants make, they reduce the risk of negative encounters and conflict with them because they have the opportunity to withdraw from a potentially harmful situation (Moore, 2009, p. 334). The Khwe knew the different sounds that elephants could make and what these sounds meant, so that people could distinguish between an elephant that is grazing, angry, chasing or intending to kill. 'If it is in the bush when you go [for] hunting and you see an elephant under a tree, you pay respect and face the other way: it will see you but not charge because you are respecting it,' (Moore, 2009, p. 335).

Avoiding lone female elephants that have gone to the bush to give birth (or especially if she is burying her calf), and avoiding resting elephants and elephants that are drinking in a group at a pan is important (Moore, 2009, p. 336). These measures would go a long way in mitigating human–elephant conflict. It is important to consult with the communities in rural Namibia in order to maximize the effects of indigenous knowledge in minimizing human–wildlife conflicts. (See also Chapter 11, this volume).

New institutional structures

Integrating indigenous knowledge into systems for addressing vulnerabilities to climate change requires the creation of institutions that can codify and make indigenous knowledge explicit. Therefore, the establishment of an indigenous knowledge centre at the University of Namibia (UNAM) is recommended. Some of the roles that could be served by such a centre would be to:

1. Support new and further research on indigenous knowledge in rural Namibia. In the past, this form of knowledge was transmitted verbally or through demonstration. However, in modern times, indigenous knowledge needs to be thoroughly researched and the information stored in maintained collections and made available using modern, user-friendly platforms.
2. Protect and restore biodiversity and communities that are responsible for reversing the consequences of climate change.
3. Use adapted information and communication technology to record, manage and disseminate indigenous knowledge in rural Namibia.
4. Create paths for the development of innovative ideas to address the need for applying indigenous knowledge in climate change context in rural Namibia.

However, certain ethical issues should be taken into account in the integration of indigenous knowledge from rural Namibia into systems to address vulnerability to climate change. Firstly, there is need for financial incentives and recognition of indigenous knowledge holders. Communities and indigenous knowledge experts in rural Namibia may be reluctant to reveal their knowledge if they see no benefits from its disclosure or if they fear that a competitor may profit at their expense (Johannes, 2010, p. 37). Secondly, there is need for gender mainstreaming. Not only should the different impacts of climate change on men and women be assessed, but men and women should also be treated equally in the disclosure of their indigenous knowledge. Finally, there is need for the synergy of indigenous knowledge and science-based knowledge. The proposed indigenous knowledge centre needs to coordinate the continuous evaluation and assessment of indigenous or diachronic knowledge and science-based or synchronic knowledge (Gadgil et al., 1993, p.151) in rural Namibia and academic institutions. It is therefore also important to conduct empirical studies around specific indigenous knowledge themes required to address climate change vulnerability.

CONCLUDING SUMMARY OF MAJOR THEMES

There are gender dimensions to the impacts of climate change. When drought and water shortages occur, women have an increased workload as they have to travel longer distances to fetch water. Droughts lead to crop failure and food shortage, particularly for many rural communities. As a consequence, many women and female-headed households become poorer. Climate change and its associated floods and rising temperatures are likely to lead to increased water- and vector-borne diseases. Since women are the main caregivers, they are expected to be most severely affected by diseases induced by climate change.

In the event of an intense drought, indigenous knowledge would be required in the harvesting of wild fruits and vegetables, and for hunting bushmeat in many African rural communities. There is knowledge of certain plants that can be useful for preserving foods for times of need.

Women can be potential contributors to mitigation measures and agents of change. However, more often than not, they are not recognized when planning mitigation measures and strategies that require community action. This needs to change. Strategies and action plans should include women in the management of forests, drainage channels and the delivery of healthcare services for flood-affected people.

References

Adams, W. M. (1993). Indigenous use of wetlands and sustainable development in West Africa. *The Geographical Journal, 159*(2), 209-218.

Aguilar, L. (2009). *Training manual on gender and climate change.* Cape Town, South Africa: IUCN.

Angula, M. (2010). *Gender and climate change: Namibia case study.* Cape Town, South Africa: Heinrich Böll Stiftung, Southern Africa.

Angula, M., Siyambango, N., & Conteh, M. (2012). *Gender and vulnerability assessment report.* Windhoek, Namibia: UNAM.

Babugura, A. (2010). *Gender and climate change: South Africa case study.* Cape Town, South Africa: Heinrich Böll Stiftung, Southern Africa.

Bollig, M. (2009). Himba lessons about drought coping strategies. *Kunene River Awareness Kit.* Retrieved from http://www.kunenerak.org/en/people/people+of+the+basin/cultural+diversity/stories/himba+oral.aspx

Byers, B. A. (1997). Environmental threats and opportunities in Namibia: A comprehensive assessment. *Research Discussion Paper, No. 21.* Windhoek, Namibia: Ministry of Environment and Tourism.

Chinsembu, K. C., & Hedimbi, M. (2010). An ethnobotanical survey of plants used to manage HIV/AIDS opportunistic infections in Katima Mulilo, Caprivi region, Namibia. *Journal of Ethnobiology and Ethnomedicine*, 6, 25. doi:10.1186/1746-4269-6-25

Chinsembu, K. C., Hedimbi, M., & Mukaru, W. C. (2011). Putative medicinal properties of plants from the Kavango region, Namibia. *Journal of Medicinal Plants Research*, 5(31), 6787-6797.

Costello, A. M., Abbas, A., Allen, S., Ball, S., Bellamy, R., Friel, S. …Patterson, C. (2009). Managing the health effects of climate change. *Lancet*, 373, 1693-1733.

Dan, V., Mchombu, K., & Mosimane, A. (2010). Indigenous medicinal knowledge of the San people: The case of Farm Six, Northern Namibia. *Information & Development*, 26(2), 129-140.

Dickman, A. J. (2010). Complexities of conflict: The importance of considering social factors for effectively resolving human–wildlife conflict. *Animal Conservation*, 13, 458-46. doi: 10.1111/j.1469-1795.2010.00368.x

Dieckmann, U., Odendaal, W., Tarr, J., & Schreij, A. (2013). *Indigenous peoples and climate change in Africa: Report on case studies of Namibia's Topnaar and Hai//om communities.* Windhoek, Namibia: LAC.

Dirkx, E., Hager, C., Tadross, M., Bethune, S., & Curtis, B. (2008). Climate change vulnerability and adaptation assessment Namibia. Windhoek, Namibia: DRFN.

Egeru, A. (2012). Role of indigenous knowledge in climate change adaptation: A case study of the Teso sub-region, Eastern Uganda. *Indian Journal of Traditional Knowledge*, 11(2), 217-224.

Erkkilä, A., & Siiskonen, H. (1992). *Forestry in Namibia, 1850–1990.* Joensuu, Finland: University of Joensuu, Silva Carelica & FAO.

Ermert, V., Fink, A., Morse, A., & Paeth, H. (2011). The impact of regional climate change on malaria risk due to greenhouse forcing and land-use changes in tropical Africa. *Environmental Health Perspectives*, 120(1), 77-84. doi: 10/1289/ehp.1103681

Gadgil, M., Berkes, F., & Folke, C. (1993). Indigenous knowledge for biodiversity conservation. *Ambio*, 22(2/3), 151-156.

Gebresenbet, F., & Kefale, A. (2012). Traditional coping mechanisms for climate change of pastoralists in South Omo, Ethiopia. *Indian Journal of Traditional Knowledge*, 11(4), 573-512. Retrieved from http://nopr.niscair.res.in/bitstream/123456789/14945/1/IJTK%2011%284%29%20573-579.pdf

Githitho, A. N. (2003). The sacred Mijikenda Kaya Forests of coastal Kenya and biodiversity conservation. In C. Lee, & T. Schaaf (Eds.), *The importance of sacred natural sites for biodiversity conservation* (pp. 27-35). Paris, France: UNESCO. Retrieved from: http://sacredland.org/PDFs/Mijikenda_Kaya.pdf

Glazebrook, T. (2011). Women and climate change: A case study from northeast Ghana. *Hypatia, 26*(4), 762-82.

Gremlowski, L. (2010). Community-based adaptation to floods in north-central Namibia: A case study in the Omusati Region (Master's thesis, University of Applied Sciences in Eberswalde, Hamburg, Germany).

GRN [Government of the Republic of Namibia]. (2004). *Namibia vision 2030: Policy framework for long-term national development.* Windhoek, Namibia: Office of the President.

GRN [Government of the Republic of Namibia]. (2010). *The government's accountability report.* Windhoek, Namibia: Author.

Huffman. T. N. (2008). Climate change during the Iron Age in the Shashe–Limpopo Basin, southern Africa. *Journal of Archaeological Science, 35*, 2032-2047.

Hunter, J. (2005). *The role of information technologies in indigenous knowledge management.* Australian Academic and Research Libraries. Retrieved from http://www.itee. uq.edu.au/eresearch/papers/2006/hunter_chapter9.pdf

Johannes, R. E. (1978). Traditional marine conservation methods in Oceania and their demise. *Ecology, Evolution & Systematics, 9*, 349-364.

Johannes, R. E. (2010). *Integrating traditional ecological knowledge and management with environment impact assessment.* Unpublished Manuscript. Retrieved from http://www. dlist.org/sites/default/files/doclib/indigenous%20knowledge%20and%20eia.pdf

Kunene River Awareness Kit. (n.d.) *Traditional knowledge.* Retrieved from http:// www.kunenerak.org/en/people/people+of+the+basin/cultural+diversity/ traditional+knowledge.aspx

Kuvare, U., Maharero, T., & Kamupingene, G. (2008). *Research on farming systems change to enable adaptation to climate change.* Windhoek, Namibia: GEF, GRN & UNDP. Retrieved from http://www.met.gov.na/Documents/Farming%20Systems%20 -%20Climate%20Change%20FINAL%20REPORT.pdf

Kyoto2. (2008). *Framework for an effective, efficient, equitable Climate Agreement.* Retrieved from http://www.kyoto2.org/page5.html.

Lambrou, Y., & Piana, G. (2006). *Gender: The missing component of the response to climate change.* Brighton, UK: Gender and Development, FAO Sustainable Dimensions. Retrieved from http://www.eldis.org/vfile/upload/1/document/0708/DOC21057.pdf

Lodhi, S., & Mikulecky, P. (2010). Management of indigenous knowledge for developing countries. *WSEAS International Conference on Communication and Management in Technological Innovation and Academic Globalization*, Puerto De La Cruz, Tenerife, 2010, pp. 94-98. Retrieved from http://www.wseas.us/e-library/conferences/2010/ Tenerife/COMATIA/COMATIA-13.pdf

MAWF [Ministry of Agriculture Water and Forestry]. (2009). *Agricultural statistics bulletin (2000–2007).* Windhoek, Namibia: Author. Retrieved from http://www.

mawf.gov.na/Documents/Agricultural%20Statistics%20Bulletin_November%20
2009.pdf

MET [Ministry of Environment and Tourism]. (2011a). *National policy on climate change for Namibia*. Windhoek, Namibia: Author.

MET [Ministry of Environment and Tourism]. (2011b). *Proposed climate change strategy and action plan*. Windhoek, Namibia: Author. Retrieved from http://
www.environment-namibia.net/tl_files/pdf_documents/strategies_actionplans/
proposed%20climate%20change%20strategy%20and%20action%20plan.pdf

MET [Ministry of Environment and Tourism]. (2011c). *The Namibia climate change adaptation youth action programme*. Windhoek, Namibia: Author.

Moore, L. (2009). Beware the elephant in the bush: Myths, memory and indigenous traditional knowledge in north-eastern Namibia. *Cultural Geographies, 16*(3), 329-349. doi:10.1177/1474474009105051

Nelson, V. (2010). Climate change and gender: What role for agricultural research among smallholder farmers in Africa? *CIAT Working Document No. 222*. Kampala, Uganda: CIAT.

OPM [Office of the Prime Minister]. (2009). *Report on the 2009 Flood Disaster Response*. Windhoek, Namibia: Author.

Palmer, C., & MacGregor, J. (2008). Fuel wood scarcity, energy substitution and rural livelihoods in Namibia. *Proceedings of the German Development Economics Conference*, Zürich, 2008, No. 32. Retrieved from http://hdl.handle.net/10419/39884

Reid, H., Sahlén, L., MacGregor, J., & Stage, J. (2007). The economic impact of climate change in Namibia. *Environmental Economics Programme Discussion Paper 07–02*. London, UK: IIED. Retrieved from http://pubs.iied.org/pdfs/15509IIED.pdf

Röhr, U. (2009). Gender in climate change mitigation and adaptation. *Dialogue on Globilization, Fact Sheet 2009(1)*. Retrieved from http://www.gendercc.net/
fileadmin/inhalte/literatur_dateien/49d356c48e54c.pdf

Ruiz-Caseres, M. (2007). How did I become the parent? Gendered responses to new responsibilities among Namibian child-headed households. In S. LaFont, & D. Hubbard (Eds.), *Unravelling taboos: Gender and sexuality in Namibia* (pp. 148-166). Windhoek, Namibia: LAC.

Scholes, R. J., & Biggs, R. (Eds.) (2004). *Ecosystems services in southern Africa: A regional assessment*. Pretoria, South Africa: CSIR.

Terry, G. (2009). No climate justice without gender justice: An overview of the issues. *Gender and Development, 17*(1), 5-18.

UNDP [United Nations Development Programme]. (2009). *Resource guide on gender and climate change*. New York, USA: UNDP. Retrieved from http://www.un.org/
womenwatch/downloads/Resource_Guide_English_FINAL.pdf

Von Oertzen, D. (2009). *Impact of climate change on human health in Namibia.* Retrieved from http://voconsulting.net/pdf/environment/Impact%20of%20climate%20 change%20on%20human%20health%20in%20Namibia%20-%20VO%20 CONSULTING.pdf

Wamukonya, N., & Rukato, H. (2001). *Climate change implications for Southern Africa: A gendered perspective.* Cape Town, South Africa: Minerals and Energy Policy Centre.

WHO [World Health Organization]. (2010). *Gender, climate change and health.* Geneva, Switzerland: WHO. Retrieved from http://apps.who.int/iris/ bitstream/10665/144781/1/9789241508186_eng.pdf?ua=1

14

Reclaiming indigenous knowledge in Namibia's post-colonial curriculum: The case of the Mafwe people

John Makala Lilemba & Yonah Hisbon Matemba

INTRODUCTION

In Namibia, as is the case in the rest of Africa, different versions of an indigenous-knowledge-based education, mainly through the formal setting of traditional initiation schools, was an integral part of community life (Amukugo, 1993; Ray, 1999). The initiation school, of which attendance was compulsory, was a system of formal education with parallels to Western forms of education. For example, initiation schools had a standardized curriculum, set times of instruction, specified age of children for instruction, assessment strategies, use of 'qualified' instructors (experienced village elders) and formal arrangements to recognize and celebrate those who successfully completed the education (Matemba, 2010).

The curriculum offered included teaching the neophytes on 'proper' use of language, survival skills, customs, values, marriage, parenting, religion, respect for others, etc. (Mbiti, 1999; Amanze, 2002). As numerous studies have shown, the arrival of missionaries and colonial political powers in Africa from the mid-1800s onwards and their attitudes towards African cultural institutions impacted negatively on the viability of the African indigenous system of education, which was condemned as barbaric, heathen and an impediment to the consolidation of Christianity and Western culture on the continent (Abernethy, 1969; McCracken, 1977; Nduka, 1980; Ball, 1983; Comaroff & Comaroff, 1986).

Despite these historical challenges facing African education under the various guises of colonial domination, it is a cruel irony that the post-colonial state in Namibia under African political leadership has not made fundamental changes in indigenous education. The result has been that, despite the rhetoric of reform, African indigenous cultural education remains marginalized in preference of Western ideals and models that continue to dominate. For example, the national curriculum is conceptualized, designed and delivered throughout the key stages of the educational sector (primary, secondary and further education) following Western ideals and models. We are not suggesting that Western education in its entirety is bad for Namibia, because in a globalized marketplace dominated by Western economic, political and ideological systems, we fully acknowledge that there is a need for Namibia to offer learners a relevant curriculum that gives them the requisite tools to compete effectively in the global arena (Altbach, 2004; Nguyen, Elliott, Terlouw, & Pilot, 2009). Thabo Mbeki, a former South African president, put it better when he said: 'We must embrace the culture of the globe, while ensuring that we do not discard our own' (Mbeki, 1998, p. 38).

However, having said this, our argument is that in order to reverse the apparent ideological loss and address the fundamental issue of cultural identity and autonomy in education, contemporary Namibia needs seriously to consider placing indigenous knowledge as the context in which the curriculum should be conceptualized, constructed and delivered. Such an approach is needed if the country is to (re)capture for its younger generation the essence of being African, mainly lost during the past century or so of colonial domination. Furthermore, this approach might also rescue indigenous knowledge from other threats in contemporary society, such as the lure of global popular culture and political compromises that have to be made towards the contested idea of 'nation' in a post-colonial and democratic state.

Here, we use the Mafwe ethnic group as a test case to demonstrate the need and relevance of an indigenous-knowledge-based curriculum for children in Namibia's post-colonial dispensation. The Mafwe are of particular interest for two main reasons: Firstly and more generally, to help understand the dynamics of culture and how cultural knowledge can be nurtured and transmitted in a post-colonial context in which political power is now in the hands of indigenous Africans themselves; and secondly, more importantly, to document cultural aspects of the Mafwe, which have not previously received any serious appraisal despite the contested political significance of the group in Namibia's post-colonial dispensation.

BACKGROUND AND CONTEXT

Located in the south-west of the African continent, Namibia is a large, mostly arid country (825,418 km^2) with a small population of 2.1 million (World Fact Book, 2012). It is a unitary state comprising 14 regions, each under a governor appointed by the state president. Politically, it is the last country in Africa to break the bonds of colonialism when it demanded full independence from apartheid South Africa. This was achieved on 21 March 1990, following a protracted, 25-year (1965–1990) liberation struggle led by the South West Africa People's Organization (SWAPO) under Sam Nujoma (Simon, 1994; Jansen, 1995; Pomuti, Shilamba, Dahlström, Kasokonya, & Nyambe, 1998; Bauer, 2001; Saunders, 2009). Ethnically, the majority of the population is Black African (87.5%), followed by people of mixed race or Coloureds (6.5%) and then White Africans (6%). Indigenous Black Africans of Namibia are from a number of diverse tribal groups, many of which comprise several subgroups. The main groups are Aawambo, vaKavango, Ovaherero, Damara, Nama, Caprivians, San and Tswana (Forrest, 1994; Suzman, 2002).

Since gaining independence, Namibia undertook a comprehensive review of education to align teaching and learning with the ethos of access, equity, quality and democracy and its aspirations of building a new, non-racial African nation (Tapscott, 1993; Dahlström, 1995; Gonzales, 2000; Fumanti, 2006; Lombard, 2011). An important task undertaken by the new Namibian Government was to fast-track educational access for the majority of the Black population who had received inferior schooling through the South African Apartheid Bantu Education system, on top of African tribal life in the country having been disrupted from the 1850s until independence in 1990. As part of this reform, structural changes were introduced, such as compulsory schooling up to the end of primary education; introduction of free primary education in 2013; increased enrolment in teacher education; and relevant curricular reforms, including changes in pedagogy, material content and introduction of new subject disciplines (Harber, 1993; Shemeikka, 2000; O'Sullivan, 2001; Howard, 2002; GRN, 2004).

We argue however, that complete educational reform has not been possible in Namibia. Instead, in line with the policy of political reconciliation adopted at independence, the country has produced a compromise curriculum in an attempt to satisfy the educational needs and ideological aspirations of all Namibians – Black, Coloured and White Africans. In fact, relevant literature suggests that given the country's recent colonial legacy under apartheid South Africa, it has been difficult to have an open, ideological debate about a new philosophy of education in Namibia (Harber, 1997). This state of affairs is due to the fact that during the first decade of independence, in particular, key government departments in education were managed largely by technocrats (mostly White Afrikaners) who had served under the previous apartheid regime. As such, it was not uncommon for these technocrats to resist or frustrate, albeit implicitly, the implementation of the more Africanized aspects of the new educational policy because this clashed with their own ideological visions of race and governance (Dahlström, 1995; Angula & Lewis, 1997; O'Sullivan, 2002; Fumanti, 2006). However, serious questions need to be asked as to why meaningful changes towards making indigenous knowledge the basic premise that informs educational policy and practice have not taken place. This is despite the fact that political power and authority in Namibia is now firmly in the hands of the (Black) African political elite (Nekhwevha, 1999; Fairweather, 2006).

The main problem in Namibia, as Fosse (1997) sees it, is that people's worldviews are conflicting due to two main competing ideologies, one addressing the 'universalist ethics of nationalism' and the other dealing with 'the particularist ethics of ethnicity'. However, as Mans (2000) observes, the issue in Namibia is that 'traditional value systems' are under the threat of being eclipsed by the need to adopt a 'global value system' for the country. Again, although largely understated, inter-ethnic problems bordering on ethnocentrism in Namibia have remained a sensitive and divisive issue (Forrest, 1994; Friedman, 2005; Melber, 2009). Consequently, this has made implementing a wholesale cultural policy difficult in a country where ethnic groups are quick to assert their singularity and semi-autonomous existence at times in sharp contrast to the idea of one nation, which the post-colonial state promotes (Lindeke, 1995; Fosse, 1997; Fairweather, 2003; Kjæret & Stokke, 2003).

Thus, similar to the situation in other African countries (Woolman, 2001), despite the rhetoric from policymakers that things in the education arena have changed dramatically, the reality is that the educational model adopted in post-colonial Namibia, despite some cosmetic changes, is fundamentally Eurocentric in its conceptualization (Sifuna, 2001; Beckman & Kurvers, 2009). For instance, the national policy 'Towards Education for All' initiated after independence placed strong emphasis in making English (as a replacement for Afrikaans) the medium of instruction in schools (GRN, 1992). Historically, in Namibia the preference of English as the lingua franca in education and business has been complex as it is a thorny political issue. For example, during the apartheid era in the 1970s, people of Caprivi Region (renamed Zambezi Region in 2013), the majority who are Mafwe, demanded to be educated in the medium of English, a demand that was met at a time when Afrikaans was the 'dominant' national language (Ntelamo, 2010). It is also worth observing that the apartheid government put effort into developing ethnology and indigenous language studies: there was a language bureau writing school textbooks in indigenous languages, and the government updated several dictionaries of indigenous languages (i.e. siLozi, Khoekhoegowab, Otjiherero and others) originally written by missionaries (Fourie, 2009).

Thus, the irony in post-colonial Namibia is that in the attempt to distance the country from its Apartheid past, the new African government led by SWAPO has not been keen to promote indigenous languages, largely in part due to the fact SWAPO's language policy '…for an independent Namibia was a policy of official monolingualism with English serving as the single official language' (Frydman, 2011, p. 182). As others have indicated (e.g. Jansen, 2003), our criticism of this policy is that vernacular languages (of which there are more than 30 distinct ones in the country) have been relegated to only the lower primary school sector (i.e. Grades One to Three) as an optional medium of instruction. Disappointingly, the much-awaited 'National Curriculum for Basic Education' – formulated in 2008 (GRN, 2008a), implemented in 2010 – has merely rubber-stamped issues in the 1993 policy, particularly regarding the status of vernacular languages *vis-à-vis* English in the education system. In addition, the textbook policy produced to accompany the new national curriculum, while stating that one of its priority areas is to produce 'mother-tongue literacy materials', has not made indigenous or cultural knowledge the key ingredient underpinning how educational policy and practice is conceptualized and implemented (GRN, 2008b). In this regard, policy makers should consider two fundamental issues in a future review of the textbook policy. Firstly, there is a need for specific policy guidelines for authors and publishing companies on the production of culturally sensitive textbooks for schools. Secondly, it should be emphasized that the material content of these textbooks should be based on indigenous knowledge – local themes; local stories, anecdotes and folklore; local historical figures, and memorable, heroic events; traditional medicines, foods, dances and attire; African values and ethos; etc.

Evidently, Namibia's post-colonial national curriculum essentially remains linguistically and ideologically Western. We agree with others who have observed (Cohen, 1993; Nekhwevha, 1999) that post-colonial education in Namibia needs to have a visible indigenous or cultural element – referred to as 'cultural capital of the African masses' by Nekhwevha (1999) – if the ideals of a truly African cultural renaissance are to be realised in the new political and social order (Shanyanana, 2011). It is encouraging to note plans are underway to recognize 'tracker schools', which when fully implemented will formalize tracking knowledge of the San by providing individuals with certificates as 'qualified' trackers (Hays, 2010). There is, however, a need for cultural policy in Namibia to adopt a comprehensive approach for schools, which should ensure that indigenous knowledge (in all its contested variety) is firmly embedded in the curriculum across the educational system. At the moment the country's arts and culture policy does not provide any guidance on how schools can implement a culturally sensitive curriculum. As it stands, it merely provides broad policy statements covering a whole host of stakeholders, including government institutions, traditional authorities, independent institutions, arts and their organizations, the media, churches and families (GRN, 2001).

Even those who have commented on this policy in as far as it can be applied in the official school curriculum have had a narrow focus on the issue. They see cultural policy only as the teaching of the arts as a distinct subject, 'Arts Education', in schools or allotting time to traditional dances and drama mainly for entertainment purposes (Mans, 2000). In fact, outside formal education this policy has engendered a proliferation of cultural groups, many of which perform for tourists in joint commercial ventures with Western tour operators keen to sell 'dream' African holidays for their tourist businesses (Fairweather, 2006, 2007).

In this context 'indigenous knowledge' is a collective theoretical and practical wisdom that has evolved over time in traditional communities, based on experience and knowledge adapted to a particular culture and environment. This knowledge is passed on from generation to generation through oral traditions, cultural rituals, farming methods, food preparation and preservation, traditional science and forms of health care, formal education through initiation schools, conservation, moral and ethical values and any other traditional activities that sustain a society and its environment. We argue that there is a real risk that, if nothing is done, critical aspects of indigenous culture may be lost forever to the young generation. Given the fact that currently only 1% of the Namibian population can converse effectively in their own indigenous language (World Fact Book, 2012) – partly due to the impact of a monolingual language policy that privileges English (Frydman, 2011) – it is our view that if left unchecked the Western model of education (in its broadest sense) could have a corrosive effect on the ability of Namibian learners to acquire indigenous knowledge and skills. Thus, notwithstanding some of the perceived but contested advantages of Eurocentric models of education – such as the marketability of those who have gone through the modern educational system in a globalized and highly competitive market (Ball, 1998; Tikly, 2001) – they potentially rob African communities of the power to educate the young generation in useful aspects of culture. Such aspects include the necessary values to help one live harmoniously with others; mastery of one's vernacular language; knowledge of traditional spirituality; etc. (Harlech-Jones, 1998).

POLITICAL AND SOCIAL LANDSCAPE OF THE MAFWE

The Mafwe are descendants of the Lozi Kingdom, which occupied much of what is now the Western Province of Zambia. Today, the Mafwe are found in Zambezi Region in Namibia, Western Province (Zambia) and in areas of Angola (Suzman, 2002). Zambezi Region has the unenviable reputation as the most politically sensitive and volatile area in Namibia, such that it has had a semi-autonomous political existence from the rest of Namibia (Harring, 2004). Its population of some 150,000 inhabitants (three-quarters of which are of the Mafwe ethnic group) had an apartheid Bantu system of education in which different races were given different school curricula, although English was the language of instruction in education here, as demanded by the people of the region (le Roux, 1999). During the long period of colonial rule, the region was ruled indirectly, in which chiefs in the area governed their people on behalf of the colonial administration (Tvedten, 2002). During the period 1940–1980, when the country was under the control of (apartheid) South Africa, Zambezi Region was ruled as a separate 'Bantustan' – a semi-autonomous puppet administration of the South African state reserved for Black Africans. South Africa took full control of the region in 1981 until Namibia's independence in 1990 (Melber, 2003).

A key issue to highlight is that, after the country gained independence, all political power was concentrated in Windhoek under the new regime with little consideration of the special circumstances regarding the level of administrative control chiefs in the region had in the previous political dispensation. Inevitably, a schism developed between the traditional leaders in Zambezi Region (mainly among the Mafwe) and the new political establishment under SWAPO-led government. This schism developed to such an extent that during the first national elections in which SWAPO was victorious throughout much of the country, it received only 40% of the votes in Zambezi Region. This per cent improved only slightly during subsequent elections when in the 1999 elections, for example, SWAPO got 52% in Zambezi while having a sweeping victory of 87% nationwide (Tvedten, 2002, pp. 424–425). Thus, after independence – and with some trepidation for fear of threatening the idealism expressed in the slogan 'one Namibia, one nation', the new African leadership conceded to allow tribal groups to retain a measure of semi-independence (van Cranenburgh, 2006). However, such was the intensity of political intrigue in Zambezi that in August 1999 Namibia witnessed the first post-independent secessionist attempt by the newly created rebel group, the Caprivi Liberation Movement (CLM). Led by Mishake Muyongo, a Mafwe and ironically SWAPO's former acting vice-president, CLM had the full support of the Mafwe chief, Boniface Mamili. Namibian security forces viciously put down the plot. A year before the plot materialized, however, Mamili and Muyongo fled into exile, first to Botswana and finally to Denmark where they were granted political asylum (Suzman, 2002; Harring, 2004).

Why the Mafwe, in particular, have been discontented with the current political establishment is an issue that has received extensive attention in the literature (Lodge, 2001; Guijarro, 2008; Melber, 2009). Clearly, the issues are complex and we have no space to detail them here, except to provide only a summary of the main points in the dispute. As an ethnic minority, some of the Mafwe resent the fact that the autonomy to rule their people, as they had historically, was subsumed by a strong central state promulgated by the SWAPO-led nationalist government. Therefore, although the role of their traditional leaders is recognized, the power of its chiefs is governed by homogenized national policies and limited by constitutional law enforced by the state (d'Engelbronner-Kolff, Hinz, & Sindano, 1998). Another serious concern is the recognition by the state of the Mayeyi and Mashi as autonomous and independent traditional authorities – previously recognized as Mafwe sub-clans. This has caused great consternation among the Mafwe because the Mayeyi and Mashi have in effect shifted their political allegiance to the SWAPO-led government when historically they were a vassal chiefdom of the Mafwe to whom their political allegiance belonged (see Kangumu, 2011; Massó Guijarro, 2013).

The Mafwe also feel politically marginalized and resent what they perceive as the state's interference in their internal affairs (Suzman, 2002; Kuteeue, 2004; van Cranenburgh, 2006; Lilemba, 2012; Sankwasa, 2012). For example, while acknowledging the appointment of a Mafwe from the Totela clan as Minister of Gender Equality and Child Welfare in 2009, generally there is a feeling among the Mafwe that the government is always reluctant to appoint people from their ethnic group into key government positions. Regarding political interference, the Mafwe cite the 2004 case when the SWAPO-led government recognized Tembwe Mayuni as the Mafwe chief when the group had already appointed its own paramount leader, Chief George Simasiku Mamili, in 2000 as a replacement for exiled Chief Boniface Mamili. Inevitably, the government's move has divided the Mafwe nation into two camps – a development some say is playing to the advantage of the SWAPO-led government because a weak, divided Mafwe nation is politically easier to control than a strong one (Fosse, 1997; Kangumu, 2011).

Ethnically, the Mafwe are divided into a number of distinct linguistic categories or clans (Fosse, 1997; Fisch, 1999; Lilemba, 2009):

1. The Mbukushu live along the Kwando River, in the north-western parts of the area around Sachona and in Angola. Essentially this group represents an eastern branch of the modern-day vaKavango ethnic group. They speak Thimbukushu and specialize in *pela* (a dance with drums and hand-clapping), *chibboli* and *mabboloma* dances. Their traditional attire, *mizyambulo*, is a coat made from animal hide.
2. The Bafwe occupy the forested central and western area of Zambezi Region in Namibia, but are also found upriver of the Kwando in Angola and also in parts of Zambia. They speak Sifwe and are known for their famous traditional dances such as *pela*, *mpuku* (a spiritual dance), *chisongo*, *chiyaya* and *nzila*.
3. The Matotela (which is divided into the bena-Luhani and bena-Chilao) live interspersed with the Bafwe in central and western areas. Their traditional dances are *pela* and *mpuku*. They are experts in carving wood for canoes and drums.
4. The Mayeyi live in the southern parts of Zambezi Region in the Linyanti swamps and on the western side of the Okavango swamps, on the border with Botswana. They perform the *chibboli*, a type of dance that involves gyrating or twisting the waist. They speak chi-Yeyi, a language that is very different from all the other languages spoken in the region because it has many clicks, like Xhosa, Zulu or San languages.
5. The Linyanti clan is from the Linyanti area, and from which all Mafwe paramount chiefs descended. During festivals women from this clan put on *misisi* (traditional skirts) while men wear *siziba* (traditional kilts).

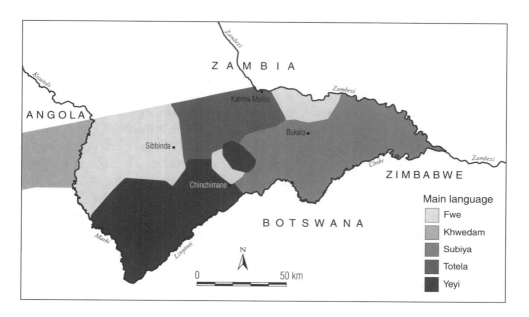

FIGURE 14.1: Map showing the distribution of Mafwe linguistic groups. Adapted from Mendelsohn, Jarvis, Roberts and Robertson (2002).

6. The Makwengo or San clan in this region is also included in the Mafwe ethnic category because they live in areas traditionally under Mafwe jurisdiction. These people are still nomadic and their diet consists mostly of meat. They are experts in making bows and arrows, which they use for hunting.

7. The Bekuhane (Basubiya or bena-Mahe) clan speak Sisubiya, a language that is also spoken in north-western Botswana. The group is found in areas such as Muyako, Lusu, Masokotwani and Sikanjabuka.

8. Finally, the Lozi clan comprises a mixture of the Matotela, Mayeyi and remnants of the Luyana clans. This clan can be traced up to Isize or Nasisangani near the Namibia–Zambia border in the north. They are subsistence farmers and also fish.

Here, we should point out that Fisch (1999), who provided some of the early documented aspects of the Mafwe, was in error when she referred to the people who live in Kaliyangile district as Mbalangwe. In Zambezi Region there is no ethnic group known by that name. The term '*mbalangwe*' is derogatory; it means 'people without a language of their own'. In fact, languages evolve and come to prominence after some time, as is the case with Swahili, Afrikaans and even siLozi. Finally, although there are slight differences in mode of dress, languages (or dialects) and foods, all Mafwe clans are galvanized by a shared sense of cultural identity.

APPLICATION OF THE PHENOMENOLOGICAL METHOD

This study adopted a phenomenological research method in the investigation of the phenomena of cultural knowledge. This method is popular in studies that 'investigate various reactions to, or perceptions of, a particular phenomenon [to help the researcher] gain some insight into the world of his or her participants and to describe their perceptions and reactions' (Fraenkel & Wallen, 2006). This method is suitable for this study because it captures data from the perspectives of people – in this case, Mafwe traditional leaders and elders, and teachers from selected schools in the areas – with expert knowledge and wisdom on Mafwe culture. The phenomenological method was also selected because the concept of phenomenology seeks to identify and describe common perceptions that people use to interpret a similar experience (Johnson & Christensen, 2008). As a study that investigated a culture and various manifestations or interpretations, the phenomenological method facilitated the capture of personal and collective experiences which, in this case, concerned how these respondents perceived and interpreted the various aspects of Mafwe traditional culture (Bogden & Biklen, 1992).

The research that informs this chapter was conducted in 2007 and 2008. Two main data collection methods were face-to-face interviews with traditional leaders and elders (13 in total) and a self-administered questionnaire comprising 14 semi-structured questions completed by 45 randomly selected teachers. Three women and ten men agreed to take part in the interviews. Of these, there were five traditional leaders and eight village elders. With the participants' consent all the sessions were recorded and lasted no longer than an hour.

The traditional leaders and elders were from 13 villages under Chief Mamili, the Mafwe paramount leader. The average age of the interviewees was 69 years. This means that on average participants for this study were born between the late 1920s and the mid-1930s. The selection of the respondents was done after consultation with the Linyanti Traditional Authority (the custodian of the Mafwe culture), which provided the researchers with 50 names of its traditional leaders and elders who were considered to have in-depth knowledge of the Mafwe culture. It is from this group that the researchers randomly selected the 13 interviewees. The inhabitants of the Zambezi Region, as in many areas of Africa, have their roots in communal areas under the jurisdiction of their chiefs (Fosse, 1997).

The teachers in the study were purposely selected because they had experienced both traditional and Western forms of education and would be able to make valid comparisons between the two educational systems. Teachers that responded to the questionnaire came from four educational inspection circuits, namely Bukalo, Chinchimani, Katima Mulilo and Sibbinda (see Figure 14.1, page 291, for approximate locations). The average age of these respondents was 49 years; five of them were women and 40 were men.

Data analysis went through two main stages consistent with phenomenological research: Firstly, the transcripts and questionnaire responses were read and re-read to understand and illuminate the data and, secondly, emergent themes and issues were identified and coded (Colaizzi, 1978; Ryan & Bernard, 2003). Regarding research ethics, the presentation of verbatim excerpts included both the use of participants' real names and other identifiable elements such as village (with full consent), and also non-identifiable codes in cases where participants wanted to remain anonymous.

One major limitation of the study concerns the gender imbalance of the sample of participants. The dominance of men in the study is attributable to the predominantly patriarchal culture of the Mafwe (Khumalo & Freimund, 2014). This explains why the majority of potential key informants that were suggested by the traditional authority were men. We also found that few female teachers completed the questionnaire. Difficulties associated with soliciting female research participants from marginalized communities have been described in previous studies. Cannon, Higginbotham and Leung (1988) suggested that female subjects require the adoption of more labour-intensive strategies involving greater personal contact and a longer stay in the community to establish familiarity. Because we only briefly visited the Mafwe community (for a total of six days), we were unable to establish personal rapport, especially with potential female participants.

Another limitation is that the views of young people were not captured in this study. It is thus possible that a parallel study of younger people would have put this work into a much wider perspective in understanding how to counter the attraction of Western culture in the lives of the younger generations. Thus, issues analysed in this chapter only reflect the views of those who participated in this study, most of whom were older men.

KNOWLEDGE, KNOWING AND PEDAGOGY

Respondents in this study stressed that the indigenous knowledge of the Mafwe has always existed, primarily as a way through which their distinct identity was confirmed. As such, a holistic paradigm of Mafwe indigenous knowledge emerged during the study, evidenced by the richness of their language; world views; philosophy and wisdom; religious practices and symbolisms; successful ways of hunting and farming; traditional medicine and healing; tribal history; ceremonies of life (birth, maturity, marriage and death); and celebrations at installing chiefs.

Respondents noted that while some of this indigenous knowledge was learnt and developed through the formal setting of traditional initiation schools, informal education systems also played a major part in this process. Knowledge was gained by taking part in traditional events (learning by doing and being involved) and by observing and internalizing spoken and unspoken assumptions about various aspects of culture. They also said that learning about culture came through other ways, such as authentic experiences, individualized instruction (from parents and elders), art, and enjoyment (e.g. when participating in the various ceremonies and festivities).

From the responses captured in this study, it could be surmised that the Mafwe place great value on the traditional ways in which people were educated about their culture. Some of the respondents even revealed that when they were young, they had attended the all-important, but 'secretive', initiation schools (*kashwi*). The following verbatim excerpts illustrate their views on this issue:

> 'I personally went through that education system. Traditional teaching was more useful than what you people call education today. It taught us everything from herding cattle, ploughing fields, respect for elders and even the right way of marriage.' Traditional leader no. 5, *c*. 79 years old.

> '[Since] before my great-grandfather's time the Mafwe had a system to educate their young ones. I went through that useful education.' Phineas Chasunda, Sibanga Village, *c*. 63 years old.

Such statements clearly gave us the impression that respondents in the study were proud to have personally gone through the traditional system of education. We also learnt that the Mafwe were not illiterate and that they had a vibrant way of transmitting cultural knowledge and values to younger generations. Perhaps, importantly, we further learnt that the process of transmitting cultural knowledge was 'well developed' and that the indigenous knowledge taught and learnt was 'very useful' to the people and the communities in which they lived.

In African traditional societies, people's psychological connectedness and response to cosmology – their philosophy regarding the origin and nature of the universe (i.e. the physical environment, spiritual reality, human existence, and so on) – usually has been the basis from which knowledge, as a philosophical entity, has emerged (see Mbiti, 1999). The Mafwe strongly believe that knowledge is derived from either real or perceived experience. Anyone who did not go through a particular experience or where the experience was not related to him/her will not know or have a personal knowledge of the experience. Hence, they have a concept '*kulobone*' – grow and see or witness for yourself. Respondents said the Mafwe use their knowledge to help them have an in-depth understanding of the world around them; become responsible people towards themselves and each other; develop a sense of unshakeable affiliation to the traditional group; respect their gods and the power of their tribal leaders; become competent to make moral decisions and solve moral dilemmas; and be competent in certain skills. Such skills noted by respondents included:

1. *kufura machinka* (skill in picking a type of red, wild fruit)
2. *kufura maka* (skill in picking wild fruit)
3. *kutafuna mungabwa* (skill in chewing a wild fruit)
4. *kumina ntete* (skill in swallowing bitter-tasting wild fruit)
5. *kutwa ngalangala* (skill in pounding wild cereals)
6. *kusa magoncela* (skill in digging wild tubers)
7. *kuhika malyacizo* (skill in cooking a wild tuber)
8. *kukoshaura maonde* (skill in cutting water lilies).

From the respondents' statements it is evident that Mafwe traditional education was advanced in its own right. As Matemba (2010) found in Botswana, it is clear that westerners were wrong to assume that the Mafwe had no activities that could be termed 'educational'. Evidently, the colonial educational authorities failed to perceive the value of Mafwe traditional education. Our research has unearthed many examples exemplifying this as the participants in this study reiterated that the Mafwe had an advanced 'education system' before the arrival of westerners. For example, activities such as *kanamundame* (type of chess played with many stones) and *mulabalaba* (chess) enhanced reasoning, logic, mathematical calculations and numeracy skills. They also had a counting system developed particularly to count livestock. Numbers, such as *ngoshile* (one), *nangala* (two), *kangala* (three), *mbuntamo* (four), *mbilimbwishwa* (five), *miyosho* (six), *chokange* (seven), *ngolilo* (eight), *mindule* (nine) and *kumi* (ten), for example, existed. Objects were counted in large numbers – as a whole or per group. The Mafwe also had a concept of time and a lunar calendar of thirteen months. They were able to tell differences and changes in seasons, as demonstrated in names given to months of the year such as *Kuzyangure* (harvesting time as in April); *Kamwiana* (a little warm in August); *Ndimbila* (very hot, as in September); *Nkumbulisa balimi* (it will rain, hence time for ploughing as in October). Certain traditional games, such as *kanamundame*, *mulabalaba* and *mayumbo* (fables) were also known to improve the agility of the Mafwe youth's counting skills. One male teacher in the questionnaire revealed that:

> 'Before I went to a formal school [i.e. Western education], I had the opportunity of playing cultural games like *mulabalaba*, *kanamundame*, *kudoda* and other cultural games with my contemporaries. These games opened my eyes that by the time I started school I could do basic counting. I could count my father's cattle because of the knowledge I obtained from the cultural games.'

As we noted previously, Mafwe knowledge was transmitted through both self-discovery (self-knowledge) and formal education (direct teaching). In this study, language was identified as the most significant factor that has enabled Mafwe indigenous knowledge to survive. Thus, Mafwe indigenous knowledge and its symbolic, verbal and unconscious orders have structured Sifwe, the Mafwe language. The language is enriched by literary expressions, the full meaning and use of which only the Mafwe can appreciate. Therefore, to fully understand Mafwe indigenous knowledge there is need for people to immerse themselves in the Mafwe language because it is the medium through which such knowledge can be fully understood and appreciated. Related to the language, Mafwe wisdom has been traditionally expressed through stories, folklore and metaphors (riddles, proverbs, anecdotes and so on). These idiomatic expressions, for example, helped to cultivate eloquence and debating skills in community affairs.

During the research for this study, respondents narrated stories, folklore and metaphors, some of which they feared were under threat of being lost forever. These narratives were given as examples to underscore the learning process regarding some of the ways people acquired traditional knowledge. The following popular Mafwe folklore was narrated by one of the participants:

'Once upon a time there was a village where the young men decided to kill all old men so that they could take control of the affairs of the village. By killing all the older men they thought that they would get rid of the nuisance, which the elders posed by advising and reprimanding them to do right things. After killing all the older men they chose one among themselves to become their chief. However, one morning the young men were awakened by the heart-breaking screams from the house of their new chief. When they rushed there they were shocked to find that a python had entangled the young chief. The chief was in terrible pain and there was no sign that the snake would let him go. He began to bid them goodbye. Then one of the young men rushed forward and said that he could help the chief if people would promise not to hurt him for what he had in mind. After being given the assurance, he told them that he did not kill his father, but hid him, and wanted to ask him for advice. The old man was quickly brought and immediately upon seeing the reptile he asked for a mouse. The mouse was dangled before the python, and on seeing the mouse it started losing its grip on the young chief. Finally it let him go and others found it easy to club it to death. The young men were amazed at the wisdom of the old man and then decided to make him their new chief.' Francis Mungu, Sibbinda Village, 82 years old.

Respondents in the study explained that this folklore is used by the Mafwe to show that the elders harbour wisdom. The old man could think quickly that the only way to save the young new chief was to bring a mouse before its eyes; because snakes like mice, hence it quickly thought of the mouse and in the process loosened its grip on the young chief. In the process the wise old man saved the life of the young and inexperienced chief and his cohorts. It was also mentioned that in the old days similar folklores were narrated to the young and at the end the narrator would pose questions, which required a certain level of wisdom to comprehend or provide a solution.

COMPETING WITH AND LOSING TO THE WESTERN 'OTHERS'

In response to the specific issue regarding how westernization impacted Mafwe traditional culture, participants indicated that the people have had an unfair deal, culturally, from their interaction with the Western 'others' (i.e. missionaries, settlers and colonial rulers). They noted that since the arrival of westerners in the mid-1860s, Mafwe traditional culture and the means through which it was transmitted has been weakened, condemned and ultimately excluded from Western knowledge systems and modern-day educational institutions. We argue that such was the contempt that westerners had for African culture in Namibia that, in the case of the Mafwe, their indigenous knowledge was 'invisible' in national life. The consequence of this was that there was no systematic means of capturing and storing rare and sensitive aspects of the culture, some of which, sadly, the Mafwe have permanently lost.

In fact we think that had it not been for the Mafwe's vibrant oral culture, even the little of their indigenous knowledge that has remained to this day, could have been lost because Western culture was determined to erase what they considered a 'pagan' and static knowledge system irrelevant to a Eurocentric vision of society (compare Abernethy, 1969; Comaroff & Comaroff, 1986). From responses in both the interviews and questionnaire a number of issues were noted which show the extent to which Western education and influence impacted on Mafwe traditional culture, as summarized below:

1. minimized *zyalyi* (communal eating system)
2. undermined *chiningamo* (evening gathering)
3. discouraged *entango* (traditional storytelling time)
4. discarded *kashwi* (initiation)
5. underrated *kushakiwa* (courting)
6. discouraged *malobolo* (bride price)
7. altered *milaka* (cattle post system)
8. undermined *njambi* (communal ploughing self-help)
9. prohibited *luwanga* (communal meat-eating place)
10. illegalized *mbelesa* (riding expedition)
11. led to the abandonment of *kanamundame*, *mulabalaba* and *kudoda* (traditional games).

In addition, the study also reveals that Western influence led to the abolition of certain traditional dances, such as *chiyaya*, *chisongo*, *likulunga*, *tuwolowolo*, *muuba/njangula* and *tuňombyo*. Europeans perceived these dances to be barbaric and tilted towards superstition, which was against their Western religion and beliefs (see Matemba (2010), for example). It was thus unsurprising to hear sentiments from the respondents in the study lamenting the onslaught of westernization on their culture. One visibly worried participant in the study stated that,

> 'Cultural activities among the Mafwe are either lost or simply neglected because they were discouraged by the German and South African education systems. Courage and bravery were tested at the cattle posts where the young men were posted to guard and protect the beasts from being mauled by lions and other wild animals. Today boys are no longer required to go to the cattle posts. Incantations and other rituals relevant for traditional healing in the community are gone. Before the arrival of the White man, the Mafwe had their way of healing the sick, using traditional medicine. Assegai-throwing for accuracy and defence in times of danger and warfare; negotiation skills in times of heated debates of marriage, succession ceremonies, bargaining or any heated dispute between and among neighbours are no more. Narration skills for remembering historical events and other important issues in one's lifespan have been lost. Skills in drumming for pleasure and informing other villages in times of death and happiness have been undermined or minimized altogether.' Elder Chataa, Makanga Village, 82 years old.

Respondents thus lamented the fact that White people (westerners) were quick to condemn Mafwe traditions and yet did not provide a relevant education for the cultural needs of Mafwe children and youth. They added that this situation contributed to the loss of traditions and cultural knowledge among the youth. They made the poignant point that having had their culture seriously undermined by missionaries and colonialists for so long, self-doubt has inevitably crept into the cultural group leading some to despair about the importance of their cultural traditions.

Many of the respondents in the study further claimed that this trend has continued to the present day because modern parents, who themselves did not receive 'proper' cultural education and are now entrapped by modern life in the cities, have neither the inclination, nor the skills to educate their own children about key cultural aspects of the Mafwe. They said that this vicious cycle is what is contributing to the further loss of Mafwe culture and traditional skills. In addition, the respondents were also quick to point out that the blame should not be on parents only, but also on the young people themselves. This is because young people have embraced 'wholeheartedly' popular global culture, which is usually fuelled by Western media (films and music) and materialistic lifestyles and which young people are reluctant or unwilling to resist. As a consequence, many young people now hold the view that indigenous knowledge is outdated and irrelevant in the current situation in terms of developmental issues in the world. Respondents in the study felt that westernization and the lure of popular culture has placed traditional culture at a great disadvantage as an alternative means of culture and community life, a reality many of the older generation find extremely hard to accept (see also Fairweather, 2006). Regarding personal relations, one respondent lamented:

> 'There is no traditional education these days. In the past, a young girl would not take herself to the house of her suitor or an ordinary boyfriend, but today it seems there are no ethical boundaries in what young people can do... Which parent allows her [girl] child [to] go like that without the suitor being charged many heads of cattle? Days have changed. We are living in difficult times, *tuli munkole* indeed! The Western system has robbed us of our own dignity and values and we are failing to teach our children the way we want them to live their lives.' Induna Sikosinyana, Sibbinda Village, 70 years old.

Whether justified or not, respondents listed several vices and issues that they blamed on westernization, particularly the perversity of global popular culture on young people:

1. Worsened dressing habits
2. Increased divorce rates
3. Increased illegitimate pregnancies
4. Worsened moral behaviour
5. Increased cases of elopement.

Clearly, the impact of westernization (in its broadest sense) on Mafwe traditional culture and consequently, the cultural loss for the younger generation, were issues that caused great concern among the respondents of this study.

RECLAIMING INDIGENOUS KNOWLEDGE

So far, we have seen how Mafwe indigenous knowledge, as indeed that of all other African groups, was marginalized and effectively excluded from formal education during the long period of missionary influence and colonial rule. In this section, we explore ways in which indigenous knowledge can reclaim its place in Namibian's modern formal education. Respondents in both the interview sessions and questionnaire provided a rich array of viewpoints on corrective measures to be undertaken in ensuring that indigenous knowledge can, once again, be part of formal education. Respondents suggested that effective policies should be introduced to encourage a moral culture to flourish in schools for Mafwe youth and other young Namibians. The respondents were sure that this would also help to teach Mafwe youth not to discriminate against others on the basis of race or tribal affiliation. They also felt that this would expose young people to moral behaviour, such as adhering to a good dress code, and avoiding vices and immorality that entrap the youth in modern times.

Given the country's previous political background under the control of apartheid South Africa in which discrimination against Black Africans was endemic, respondents felt that an indigenous-based moral code of *ubuntu* (an African philosophy that stresses the importance of community, selflessness, kindness and humanity towards others) would help heal the wounds of the past. In particular, they mentioned this healing was necessary because, due to the perversity of apartheid at play in pre-independent Namibia, young Black policemen were used to torture other Black Africans, in particular by beating old Black men and women, which is taboo in the Mafwe culture.

On a different point, respondents indicated that there was need for the Mafwe and other Namibians to purge themselves of the colonial mentality they may have towards traditional culture. For this to happen they indicated that there was need to dismantle White supremacist beliefs and Western attitudes and structures, which suppress the viability of African indigenous culture. When pressed on the point whether they thought that Western structures were bad in their totality for education, respondents were quick to clarify that while decolonization does not mean ignorance of foreign traditions, the important point was that there was need for Namibia to overthrow the alien authority (i.e. Western education), which has exercised its control over African community life and its traditional culture.

Respondents further advocated the need for Namibia to introduce cultural education as a compulsory subject for all learners in public education and, more importantly, ensure that indigenous knowledge is used as the key factor underpinning how the curriculum is developed (content) and delivered (pedagogy). Several examples and advantages of an African-orientated curriculum were given. Respondents noted that, if taught as part of cultural education, traditional dances had curative effects as well. For example, besides providing entertainment in African communities, they claimed, though unsubstantiated, that Mafwe dances such as *pela*, *chiyaya*, *chisongo* and *chingubu* were known to reduce high blood pressure and stress. They also observed that the time was ripe for education in Namibia to include the teachings of traditional religions, which for a long time had been condemned as heathen and completely omitted in preference of Christianity as the main subject in Religious Education at school (Hartman, 2011). In doing so, they pointed out, people would have greater awareness and respect for traditional religion as the driving force, which historically has united tribal communities and provided them with a coherent and systematic structure that embodied a measure of African identity and belonging.

Respondents were also quick to point out that an indigenous-based curriculum will help the Mafwe community and other tribal groups in Namibia to recapture and document traditional knowledge, which at the moment is on the verge of being lost forever. They feared that vital traditional science and medicine knowledge might already be lost. They said that it is a known fact that traditional healers had knowledge to heal and cure some illnesses and yet since the advent of western medicine, this knowledge and those that possessed it were condemned. Respondents wished to see the day when schoolchildren would be able to identify trees and other plants that the Mafwe traditionally used for medicine and, even better, were able to use this knowledge.

Controversially, respondents condemned the current structure of formal education, which in their view aims only to produce 'qualifications' without 'real learning' having taken place. In its place, they advocated a work-oriented indigenous curriculum, which promotes independent learning, self-reliance and physical work. Respondents were also clear on the point that young Mafwe should learn to combine practical and intellectual activities.

For the respondents in the study, a relevant curriculum would be one that inculcates and reinforces traditional African socialist values of equality, cooperativeness and self-reliance; that foster the social goals of living together as a community or nation in line with the ethics of *ubuntu*.

INDIGENOUS KNOWLEDGE AND EDUCATIONAL REFORMS

The main purpose of this chapter is to argue for the necessity of an indigenous-knowledge-based curriculum for post-colonial Namibia. To that end we have provided evidence of the nature of indigenous knowledge, the various ways this knowledge has been repressed in a Western political and social context and finally how such knowledge can be reclaimed in the contemporary Namibian educational framework. Crucially, we challenge the Eurocentric assumptions and prejudices that it is only Western societies that have 'proper' knowledge worthy of study. Using the Mafwe as a test case, we have demonstrated the richness, viability and importance of African indigenous knowledge in Namibia. Clearly, the findings in this study suggest the need for a comprehensive theory regarding how indigenous knowledge can become the bedrock – and not merely an ancillary – to a modern education in Namibia. We must emphasise here that learning about indigenous knowledge enables children and the communities they represent to feel authentic, respected and connected.

Examining the evidence we have presented in this chapter more critically, it is clear that the issue about knowledge is actually an issue about power. This is the point made by Foucauldian theory – based on the work of Michel Foucault, an influential 20th Century French philosopher – which emphasizes the relationship between power and knowledge and the implication of this on the social and political functions of education (Deacon, 2006). For Foucault, power offers a strategic situation in a given society and power relations maintain social hierarchy through day-to-day activities of the individuals in the society (Foucault & Gordon, 1980; Foucault, 1984). Foucauldian theory argues that power and knowledge are intertwined entities, and as such power may limit what is acceptable to be known and in turn knowledge can develop as response and resistance to the limits set by power (Foucault, 1982).

Foucauldian thinking on the nexus of power and knowledge when applied to the field of education informs us that formal schooling provides the structure that the state might use to regulate social conduct in practice. This is done when the state exercises its power by controlling and managing the schooling process, which includes (but not exclusively) decisions about the aims of education, nature of the curriculum and its material content, approval of particular textbooks for schools and how knowledge is evaluated (i.e. scholastic performance and assessment) (Apple & Aasen, 2003). Thus, the idiom 'knowledge is power' and conversely 'he who controls knowledge, has power', underscores the power play that exists between those who create and control knowledge – the state and schools – and those who consume that knowledge – the learners.

As we have shown, given the background of education in Namibia, African indigenous knowledge was condemned and marginalized. We argue that this situation gave westerners (missionaries, colonialists and settlers) not only political but also ideological power. In other words, for over a century, African children were denied the opportunity to receive an education that was relevant to and consistent with their cultural setting. And yet, disappointingly, even after independence in 1990 and in spite of some attempts to reform education, the curriculum in Namibia has essentially remained Eurocentric. This means that, sadly, ideological power has not yet been completely transferred to indigenous Africans in Namibia, similar to what Philip Altbach (1977) has described as 'servitude of the mind'. Altbach (1977) makes the convincing point that in post-independent Africa, education serves the neo-colonial interests of the political elite who, instead of transforming education, have merely adjusted it to suit their needs as a weapon of power and social control in tune with a Eurocentric framework.

Evidently, in line with the Foucauldian dictum that knowledge is power, there is need for fundamental reforms in Namibian education so that, ideologically, power can be returned to the African masses. This is an important point to emphasize because the current format of education in Namibia has failed to address the specific needs of its people. This is also the point independent commentators have made about Namibian curriculum for basic education (GRN, 2008a) implemented in 2010 (Engelhardt, 2012; Hango, 2012). Thus, it is small wonder that even before the new curriculum has been fully implemented, there are already criticisms that it is not fit for its purpose. For example, it lacks clarity on the language policy in education and if nothing is done schools will continue to use English as the 'official' language in education even in the Lower Primary Grades 1–3 (Sasman, 2012).

If indeed further curriculum reform is to be undertaken sooner than the mandated 2021 official review circle, as we recommend, indigenous knowledge should feature prominently in that reform agenda. However, in pondering such a development there are two questions that must be seriously considered:

1. How should indigenous communities in Namibia transform their traditional structures to enable them to adopt effective ways of capturing and storing their indigenous knowledge in such a way that it is accessible not only to themselves but to wider society?
2. How should Namibia's modern education create spaces, which not only incorporate indigenous knowledge, but also guarantee that such knowledge will be respected within a common and multi-ethnic schooling experience?

We stress here that in the context of further educational reform there is need to acknowledge how perverse Eurocentric education has been to African education, particularly as far as the curriculum is framed and how schools, perhaps unwittingly, are the conduit of information that promotes Western culture and the ideals it entails at the expense of African traditional culture. We also think that educators, policy makers and educational technocrats need to make a conscious decision to nurture indigenous cultural knowledge by making fundamental changes to the curriculum and schooling philosophy, pedagogy and practice. Only then, will real power return to the hands of indigenous communities.

RECOMMENDATIONS

Finally, in order to take the issue of indigenous knowledge as a central part of formal education forward, we make some recommendations:

1. Specific policies that address the issue of indigenous knowledge in education should be introduced. Such policies will compel the government to commit itself and its resources to supporting ways in which indigenous knowledge can become the backbone of formal education. The policies should also ensure that

indigenous knowledge is respected and promoted in the school system in both rural and urban settings.

2. Indigenous community leaders – traditional leaders, elders and other 'keepers' of indigenous knowledge – should be consulted in any future reforms to make the national curriculum culturally sensitive and based on indigenous knowledge.

3. The use of traditional languages should be encouraged throughout the education system, not only for Grades 1–3, as is currently the case.

4. Schools, teachers and textbook writers should be encouraged to use traditional pedagogies and languages. This can involve the use of traditional leaders and elders as content editors for curriculum materials and school textbooks. Also, given that much of the indigenous knowledge is unrecorded and remains in the memories of elders and traditional leaders and is therefore not easily accessible to others, there is need for the government to invest in oral history and cultural knowledge projects. Such projects would help capture indigenous knowledge and culture for posterity, before critical aspects are lost forever to younger generations. There is also perhaps the need for protected funding to facilitate in-service education in indigenous knowledge and culture of teachers.

5. Where possible, indigenous leaders and elders should be used to provide cultural inputs to schools. This could include the leaders and elders giving instruction on traditional dances, demonstration in making local crafts and talks on oral history and culture. To make this sustainable and attractive, traditional leaders and elders could be given an honorarium for their services and, in some cases, be employed as part-time teachers in cultural studies.

6. Schools in urban areas that are using European languages as media of both instruction and communication should be encouraged through a national policy to bring in the use of indigenous languages. In effect, in Namibia all learners should be compelled to take an indigenous language (as determined by the local education department) as part of the curriculum. To facilitate this, a national programme to train indigenous language teachers should be initiated.

7. Measures should be taken to indigenize tertiary education, in particular, the curriculum of pre-service teacher education.

References

Abernethy, D. (1969). *The political dilemma of popular education: An African case.* California, USA: Stanford University Press.

Altbach, P. (1977). Servitude of the mind? Education, dependency and neocolonialism. *Teachers College Record, 79*(2), 187-204.

Altbach, P. G. (2004). Globalisation and the university: Myths and realities in an unequal world. *Tertiary Education and Management, 10*(1), 3-25.

Amanze, J. (2002). *African traditional religions and culture in Botswana*. Gaborone, Botswana: Pula Press.

Amukugo, E. (1993). *Education and politics in Namibia: Past and future prospects*. Windhoek, Namibia: Gamsberg Macmillan.

Angula, N., & Lewis, S. G. (1997). Promoting democratic processes in educational decision making: Reflections from Namibia's first 5 years. *International Journal of Educational Development, 17*(3), 233-249.

Apple, M., & Aasen, P. (2003). *The state and the politics of knowledge*. London, UK: Routledge Falmer.

Ball, S. J. (1983). Imperialism, social control and the colonial curriculum in Africa. *Journal of Curriculum Studies, 15*(3), 237-263.

Ball, S. J. (1998). Big policies/small world: An introduction to international perspectives in education policy. *Comparative Education, 34*(2), 119-130.

Bauer, G. (2001). Namibia in the first decade of independence: How democratic? *Journal of Southern African Studies, 27*(1), 33-55.

Beckman, D., & Kurvers, J. (2009). Growing roots and wings: A case study on English literacy in Namibia. In I. van de Craats & J. Kurvers (Eds.), *Low-educated second language and literacy acquisition* (pp. 201-212). Utrecht, The Netherlands: LOT.

Bogden, R. & Biklen, S. (1992). *Qualitative research for education: An introduction to theory and methods*. Boston, USA: Allyn and Bacon.

Cannon, L., Higginbotham, E., & Leung, M. (1988). Race and class bias in qualitative research on women. *Gender & Society, 2*(4), 449-462.

Cohen, C. (1993). 'The natives must first become good workmen': Formal educational provision in German South West and East Africa compared. *Journal of Southern African Studies, 19*(1), 115-134.

Colaizzi, P. (1978). Psychological research as the phenomenologist views it. In R. Valle & M. King (Eds.), *Existential–phenomenological alternatives for psychology* (pp. 48-71). New York, USA: Oxford University Press.

Comaroff, J., & Comaroff, J. (1986). Christianity and colonialism in South Africa. *American Ethnologist, 13*(1), 1-22.

Dahlström, L. (1995). Teacher education for independent Namibia: From the liberation struggle to a national agenda. *Journal of Education for Teaching, 21*(3), 273-288.

Deacon, R. (2006). Michel Foucault on education: A preliminary theoretical overview. *South African Journal of Education, 26*(2), 177-187.

d'Engelbronner-Kolff, F. M., Hinz, M. O., & Sindano, J. L. (Eds.). (1998), *Traditional authority and democracy in southern Africa*. Windhoek, Namibia: New Namibia Books, UNAM.

Engelhardt, C. (2012). Protestant education in Namibia: Serving church and state. In W. Jeynes & D. Robinson, (Eds.), *International handbook of Protestant education* (pp. 341-360). Dordrecht, The Netherlands: Springer Netherlands.

Fairweather, I. (2003). 'Showing off': Nostalgia and heritage in north-central Namibia. *Journal of Southern African Studies*, *29*(1), 279-296.

Fairweather, I. (2006). Heritage, identity and youth in postcolonial Namibia. *Journal of Southern African Studies*, *32*(4), 719-736.

Fairweather, I. (2007). We all speak with one voice: Heritage and the production of locality in Namibia. In U. U. Kockel & M. Nic Craith (Eds.), *Heritages of conflict: History, identity and the future of divided societies*. London, UK: Macmillan.

Fisch, M. (1999). *The Caprivi Strip during the German Colonial period 1890 to 1915*. Windhoek, Namibia: Out of Africa Publishers.

Forrest, J. B. (1994). Ethnic state political relations in post-apartheid Namibia. *The Journal of Commonwealth & Comparative Politics*, *32*(3), 300-323.

Fosse, L. J. (1997). Negotiating the nation: Ethnicity, nationalism and nation-building in independent Namibia. *Nations and Nationalism*, *3*(3), 427-450.

Foucault, M. (1982). The subject and power. *Critical Inquiry*, *8*(4), 777-795.

Foucault, M. (1984). *The Foucault reader*. London, UK: Pantheon.

Foucault, M., & Gordon, C. (1980). Power/knowledge: Selected interviews and other writings, 1972-1977. London, UK: Vintage.

Fourie, D. (2009). Educational language policy and the indigenous languages of Namibia. *International Journal of the Sociology of Language*, *125*(1), 29-42.

Fraenkel, J., & Wallen, N. (2006). *How to design and evaluate research in education* (6th ed.). New York, USA: McGraw-Hill.

Friedman, J. T. (2005). Making politics, making history: Chiefship and the post-apartheid state in Namibia. *Journal of Southern African Studies*, *31*(1), 23-52.

Frydman, J. (2011). A critical analysis of Namibia's English-only language policy. In E. G. Bokamba, R. K. Shosted, & B. T. Ayalew (Eds.), *Selected Proceedings of the 40th Annual Conference on African Linguistics: African languages and linguistics today* (pp. 178-189). Somerville, MA, USA: Cascadilla Proceedings Project.

Fumanti, M. (2006). Nation building and the battle for consciousness: Discourses on education in post-apartheid Namibia. *Social Analysis*, *50*(3), 84-108.

Gonzales, M. (2000). Re-educating Namibia: The early years of radical education reform, 1990–1995. *Africa Today*, *47*(1), 104-124.

GRN [Government of the Republic of Namibia]. (1992). *Toward education for all: A development brief for education, culture and training*. Windhoek, Namibia: Ministry of Education and Culture.

GRN [Government of the Republic of Namibia]. (2001). *Unity, identity, creativity for prosperity: Policy on culture and arts of the Republic of Namibia*. Windhoek, Namibia: Ministry of Basic, Sports and Culture.

GRN [Government of the Republic of Namibia]. (2004). *National report on the development of education in Namibia*. Windhoek, Namibia: Ministry of Education, Sport and Culture.

GRN [Government of the Republic of Namibia]. (2008a). *The national curriculum for basic education*. Windhoek, Namibia: Ministry of Education.

GRN [Government of the Republic of Namibia]. (2008b). *Textbook policy: Building a learning nation*. Windhoek, Namibia: Ministry of Education, Windhoek.

Guijarro, E. M. (2008). Relato etnográfico de un encuentro real: visita al Khuta Mafwe, región de Caprivi, Estado de Namibia. *Etnográfica*, *12*, 525-561.

Hango, W. (2012, 23 April). Proposed basic education curriculum reform. *Namibian Sun*. Retrieved from http://www.namibiansun.com/content/letters/proposed-basic-education-curriculum-reform

Harber, C. (1993). Lessons in Black and White: A hundred years of political education in Namibia. *History of Education*, *22*(4), 415-424.

Harber, C. (1997). *Education, democracy and political development in Africa*. Brighton, UK: Sussex Academic Press.

Harlech-Jones, B. (1998). Viva English! Or is it time to review language policy in education? *Reform Forum: Journal for Educational Reform in Namibia*, *6*, 1-10.

Harring, S. (2004). Indigenous land rights and reform in Namibia. In R. Hitchcock & D. Vinding (Eds.), *Indigenous people's rights in southern Africa* (pp. 63-81). Copenhagen, Norway: International Work Group for Indigenous Affairs.

Hartman, A. (2011, 26 January). Bible to be reintroduced in schools. *The Namibian*. Retrieved from http://allafrica.com/stories/201101260190.html

Hays, J. (2010). Educational rights for indigenous communities in Botswana and Namibia. *The International Journal of Human Rights*, *15*(1), 127-153.

Howard, L. M. (2002). UN peace implementation in Namibia: The causes of success. *International Peacekeeping*, *9*(1), 99-132. doi:10.1080/714002698

Jansen, J. D. (1995). Understanding social transition through the lens of curriculum policy: Namibia/South Africa. *Journal of Curriculum Studies*, *27*(3), 245-261.

Jansen, J. D. (2003). What education scholars say about curriculum in Namibia and Zimbabwe. In W. Pinar (Ed.), *International handbook of curriculum research* (pp. 471-476). New Jersey, USA: Lawrence Erlbaum Associates.

Johnson, B., & Christensen, L. (2008). *Educational research: Quantitative, qualitative, and mixed approaches* (3rd ed.). Boston, USA: Pearson Education Inc.

Kangumu, B. (2011). *Contesting Caprivi: A history of colonial isolation and regional nationalism in Namibia*. Basel, Switzerland: Basler Afrika Bibliographien.

Kjæret, K., & Stokke, K. (2003). Rehoboth Baster, Namibian or Namibian Baster? An analysis of national discourses in Rehoboth, Namibia. *Nations and Nationalism, 9*(4), 579-600.

Kuteeue, P. (2004, 5 August). 'Duplicate' Mafwe chiefdom spreads confusion. *The Namibian*. Retrieved from http://www.namibian.com.na/indexx.php?archive_id=3444&page_type=archive_story_detail&page=6977

Khumalo, K. E., & Freimund, W. A. (2014). Expanding women's choices through employment? Community-based natural resource management and women's empowerment in Kwandu Conservancy, Namibia. *Society & Natural Resources, 27*(10), 1024-1039.

Le Roux, C. (1999). The Botswana–Namibian boundary dispute in the Caprivi: To what extent does Botswana's Arms Procurement Program represent a drift towards military confrontation in the region? *Scientia Militaria – South African Journal of Military Studies, 29*, 53-70.

Lilemba, J. M. (2009). *Indigenous Mafwe philosophy of education: Impact of Western education from 1860 until 1990* (PhD thesis, University of Namibia, Windhoek, Namibia). Retrieved from http://wwwisis.unam.na/theses/lilemba2009.pdf

Lilemba, J. M. (2012, 10 May). Lilemba clarifies 'Mafwe' name. *The Caprivi*. Retrieved from http://www.caprivivision.com/lilemba-clarifies-mafwe-name/

Lindeke, W. (1995). Democratization in Namibia: Soft state, hard choice. *Studies in Comparative International Development, 30*(1), 3-29.

Lodge, T. (2001). The Namibian elections of 1999. *Democratization, 8*(2), 191-230.

Lombard, C. (2011). Namibia and South Africa as examples of religious and moral education in changing societies. In K. Sporre & J. Mannberg (Eds.), *Values, religions and education in changing societies* (pp. 129-144). Netherlands: Springer.

Mans, M. E. (2000). Creating a cultural policy for Namibia. *Arts Education Policy Review, 101*(5), 11-17.

Massó Guijarro, E. (2013). An independent Caprivi: A madness of the few, a partial collective yearning or a realistic possibility? Citizen perspectives on Caprivian secession. *Journal of Southern African Studies, 39*(2), 337-352.

Matemba, Y. (2010). Continuity and change in the development of moral education in Botswana. *Journal of Moral Education, 39*(3), 329-343.

Mbeki, T. (1998). *Africa the time has come: Selected speeches*. Johannesburg, South Africa: Mafuba.

Mbiti, J. (1999). *African religions and philosophy* (2nd ed.). Oxford, UK: Heinemann Educational Publishers.

McCracken, J. (1977). Underdevelopment in Malawi: The missionary contribution. *African Affairs, 76*(303), 195.

Melber, H. (2003). From controlled change to changed control: The case of Namibia. *Journal of Contemporary African Studies, 21*(2), 267-284.

Melber, H. (2009). One Namibia, one nation? The Caprivi as contested territory. *Journal of Contemporary African Studies, 27*(4), 463-481.

Mendelsohn, J., Jarvis, A., Roberts, C. & Robertson, T. (2002). *Atlas of Namibia: A portrait of the land and its people.* Cape Town, South Africa: David Philip Publishers.

Nduka, O. (1980). Moral education in the changing traditional societies of sub-Saharan Africa. *International Review of Education, 26*(2), 153-170.

Nekhwevha, F. (1999). No matter how long the night, the day is sure to come: Culture and educational transformation in post-colonial Namibia and post-apartheid South Africa. *International Review of Education, 45*(5-6), 491-506.

Nguyen, P. M., Elliott, J. G., Terlouw, C., & Pilot, A. (2009). Neocolonialism in education: Cooperative learning in an Asian context. *Comparative Education, 45*(1), 109-130.

O'Sullivan, M. C. (2001). The inset strategies model: An effective inset model for unqualified and underqualified primary teachers in Namibia. *International Journal of Educational Development, 21*(2), 93-117.

O'Sullivan, M. C. (2002). Reform implementation and the realities within which teachers work: A Namibian case study. *Compare: A Journal of Comparative and International Education, 32*(2), 219-237.

Pomuti, H., Shilamba, P., Dahlström, L., Kasokonya, S., & Nyambe, J. (1998). Critical practitioner inquiry – the first steps towards a critical knowledge base of education in Namibia. *Reform Forum: Journal for Educational Reform in Namibia, 6*, 1-5.

Ray, B. (1999). *African religions: Symbol, ritual and community.* Upper Saddle River, USA: Prentice Hall.

Ryan, G., & Bernard, R. (2003). Techniques to identify themes. *Field methods, 15*(1), 85-109.

Sankwasa, F. (2012, 3 February). Katima couple burns down traditional court. *Namibian Sun.* Retrieved from http://sun.com.na/content/national-news/tribal-tension-tightening

Sasman, C. (2012, 24 April). Basic education to be overhauled. *The Namibian.* Retrieved from http://www.namibian.com.na/indexx.php?archive_id=94401&page_type=archive_story_detail&page=982

Saunders, C. (2009). Namibian solidarity: British support for Namibian independence. *Journal of Southern African Studies, 35*(2), 437-454.

Shanyanana, R. (2011). *Education for democratic citizenship and cosmopolitanism: The case of the Republic of Namibia* (Master's thesis, Stellenbosch University, Stellenbosch, South Africa). Retrieved from https://www.academia.edu/713260/Education_for_democratic_citizenship_and_cosmopolitanism_the_case_of_the_Republic_of_Namibia

Shemeikka, R. (2000). Education in Namibia. In B. Fuller & I. Prommer (Eds.), *Population–development–environment in Namibia: Background readings* (pp. 153-164). Laxenburg, Austria & Windhoek, Namibia: International Institute for Applied Systems Analysis & University of Namibia Multidisciplinary Research and Consultancy Centre.

Sifuna, D. (2001). African education in the Twenty-first Century: The challenge for change. *Journal of International Cooperation in Education, 14*(1), 21-38.

Simon, D. (1994). Namibia regains Walvis Bay at last. *Review of African Political Economy, 21*(59), 127-129.

Sitwala, J. N. (2010). Language maintenance in the Malozi community of Caprivi, Master of Arts (Sociolinguistics) dissertation, University of South Africa.

Suzman, J. (2002). *Report: Minorities in Namibia*. Cambridge, UK: Minority Rights Group International.

Tapscott, C. (1993). National reconciliation, social equity and class formation in independent Namibia. *Journal of Southern African Studies, 19*(1), 29-39.

Tikly, L. (2001). Globalisation and education in the postcolonial world: Towards a conceptual framework. *Comparative Education, 37*(2), 151-171.

Tvedten, I. (2002). 'If you don't fish, you are not a Caprivian': Freshwater fisheries in Caprivi, Namibia. *Journal of Southern African Studies, 28*(2), 421-439.

Van Cranenburgh, O. (2006). Namibia: Consensus institutions and majoritarian politics. *Democratization, 13*(4), 584-604.

Woolman, D. (2001). Educational reconstruction and post-colonial curriculum development: A comparative study of four African countries. *International Education Journal, 2*(5), 27-46.

World Factbook. (2012). *Namibia: People*. Washington, USA: United States Central Intelligence Agency. Retrieved from https://www.cia.gov/library/publications/the-world-factbook/geos/wa.html.

15

Developmental issues facing the San people of Namibia: Road to de-marginalization in formal education

Anthony Brown & Cynthy K. Haihambo

INTRODUCTION

As for other indigenous people in the world, the living standards of the San in Namibia have drawn attention as they have been viewed as contravening basic human rights. Since its independence from apartheid South Africa, the Namibian Government, as a member of the United Nations (UN), has embarked upon various projects and interventions in order to secure the rights of their indigenous communities, including those of the San.

One of the most progressive conventions of the UN, the Salamanca Statement of 1994 on inclusive education (UNESCO, 1994), promulgates that schooling should cater for all children regardless of their differences or difficulties and serves as a driver towards such efforts. It is worth noting that this global educational transformation came at a time when Namibia was in its fourth year of independence from apartheid South Africa, and was attempting to deconstruct and redress the fragmented education system that it had inherited. It was an education that separated learners depending on their race, gender, ethnicity and language, and if they had a disability (MEC, 1993). It is through this historical backdrop that the San face current challenges as agents in an inclusive space.

The educational experiences of indigenous San children in Namibia reflect discrimination, isolation and a compromised quality of education, and their identity and their indigenous knowledge is not fully embraced in the broader education system. As a result many of them fall through the safety net of this all-embracing educational philosophy. It is for this reason that San children have become a heightened concern and responsibility for the education authority in Namibia.

Through the educational framework "Inclusive Education", Namibia now embodies an educational provision which aims to be free from discrimination and strongly secured in the values of social justice, equality and human rights (UNESCO, 1994). In redressing educational disadvantage, the Government of Namibia has identified increasing the educational participation of San children and retaining them in the education system as a special priority. Various commitments by the Ministry of Education (ME) have been made to support San children so that they have access to formal education in an inclusive society. Some of these interventions included placing San children in public schools and hostels, and waiving their school fees. On a broader societal level, San communities have been provided with other basic needs, such as houses. Furthermore, having recognized the San as a group 'at risk', the government established a department in the Office of the Deputy Prime Minister to specifically address their issues. Most of these interventions have had a low rate of success (Graham-Brown, 1991).

Education in Namibia has to critically analyse the barriers to providing an education that would foster access, equality, equity and democratic participation. How would the assimilation of the San community into a dominant culture and lifestyle support their increased and meaningful participation when the San's cultural beliefs and values are in limited consideration? Could this be one of the major factors that minimize the chances of educational success and social inclusion of San children?

In this chapter, we use the terms 'marginalized people', 'indigenous people' and 'minority groups' interchangeably, and in the context of 'few in numbers' and not 'inferior to' in comparison with other groups. We thus assume the views of social and human rights models as opposed to the views of medical models. In the case of the medical model 'deficit' is central to addressing barriers with the view that the challenges experienced by the San people will be due to the fact that they are of San origin and their difficulties are situated in being San. The human rights model emphasizes human dignity as an entitlement of everyone by virtue of being human. Proponents of the social model would view San communities as being 'marginalized' by the environment and society. The chapter further aligns itself with the definition of indigenous people, by stating that:

'Their cultures and ways of life differ considerably from the dominant society and their cultures are under threat, in some cases to the extent of extinction. A key characteristic for most of them is that the survival of their particular way of life depends on access and rights to their traditional land and the natural resources thereon. They suffer from discrimination as they are being regarded as less developed and less advanced than other more dominant sectors of society. They often live in inaccessible regions, often geographically isolated and suffer from various forms of marginalisation, both politically and socially. They are subject to domination and exploitation within national, political and economic structures that are commonly designed to reflect the interests and activities of the national majority. This discrimination, domination and marginalisation violate their human rights as peoples/communities, threaten the continuation of their cultures and ways of life and prevents them from being able to genuinely participate in deciding their own future and forms of development.' (ACHPR, 2005, p. 89).

Considering the definition above, which comprehensively depicts the life of the San people in Namibia, there is a need to treat the San as a special group not with the aim to further marginalize or provide them with preferential treatment, but with the aim to ensure that their basic rights and subsequent needs are restored. Their educational needs thus cannot be addressed as those for mainstream communities. Rightly so, the ME's National Policy Options for Educationally Marginalized Children lists children of San and Ovahimba communities as specialized groups that could be excluded from education if no intensified efforts are made to deliberately include them in educational programmes (GRN, 2002).

THE CONTEXT OF THE SAN PEOPLE OF NAMIBIA

The San are southern Africa's indigenous people, mostly living today in Angola, Botswana, Namibia and South Africa, with smaller numbers in Zambia and Zimbabwe. Former hunter–gatherers, the San are currently living in conditions of extreme marginalization and poverty, and are struggling to adapt to a fast-changing world. The name 'San' is the name that the Damara used, meaning 'gatherers'. The Ovaherero people refer to the San people as *Ovakuruveha* or, in short, *Ovakuruha* – 'the ancient people of the land'. In Botswana, they are referred to as the Basarwa (Amathila, 2012, p. 193). In all of the countries in which they live, San communities experience problems with formal education, leading to low levels of success and very high dropout rates from both school and employment. They live at the margin of society and are often unemployed, and have poor living and health conditions. Most countries in which the San live have put programmes in place to help put them on a par with the rest of society.

In Namibia, there are an estimated 38,000 San people, making up about 2% of the population (Diekmann, Thiem & Hays, 2011). They live mainly in eight of Namibia's 14 political regions: Kavango East, Kavango West, Kunene, Ohangwena, Omaheke, Oshikoto, Otjozondjupa and Zambezi. The intensive interviews and observations on which the information in this chapter is based were done in the Ohangwena, Oshikoto and Otjozondjupa regions. Interviews and observations were conducted with various, purposefully composed groups consisting of traditional and regional council leaders; San of different age groups and consisting of both genders; San learners; non-San in the areas where the San reside (dominant groups); education officials such as school principals, life skills teachers, people at the helm of programmes targeting San development issues; representatives of line ministries including: Ministry of Health (Rehabilitation Division); Ministry of Education; Ministry of Safety and Security.

The San people live primarily in remote areas and, these days, make their livelihoods as farm workers. They can no longer practise their hunting and gathering lifestyles due to strict conservation regulations. They are absent from many spheres of life and are mostly employed in unskilled or semi-skilled activities (GRN, 2008, p. 13). As a result, they are paid very low wages with which they routinely buy home-brewed alcohol (Amathila, 2012, p. 195).

The literature repeatedly reveals that the San have the lowest educational attainments of any ethnic group in Namibia. In the past, when each ethnic group administered the needs of their own people, the San had no administration of their own. Le Roux (2000) describes how the San were used as trackers by the South African army and were given food rations and alcohol as remuneration for their services, which some believe created the San's dependency on hand-outs, which continues today. They barely had material resources, or contemporary skills to build on at independence. The skills and indigenous knowledge they possess was not valued enough to be used in moving the newly formed nation forward. Ironically, the skills of the San people are sought after by both communal and commercial farmers, yet these are not valued enough to warrant compensation at market-related rates. This suggests that a degree of inferiority and stigmatization is imposed on the San.

Since independence when the Government of Namibia committed itself to equality and equity through the Namibian Constitution (Article 10), the San have been faced by the difficulties of securing basic needs, such as land and a means to survive. Hence, school attendance and literacy are not their highest priorities.

Statistics from ME's Education Management Information System (EMIS) showed that the enrolment rate of San learners in 2011 was only 1.3% of the total learner population compared to learners of other home languages, for example, Khoekhoegowab (11%); Otjiherero (7.4%) and Afrikaans (6.3%) (ME, 2011, p. 41). While the total population of the San is considerably lower than that of other ethnic groups, and taking the barriers experienced in accounting for the San in population and housing censuses, the low number of San learners in schools remains a cause for concern. Equally, the dropout rates of San children from educational institutions, especially at secondary and post-secondary levels, remain worrying.

The high dropout rate is linked to a variety of factors, including language, poverty, remoteness, stigma and other social and cultural factors (Kavari, 2012, p. 3). Several concerted efforts by the government and supporting organizations have attempted to increase numbers of San children in formal education. These include exempting San children from school and hostel fees; creating community hostels for them; providing them with free transport to school; providing school feeding programmes; and making children from marginalized communities automatic beneficiaries of such programmes. Unfortunately, these initiatives have had limited success, and the vast majority of San youths and adults have very low levels of education. San children are often faced with extreme forms of bullying at school because of their differing cultural lifestyle and appearance, and lack of material means amongst other factors (IWGIA, 2011). It is therefore not surprising to find that only 1.8% of the San learners that enrol in Grade One manage it through to secondary school (Cupido, 2013).

Employment opportunities for San adults are also limited, and the majority of San have little, inconsistent, or no cash income. Many families are dependent on erratic state-run, food-aid programmes, and pensions and disability grants. It was also revealed through the various community meetings we held that many San who should be eligible for pensions, or grants as orphans or vulnerable children, etc. have not been able to benefit as they do not have the necessary information regarding dates of birth, death, etc. needed to obtain documents, which in turn enable access to grants; such details are not recorded in the same manner in San culture.

As plans to develop land through economically productive activities intensified prior to independence, the Namibian San were moved from their ancestral lands into settlements closer to towns and villages. For example, some were moved from Etosha National Park to small settlements in Oshivelo, Tsintsabis and others to Tsumkwe and Mangetti areas. In these settlement areas, restrictions made it impossible for the San to continue their traditional lifestyles. Yet, they were not equipped with relevant skills and opportunities to make alternative livelihoods. Ostensibly the San are faced with many challenges in adapting to contemporary lifestyles and a cash economy.

San men are most commonly employed by well-off farmers as farm workers erecting fences for kraals and boundaries, herding animals and rendering other services, such as collecting water (le Roux, 2000). Women are often employed as domestic workers rendering childcare and other domestic services in their 'host's' houses (le Roux, 2000). Ironic narratives told by the San suggest that while they are the original owners of the land, they have become 'guests' and 'slaves'. One young (23-year-old) San man from Oshivelo stated, 'that whole fenced land of Etosha is where our parents were chased from to make way for animals and tourists who come to see them'.

Because of their culturally nomadic lifestyles, they continue to struggle with settling at one particular place. As one respondent in the focus group discussion in Tsintsabis said: 'We were not made to stay in one place. After all, we do not have cattle and property to look after.' This and other similar statements indicate that the San perceive themselves as having been pushed to the periphery of society.

The Namibian Government and non-governmental organizations (NGOs) have made efforts to alleviate the transitional difficulties of the San. Amongst others are conservancy rights in certain areas (around Tsumkwe, for example); poverty alleviation programmes; food for work schemes; and free access to education (le Roux, 2000). The government has gone the extra mile in recognizing the San as a marginalized or minority group with the intention of addressing their exceptional struggles, which, here, we liken to potholes. Despite the constitutional and educational reforms promoting the social inclusion and equality of the San, they remain a significantly disadvantaged group. They face difficulties with access to work and services. In addition to these, they face harsh treatment by their 'host' communities. Graham-Brown (1991, p. 57) confirmed this when she referred to experiences of refugees and displaced persons in southern Africa. This is ironic in the sense that it is commonly believed that the San are held to be the original inhabitants of most countries in southern Africa, yet they now lead livelihoods of displacement in these countries.

Minority or marginalized groups are often viewed homogenously, having similar needs and challenges (Gaviria-Soto & Castro-Morera, 2005) because they are seen to have a number of attributes in common that set them apart from other people (Olney & Kim, 2001). Their exterior features are different from the majority of other ethnic groups; their language and dialects contain unique features and sounds; and their social behaviour is characterized by group cohesion (large families, inclusive of all generations moving together). As a result, various critical issues of minority groups are not regarded highly, including factors related to disability, chronic conditions, and gender issues. Neglecting to uproot such intersections of gender, disability and, often, class could contribute to immense challenges for individuals to live in an embracing social and just society.

Although the case of the San people has been studied, literature specifically on perceptions of disabled San people is lacking. As part of discussion on inclusive education, we also investigated the binary of social exclusion and disability within the San community. While the San are known for natural skills in the areas of healing, physiotherapy and other habilitation and rehabilitation processes, our research did not manage to source much of this kind of information from the San communities that participated in the study. Many referred to certain practices their grandparents or great grandparents used to restore mental or physical health, but they did not know the details. Part of this could be attributed to the lack of appreciation by the larger society, prompting the San to start viewing their indigenous knowledge and practices as of minimal importance.

One major finding in the area of inclusion, though, was the fact that differentia is not a factor to them, and would thus not be stigmatized. Participants across the sample were able to identify people amongst them who were different in terms of physical conditions (impairments); health status (tuberculosis or HIV); or mental composition (lower cognitive functions judged by the way they carried out daily tasks). Yet, for them this diversity was part of the complete picture of their communities. When prompted about special schools, many were not aware of such schools and the function they would perform, while those who heard about such schools understood that these are schools that could relieve parents from the burden of childcare. Their culture thus forms a good basis for inclusion as 'being together' is a very important component of it, and separation anxiety is experienced quite severely by group members if one or some members of the group have to be removed.

In this chapter, however, we focus on education as a developmental issue and on the barriers San people experience in this area. We thus provide a brief overview of the education of San children, while reflecting on barriers to education. We further highlight the need for marriage of inclusive indigenous educational theories with the rest of conventional inclusive education issues, such as learning difficulties, giftedness and impairments. Lastly, we provide a lens into the binary of inclusive education and disability as an emerging discourse, especially in relation to 'marginalized' communities, such as those of the San.

EDUCATION

Education is a basic human right as recognised in the Namibian Constitution (GRN, 1990, Article 20), Convention on the Rights of the Child (UNICEF, 1990), the UN Millennium Development Goals (UN, 2008) and the Dakar Framework for Action (UNESCO, 1990). Education has been used by many nations around the globe to overcome challenges such as poverty, disease, social cohesion, social justice and citizenry.

In Dakar, a commitment was made to the pursuit of broad-based strategies for achieving learning needs for all, through expanding and improving early childhood education, especially for the marginalized and most vulnerable. This could be achieved by ensuring that all children, including those of marginalized communities, have access to and complete free primary education. Also deemed important was to offer equitable access to learning for both children and adults, eliminating gender disparities and improving the quality of education, especially recognized and measurable learning outcomes (UNESCO, 2000, pp. 15–17). Namibia is signatory to the Dakar Framework. In this respect, the government provided an amount of N$400,000 to kick-start the San Development Programme through the Office of the Deputy Prime Minister (Amathila, 2012, p. 202). Through this programme, schools, farms and houses were erected, and San were provided with identity documents to enable them to access state grants and other services.

These innovations were not without opposition as some San perceived development as interfering with their cultural institution. The San presently form a non-dominant sector of Namibian society and are determined to preserve, develop and transmit to future generations their ancestral territories and their ethnic identity, as the basis of their continued existence as a people, in accordance with their own cultural patterns, social institutions and legal systems (Martinez-Cobo, 1984, quoted from the University of Minnesota Human Rights Center, 2003). From this perspective, they are often caught between current developments and the interference of these with, and dilution of, their cultural lifestyles. It took perseverance to convince some San leaders to participate in the development programmes.

SCHOOL ENROLMENT AND DROPOUT

The educational experience in schools will be different for every child. How they adapt and engage in such structures is much determined by the type of school they attend, the relationships they build with teachers and peers and the reflections of family background and prior knowledge (Rhaman, 2013). In mainstream education structures, learners are found to abandon their culture of speech and learning to conform to the values and practices of mainstream society (Vange, 2006, cited in Rhaman, 2013, pg. 661). We argue that if an individual's identity is not valued, he or she is more likely to reject the institution. Guided by the hypothesis that the San do not want to go to school and would rather be left alone to continue free roaming, hunting and searching for *veldkos* (food harvested directly from the natural environment), we question this predisposition and were interested in finding out through face-to-face narrative interviews the position of San communities in Oshivelo and Tsintsabis (Oshikoto Region), Tsumkwe and Mangetti Dune, (Eiseb Block and Gam in Otjozondjupa Region), and Ouhalamo (Ohangwena Region) regarding education.

When posed with the question, 'Do you want your children to go to school?' (translated to them by a research assistant from their own community), both body language and words affirmed almost in a chorus: 'Yes, we want our children to go to school like other Namibians.'

An automatic follow-up question was: 'Why do you want your children to go to school?' They responded as follows:

'They can help us become like other groups in Namibia.' ['How are the other groups?'] 'They are advanced; they don't live in poverty like us.' Community leader, Tsintsabis.

'They can help us sign when collecting our pension grants.' Parent, Oshivelo.

'We want our children to become scientists. But tradition is in our blood and education and tradition should go together.' Nurse, Mangetti Dune.

'Yes, we want our children to go to school so that they become educated and come to take care of their parents.' Community leader, Ouholamo.

The responses above did not correspond with observations and findings when data were triangulated. For example, while the San people expressed the desire for their children to receive education, teachers reported that some parents came to fetch their children out of school to visit drinking places with them. Teachers also reported that parents from the San communities rarely attended school activities, neither did they send children back when the latter ran away from school. It was also reported that some parents visit the schools when food through the school-feeding programme is being distributed, shared the meal with their children and then left, sometimes with the children. Teachers and school principals of all the schools that formed part of the sample repeated these findings. The dropout rate of San learners from schools continues to rise despite various concessions and exemptions by government and donations from NGOs and concerned groups, such as WIMSA (Working Group of Indigenous Minorities in Southern Africa) and FAWENA (Forum for African Women Educationalists Namibia), in attempts to make attendance easier for them.

Statistics obtained from Tsumkwe Secondary School indicated that while the majority of their enrolment (70%) was San children in 2011, for example, few of them were enrolled in the higher grades. In 2011, there were 138 San learners in Grade 8, 77 in Grade 9, 55 in Grade 10, only one in Grade 11 and none in Grade 12. This finding is supported by Kavari (2012) who found that San children in Omaheke Region had fewer difficulties attending primary schools as these are close to their villages, but secondary school attendance was impaired by the long distances of schools from their homes, necessitating children to board in the school hostel for a whole term without seeing their family members. Problems related to puberty and adolescence were also factors at secondary school. Kavari's research revealed that San learners experienced more discrimination, sexual and emotional abuse and other forms of exclusion from social spheres of school life in secondary school, compared to primary school. Learners from other ethnic groups regarded themselves superior to San learners (Kavari, 2012).

San learners we met who communicated in Afrikaans confirmed this finding. When asked why they were not speaking their mother tongue, their response was:

> 'Here, life is better when you say you are Nama or Damara. Otherwise you will be treated like nothing. You can't even borrow a comb from someone then people start to laugh at you. One girl told me that she only has one comb and if I use it for my Bushman hair, it will break. So, when I came to this school [secondary school] I tell people I am Nama.'

The picture of enrolment and dropout is not the only indicator of exclusion within inclusion. Although the Ministry of Education has attempted to enrol San learners in schools together with other ethnic groups, there could be a point which is being missed: that visibility and presence of a minority group does not necessarily secure social inclusion. Most teachers who participated in this study described the San learners to be academically able, but often shy to participate in classroom activities. They rarely spoke their own language and rarely answered questions in class, even when they knew the answers, as the female head of department at Uukumwe Primary School, Oshivelo, stated in an interview:

> 'San children are very clever. But they will never answer. They will always look at other children and some will even tell their friends the answers instead of raising their hands and providing the answers. Wait until they write a test, then you will know who they truly are. I think it is their culture. They don't boast. They are reserved. And when they are not happy with something, they will get up and leave, just go away never to come back to school'.

Another teacher at a secondary school in Eenhana shared the following:

> 'Last year we had a very clever girl from the San community here in Grade 11. She was the only one we had left from the more than thirty that came here to start Grade 8 from Oshivelo in 2008. She was out-performing everybody here. We were proud of her. Then at the beginning of the third term, she started staying out of school. By the time of examinations, she only wrote two subjects. Then she disappeared again. I drove myself to go and look for her and convince her to come back. The whole family came to listen to me. Then she came the Monday after my visit to her homestead and disappeared again. If she comes back, I will enrol her. But for now, she is gone. Some say she got married, others say she went to look for food in the field'.

These narratives are indicative of the negative impacts of marginalization on the self-esteem of San learners. Even if the school environment is welcoming, poor self-esteem limits the San learner's performance and achievement. A critical ingredient for indigenous people is that they exist and therefore self-belief and confidence are intrinsic contributing factors to success (Bethel, 2006, p. 35). It appears that even when the learner is needed and embraced, the pull factors outside school are stronger; the dominant school culture has to transform in order to accommodate a greater multicultural awareness.

Another characteristic of marginalization is the pattern of poverty and dependence that are associated with unemployment and the culture of destitution. Parents coming to school to share their children's food could be partly a good practice of caring and bonding. On the other hand, if this practice is indicative of a lack of basic needs in the family, it raises concerns for the continuous relationships between children and their parents, motivation of children to remain in school and role modelling. Parents who own cattle or have other means would not need to come to school to eat with their children. Thus, in multi-ethnic schools attended by children of families with different economic means, as is the case here, the minority status, imbalances and gaps of the poverty-stricken are widened, rather than narrowed.

Perhaps mainstream schools should look beyond conventional efforts of encouraging San learners to return to school by looking inside the schools. Many San learners we spoke to disclosed frequent experiences of bullying by other learners. Most forms of bullying were emotional in nature and attacked the character of the victims. As one 16-year-old boy from Eenhana narrated,

> 'Sometimes they call us *uukwanghala* [(a derogatory term which directly translates into 'those that do not save anything for tomorrow')] and, when you are not paying attention, some teachers ask whether you are looking for wild animals in the field.'

A 14-year-old girl from Tsumkwe told us, 'The majority of the children and teachers are really nice, but some girls laugh at our hair and some say we smell like fire.'

Although on the surface it appeared that social inclusion of the San was taking place, many respondents reflected negatively or derogatively towards the San. Some examples of these are:

1. Names such as 'aakwangala' and 'ovakuruha' have derogatory connotations and imply lower status, a begging culture, etc.
2. San are likely to be requested to provide unskilled labour, irrespective of the capacity in which they are attending a particular function, for instance, and (non-San) people are either surprised or offended if they refuse. One man mentioned that people tend to say, 'Okakuruha kahapavi?' which means, 'What's wrong with this Bushman?'

3. One San woman with a disability who visits the hospital on a regular basis explained how she is often neglected by health personnel and has to wait for one specific nurse who is willing to attend to her needs and treat her humanely. She believes that, if she were not San, she would receive better services.

At each research site, focus group discussions were held with non-San community members on the scenarios told by San communities. Respondents in these non-San groups raised issues of what they referred to as 'typical San behaviour' that warranted inferior treatment. Five of these are listed below:

1. They disappear mysteriously.
2. Even if you build them a proper house, they won't sleep in it. They would rather erect a shack next to it or sleep in the open air.
3. They do not complete education, irrespective of the investments. Even if you raised them with other children, by the time they reach puberty, they will distinguish themselves as San through their behaviour.
4. They are more vulnerable to alcohol abuse and early sexual activities than children in other ethnic groups.
5. Even when they are professionals, when they decide to walk off their jobs, they just go, even for months, and come back whenever they want.

It is common knowledge that attitudes and actions of adults in a community are reflected in the interactions between and among children. As a result, inferior treatment of the San finds its way into schools, as deduced from the statements below:

'When there was this outbreak of TB, some children were saying we are the ones spreading it and they did not want us to come near them.' Boy, 15, Tsumkwe.

'Some teachers never ask us anything, even if you raise your hand until it gets numb.' Girl, 12, Oshivelo.

'When a[n] [Ova]herero or [Aaw]ambo child is absent, the teachers say, maybe she or he is sick. But if it is one of us, the teachers says, she or he is gone forever.' Boy, 19, Tsintsabis.

If learners from diverse backgrounds are labelled negatively and experience rejection, it is a normal reaction for them to flee and be with those that accept them. And for the San children, safety and security can be found at home, even if that home is a shack made of plastic bags.

INTRINSIC AND EXTRINSIC FACTORS HINDERING SCHOOL ATTENDANCE

The fact that there was a will to attend school, accompanied by the required intellectual capacity to succeed in school, it was deemed necessary to identify factors that contributed to the current status quo of limited visibility of San learners in educational circles. Hence, we arranged both San-specific and mixed group community meetings in an attempt to find answers to reasons why the San remain invisible in secondary schools and ultimately the white-collar employment sector.

One community meeting that consisted largely of young people summarized causes for San children's school dropout as follows:

1. **Poverty:** No clothes, extra food and other necessities.
2. **Nomadic lifestyle:** When parents move, they move with their children and come back after a long time. They are stigmatized upon return and will have fallen behind with schoolwork.
3. **Early marriages, an acceptable norm:** 'Parents don't have that much control over their children. If we tell our parents that we do not want to go back to school, most parents will lift their shoulders and that is the end of the story,' a 23-year-old San woman said.
4. **Hand-outs:** 'People drop out because they know they will survive on food hand-outs, oranges and mattresses! The young people do not want to think beyond today.' Female traditional leader of the San people, Omatako.
5. **The portrayal of San:** Although it is the most sustainable gateway to development, school is alien and irrelevant to the San. In school, they are always portrayed as gatherers and hunters, as one female from a youth group in Mangetti Dune explained:

   'History and other books are full of pictures of San people with a bow and arrow. San people who have education come here and drink alcohol. It is as if we will be forever hunters, even now when there is nothing to hunt as the whole land has been declared as conservancies or belong to rich people.'

6. **Child labour:** People leave school because they work for others as related by a physically disabled woman in Ouholamo:

   'Early pregnancy, early cattle herding, looking after the house of the Kwanyama employers and not [being] able to attend school. Girls work in the house and till the land. Boys also work in the land and herd animals. Sometimes a boy or girl attends to the whole house.'

Although these factors cannot be ignored, Muthukrishna (2008) urges educationists to view inclusive education through the lenses of social justice and human rights, empowering individuals and institutions to question systems of oppression, how they work, how they are sustained and how they can be contested. Often mainstream education structures are inflexible and cannot accommodate alternative student experiences and, as a result, endanger cultural identities of minority learners (Rhaman, 2013). If the nomadic lifestyle of the San and early marriages are regarded as part of their cultural heritage, how does policy cater for such practices so as not to penalise learners for absences?

Martin (2014) insists that the effective inclusion of indigenous learners in mainstream education structures cannot be accomplished simply by providing more resources. Consideration of incorporating indigenous knowledge into the school system could reinforce the values, beliefs and ideologies of the San people in relation to mainstream society. Although pockets of San history are infused in the curriculum, much more is needed to bring value to the existence and life of this indigenous group to be appreciated alongside other Namibian cultures and identities. El-Ayoubi (2008) advocates that pedagogies should include comprehensive indigenous knowledge. She suggests that such indigenous knowledge should not serve as mere information about the indigenous groups, but be validated as legitimate knowledge structures. Such an approach has the potential to reduce the stigma that the San lifestyle is inferior and help to break down the dominant culture in the school that often perpetuates class and meritocratic values. Using the knowledge of indigenous cultures and lifestyles through inclusive education would narrow the gap in indigenous disadvantage.

DISABILITY AS DEVELOPMENTAL ISSUE

During a set of community meetings in which researchers explored various developmental issues including disabilities, it became clear that congenital disabilities were rare amongst the San. It also became clear that there was no stigma attached to disabilities. Those that had disabilities acquired them through human–animal conflicts or in accidents and they were treated in the same way as those without disabilities. The headman at Oshivelo said that, 'those with disabilities are better off because they receive a grant from Government'. This statement not only affirms the acceptance of disability as a normal course of life, but also points out that in poverty-stricken communities the disability grant is a useful commodity.

Although a few infants and toddlers with conditions ranging from central nervous system to sensory disorders accompanied parents and grandparents to the community meetings we called, we did not come across children with obvious disabilities in schools. Researchers, however, observed a few hidden disabilities such as intellectual impairments and emotional disorders, but teachers did not seem to be aware of these impairments and their possible impacts on learning as a result of those conditions. We believe that learning difficulties were automatically attributed to 'being San' (medical model) and not much effort was put into investigating why learners, whether they were San or not, had difficulties learning. Perhaps this explains why we observed no different learning and teaching strategies.

Based on our in-depth interviews, it can be concluded that disability was not very common, but San culture is also inclusive in nature. When asked whether children with disabilities should attend school in their community, some participants shook their heads in disagreement. Some indicated that they had heard of schools where blind children could go and learn how to read and write and thought children with impairments should be sent to such (special) schools. While respondents expressed ideas of integration and special schooling for children with characteristics that are not typical, these ideologies seemed to be adopted rather than based on their cultural beliefs. We arrived at this conclusion because we did not observe or hear in our interviews any reference to the identification of needs with the aim of separating those affected. The same principle was observed with regard to HIV/AIDS.

With regard to gender issues, the San manifested more equality than many other groups in Namibia. Women and men shared more socialization spaces and they moved together as one group consisting of both genders. When a man or woman was carrying out chores, their partner and children kept them company. The same was observed at places of recreation, mostly *shebeens* (community bars) and events in communities.

CONCLUSIONS AND RECOMMENDATIONS

The findings of this research supported evidence that factors in their environment ranging from external to intrinsic factors, were responsible for high dropout rates of San learners as advanced by Kavari (2012). Also, internalization of their 'marginalized status' has gone a long way in conditioning San, both young and old, so that they believe their place in society is either to work for others for meagre salaries or to receive hand-outs.

The current research also showed that Namibia's colonial history introduced a charity model: receiving goods for free or after rendering a service. These included payments in kind such as in the form of food, second hand clothing, tobacco and alcohol. Namibia's current democratic government, to a large extent, seems to maintain the status quo, given that a number of concessions have been made available to marginalized communities without time frames or processes to empower these communities to move from dependency to independence. However, some of the San people do not want to continue with this status, as expressed below:

> 'We are tired of mattresses and oranges! We want education to sustain ourselves.'

> 'The government should provide for us. We do not have jobs, no IDs [identification documents], no cattle! They should give us food and clothing. We want to be like other [ethnic groups] in Namibia.'

> 'We cannot remain a tourist attraction, demonstrating to them how we make fire without matches! We want to move together with other nations in the world, but not forgetting our culture.'

> 'We are poor, we don't find jobs, we don't have cattle. How are we supposed to survive? We thank Libertine [the former Deputy Prime Minister] for making Namibia aware that we are people, even though we live in the bush!'

The San communities face various challenges as they attempt to move from their traditional lifestyles towards modernization. Many youths expressed the willpower to be on a par with other ethnic groups in the country. All they need now is to continue negotiating for the penetration of their culture in the school system.

We also found that learners from marginalized communities in mainstream schools need to be empowered to apply themselves in accordance with the human rights model. This will only be possible if the playing field is levelled, for example, through the provision of basic needs to all children irrespective of their culture. It would be important to facilitate more dialogue between San people and government in order to identify challenges and to address them accordingly. Surely, San people can advise government on inclusive practices that are likely to support the retention of learners from San communities! Equal collaborations and partnerships between schools and San parents and communities can redress current statistics that reflect high dropout or perhaps 'push-out' factors of San children from education institutions. The impacts of marginalization on people should not be underestimated when dialogues are planned. Hence, care should be taken to ensure equity in discussions if we are to gain the maximum from the San about how the education system could be restructured to better retain San children in schools. To this end, it is crucial for educated San people to become the mouthpieces of their communities and to play a significant role in uplifting them.

Among possible inclusive practices that can assist in retaining San learners in schools and ensure their full access, participation and achievement, is to empower San learners to manage stigma and labelling, and claim their rightful citizenship in order to demand their right to education. This should be coupled with teaching all children the values of respect for diversity. Until such a time, inclusive education will remain a political rhetoric that applies to a selected few.

It is advisable that all education stakeholders plan together, guided by the wise words of Martin Luther King, as quoted by Apple Seeds (2000):

> 'If you want to move people, it has to be toward a vision that's positive for them, that taps important values, that gets them something they desire and it has to be presented in a compelling way so that they feel inspired to follow.'

Perhaps these questions for us remain unanswered and call for further exploration: Is the education we offer relevant to the San? How can it be improved in order to make sure that the San accept it and use it to overcome barriers that are holding them back? Education in Namibia will have to reconsider how the identity and culture of indigenous people are incorporated in the mainstream curriculum. Such knowledge should move away from simply informing what their lifestyles are and acknowledge and embrace indigenous knowledge as a valid and formal knowledge construction through which the world could be viewed.

The culture of the San offers a good lesson for inclusive education in the sense that disability is not viewed as a curse or something requiring persons to be excluded. People who were said to be infected with HIV or tuberculosis (multi-drug-resistant TB was rife in the Tsumkwe area at the time of data collection) were treated with dignity. With awareness regarding identification and provision of support, the San culture will become a good model for inclusion.

This study did not only contribute to the body of knowledge in inclusive education from the perspective of marginalized communities, but it also played a participatory role in the sense that data were gathered from the respondents themselves, in their own environment (territory and ownership) and at the same time helped them identify the loopholes on their way to development. In educational psychology we believe that identifying one's problem is the first step towards positive intervention.

This research seemed to have served a good purpose in giving a voice to San communities to identify and confront challenges in their lives. How the values of inclusive education could infuse indigenous knowledge and cultural values of the San communities in the current education curriculum to enhance and value the identity of the San alongside the dominant cultures in Namibia remains a challenge.

We believe that preserving and appreciating the San's indigenous cultural knowledge could lead to a restored image of the current disrespectful, ungenerous and harmful experiences of San learners in schools. It is of cardinal importance that San people are included in critical dialogues of educational design and development with the construction of knowledge that truly and inclusively depicts Namibia as a country with good policies and democratic and inclusive values. We as citizens have a collective responsibility to ensure that we respect and embrace diversity. Inclusive education in Namibia commits itself to the removal of barriers caused by systemic, organizational, pedagogical, curriculum-related, environmental, financial, societal, cultural and attitudinal barriers (ME, 2013: iii). Framing inclusive education through the lenses of social justice and human rights empowers individuals and institutions to question systems of oppression, how they work, how they are sustained and how they can be contested (Muthukrishna, 2008).

References

ACHPR [African Commission on Human and Peoples' Rights]. (2005). A protocol to the Charter on Human and Peoples' Rights. Organization of African Unity.

Amathila, L. I. (2012). *Making a difference*. Windhoek, Namibia: UNAM Press.

Bethel, B. (2006) Critical approaches to inclusion to indigenous teacher education in Queensland: The case of RAPTEP. *International Journal of Learning and Pedagogies*, *2*(3), 30-41.

Cupido, D. (2013). Namibia Still Failing Indigenous Peoples. In *Open Society Initiative of Southern Africa OSISA and the Indigenous World* 2013.

Diekmann, U., Thiem, M., & Hays, J. (2011). "Scraping the Pot": San in Namibia two decades after independence. Legal Assistance Centre.

El-Ayoubi, M. (2008). Inclusive pedagogies: The development and delivery of Australian indigenous curricula in higher education. *Learning and Teaching in Higher Education*, *2007-08*(3), 33-48.

Gaviria-Soto, J. L., & Castro-Morera, M. (2005). Beyond over-representation: The problem of bias in inclusion of minority group students in special education programs. *Quality & Quantity*, *39*(5), 537-558.

Graham-Brown, S. (1991). *Education in the developing world: Conflict and crisis*. London and New York: Longman.

GRN [Government of the Republic of Namibia]. (1990). *Constitution of the Republic of Namibia*. Windhoek, Namibia: Author.

GRN [Government of the Republic of Namibia]. (2002). Educationally Marginalized Children in Namibia: An Inventory of Programmes, Interventions and Data. Windhoek, Namibia: UNICEF/Ministry of Basic Education, Sport and Culture (MBSC).

GRN [Government of the Republic of Namibia]. (2008). Committee Report on the Elimination of Racial Discrimination. Windhoek, Namibia: Author.

GRN [Government of the Republic of Namibia]. (2011). Education Statistics 2011. Education Management Information system. Windhoek, Namibia: Author.

Kavari, E. (2012). *Issues associated with school dropout of San children in the Omaheke Education Region.* Action research paper presented at the Inclusive Education and Democracy workshop in Swakopmund, 28 October – 3 November, 2012.

IWGIA [International Work Group for Indigenous Affairs]. (2011). The Indigenous World Update 2011. www.iwgia.org Accessed 29 August 2015.

Le Roux, W. (2000). *Torn apart: San children as change agents in a process of acculturation.* Gaborone, Botswana: WIMSA.

Martin, C. (2014). Transitional justice and the task of inclusion: A Habermasian perspective in the justification of Aboriginal educational rights. *Educational Theory, 64*(1), 33-53.

ME [Ministry of Education]. (2002). *National policy options for educationally marginalized children.* Windhoek, Namibia: GRN.

ME [Ministry of Education]. (2011). Education Management Information System (EMIS). Windhoek, Namibia: GRN.

ME [Ministry of Education]. (2013). Sector Policy on Inclusive Education. Windhoek, Namibia: GRN.

MEC [Ministry of Education and Culture]. (1993). Towards Education for All: A Development Brief for Education, Culture and Training. Windhoek, Namibia: GRN.

Muthukrishna, N. (Ed.). (2008). *Educating for social justice and inclusion in an African context.* New York, USA: Nova Science Publishers, Inc.

Olney, M. F., & Kim, A. (2001). Beyond adjustment: Integration of cognitive disability into identity. *Disability & Society, 16*(4), 563-583.

Rhaman, K. (2013). Belonging and learning to belong in a school: Implications of the hidden curriculum for indigenous students. *Discourse: Studies in the Cultural Politics of Education, 34*(5), 660-672.

UN [United Nations]. (2008). Defining an Inclusive Education Agenda: Reflections around the 48th Session of the International Conference on Education. Geneva: UNESCO International Bureau on Education.

UNESCO [United Nations Educational, Scientific and Cultural Organization]. (1990). Summary of Progress towards Education for All. Tenth Meeting of the High Level Working Group on Education for All. Jomtien: Author.

UNESCO [United Nations Educational, Scientific and Cultural Organization]. (1994). Salamanca Statement and Framework for Action on Special Needs Education. Adopted by the World Conference on Special Needs Education: Access and Quality. Salamanca, Spain, 7-10 June 1994. Salamanca: Author.

UNESCO [United Nations Educational, Scientific and Cultural Organization]. (2000). *Education for All. Dakar Framework*. Paris: Author.

UNICEF [United Nations Children's Fund]. (1990). *Convention on the Rights of the Child*. Author.

University of Minnesota Human Rights Center. (2003). *The Rights of Indigenous People: A Study Guide*. Retrieved from http://www1.umn.edu/humanrts/edumat/studyguides/indigenous.html. Accessed 19 October 2015.

16

Messages given to adolescents and young adults during initiation ceremonies and their relation to HIV/AIDS

Cynthy K. Haihambo

INTRODUCTION

According to Namibia's national population census, the total population of the country stood at 2,113,077 people distributed over its 14 political regions (NSA, 2014). Of this, 43.1% of the population inhabited urban areas, and 56.9% lived in rural areas. The average household size in Namibia is 4.4. The population under the age of 15 stands at 760,707 (36%) while the population aged 15 years and above is 1,352,369 (64%). The employed population, which includes part-time and seasonal employment, stands at 690,019 (70.4%) and the total population that is unemployed is 290,762 (29.6%) (NSA, 2014).

Human immunodeficiency virus and acquired immunodeficiency syndrome (HIV/AIDS) is regarded as one of the biggest threats to economic development in sub-Saharan Africa. HIV is acquired through the transmission of bodily fluids such as blood, vaginal fluids and semen. It is mostly contracted through sex (both hetero- and homosexual) that involves the exchange of bodily fluids between individuals. Once it has entered the body, it compromises the individual's immune system and weakens the body's ability to fight diseases. In its most advanced stage, it develops from a viral infection to a disease that can lead to disability and death. Sub-Saharan Africa has the highest HIV prevalence, globally, and is termed the worst affected region and is widely regarded as the 'epicentre' of the global HIV epidemic.

In 2012, Swaziland had the highest HIV prevalence rate of any country in the world (26.5%). HIV prevalence is also particularly high in Botswana (23%) and Lesotho (23.1%). With 6.1 million people living with HIV in South Africa – a prevalence of

17.9% – it has the largest HIV epidemic of any country. The remaining countries in southern Africa have an HIV prevalence between 10% and 15% (ICASA 2013).

It is believed that polygamous relationships, as well as multiple concurrent partners, are the key drivers of HIV transmission in these countries. Sexual networks of men seem to be both extensive and socially accepted (CDC, n.d.). Many adults and children are directly or indirectly affected by HIV/AIDS. Statistics of the Centers for Disease Control and Prevention (CDC) reveal that HIV remains the number one cause of death in Namibia (23%), followed by cancer (8%), strokes (7%), lower respiratory infections (5%), diarrhoeal diseases (5%), tuberculosis (5%); ischemic heart disease (4%); diabetes (3%); interpersonal violence (3%) and malaria (3%). Source: Global Burden of Disease Compare: http://viz.healthmetricsandevaluation. org/gbd-compare, 2010.

Although Namibia has made tremendous efforts in providing life prolonging antiretroviral therapy (ART) as well as mother to child transmission drugs, HIV/AIDS remains a challenge to contain and as a result, remains a priority area in Namibia's Fourth National Developmental Plan (GRN, 2014).

Like many other African countries, Namibia is a multicultural democracy, and each cultural group has its own methods of life orientation at different stages, and perceptions, beliefs and myths, which in turn shape human behaviour. According to Sharpley (2010), 'traditions, norms, beliefs and values are inherited by contemporary societies from previous generations through the sociological vehicle called culture.' I concur with Sharpley (2010) in assuming that there is a correlation between the content of traditional life-skills programmes (which are not written) and HIV infection in Namibian society. Sharpley (2010) states that:

'As adults, it is not just what we verbally articulate that directly impacts our world and more specifically our children, but our actions which are dictated by our world which in turn has been impacted by our past and present experiences, as well as our exposure to the world beyond our world.'

One form of transmitting information, knowledge and skills regarding the world of adults to the youth in Namibia is through traditional life-skills and counselling programmes at various stages of life. Such programmes not only provide precious indigenous knowledge carried over from generation to generation, but they also provide a sense of belonging, ownership and accountability to those that participate in them. This chapter provides a description of how various sampled cultural groups in Namibia provide essential culture-specific information, and also how information on HIV/AIDS is included or excluded from such education and rites of passage involving adolescents and young adults.

Ethnic groups and languages in Namibia

For the sake of national reconciliation and healing from the wounds of apartheid, it is a commonly accepted norm in Namibia to identify people by their primary language of communication as opposed to by their ethnic origin or group. According to the national census of 2011 the Oshiwambo languages are spoken by 49% of the population, Khoekhoegowab (the Nama and Damara language) by 11%, Afrikaans by 10%, Kavango languages by 8.5% and Otjiherero by 8.6%. English, the official language, is spoken by less than 3.4% of people as their native language (NSA, 2014). Among White Namibians, 60% speak Afrikaans, 32% German, 7% English, and 1% Portuguese.

Figure 16.1 provides a visual representation of the political regions of Namibia, their population sizes and the main languages spoken.

The Aawambo are the largest ethnic group, and they traditionally occupy the central northern part of the country in four regions, namely Oshikoto, Oshana, Omusati and Ohangwena. The total population of these four regions is 847,259 (NSA, 2014). They are closely attached to the land and their cattle.

The Damara people traditionally populate the central part of the country and are mostly concentrated in two regions, namely Erongo and Kunene.

The Ovaherero and Ovahimba are closely related, although they are concentrated in three different regions: the Ovaherero in Otjozondjupa and Omaheke regions and the Ovahimba in Kunene region. The two share a language, differing only in dialect, while their cultures and traditions are largely the same. Another significant difference between the Ovahimba and Ovaherero is the fact that the Ovahimba largely maintain a semi-nomadic lifestyle and have distinct dressing and grooming styles that set them apart from other cultural groups in Namibia. Amathila (2012, p. 221) describes Ovahimba as '… friendly, handsome, tall and strong. They walk many kilometres on foot. The women are strong-minded with their own views.' The Ovaherero on the other hand, have adopted modern lifestyles, at least those living in towns. Because of the overwhelming similarities between the Ovaherero and Ovahimba especially with respect to their traditional ceremonies, I combined the information acquired from these two groups. As a result of this decision, I will refer to three cultural groups rather than four.

The Constitution of Namibia makes provision for free movement and settlement of citizens anywhere in the country. Therefore, no particular ethnic group is restricted to a particular region, however, people continue to live where they have lived historically. The colonial division of ethnic groups and enforcement of this has also contributed to the current patterns of dominance of certain ethnic groups in particular regions as indicated above.

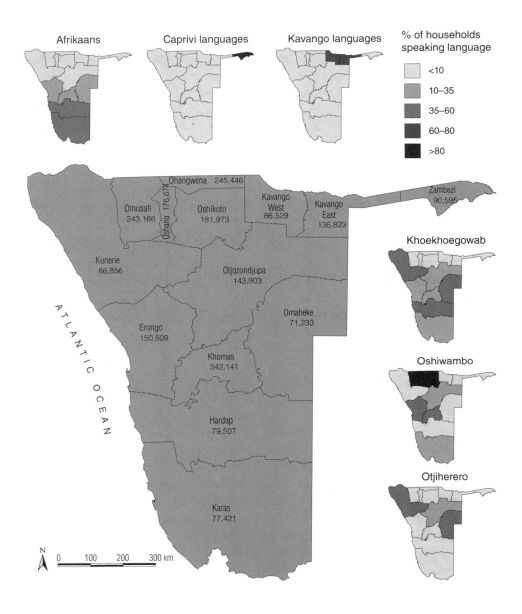

FIGURE 16.1: The 14 regions of Namibia and the population size of each. The distribution of main languages spoken in Namibia are shown in the small maps. Adapted from information from NSA (2014).

Spiritual beliefs

The majority (90%) of Namibians follow various Christian denominational beliefs, while 10% follow other beliefs, as shown in Figure 16.2 (Haihambo, 2010). It should, however, be noted that many people practise Christianity, as well as following other beliefs – for example, the belief in the power of the ancestors over their lives. It is the relationship between spiritual and traditional beliefs and practices, from the perspective of their roles in HIV mitigation that this research has explored.

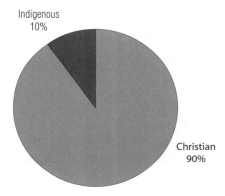

FIGURE 16.2: The spiritual beliefs of Namibians. Adapted from Haihambo (2010).

Indigenous knowledge systems and HIV/AIDS

In the light of the multisectoral approaches to HIV/AIDS mitigation in Africa and Namibia (Iipinge, Hofnie, & Friedman, 2004), this chapter was based on the acknowledgement of African models of life skills as it manifests in three main ethnic groups in Namibia namely the Aawambo, the Ovaherero and Ovahimba, and the Damara people. According to Rooth (2007, p. 18), 'Indigenous knowledge systems emphasize the interrelatedness and interdependence of all phenomena – biological, physical, psychological, social and cultural with indigenous cosmology centring on the evolution of spiritual, natural and human worlds.' The research on which this chapter is based sought to study these interrelations with specific reference to traditional life skills in Namibia.

I had been puzzled by the disconnection between the various HIV/AIDS prevention programmes, in which substantial amounts of money are being invested year after year, and the numbers of new cases of HIV infection, as well as teenage pregnancies and baby dumping, which are illustrative of risky sexual behaviour and are likely to increase HIV exposure. A study by Parker and Connolly (2007) of adolescents and young adults between the ages of 18 and 24 years confirmed the youngsters' high level of HIV knowledge, but little evidence of application of such knowledge in their behaviour. The same study also pointed to high numbers of females that had sexual partners who were ten years or more older than themselves, thus increasing the threat of power relations, including negotiations over condom use and open discussions of threats to the relationship, to mention just a couple.

In her preface to the book in which women wrote their stories related to culture, violence and HIV/AIDS, the UNICEF representative to Namibia in 2008, Khin Sandi Lwin, remarked (!Khaxas, 2008, pg. xvi):

'Culture and tradition have wonderful and beautiful aspects to offer. Wherever we may come from, be it Africa, Asia, Europe, the Americas or "Down Under", there is much to appreciate, cherish and preserve in our cultures and traditions. We must not lose these precious gifts handed down over generations; they should not be threatened by our rushed life of constant change and by globalization of "Western" culture. But whether in the west, east, north or south of the globe, there are elements of negative attitude, beliefs and practices – defended by the so-called aim of "preserving culture and tradition" – these must be challenged and changed. Whatever practices do not treat humans with dignity, respect and equality because of their gender (or race, religion or creed) have to be challenged and changed.'

This quote calls for reflection and, if need be, review of our cultural practices, should they be found to violate our human rights or make people vulnerable and susceptible to HIV/AIDS.

Statistics indicate that 71% of the worldwide cases of AIDS occur in sub-Saharan Africa (Haihambo, 2002; UNAIDS, 2012). Namibia has responded to the call for mitigation by implementing various educational, preventive and intervention programmes. Programmes have assumed various formats and ranged from video and other visual media material, to pamphlets and posters, and life-skills programmes for children and youths, such as 'Window of Hope' and 'My Future is My Choice'. Development partners, such as UNICEF (United Nations Children's Fund), UNESCO (United Nations Educational, Scientific and Cultural Organization), UNAIDS (Joint United Nations Programme on HIV/AIDS), Global Fund, GIZ–InWEnt (Deutsche Gesellschaft für Technische Zusammenarbeit – Capacity Building International, Germany) and many others, have invested both material and financial resources to support communities in raising awareness of HIV, provide knowledge through information and skills, and promote behavioural changes. In most cases, these programmes are formal and occur within official spheres of educational, health and religious institutions. Although Namibians are attached to their cultures, there have been very few approaches or mitigation strategies from a cultural perspective. This realization prompted me to explore HIV content in traditional guidance and counselling programmes.

It is my conviction that, in the pre-HIV/AIDS era, concepts of guidance, counselling and life skills as psychological concepts rarely took place in community conversations. This was confirmed by observing participants in a pilot study at the initial stages of this research in which I discovered that these concepts were perceived as alien or associated with HIV testing (even in their translated forms). While this was the case, activities of advising, guiding, counselling and imparting life skills have been in existence for as long as human beings existed and groups had organized platforms of skills and knowledge transfer. The new form of counselling – which involves a designated helper and a help-seeker engaging in finding a solution to a problem the help-seeker is facing – became common in the 1990s when HIV/AIDS started to pose challenges to people in African societies and to the institution of extended families, especially in Namibia. Whereas in the past it was unheard of for children and the elderly to live alone, the current rise in the number of child-headed households and orphans fending for themselves is living proof of the scourge of HIV/AIDS. In my work, I soon learnt to refer to traditional, life-skills ceremonies, a concept with which participants associated easily, rather than counselling. In the context of this chapter, these terms are, however, used interchangeably. Prior to the appearance of HIV/AIDS in Namibia, guidance, counselling and life orientation were present through all phases of human development in all Namibian cultures, although it was never described as such. The unwritten 'curriculum' was carried over from one generation to the next through social structures. It took various formal and informal forms. For example:

1. When a woman was pregnant, she received a lot of advice, guidance and counselling from women with experience about a 'proper' diet, child birth and delivery, childcare and child-rearing practices, and dealing with a husband during pregnancy and after childbirth, to mention just a few. These lessons were often informal in nature and took place during a brief encounter on the way to the water point, in the compound or on the side during a mourning ceremony, for example.

2. When a baby was born, in many Namibian cultures, the mother or aunt to the new mother would go and live with the couple or the new mother and provide counselling and support, mainly in the form of scaffolding – a process by which an experienced person in a particular area shows the way to a novice (Vygotsky,

1982, cited by Mwamwenda, 2004). The experienced mother or aunt would teach the new mother how to take care of her baby and provide counselling to deal with postnatal 'blues' that the mother might experience.

3. Initiation ceremonies – mostly following or preceding menarche for girls and circumcision for boys – were held. These were more formal forms of life orientation with clear separate groups – one of young people at the brink of entering adulthood and the other of carefully selected and qualified mentors to lead the young people into adulthood.

4. When a son proved that he was capable of starting and maintaining his own family, his uncles would involve him in all they were doing and in the process told him what was expected of a man in his particular culture. Sometimes a girl who had already been studied and identified as the most appropriate wife for a son would be indirectly introduced to him while he was undergoing this training and preparation for becoming a good husband and man in his culture.

5. When someone died in a particular homestead, the whole village participated in comforting the bereaved and organizing the funeral. After the funeral, the community members kept coming to the homestead to continue comforting and helping them cope with their loss.

This chapter focuses on two types of ceremonies – adolescent initiation ceremonies, and premarital and perimarital counselling, guidance or life-orientation sessions – amongst the Aawambo, Ovaherero, Ovahimba and Damara peoples of Namibia.

METHODOLOGY

This descriptive, qualitative ethnographic study was conducted over a period of six months in six regions of Namibia – Khomas, Kunene, Oshikoto, Oshana, Erongo and Otjozondjupa. Initiation ceremonies of adolescents and adults of the Aawambo, Damara, and Ovaherero and Ovahimba peoples in Namibia were targeted, but the majority of the data were acquired during traditional wedding ceremonies.

In each ethnic group, the study was conducted in two phases. In the first phase, in-depth interviews were conducted either with an information-rich group or individual from whom information was acquired regarding the various life orientation and guidance and counselling ceremonies in their particular culture, specifically for adolescents and those entering marriage. In the second phase, the researcher, accompanied by a resource person, observed identified ceremonies and interpreted the data with respect to the inclusion of HIV/AIDS content. In the final phase, in-depth interviews were conducted with all four groups, but in phase two only ceremonies for the Damara, Aawambo and Ovaherero could be observed.

Sampling

The guiding principles for selecting particular ethnic groups (four out of the eleven main ethnic groups in Namibia) were language and culture. In indigenous knowledge studies, it is important for the researcher to have an in-depth understanding of the context in which events are taking place in order to interpret actions and lessons from an informed position. I have an in-depth indigenous knowledge and understanding of the language, cultures and traditions of the Aawambo, Ovaherero and Ovahimba. For each ethnic group, a resource person was identified who served the role of gatekeeper and at times also as translator and interpreter of actions and expressions.

The Damara was the only group included in the study of whose language I had minimal understanding. The Damara people speak a Khoisan language with clicks, called Khoekhoegowab, which I did not speak nor understand, with the exception of a very basic vocabulary. This group was included mainly out of curiosity, but also to reduce the degree of bias that could be introduced when a researcher possesses an in-depth and thus preconceived knowledge about the research site or group. However, I had, through other indigenous knowledge work and through socialization, learnt much about the Damara culture and was interested in investigating the differences and similarities with other ethnic groups in Namibia. Many of the Damara people are conversant in Afrikaans – the lingua franca in many areas of Namibia – in which I am proficient. In an attempt to break the language barrier, an interpreter with an in-depth knowledge of the language, culture and qualitative research was appointed and accompanied me throughout all phases of the study where her services were required. The resource person for the Damara group was a female education officer. A male media practitioner was used in the Ovaherero and Ovahimba groups. For the Aawambo study sessions, only a gatekeeper was used to introduce me to key role players in each family and explain my intentions. At each ceremony, one gatekeeper was used.

I attempted to target at least three ceremonies per ethnic group, although this was not always possible (see Table 16.1). During the ceremonies I assumed the position of a non-participating observer. (It is common in such ceremonies to have some members of the group present who do not actively participate and who are not necessarily known to every participant or key group – in this case, those that were being initiated.) It could have been to my advantage if I had been able to understand the language and follow procedures without the use of a translator. However, it transpired that the translator played a crucial role and enabled me to understand the deliberations to the required depth.

In cases where I was not allowed access, for example into a circumcision ceremony of adolescent boys from which women are excluded, I relied on a resource person (an insider with rich information about the group being researched) for information.

I attended six traditional marriage-counselling ceremonies of which four were of the Aawambo culture, one of Ovaherero culture, and one of the Damara culture

TABLE 16.1: The numbers and types of ceremonies observed and numbers of resource people consulted.

Cultural group	Region	Numbers of resource people		Key informant or focus group interview	Ceremonies observed	
		males	females		number	nature
Aawambo	Oshana	1		x	4	wedding
Ovaherero	Otjozondjupa	1		x	1	wedding
	Kunene				1	peer-group meeting
Ovahimba	Kunene	1	2	x	–	–
Damara	Kunene	1	2	x	1	wedding
	Erongo				1	briefing on adolescence ceremony
	Khomas	1	1	x		discussion on premarital guidance
	Erongo		1	x		discussion on premarital guidance
	Oshikoto	1	1	x		discussion on premarital guidance
	Omusati	1	2	x		discussion on premarital guidance

Key: x indicates either a key informant or a focus group interview was used.

with the help of an interpreter. Theoretical data were collected from key respondents in the Ovahimba group, but unfortunately, no ceremony could be observed.

In cases where I did not qualify to sit in, based on my gender, age or relationship to the bride or groom, or group targeted for observation, information was obtained from a third person and confirmed with the resource person as explained above. Sometimes the third person was also the resource person, but not in all cases.

Research procedures and limitations

The research was carried out from December 2009 to May 2010. December is known as the 'month of festivities', and numerous festive ceremonies take place during the December summer holidays when people are on leave from work. This is also the time that many people leave the cities, which are for them places of work only, to go 'back to their roots' – their villages. I conducted key informant interviews with various resource persons in each of the cultural groups in the study in order to understand their practices. These resource persons also served as gatekeepers and invited me to the ceremonies.

I observed various ceremonies to explore the content of their life-skills (life) orientation or guidance and counselling programmes with a specific interest in the inclusion or exclusion of HIV/AIDS-related themes. When attending these ceremonies, I was introduced as a relative, or a friend of a relative, to the large group of participants. However, in each case, a key group responsible for the affairs of the family was informed that I was conducting research on their ceremonies and that the outcome of the research would be published in a book or academic article. The HIV/AIDS component of the research was not revealed to the participants of the ceremony because it was thought that doing so would influence the manner in which the ceremonies would be conducted and ultimately lead to the contamination of data. In all cases, I was welcomed and my presence honoured. In most cases, especially in the Damara culture, members of the family were delighted to have someone from a different ethnic group showing interest in how they conducted their ceremonies. They were impressed with this 'person from a different Namibian culture' wearing their traditional outfit and eating their traditional food. As is the practice in ethnographic research, I blended in with my respondents without attempting to make adjustments to the way in which things were done (Baker, 1999, p. 81). For example, I dressed appropriately for the ceremony of that particular cultural group; assumed the expected sitting position; danced and sang as the group did (at least I tried to copy what they were doing); and so on.

The main tools of data collection were participatory observation and in-depth, narrative interviews (following Creswell, 2011), which were conducted over a six-month period with identified resource persons in the Oshana, Kunene and Khomas regions. These were specifically intended to gain a better understanding of the purpose of events that I had observed during the ceremonies. It also provided me with an opportunity to gain more knowledge on the initiation ceremonies that I could not attend.

There were some limitations to the study. In some cases, language posed a limitation, as translators often interpreted instead of translating directly to me. The fact that I assumed the position of a member of the group, and not as a researcher (although the key committee of the family or clan was informed about my presence and my actual role and intention), meant that I could not use recording instruments except for a camera, which I only used with their permission. The majority, however, seemed to appreciate the opportunity of the events being recorded on camera; many were delighted to be photographed and started posing as soon as I came around with the camera. I believe that videos, audio-tapes and complete field notes would have enhanced the quality of the research. In some cases, contradictory information was received from different people in the same ethnic group; it took a lot of time to find consensus. It also highlighted that although groups might appear homogenous, they were indeed different in some aspects depending on where they originated and where they passed on their journey to where they finally settled.

Ethical considerations

In a study of this nature, the researcher gains access into the private lives of the respondents. To prevent participants from feeling that their privacy was being invaded, I was introduced to key persons in the families and confided in them who I was and that I was carrying out research.

The participants were assured that their identities would be protected through anonymity, although most of them said they did not mind their identity being revealed.

I thanked the gatekeepers and, where possible, went back to them to verify the accuracy of the data collected. Where data verification was not done with the main participants of a ceremony, as in the case of the Damara in Kunene Region, data was verified with key resource persons identified in Windhoek.

I took photographs of events as they unfolded. I returned to most of the communities that I could re-access at a later date to show them the pictures, explain how I would like to use them in publications and ask their permission to do so; they all agreed. I tried, as far as possible, to send or take copies of the photographs to the participants during my debriefing sessions or via e-mail, a token that was highly appreciated.

I went back to the key respondents several times (with the exception of the northern Kunene Region, where I only returned once and found only one of the original participants) to verify information and ensure that a rich contextual understanding was attained. The key respondents valued this and referred to other researchers who spent a day with them and then wrote as if they knew it all.

RESULTS

The results are presented according to three ethnic groups explained above, starting with adolescent initiation ceremonies, followed by premarital or perimarital counselling ceremonies.

Aawambo ceremonies

Adolescent ceremonies

The respondents referred to ceremonies that were not commonly practised anymore, such as the 'olufuko' (a 'marriage feast' for girls). The original data were collected in 2011 before the return of olufuko in 2012, around which there was a lot of debate.

Girls in a particular village who had reached the early stages of adolescence gathered at one homestead, performed traditional dances and were advised that they were old enough to get married. Older women in the village used to guide the girls in carrying out their traditional roles and chores once they got married, and the ways of treating their husbands with respect (irrespective of what the husband might do), for example, not questioning them, not talking back, and, most of all, serving them and satisfying all their needs at all times. It was taboo for a girl to fall pregnant before they had participated in the *olufuko*. Young men or their parents attended the ceremony with an intention to identify a bride for themselves or their sons. The respondents believed that this ceremony prevented girls from falling pregnant at an early age.

Although the missionaries discouraged the *olufuko*, replacing it with Christian ceremonies, some clans still continue to practise them. Many respondents maintained that the church does not have the same impact on communities that traditional ceremonies had, and continue to have today. Where Christian ceremonies – such as church confirmations and weddings – have replaced traditional ones, girls are guided by their mothers and aunts and are socialized into their roles as wives and mothers. The church provides classes teaching biblical norms, which have a strong emphasis on abstinence from sex. Explicit talks about sex are taboo from both the family and church perspectives. Community counselling and guidance (offered by parents and other close relatives) often perpetuates community norms that encourage male dominance and power while limiting women's abilities to make their own decisions and lead lives independent from those of their husbands or male partners.

Similar findings were reported in an article on a study in Tanzania in which, for example, one female respondent confirmed: 'What he says, you do fulfil,' (Hutchinson, Weiss, Barker, Segundo, & Pulerwitz, 2004). Although these societal norms are highly valued by elders, and women that follow them are praised and upheld as good women or Aawambo wives, and 'preferred' over those that demonstrate critical thinking, they seem to bring negative consequences with respect to HIV/AIDS.

In August 2012, some traditional authorities hosted *olufuko* ceremonies for the first time after a long interval. This 'Olufuko Festival' was hosted in Outapi (Omusati Region). The reintroduction of the *olufuko* ceremony was followed by heated debates. It received support from many communities in the four northern regions, and some traditional authorities were in favour of its return. Churches and women's rights groups, however, expressed their reservations. They labelled it as an abuse of young women, which portrayed them simply as tools to satisfy men; a form of 'early marriage', which could compromise girls' education. Those who supported the return of this old, traditional ceremony argued that it serves as a deterrent for early and premarital pregnancies as it provides information on pregnancy prevention and emphasizes the importance of virginity. However, opponents of the traditional practice argued that girls who go through this process often lose interest in school as they feel that after they have gone through the ceremony, they are ready for marriage and do not need an education. Nevertheless, the ceremony has continued to take place annually and has become known as the 'Olufuko Festival'. In 2015, 262 'brides' from the Omusati, Oshana, Oshikoto, Ohangwena and Kunene regions participated in the festival. The festival also attracted observers from other regions in the country.

In addition to *olufuko* that traditionally took place once every two years or so, there were other forms of continuous life-skills lessons. At family or clan level, girls were guided by their aunts and mothers into adulthood, while boys literally 'understudied' their fathers and uncles in all respects. The boys were socialized in terms of their roles and responsibilities, but also in their behaviour towards women and other members of their community. Power relations were reinforced.

For both sexes, gender norms were also indirectly conveyed through folklore shared in the evenings at a meeting point in each homestead, known as *olupale*. Much of the folklore portrayed good women as those who were submissive, obedient and hardworking. Men with multiple partners were held in high esteem or portrayed as heroes in much of the folklore.

It is important to note that respondents in the study that led to this chapter expressed a concern for the absence of traditional ceremonies in modern communities without being replaced with equally effective life-skills, guidance and counselling programmes. Some made reference to what is learnt in schools and through public media and criticized these as insensitive to the cultural norms and beliefs of learners. They also criticized them for providing youth with knowledge about HIV/AIDS without addressing behaviour and good values.

When the key respondents were asked what they would regard as the most appropriate life skills, guidance and counselling systems for Aawambo youth, they said that the best way forward would be to go back to traditional methods, but with the inclusion of HIV/AIDS messages. One respondent – a retired teacher of 63 in Oshana Region – made the following statement:

'Look at us. We went through *olufuko*. And we are well balanced and most of us are still married, or widowed. What is wrong with teaching young people the right things? Today, they marry this Saturday and divorce after a month. In our days, divorce did not even exist!'

Premarital counselling ceremonies

In the modern Aawambo tradition, the wedding assumes a dual format: The traditional wedding (different from *olufuko* with regard to age and format), starts a week or two before the official date – the date of the 'Western wedding', which takes place in a church or magistrates' court, although the latter venue is perceived as inappropriate.

The traditional wedding officially starts with a public announcement in church, which is followed by hoisting white flags at the houses of both the bride's and the groom's parents. This informs and invites the community members to the wedding celebrations. Members of the communities start to visit the families and directly or indirectly provide advice to the couple on how to conduct themselves in their married life.

The night before the (Western) wedding, close relatives of the groom come to the homestead of the bride to ask for the wife's hand in marriage from her parents and uncles. This is a session that is attended by many people. At this stage, some counselling takes place. The family of the husband-to-be will be asked questions regarding their intentions with the bride. Different members of both families then express their expectations.

A day after the official Western wedding, the husband returns to the homestead of the wife to fetch her officially with her personal belongings. While the guests are being entertained with food and drink, the wife packs her belongings and bids farewell to the people in her homestead – an indication that she now belongs to another family. During that process, everyone gives a word of advice. In the meantime, a place is prepared where further guidance and life skills are given by a carefully selected group of representatives from both families. At the end of this life-skills session, the husband and his family leave with his wife. In Aawambo culture, she is allowed to come back and visit her family at anytime, but preferably with her husband. This practice is different to that of the Ovaherero and Ovahimba in which a wife is discouraged from visiting her family as she is viewed as no longer belonging to the family into which she was born and she should rather invest her energy into bonding with her new family, that of her husband.

In the four wedding sessions attended, the researcher observed that the couples were advised to:

1. always respect their in-laws and not embarrass their families;
2. have children;
3. keep their disagreements to the privacy of their homes;
4. return to this group of elders if they have problems rather than discussing their problems with friends and/or neighbours.

Specific advice to the husbands included to:

1. provide for his wife and family;
2. protect his family;
3. refrain from violence (mostly referring to physical violence) and bring back the wife to this group of elders if he does not want her any longer. In one particular case the message was very clear regarding physical violence as follows: 'Look at

FIGURE 16.3: Family members bid the Aawambo bride farewell. (© Cynthy Haihambo.)

this beautiful girl properly. She has no marks on her body. She has all her body parts. When you do not want her anymore, do not harm her. Bring her back the way she is.'

Specific advice to the wife included:

1. Respect your husband and his family.
2. Do not confront your husband or back-chat (*aalumentu ihaya yamukulwa*, meaning 'it is not acceptable to answer or talk back to men and/or husbands'). Furthermore, 'If your husband goes somewhere, even if he does not tell you, wait in your house, he will come back. And do not ask him where he comes from. If he dies, his body will be brought to you to bury!' Iipinge et al. (2004), whose participants indicated that the inability of women to negotiate safer sex practices placed them in a hopeless position for HIV infections, supports this finding.
3. Do not listen to stories about your husband.
4. Do not deny your husband food. 'If you do, he will eat somewhere else.'
5. Have a good relationship with your neighbours.

A summary of observations

There was no mention of how to protect oneself against HIV infection in any of the sessions observed. On the contrary, there was emphasis on satisfying the husband's needs; respecting the husband and his family at all times; having children; and not asking for explanations about a partner's (especially a husband's) behaviour. These lessons continued to reinforce the unequal power relations between men and women, in spite of it being common knowledge that this inequality leaves women with their hands tied behind their backs and open to infection by HIV. This was

FIGURE 16.4:
Aawambo women
conferring before
joining a larger group
for counselling.
(© Cynthy Haihambo.)

deduced through the interviews. For example, one 42-year-old female respondent in Oshikoto Region explained in detail that, 'A woman should never confront her husband about his behaviours and movements. She should wait for him at home, and make him happy.'

Badcock-Walters, Kelly and Görgens (2004, p. 6) similarly found that although Africa has made huge financial investments in life-skills programmes to target HIV/AIDS reduction, they have had inadequate impact on modifying behaviour, which would ultimately lower infection rates. Traditional customs thus appear to hold precedence over formally organized HIV-prevention programmes.

I also observed that the advice and guidance given during both adolescent and wedding ceremonies were largely non-interactive. The recipients of such information did not ask questions or make comments, at least not at that platform. The researcher noticed that the brides simply smiled when it was obvious that they disagreed with the advice because they were expected to be polite. While the brides or grooms did not always agree with the lessons handed to them, they still demonstrated respect by not engaging in a discussion. I believe that they set their own rules in their house once the wedding is over and they are on their own, but that would depend on the relationship between the two and what they perceived as respect and dignity. Some partners who are bound to their tradition, still apply these traditions, even if those practices no longer respond to the realities of modern-day society – HIV being a case in point.

The exclusion of young people from these life-skills and guidance sessions did not allow for the infusion of newer ideas. The elderly retained old ideas and passed them on to the young generation. It did, however, seem that the theme of violence was infused in these sessions. This could be attributed to two possible factors. Firstly, it could be easier to talk about violence than about HIV/AIDS because addressing HIV/AIDS would imply addressing the social construction of male dominance, which is central in the Aawambo culture. Secondly, violence not linked to sex is less stigmatized than HIV despite the fact that most passion murders and other family-related violence could be related to sex and power as is the case with some HIV/AIDS cases.

In conclusion, since there was no room for interactive discussions of these issues during the official counselling sessions, as the couple were not expected to respond or ask any questions whatsoever, it would serve the youth better if these sessions happened earlier than during the actual ceremonies.

Damara ceremonies

Adolescent ceremonies

The respondents revealed that there were a few initiation ceremonies for the youth and young adults in the Damara culture. The different clans dealt with life-skills issues differently. The main form of training was through copying the behaviour of adults. This instils values of hard work for both boys and girls at a very early age, for example. Of the different ethnic groups studied, the extended family system of the Damara people was the least close-knit. As indicated in the introduction, there are fewer Damara than people from the other groups that participated in the study. Because they are few, there were not many adults available to maintain traditional ceremonies. All key-informant interviewees lamented the lack of people and resources to perform these much-needed ceremonies. Life skills were largely acquired through older, close relatives, such as parents, aunts and uncles, where they were available, No adolescent ceremony was observed, although one such adolescent ceremony had been planned close to Christmas and the programme for it was shared with me. Most of the information regarding adolescence shared in this chapter was obtained through the different key-informant or focus group interviews.

Initiation ceremony for Damara girls

In the past, girls who experienced menarche within a particular time frame in the village would be gathered at one household. The women in that village would prepare a big feast and celebrate the transition of these girls into adulthood. During the time of the feast, the elder women would provide the girls with advice on womanhood. These talks focused on hygiene; how to take care of themselves in terms of refraining from sex until marriage; submissiveness; and the qualities of a 'good woman'.

Families generally observed that when their girls entered puberty and adolescence, they tended to talk a lot. This was perceived as negative and the grandmother would put the shell of a tortoise in the girl's mouth to stop her from talking too much.

Menstruation is referred to as a 'disease' in Damara culture. On having her first menstruation, a girl would inform an elder sister, niece or aunt. This would be the official start of the initiation ceremony. The young girl would be isolated in a room or hut and would be left alone with the tortoise shell in her mouth. Her grandmother would then bring her herbs with a nice smell (!gau, sai – a traditional perfume) and expensive jewellery (sakara – made by Ovahimba women). This rite of passage is similar to a wedding. During the time of isolation, elderly women would visit the girl, either singly or in a group, and provide guidance on womanhood. The main message would be that, 'You should be a woman who studies the world around you and not talk too much.' She would also be given a pot as a gift symbolizing her womanhood.

There would be limited sex education during this initiation ceremony, but messages about sex would be given in puzzles. Messages to the young adult included the following:

1. Learn that you can fall pregnant easily. Take care of yourself like an egg. A woman is fragile. Virginity is valued.
2. Parents are proud if you get married without the sacrifice of the blood of a white sheep! If a man had sex with a woman before marriage and conceived a child with her, he should slaughter a white sheep and put some blood at the door of her parent's house. The man should apologize. The man should earmark cattle for the child he had conceived with this woman. Parents used to be embarrassed if this happened because it revealed that their daughter had engaged in sex before marriage.

Initiation ceremonies for Damara boys

Key respondents revealed that there were no ceremonies for boys. Some clans still practised circumcision and other cuts to 'protect the boys against evil spirits', but these customs were also said to be fading away. These days, most people only use circumcision as a medical procedure to be done at hospitals under anaesthetic, and it is no longer done as an initiation ceremony.

The respondents regretted the slow fading of such traditional practices, as teenage pregnancy, alcohol and drug use among the youth, and rates of HIV infection were perceived to be high, despite the education programmes offered at school. When asked why traditional life-skills programmes were no longer valued and practised, the respondents blamed modernization. They said that both elders and children would rather watch television than interact with one another; that the world of employment had taken away valuable time that in the past was available for interactions; and the prevalent moral decay. One respondent from Khorixas (Kunene Region) exclaimed:

'We have dropped our own cultures and try to be like Americans. But we are not exactly doing what the Americans are doing. So we are somewhere in the middle. Our children are left to television and schools to educate

[them]. But they teach curriculum and no life skills, at least not within the context of our culture.'

Another respondent in Windhoek (Khomas Region) blamed the commercialization of the communities:

'We have to acknowledge that nowadays everything costs money. To bring young people together like in the past costs money, which we do not have. In the past, women would gladly do these sessions and even bake bread and slaughter cattle for these. Nowadays, people want to be paid for such community work. And the men demand money for their cattle. Besides, the young people think we are wasting their time.'

Premarital guidance

Traditionally in the Damara culture, women who were about to enter matrimony were isolated for about three months before the wedding. Although the time frame has been shortened due to employment obligations, the core of the preparation process remains largely unchanged.

The Damara wedding starts perhaps three months before it is officiated. The bride-to-be introduces her future husband to her family. The family then starts to research his family and his past. If they have an objection, they discuss it with her to discourage her from marrying him. If the family accepts him, the future husband negotiates a wedding date with them.

Representatives of the two families then meet with the couple and discuss the importance of marriage. The couple is called each to ask permission from their family members to marry their partner. This is to make sure that they intend to marry willingly. Married people from both families will start the guidance process. The messages conveyed to the wife may include among others the following:

1. The wife should be submissive to her husband.
2. The husband is the head of the family and should be treated according to this status.
3. The husband should be respected at all times and his advice should be followed without question.

'If you disagree with his suggestions, you have to identify an elder woman and register your concerns. That elder woman and her husband or one of your uncles or a traditional elder will come and explain your position to your husband.' Key respondent, Khorixas, Kunene Region.

4. The woman should always keep quiet when her husband is shouting at her in the presence of other people. As an advisor during a guidance session to the bride (Okombahe, Erongo Region) advised, 'You should wait for an appropriate time, study his mood and raise your concern in the privacy of your bedroom.'
5. A good woman looks after her husband's family, including his children from other women.
6. A good woman responds to the sexual needs of her husband whenever it suits him.
7. A good woman washes and irons his clothes in time.
8. The husband is the image of God.
9. You have to serve him.
10. Marriage requires perseverance, as stated by the respondent using the following Afrikaans expression: '*Volhou, moedhou en bekhou!*' 'Persevere, remain courageous and shut your mouth!' (Reminiscent of the tortoise in the mouth.)
11. 'Don't think you are going to collect wild berries or grapes. Marriage is not [an] easy thing!'

Messages to the husband included:

1. He should take good care of his wife.
2. He should only eat from the pot of his wife.
3. Husband and wife should do budgeting together. 'Don't do things on your own. Consider your wife.'
4. 'Remember where you got her from.' This means that the man should not let his wife suffer as he found her having a good standard of living.
5. 'Bring back the bones.' Mostly grandmothers request that, when the wife dies, they want to bury her.

At the end of the guidance session, two couples from each family are identified as the ones the new couple should consult as mentors. These mentors should take care of them and show them the way – scaffolding.

When the marriage is approved, the husband should give a white goat and a white cloth or headgear with other basic necessities (sugar, salt, a box of matches, oil for a lamp, etc.) to one of the grandmothers of his wife-to-be. This is a sign of his intention to respect and take care of his wife and her family.

In one session, one of the respondents brought up the issues of HIV and suggested that the couple should go for HIV testing and report on the results at the next session. This was the only time that this topic was brought up. When this issue was brought up, the participants clearly felt uneasy and some said it was inappropriate to bring up such a 'sensitive topic'. Another participant claimed that the particular participant who brought up the issue was drunk and wanted to spoil the celebratory wedding mood. This was a clear indication that it was almost unheard of to discuss

FIGURE 16.5:
Ovaherero women
clapping in
accompaniment to a
traditional dance at a
wedding celebration.
(© Cynthy Haihambo.)

FIGURE 16.6:
Ovahimba women
in traditional attire,
advising the new bride.
(© Cynthy Haihambo.)

FIGURE 16.7: Core
group approaching a
house to provide coun-
selling and guidance
at a mixed Ovaherero–
Aawambo wedding.
(© Cynthy Haihambo.)

HIV/AIDS at such an event, although the researcher did overhear discussions about it in private and behind the scene at weddings.

When asked about the absence of HIV/AIDS-related discussions in the ceremonies, key respondents maintained that private issues are discussed in the early hours of the morning (two or three o' clock). By then, outsiders will have left. When I insisted that in all cases I had not left the group at any stage and the issue rarely came up and, when it did, it was perceived negatively by group members, key respondents admitted that the private issues discussed rarely had anything to do with HIV/AIDS. In most cases, they related to a history of unacceptable behaviour or if the husband- or wife-to-be, for example, had children from previous relationships and they were asked to pronounce themselves on those.

In conclusion, with regard to the sample of this research, it is safe to conclude that in the case of the Damara culture, guidance sessions emphasized female submission and male dominance. It also clearly demonstrated that from adolescence right through to marriage, the family and community played very important roles. It can also be concluded that the inclusion of HIV/AIDS in these sessions to attempt to mitigate it, is yet to be considered.

Ovaherero and Ovahimba ceremonies

The Ovaherero and Ovahimba cultures are very similar as the two groups share the same roots. The difference is that the Ovahimba settled in Kunene Region, in the area formerly known as the Kaokoveld, and retained their traditional lifestyles of keeping livestock, distinct traditional attire and a nomadic lifestyle. The Ovaherero, on the contrary, moved to areas further south and settled in Otjozondjupa and Khomas regions and run urban lives (employment in cities) while maintaining a very close link to their villages and livestock, which they visit at every possible opportunity. The Ovaherero and Ovahimba can be distinguished by their respective and unique traditional outfits, as shown in Figures 16.5 and 16.6.

Based on the overwhelming similarities of these two groups, they were treated as one with specific reference given to any differences in the traditional ceremonies studied. The culture of these groups is complicated as it pertains to relationships between women and men and marriage. Cultural values determine sex practices. There exists a very complicated system, known as *otjiramwe*, of intimate relationships between traditionally defined cousins. According to this culture, a woman marries into the family and not necessarily to her husband. Male cousins of the husband may have access to the wife for sexual relations if they meet particular, culturally set criteria. A man is allowed to marry more than one wife.

In the Ovaherero and Ovahimba culture, marriage counselling officially takes place a week before the wedding. The prospective wife is isolated in a hut with a younger girl who serves as her assistant. During this time, she may not appear in public and her face must not be seen by anyone. This will protect her from 'evil spirits' and people with bad intentions. During this period of isolation, older women are allowed to come into the hut and advise her. This combination of orientation to married life and counselling entails:

1. identifying articulated and unarticulated needs of your husband and serving him at all times;
2. listening to and trusting your husband at all times;
3. not confronting him.

Observations and interviews with the key respondents revealed that HIV did not really feature in these premarital counselling sessions. The message given was that it was more important to satisfy the needs of one's husband than to worry about HIV/AIDS. Upon enquiry, key respondents confirmed that HIV/AIDS was brought in by those who ventured out of traditionally defined boundaries, such as those having sex with people outside the traditionally defined structures (not necessarily single partnership), or as a result of a curse or bad omen emanating from unacceptable behaviour.

Initiation ceremonies of Ovaherero and Ovahimba boys

Male circumcision played a central role in the lives of Ovaherero and Ovahimba people. This is demonstrated in their belief that women from these ethnic groups who marry outside of them, were almost completely isolated and looked down upon. It is assumed that their 'alien' husbands were not circumcised, making them lesser men than those who were circumcised.

Circumcision symbolizes the beginning of peer-group formation. The peer group of boys, who were circumcised together, plays a very important role throughout life. For these two ethnic groups, circumcision is not performed for medical or cosmetic reasons. On the contrary, it is related to power, as expressed by a key respondent in Windhoek (Khomas Region): 'It binds us together, for life! It tests your manhood and initiates you into manhood and [a] peer group.'

In the past, boys used to be circumcised after the age of ten, at the beginning of puberty. Although most of the children are circumcised much earlier nowadays (between the ages of one and two), parents keep track of the peers with whom they were circumcised, and they are raised with the awareness that they belong to a particular peer group who band together during puberty and adolescence to establish their peer group. Thus, circumcision continues to be an initiation process marking their entry into adulthood, known as '*okuhitamotjoto*'. It is also referred to as a process of marriage into one's culture.

Boys born within the same year (or within two years) in a particular village or area, leave the homestead and go out to the bush (wilderness). At the camp, an expert circumcises them. A sheep is slaughtered and they eat together. They also wrestle with each other to prove their manhood and, through this, identify the leader of the group. This is the first step of forming their peer group. As a resource person in Khomas Region explained, 'The winner [of the wrestling] remains the leader until the [boys of the] group are about 15–16 years old when they are formalized into a peer group' known as *omakura*.

At this stage, when the peer group or *omakura* is formalized, the boys are adolescents and are acknowledged as such. They decide on a name for their peer group, which is often based on major happenings during the year in which they were circumcised, or born. For example, the peer group of boys born around the years of Chief Hosea Kutako's death was named after him and are known as *'otjiuondo tja Hosea'* or *'Katjikururume'* (the grandfather). This means that boys born in the same year or two will be circumcised together and form the peer group. They also establish rules for their group, which might include:

1. Never swear at each other.
2. Stand by each other through thick and thin.
3. Allow one specific peer (*ekura*) to sleep with your wife during adulthood.

The Ministry of Health and Social Services, in collaboration with the World Health Organization has rolled out a voluntary, male-circumcision programme nationally. It is based on researched evidence that circumcision reduces the chances of HIV infection by 60%. The programme is offered free of charge at hospitals, clinics and also through mobile clinics at schools and communities. I have understood that most of the Ovahimba and Ovaherero do not participate in this programme as the majority will have been circumcised already during early childhood or puberty.

During their meeting to formalize the peer group, the adolescents are joined by adult men who teach them about manhood, marriage, etc. HIV is not mentioned at all. When the researcher questioned the key respondents regarding the absence of HIV/AIDS messages during both sets of ceremonies, the two key respondents regretted such omission and indicated that, in this era, it was indeed important to make that mind shift as human behaviours have changed. They indicated that the peer group and circumcision ceremonies had great potential for including HIV/AIDS themes by virtue of the nature of their construction: a single-sex, open platform for discussion in isolation. The meetings are also driven by a strong sense of bravery, which is required in addressing HIV/AIDS. This position gave me hope that, if awareness is raised, there is a chance that HIV/AIDS content will be included in traditional life-skills programmes in the near future.

Premarital guidance

In the Ovaherero and Ovahimba ethnic groups, marrying a cousin was the most preferred and approved norm. Matchmaking was the order of the day. Elderly people in the family initiated the process based on their knowledge of the two young people, as a male key respondent in Khomas Region explained: 'They [uncles and aunts] know your temperaments. Women were very important in that process. They come closer to the targeted woman and tactfully introduce you. They actually do a psychological mapping and family research.'

Marrying outside the family network was allowed (if the couple insisted), but continues to be regarded as inappropriate or far from ideal. The resource person revealed that in modern times, the practice of marrying outside the expected network is becoming more and more acceptable or at least tolerable.

Messages given to men prior to marriage included:

1. Domestic violence is a taboo. It breaks social rules. Elders used to step in when this happened, but now working life has created loopholes. Couples now argue in their homes and heal their differences with sex. Public displays of anger are not allowed.
2. According to the Ovaherero, if they see that a man cannot manage anger, he is allowed to marry another wife. This is seen as a way of managing his anger. In the past, promiscuity was not the norm. It should be noted that relationships with cousins were not regarded as promiscuous. Further investigations into the matter of sex with cousins other than the wife, showed that this was not regarded as promiscuity; if people stuck to the rules of the game, no harm was caused to anyone.

Messages to wives included:

1. Be submissive.
2. The man is the head of the family and all property belongs to him or is referred to as his.
3. When you are married, you do not divorce and go back to your family. You sort out your issues; after all, you and your husband are most likely cousins.
4. You are part of a social network and you have to behave as such.

HIV messages did not feature in the life-skills training of the Ovaherero and Ovahimba. Ovaherero and Ovahimba rely mostly on circumcision and on staying within the intra-family sexual network for protection against HIV/AIDS.

Key respondents regretted that there were few initiation ceremonies for girls in their culture. The ceremonies have become reduced to cosmetic enhancement.

These comments were made in reference to the 'fitting of headgear on the girls' when they reach adolescence, and dressing up in the famous Ovaherero dresses, and the headdresses (known as *otjikaiva*) and beads of the Ovahimba.

CONCLUSIONS AND RECOMMENDATIONS

Over the past three decades, HIV/AIDS has presented itself as the biggest threat of our time. Yet many traditional structures have not adapted to fight it, in spite of evidence that formal or external HIV/AIDS programmes increase knowledge of the disease, but do not change people's behaviour or reduce HIV infection rates. The omission of HIV/AIDS content in traditional rites of passage was starkly evident in this research. Of all the sessions attended, HIV/AIDS was mentioned only once and when this happened, the majority of the participants criticized it. When key respondents were asked about the omission and how this might increase the risk of infection especially for women who are clearly advised to be passive in their relationships with men, they acknowledged that their culture and traditions have been very slow in making the mind shift to address HIV/AIDS prevention directly in traditional life-skills sessions.

Clearly, traditional structures vest power in boys and men and by so doing disempower women. Even when women acquire information and skills through gender equality programmes, culture and tradition make it difficult for them to apply such knowledge in their relationships. This makes it crucial that efforts are made to enable the infiltration of HIV/AIDS content in traditional life-skills programmes.

It is important that opportunities are found to bridge the gap between public, scholastic and media HIV/AIDS prevention campaigns and existing traditional structures. It is clear that there is a disjuncture between HIV knowledge and behavioural change (Badcock-Walters et al., 2004, p.5). Cultures and traditions continue to place the power in relationships with the men. At the same time, most of the 'teachers' observed in the life-skills programmes during this research were women who continued to pass on the values of male dominance from generation to generation. It is obvious that HIV/AIDS cannot be overcome in systems where unequal relations between men and women exist. Some key respondents suggested that women should create platforms for girls and women to start influencing traditional life-skills curricula by integrating what they learn in the public sector.

Boler and Aggleton (2005) state that current HIV/AIDS prevention campaigns are based on the assumption that people lack skills, such as assertiveness, which if they had and would apply would reduce their chances of infection. The findings of this research confirmed this position, but further suggest that although participants might have the skills, traditional social structures do not make provision for them to exercise such skills. Clearly in this research, it was discovered that men had all the rights to demand sex whenever they wished, while community norms encourage women to remain submissive. The impact of these power dynamics should be openly confronted and discussed during traditional ceremonies.

More opportunities should be made to create safe spaces for women to discuss issues that affect them, such as protecting themselves against HIV infection within their social cultural settings, and communication and conflict resolution strategies.

This research confirmed the vulnerability of women to HIV infection. It remains a challenge to education, communities and the country to bridge the gaps between laws and cultural practices.

While the school curriculum offers rich life-orientation programmes, such school-based programmes do not consider cultures and traditions. As long as learners and teachers are not empowered to confront the negative aspects of their cultures, the vicious circle of inequality and oppression of women will continue from one generation to the next. In the same vein, the positive aspects of culture can go a long way in informing school curricula and, by so doing, ensure quality education to both girls and boys.

ACKNOWLEDGMENTS

The key respondents, resource persons and wider participants in this research showed me compassion and carried me through tough situations, even when I felt insecure. They accepted me as one of their own and shared their lives with me. Was it not for the sake of confidentiality, I would mention their names. Nevertheless, I thank them all for the passion they demonstrated during this project, and for being the windows through which I, and the readers of this chapter, could view their cultures.

References

Amathila, L. I. (2012). *Making a difference*. Windhoek: University of Namibia Press.

Badcock-Walters, P., Kelly, M., & Görgens, M. (2004). *Does knowledge equal change? HIV/AIDS education and behaviour change*. Background paper for the EFA Global Monitoring Report. UNESCO, Paris, 31 April 2004.

Baker, T. L. (1999). *Doing social research* (3rd ed.). California, USA: McGraw-Hill College.

Boler, T., & Aggleton, P. (2005). *Life skills education for HIV prevention: A critical analysis*. London, UK: Save the Children & ActionAid International. Retrieved from http://www.actionaid.org.uk/sites/default/files/doc_lib/168_1_life_skills.pdf

CDC [Centers for Disease Control]. (n.d.) *CDC in Namibia Fact sheet*. Retrieved from http:/viz.healthmetrics and evaluation.org/gbd-compare/2010. Atlanta. Centers for Disease Control and Prevention.

Creswell, J. (2011). *Educational research: Planning, conducting, and evaluating quantitative and qualitative research* (4th ed.). Boston, USA: Pearson.

GRN [Government of the Republic of Namibia]. (2014). *Namibia's fourth national development plan 2012/2013–2016/2017.* Windhoek, Namibia: National Planning Commission, Office of the President.

Haihambo, C. K. (2002). Children infected and/or affected by HIV/AIDS in Namibia: A case study. In M. L. Mostert and C. D. Kasanda (Eds.), (2005), *Education in Namibia: A collection of essays.* Windhoek, Namibia: University of Namibia Press.

Haihambo C. K. (2010). *Inclusive education: Challenges of students with disabilities in higher education institutions in Namibia.* Saarbrucken, Germany: Lambert Publishing.

Hutchinson, S., Weiss, E., Barker, G., Segundo, M., & Pulerwitz, J. (2004). Involving young men in HIV prevention programmes. Operations research on gender-based approaches in Brazil, Tanzania, and India. USAID, John Hopkins Bloomberg School, Center for Communication Programs.

ICASA (2013). *Africa HIV & AIDS Multiple Indicator Score card.* Nigeria & London: Africa Health, Human & Social Development (Afri-Dev) Information Service & Parliamentary Support Network.

Iipinge, Hofnie, & Friedman. (2004). The relationship between gender roles and HIV infection in Namibia. Windhoek: University of Namibia Press.

!Khaxas E. (2008). *We must choose life: Writings by Namibian women on culture, violence, HIV/AIDS.* Windhoek, Namibia: Women's Leadership Centre.

Mwamwenda, T. S. (2004). *Educational psychology: An African perspective* (2nd ed.). Durban, South Africa: Butterworths.

NSA [Namibia Statistics Agency]. (2014). *Namibia 2011 national population and housing census main report.* Windhoek, Namibia: Government of the Republic of Namibia.

Parker, W., & Connolly, C. (2007). *Namibia: HIV/AIDS Community Survey Report for Rundu, Keetmanshoop, Walvis Bay and Oshakati.* Windhoek, Namibia: NawaLife Trust.

Rooth, E. (2007). *Life skills in the time of AIDS: Training course for teacher educators in Malawi – Workbook.* Berlin, Germany: in Went Capacity Building International.

Sharpley, M. W. (2010, July 9). We are the struggle kids: Paranoia of the youth warrants attention. *New Era*, p. 9.

UNAIDS [Joint United Nations Programme on HIV/AIDS]. (2012). *Regional fact sheet 2012.* Retrieved from http://www.unaids.org/sites/default/files/en/media/unaids/contentassets/documents/epidemiology/2012/gr2012/2012_FS_regional_ssa_en.pdf

17

To integrate or not: Exploring the prospects and challenges of integrating indigenous knowledge at the University of Namibia

Grace M. Mukumbo Chinsembu & Miriam Hamunyela

INTRODUCTION

Namibia has a population of about 2.1 million people of which 87.5% belong to one of nine main indigenous ethnic groups: Aawambo (50.0%), vaKavango (9.0%), Ovaherero (7.0%), Damara (7.0%), Nama (5.0%), Lozi (4.0%), San (3.0%), Baster (2.0%) and Tswana (0.5%) (UNDP, 2000). In Namibia, ethnic identity is stronger than national identity, with 75% of Namibians feeling much stronger ties to people of their own ethnic group than to fellow compatriots of other ethnic groups (Shaw-Taylor, 2008). Undoubtedly, a lot of indigenous knowledge is embedded within these strong ethnic and cultural precincts.

Over the past two decades, many Namibian policy makers and knowledge workers have begun to realize the importance of indigenous knowledge in the country's development process. In 2011, the Polytechnic of Namibia hosted a three-day conference on the technology of indigenous knowledge under the theme, 'Embracing indigenous knowledge systems into a new technology design paradigm'. During this conference, Namibians were urged to nurture the knowledge of their ancestors and ensure that it is protected and preserved. At the University of Namibia (UNAM), the Multidisciplinary Research Centre (MRC) conducts annual indigenous knowledge symposia. The MRC also has a research programme on indigenous knowledge systems (IKS), which is funded by the Ministry of Education (ME).

Nowadays, more plans are being devoted to the documentation of indigenous knowledge before it disappears. However, it remains largely tacit, wordless, unstated and undocumented, even as it increasingly disappears with the death of older people

– the bearers and libraries of this important resource. Here, our thesis is that the integration of indigenous knowledge into formal educational curricula can become one of the avenues to capture and document it for future generations. Be that as it may, integration of indigenous knowledge is still a contentious matter and should be approached cautiously, and the question of whether an institution of higher learning should integrate it or not into its pedagogy needs to be answered within the prism of empirical evidence.

In this chapter, we revisit the definitions of indigenous knowledge; interrogate the significance of it in traditional Africa and the African Renaissance; discuss its links to formal education; and present findings that shed light on the prospects and challenges of teaching indigenous knowledge at the University of Namibia (UNAM). The chapter closes with a recommendation for UNAM to introduce a new degree programme in indigenous knowledge.

CONCEPTS OF INDIGENOUS KNOWLEDGE

The scope of indigenous knowledge remains a debatable issue in many circles, but the canonical definitions, characteristics and meanings of it remain the same, namely:

1. Indigenous knowledge is a set of perceptions, information and behaviours that guide a local community's use of land and natural resources. It is therefore created and sustained by local community members as a means to meet their needs for food, shelter, health and spirituality (Burger, 1990).
2. Indigenous knowledge is often referred to as indigenous wisdom, as it is the result of human observation of patterns in nature and society. This knowledge is transmitted through narratives that are told from the heart and in the voices of the indigenous people themselves (Burger, 1990).
3. Indigenous knowledge is part of agriculture, health care, food preparation, education, environmental conservation and a host of other activities (Warren, 1987). Much of this knowledge is unique to a given culture or society and is passed down from generation to generation, usually by word of mouth, because it is mostly tacit and not documented (Rajasekaran, 1993).
4. Indigenous knowledge is synonymous to the local knowledge that is unique to a given culture or society. It is a basis for local-level decision-making in agriculture, healthcare, food preparation, education, conflict resolution, natural resource management, environmental problems and other activities in local communities (Warren, 1991).
5. Indigenous knowledge is a systematic body of knowledge acquired by local people in a given culture through accumulation of informal experiences and intimate understanding of the environment (Rajasekaran, Warren, & Babu, 1990).

6. Indigenous knowledge is usually adapted and specific to local ecological conditions and to a community's socioeconomic situation and cultural beliefs (Piso, 2008).
7. Indigenous knowledge reflects a set of resource-use strategies that may be sustainable in certain contexts and therefore can help promote biodiversity conservation when they are appropriate for a particular local landscape.
8. Indigenous knowledge is dynamic, changing through local mechanisms of creativity and innovativeness as well as through contact with other traditional and international knowledge systems (Warren, 1991).
9. Indigenous knowledge systems (IKS) are tailored to the needs of local people, including the quality and quantity of available resources (Pretty & Sandbrook, 1991). They pertain to various cultural norms, social roles and physical conditions. Their efficiency lies in the capacity to adapt to the changing circumstances.
10. IKS may appear simple to outsiders, but they represent tested mechanisms to ensure resilient livelihoods of the local people.
11. IKS are often elaborate and they are adapted to the local cultural environment and conditions (Warren, 1991). Indigenous knowledge can be simple or complex, but it is not static. It evolves in response to changing ecological, economic and sociopolitical circumstances based on the creativity and innovation of community members and as a result of the influence of other cultures and outside technologies (The World Bank, 2004).

These definitions indicate that indigenous knowledge is knowledge generated and developed through, rooted in and stems from local practices of local people, and strives to optimize the dynamics of locally available resources. As intellectual property, indigenous knowledge has value in enhancing cultural diversity, human welfare and ecological stability. The value of indigenous knowledge is not only for the culture in which it develops. It can also include knowledge originating from elsewhere, which has been internalized by local people seeking solutions to community problems, such as overexploitation of resources and environmental events.

INDIGENOUS KNOWLEDGE IN 'TRADITIONAL' AFRICA

According to Burger (1990), there are about 250 million indigenous people in the world, making about four per cent of the world's population. This should be viewed in a larger context, however, because all knowledge and practices accumulated in a place over many centuries are now considered indigenous knowledge. Rajasekaran and Warren (1993) contend that Africa has a relatively richer body of indigenous knowledge than other continents. This is not surprising given that Africa is the birthplace of humankind. In Africa, indigenous knowledge has been used for thousands of years to address challenges, such as disease, improve food production and stem environmental degradation (Chinsembu, 2012).

Overall, the most important element in understanding African indigenous knowledge rests on the principle that land is the backbone of livelihoods, a source of life, history and spirituality (Warren, 1991). There is a close relationship between the people, their land and the spiritual world. This is vividly reflected in many of our African languages – not only in the content of their vocabularies, but also in structure, including the nature-based noun class system.

Evidence has shown that indigenous knowledge is particularly important in environmental management. According to Hall, Sefa Deo and Rosenberg (2000), indigenous people have usually lived in one bioregion for many generations and thus learnt how to live there sustainably. These same authors noted that in modern times, this ability often puts indigenous people in a unique position to understand the interrelationships, needs, resources and dangers within their bioregion. However, they cautioned that this is not necessarily true of indigenous cultures that have been eroded through colonialism, genocide or displacement (Hall et al., 2000).

IKS provide the basis for grass-roots decision-making. Posey (1995) argued that indigenous ecological zones, natural resources, agriculture, aquaculture, forest and game management were far more sophisticated than previously assumed. He further stated that indigenous knowledge offers new models for development that are both ecologically and socially sound. He also alluded that it is a well-known fact that development activities that work with and through IKS have several important advantages over projects that operate outside them (Posey, 1995).

One such classic example is the shift from 'green revolution' monocultures to indigenous multiple-cropping or mixed-cropping systems (Obomsawin, 2001). According to Obomsawin (2001), following the euphoria of high crop yields that came with the 'green revolution', agricultural researchers in developed and developing countries quickly ignored the characteristics of traditional multiple-cropping system that make them desirable. However, more recent research has shown monocultures to be ecologically misplaced and that the benefits of polycultures, such as biodiversity enrichment, have become clearer and more widely accepted.

Yet, even before any research could vindicate indigenous-knowledge-based polycultures, Africans already knew that these mixed-cropping systems had many sustainable characteristics. These include diet diversity, diversified income generation, production stability, minimization of risk, low incidences of pests and diseases, efficient use of labour, maximized production with limited natural resources and low levels of technology (Posey, 1995; Obomsawin, 2001).

Eyford (1990) maintained that the value of indigenous knowledge is not just limited to agriculture, environment and biodiversity. On the contrary, it has immense value in education and medicine as well. Indigenous peoples' traditional framework of education is a balanced and complementary model acceptable to the local community. It leads to the development of a well-rounded person in a dynamic family and community context. Indigenous knowledge incorporates principles of holism, integration, respect for the spiritual and natural world, order and balance. For an individual, indigenous knowledge encompasses total preparation of the whole person for living a fulfilling life (Obomsawin, 2001).

Thus, Muya (2006) stated that in traditional African societies, children acquire indigenous knowledge through their constant interactions with both the adult world and the physical environment around them. This knowledge includes an understanding of ecological systems; the methods of harvesting natural resources without depleting biodiversity or significantly damaging the natural balance; the skills required to use various tools and devices; familiarization with customs and practices of their society; coming to grips with societal values or beliefs; and the development of a world view that reflects the experiences of the society in which they live.

Le Roux (2003), however, bemoaned that this indigenous mode of linguistic, cultural and nature-based knowledge has been affected in recent years by a reduction in cultural diversity through the adoption of Western-based lifestyles in most African societies. The same author stated that children have less contact with their natural and cultural environments, even in their home environments, due to the exotic trends in the lifestyles of most Africans and, as a result, younger generations are rapidly losing their competencies in African indigenous knowledge (le Roux, 2003). They are also losing interest in their cultural backgrounds and traditions because their current lives are focused on the Western-oriented school system, urban living and the internet.

Many knowledge workers thus lament that despite the contributions and importance of indigenous knowledge, it has not been adequately promoted and protected in most African countries because most Western-educated people believe it is unscientific. Institutions that could safeguard the rights of indigenous-knowledge holders do not exist in most African countries. Furthermore, the links between formal institutions and local communities that hold and use indigenous knowledge are weak. These factors have denied Africans the opportunity to better understand and use their indigenous knowledge base.

INDIGENOUS KNOWLEDGE IN THE AFRICAN RENAISSANCE

Ntuli (2002) defines the African Renaissance as a rebirth or renewal to overcome Africa's current challenges and problems. This, according to Ntuli (2002, p. 54), 'requires of us to re-examine our knowledge systems anew, with a view to extracting some lessons from our past to distil what can be used at this current moment and what has to be jettisoned.' Here, we also concur with Ntuli (2002) that IKS are a counter-hegemonic discourse in the context of the African Renaissance. Along this counter-hegemonic thinking, African leaders are beginning to recognize the importance of protecting and promoting indigenous knowledge in order to solve specific problems and improve the continent's economies.

Given this renewed interest in indigenous knowledge, it is essential to protect and nurture all tradition-based innovations and creations. Studies conducted in South Africa for the New Partnership for Africa's Development (NEPAD) reveal that the majority of people in Africa, especially the poor, depend on indigenous knowledge for survival (Muya, 2006). Indeed, indigenous knowledge contributes to problem-solving strategies for local communities, helps the poor meet their food requirements, and offers opportunities for strengthening local experiences, practices, moral values and decision-making.

Reports suggest that more than 65% of the poor people in sub-Saharan Africa depend on knowledge of traditional medicine and food for their basic healthcare needs (Kaya & Materechera, 2005). The World Bank (2004) reported that in most African countries, traditional medicine is used by nearly 70–80% of local populations to deal with their basic healthcare needs. Moreover, of the over 120 pharmaceutical products that are derived from plants, 74% were first utilized by indigenous cultures (The World Bank, 2004).

As an example, the San people of southern Africa have used the plant *Hoodia* as an appetite suppressant for many centuries, especially during hunting expeditions when little food is available for many days (Rodolo, 2007). Following the San people's ethnomedicinal knowledge of the plant, pharmaceutical companies now extract the appetite-suppressing chemicals of *Hoodia* species to make weight-loss tablets (Rodolo, 2007).

According to The World Bank (2004), the Nigerian National Institute for Pharmaceutical Research and Development in Abuja conducted scientific and clinical investigations into the use of a standardized herbal extract for treating sickle-cell anaemia. The phytochemical developed, under the name Niprisan, showed very good efficacy and safety profiles such that it was subsequently licensed to an American company for commercial production.

Suffice to state that these two examples of *Hoodia* and the herbal extract for treating sickle-cell anaemia clearly illustrate the importance of indigenous knowledge on two frontiers: (1) to drive drug innovations for human and animal healthcare needs, and (2) to generate monetary wealth from bio-trade and the bio-economy (Chinsembu, 2012). Thus, in order to add value to their indigenous knowledge of medicinal plants, African countries under the auspices of NEPAD are being urged to invest into the research and development of phytomedicines and biotechnology. Moving forward, many African countries now view indigenous knowledge as an important resource that should derive socioeconomic benefits. However, in order to ensure sustainability of the contributions of indigenous knowledge to the new

African Renaissance and economy, many countries are now planning to or currently experiment with the integration of indigenous knowledge into formal education.

INDIGENOUS KNOWLEDGE AND FORMAL EDUCATION

Kimenyi (2003) stated that conventional curricula and assessment tests in many countries do not support the students' indigenous-knowledge base. If learning environments, however, were adapted to help students build on their community knowledge, it would encourage students to learn from their parents, grandparents and other adults and, by so doing, students could appreciate and respect their community knowledge. Such a relationship between the young and the older generations could help reduce the generation gap and develop inter-generational harmony (Muya, 2006).

In fact, many Western educational experts now realize the value of the holistic nature of IKS to such an extent that they have cleverly sneaked IKS into Western and modern education systems under the title of 'affective learning' (Eyford, 1990). The concept of affective learning entails a holistic approach to develop character, conscience, attitudes and moral values. According to Eyford (1990), affective learning contains the forces that determine the nature of an individual's life and ultimately the life of an entire people. It was postulated that the neglect of affective learning has contributed to escalating crime, drug dependency, and family and social breakdown in many developed countries (Eyford, 1990).

Kaya (2009) also argued that the dominance of Western knowledge systems has led to the marginalization of African IKS in the search for sustainable solutions to development and poverty eradication. Currently, however, there is an increasing interest and realization among policy makers, researchers and academics that any developmental strategy that is not based on local experiences, knowledge and culture will not be sustainable (The World Bank, 1998). One of the major challenges facing the promotion of indigenous knowledge for sustainable development is the lack of trained person power at several rungs in the ladder of formal education. We think that in order to meet this challenge, African indigenous knowledge should be integrated into our school and university curricula.

Our view is consistent with that of Seleti (2010) who espoused that indigenous people have a broad knowledge on living sustainably. It is disappointing that formal education systems have disrupted the practical, everyday-life aspects of indigenous knowledge and ways of learning, and replaced them with abstract knowledge and academic modes of rote learning. Moreover, there is a grave risk that much indigenous knowledge is being lost because it is not documented. Both Seleti (2010) and Kaya (2009) emphasize that there are pertinent issues regarding the management of IKS in Africa. One of these is the threat of indigenous knowledge becoming extinct – more so because it is not in a written form, as it is transmitted orally from one generation to the next (Kimenyi, 2003).

It is evident that despite the importance of indigenous knowledge, there are not many programmes and institutions designed to collect, document, develop and disseminate such knowledge. Specifically, Kitula (2007) was concerned that there have been few attempts by formal educational systems to integrate indigenous knowledge into school and university curricula. This is despite the fact that it can act as a powerful foundation in formal teaching and learning environments. In this light, Chinsembu, Shimwooshili-Shaimemanya, Kasanda and Zealand (2011) asserted that the use of IKS can help students to form schemata for interpreting local phenomena through the prism of what they already know.

One of the most eminent African indigenous knowledge scholars of our time, Nkondo, has repeatedly cautioned that the quest to understand and use IKS should not be likened to 'primitive anthropology'. According to Nkondo (2010), indigenous knowledge has a clear link between thinking and action, theory and practice, and mind and body. Nkondo (2010) and Teffo (2010) argued that African indigenous knowledge adequately fits into the two epistemological denominations of rationalism and empiricism. They asserted that African IKS are not static. On the contrary, African IKS are situation-dependent, continuously evolving and actively adapting to the ever-changing world (Nkondo, 2010; Teffo, 2010). As a result, African research and educational institutions have now reinvigorated efforts to interface and mainstream IKS into their programmes.

In South Africa, the Department of Science and Technology (DST) has positioned IKS at the core of their vision and blueprint for scientific development and innovation (Seleti, 2010). The national IKS policy, adopted in 2004, mandates the DST to establish a National Indigenous Knowledge Systems Office (NIKSO). The main strategic objective of NIKSO is to coordinate the South African research agenda on IKS within the DST and throughout South Africa (Muya, 2006). To this end, DST and the University of Zululand have established the IKS Documentation Centre situated at the University of Zululand. According to Muya (2006), this centre was established as a vehicle through which the wealth of indigenous knowledge located in various communities can be captured and stored. The objectives of the centre include:

1. Mobilizing resources in order to realize the goals and objectives of IKS;
2. Integrating IKS into the research and teaching agenda of the university;
3. Enhancing the partnership between the university and the community with regard to IKS; and
4. Exploring collaborative activities, particularly within the continent of Africa.

Kaya and Materechera (2005) reiterated that integration of African indigenous knowledge into the educational curricula would ensure that the value and importance of indigenous knowledge is understood and appreciated among African students who should be equipped with the necessary intellectual and research tools to recognize, conserve and develop it. Hence, in South Africa, the Universities of Venda, Zululand and North-West have integrated indigenous knowledge into their curricula to the extent that a Bachelor of IKS (BIKS) degree programme has been introduced at each.

It goes without saying that South Africa has set a shining example in terms of mainstreaming IKS into development, research and teaching. While the spotlight is on South Africa, we contend that some of the ideas implemented there are relevant to neighbouring Namibia. On a par with South Africa, we strongly argue that if IKS is to be captured from various Namibian communities, UNAM should establish an IKS documentation centre, which should work in close collaboration with rural communities. In this way, the teaching and learning environment will adapt and help students to build on their indigenous knowledge, cultures and value systems.

Altogether, it is imperative for educators to recognize the various forms of indigenous knowledge that students bring with them to the school environment; this will serve as a stepping stone to help students succeed academically. According to Piso (2008), there are different forms of knowledge that students gain from living and working in their communities and homes, and from other local activities. Educational research on forms of learning has shown that teaching supported by prior knowledge increases a student's ability to form schemata and grasp the material and concepts taught to them (Rodolo, 2007).

Integrating indigenous knowledge into the learning environment can also help students feel a sense of ownership of the knowledge they bring there. For example, in *Pedagogy of the oppressed*, Freire (1970) suggests that allowing learners to have ownership of their knowledge is equivalent to respecting their culture, tradition and identity. He further warned that educators should avoid the misconception that learners are 'empty vessels' and the goal of education is 'deposit-making'. When material is taught merely as 'banking' information, learners do not have the opportunity to understand the relevance and meaning of the knowledge being imparted (Freire, 1970). Furthermore, educators should use the student's prior knowledge as a foundation to build on and introduce new concepts. This process, according to Fasokun, Katahoire and Oduaran (2005) is known as constructivist learning. This type of learning creates a systematic process that allows students to slowly and accurately grasp the concepts being taught at school and university.

On the other hand, Sillitoe (1998) argued that the incorporation of indigenous knowledge into the school and university curricula at a larger scale should not only depend on the attitude of the African governments, but also on the results of further research into the characteristic features of indigenous cultures and knowledge systems. Sillitoe pointed out that while the potential of indigenous knowledge has been grossly underutilized in the past, the contributions of indigenous culture and knowledge systems in relation to sustainability and development should not lead to the temptation 'to overvalue our heritage'; we should bear in mind that indigenous knowledge 'can be less systematic than scientific knowledge' (Sillitoe, 1998, p.227). Sillitoe also advised that 'we need to guard against any romantic tendency to idealise IK [(indigenous knowledge)] it may be inadequate, especially in situations of rapid change' (Sillitoe, 1998, p. 227).

Despite Sillitoe's caution, Nakashima and Rou'e (2002) make a strong case for the growing recognition of the value of indigenous knowledge for sustainable development. They argue that it is wise not only to sustain indigenous knowledge in traditional communities, but also to integrate it into the school curriculum. There are several ways in which indigenous knowledge can help enhance the curriculum. For instance, students can learn from fieldwork in local areas; this will call for some prior knowledge and understanding. To be able to understand the relationship between indigenous people, soils and plants, students need to identify the plants and soil types in the local area. One way to get preliminary knowledge of plants and soil types in the local environment is to consult indigenous people and invite them to teach students in the field (Nakashima & Rou'e, 2002).

The teaching principle of the 'known to the unknown' should be adopted if education is to be effective. Therefore, it is imperative to start with knowledge of the local area that students are familiar with, and gradually move to the knowledge pertaining to regional, national and global environments. Indigenous knowledge can play a significant role in education about the local area. Muya (2006) posited that in most societies, indigenous people have developed enormous volumes of knowledge over centuries by directly interacting with their local environment. This ready-made knowledge system, as is often the case when harvesting low-hanging fruits, can easily be used in formal education as long as appropriate measures are taken to unlock it from the memories of the local people.

For indigenous learners and instructors, the inclusion of indigenous knowledge into schools often enhances educational effectiveness by providing an education that adheres to an indigenous person's own inherent perspectives, experiences, language and customs. Indigenous knowledge makes it easier for children to transit into the realm of adulthood. For non-indigenous students and teachers, such education often has the effect of raising awareness of individual and collective traditions of indigenous communities and peoples, thereby promoting greater respect for and appreciation of various cultural realities. In terms of educational content, the inclusion of indigenous knowledge into instructional materials, such as textbooks, enriches the preparation of students for the greater world.

TO INTEGRATE INDIGENOUS KNOWLEDGE INTO THE UNAM CURRICULUM OR NOT

A descriptive and qualitative study was conducted at UNAM to describe the prospects and challenges of teaching indigenous knowledge there.

Permission to conduct the study was obtained from the Office of the Vice-Chancellor through a written letter. Ethical attributes, including participants' rights to privacy, voluntary participation, confidentiality and anonymity, were maintained.

A total of 37 lecturers participated in the study: 16 were from the Faculty of Agriculture and Natural Resources and 21 were from the Faculty of Education. Using convenience sampling, which includes whoever happens to be available into the sample, the number of participants was largely determined by the availability of the lecturers and their willingness to participate in the study.

Qualitative data were collected through semi-structured questionnaires and interviews. Questions in the interview guide and questionnaire were piloted with a small group of five respondents from the Department of Biological Sciences at UNAM's main Windhoek campus. Lecturers from the Faculty of Education were interviewed, but due to time constraints, those from the Faculty of Agriculture and Natural Resources were given questionnaires to complete. Both interviews and questionnaires consisted of the same questions. The data were examined, and common themes and ideas expressed by the participants were identified.

Lecturers' perceptions on integrating indigenous knowledge

The results of the study showed that 30 out of 37 lecturers (81.1%) supported the integration of indigenous knowledge into the curriculum:

> 'It is a good idea. It will need to be developed properly as a body of knowledge; the challenge of documentation and references might arise, though.'

> 'It is good since it is based on local-level decision-making in local areas, e.g. agriculture and health.'

> 'No objection, however, it goes with a lot of research.'

About 11% of the lecturers (4 out of 37) did not support the integration of indigenous knowledge into the UNAM curriculum. They indicated that the inclusion of indigenous knowledge into the university curriculum would be difficult because one would have to incorporate aspects of indigenous knowledge from several different Namibian cultures. Negative perceptions of a few lecturers were as follows:

'The idea of integrating IK [indigenous knowledge] into the university curricula could be valueless since many people may not appreciate it, especially the young generation.'

'It would be difficult to incorporate all aspects of IK from different indigenous set-ups of Namibia into the university curricula, since IK systems are peculiar to a group of people in a locality.'

'Indigenous education often takes different forms than a typical Western model of education because children learn through example; traditional education is less formal than the standard Western model. In contrast to structured hours and a classroom setting, learning takes place throughout the day, both in the home and in adults' workplace.'

Two respondents indicated that indigenous knowledge was already integrated into the curriculum albeit at a limited level. They said that the teaching of local languages includes indigenous knowledge:

'The idea is already included in teaching linguistics. It is incorporated already because IK is very useful. At the Language Centre, for instance, a doctorate degree in the Khoekhoe language [Khoekhoegowab] is offered. A number of local Namibian language courses are being offered at the Language Centre, for example, Oshindonga, Oshikwanyama and Otjiherero.'

'As far as I know it is already integrated in linguistics syllabi at a very limited level.'

Overall, the results indicated that the majority of the lecturers at UNAM supported the inclusion of indigenous knowledge into the university curriculum, although they recognised that it would be challenging and require research.

Challenges regarding the integration of indigenous knowledge

All participants responded to the question that asked them to explain the challenges of integrating indigenous knowledge into the curriculum. Some of the challenges identified, were:

'Content, material, the syllabus and availability of qualified staff to handle the courses.'

'Locating examples of IK; finding people who would share IK with UNAM; lack of capacity at UNAM to understand and impart it.'

Nine respondents (24.3%) indicated that unskilled person-power would be a challenge in teaching indigenous knowledge at UNAM. Twelve respondents (32.4%) felt that since indigenous knowledge was mostly not documented, it would be a big challenge to integrate it into the curriculum:

> 'Much of IK is not documented, so it will be a challenge to list down what is not documented. Hence a lot will be missed.'

> 'Encounter[ing] resistance, especially from youths. IK not documented; do research first, interview people to have it documented'.

> 'Documentation will be a challenge because those who possess the knowledge can resist sharing it.'

Ten respondents (27.0%) indicated that indigenous knowledge is not scientific; therefore it will be difficult to integrate it into the curriculum.

> 'Stigma and stereotypes – [indigenous knowledge] may be stereotyped as poor peoples' ideas.'

> 'Some people think it is out-dated knowledge and it's irrelevant, but if made compulsory in some subjects, knowledge can be turned into power.'

> 'Our educators are too focused on science and technology, which greatly focuses on Western ideas and technology.'

Four respondents (10.8%) suggested that lack of funding would be a challenge to integrating indigenous knowledge into the university curriculum.

> 'The challenge is to convince UNAM management and academic staff of the value of IK; secondly, there is the non-availability of resources to develop such a programme or curricula.'

> 'Resources are needed for forums and seminars to take place.'

Four respondents (10.8%) alluded to the fact that indigenous knowledge varies from culture to culture and therefore it will be a challenge to integrate it into the university curricula.

> 'Consolidating different values, beliefs and practices will be a big challenge.'

> 'A nation like Namibia with many different cultures – which one will be chosen and which one can be left out?'

'Acceptance, because of different cultures; time, a lot of people to accept other IK from other cultures.'

One respondent (2.7%) noted that indigenous knowledge is not uniform; therefore it will be a challenge to integrate it into the university curricula:

'IK practices may not be uniform among Namibian communities from [different] parts … ; scanty or no research done on subject of IK systems.'

'Because of many different cultures and tribes in Namibia, … it will be difficult [to] incorporate the different IK from the different cultures and tribes into the university curricula.'

CONCLUSIONS AND RECOMMENDATIONS

Most of the lecturers support the integration of indigenous knowledge into the UNAM curriculum. This finding indicates strong prospects for teaching and learning indigenous knowledge at UNAM. In order to operationalize these prospects, we recommend that UNAM should introduce indigenous knowledge as one of the major courses in the Bachelor of Education (Adult Education) Honours Programme, which could lead to a Master's Degree in Indigenous Knowledge Systems.

Integrating indigenous knowledge at UNAM, however, would have to overcome a variety of identified challenges, such as the lack of adequate human and financial resources. Government should provide more financial resources to permit UNAM to hire new academic staff who will embark on new academic programmes related to indigenous knowledge. Also, because there are several different cultural identities in Namibia, it would be important to carefully agree on the indigenous knowledge content to be integrated into the curriculum. Finally, there is a need for more research to elucidate the perceptions of UNAM students towards learning indigenous knowledge. This is important if students are to believe that there are important career prospects in the field of indigenous knowledge.

The conclusions and recommendations of this study are based on a small sample of two faculties (Agriculture and Education). More studies consisting of bigger sample sizes are needed to understand specific strategies and organizational structures for integrating indigenous knowledge at UNAM.

ACKNOWLEDGMENTS

We thank all the lecturers who participated in this study. This work was part of Grace Chinsembu's thesis towards her Master's degree in Education (Adult Education) submitted to the University of Namibia.

References

Burger, J. (1990). *The Gaia atlas of first peoples: A future for the indigenous world*. Ringwood, UK: Penguin Books.

Chinsembu, K. C. (2012). Indigenous knowledge systems as a platform for biological innovations in Africa. *Journal of Inventions and Discoveries in Biology, 1*(1), 012-025.

Chinsembu, K. C., Shomwooshili-Shaimemanya, C., Kasanda, C. D., & Zealand, D. (2011). Indigenous knowledge of HIV/AIDS among High School students in Namibia. *Journal of Ethnobiology and Ethnomedicine, 7*, 17. doi:10.1186/1746-4269-7-17

Eyford, G. (1990). Cultural dimensions of learning. *International Review of Education, 36*(2), 195-205.

Fasokun, T., Katahoire, A., & Oduaran, A. (2005). *The psychology of adult learning in Africa: African perspectives on adult learning*. Cape Town, South Africa: CTP Book Printers.

Freire, P. (1970). *Pedagogy of the oppressed*. New York: Continuum International Publishing.

Hall, L. B., Sefa Deo, G. J., & Rosenberg, D. G. (2000). *Indigenous knowledge in global contexts: Multiple readings of our world*. Toronto: University of Toronto Press.

Kaya, H. O. (2009). Indigenous knowledge (IK) and innovation systems for public health in Africa. In F. A. Kalua, A. Awotedu, L. A. Kamwanja, & J. D. K. Saka (Eds), *Science, technology and innovation for public health in Africa* (pp. 9-110). Pretoria, South Africa: NEPAD (New Partnership for Africa's Development).

Kaya, H. O., & Materechera, S. A. (2005). *Documentations of IKs best practices in the SADC region* (unpublished manuscript), National Indigenous Knowledge Systems Office (NIKSO), Department of Science and Technology, National Research Foundation of South Africa.

Kimenyi, M. S. (2003). Research and development in the south: The case study of sub-Saharan Africa. Background paper Commissioned by IDRC in preparation of its Cooperate Strategy and Program Framework (2005–2010).

Kitula, R. A. (2007). The use of medicinal plants for human health in Udzungwa Mountains Forests: A case study of New Dabaga Ulongambi Forest Reserve, Tanzania. *Ethnomedicine, 3*(7), 45-58.

Le Roux, C. J. B. (2003). Tapping indigenous knowledge on the world-wide web. *Indilinga African Journal of Indigenous Knowledge Systems, 2*(1), 107-113.

Muya, P. (2006). *Contributions of IKS to community livelihood in Africa* (Master's thesis, University of Dar es Salaam, Dar es Salaam, Tanzania).

Nakashima, D., & Rou'e, M. (2002). Indigenous knowledge, people and sustainable practice. In P. Timmerman (Ed.), *Encyclopedia of global environmental change, Volume 5: Social and economic dimensions of global environmental change* (pp. 314-324). San Francisco, USA: Wiley.

Nkondo, O. M. (2010, August). *The future of indigenous knowledge systems in global knowledge innovations.* Paper presented at the Regional Symposium on Indigenous Knowledge and Community Innovations in the Biosciences and Biotechnology in Southern Africa, KwaMaritane Game Lodge, South Africa.

Ntuli, P. P. (2002). Indigenous knowledge systems and the African Renaissance. In: C. A. Odora Hoppers (Ed.), *Indigenous knowledge and the integration of knowledge systems: Towards a philosophy of articulation* (pp. 53-67). Cape Town, South Africa: New Africa Books.

Obomsawin, R. (2001). *Indigenous knowledge systems: Harnessing the wisdom of the ages for sustainable development.* Unpublished discussion paper.

Piso, F. S. (2008). *The contribution of African vegetables in food security and nutrition in the North-West Province: Cases from Sannieshof and Lokgopung (Central District Municipality)* (Master's dissertation, North-West University, Mahikeng, South Africa).

Posey, D. A. (1995). Nature and indigenous guidelines for new Amazonian development strategies: Understanding biological diversity through ethnoecology. In. J. Hemming (Ed.), *Change in the Amazon Basin* (pp. 156-181). Manchester, UK: Manchester University Press.

Pretty, J., & Sandbrook, R. (1991, October). *Operationalising sustainable development at the community level.* Paper presented at the DAC Working Party on Development Assistance and Environment, London.

Rajasekaran, B. (1993). *A framework for incorporating indigenous knowledge systems into agricultural research, extension, and NGOs for sustainable agricultural development studies in technology and social change.* Studies in Technology and Social Change No. 21. Ames, IA: Technology and Social Change Program, Iowa State University, Iowa. Ames. Retrieved from http://www.ciesin.org/docs/004-201/004-201.html

Rajasekaran, B., & Warren, M. (1993, March). *A framework for incorporating indigenous knowledge systems into agricultural extension organisation for sustainable agricultural development in India.* Paper presented at the 9th Annual Conference of the

Association for International Agricultural and Extension, Education, Arlington, Virginia, USA.

Rajasekaran, B., Warren, M. D, & Babu, S. C. (1990). Indigenous national resource management systems for sustainable agriculture development: A global perspective. *International Journal of Development*, *3*(1), 1-14.

Rodolo, S. (2007). Setting up the terms of reference for task team for developing *sui generis. Proceedings of the Workshop on Developing Strategies for Promoting Community Knowledge and Awareness of IKS Policy and Implications of IPR on IKS Issues* (pp. 38-44). Mahikeng, South Africa: IKS Centre of Excellence, North-West University.

Seleti, Y. (2010, August). *The role of higher education and research institutions in promoting indigenous knowledge and innovation in the bio-economy in southern Africa.* Paper presented at the Regional Symposium on Indigenous Knowledge and Community Innovations in the Biosciences and Biotechnology in Southern Africa, KwaMaritane Game Lodge, North-West, South Africa.

Shaw-Taylor, Y. (2008). Measuring ethnic identification and attachment in sub-Saharan Africa. *African Sociological Review*, *12*(2), 155-166.

Sillitoe, P. (1998). The development of indigenous knowledge: A new applied anthropology. *Current Anthropology*, *39*(2), 223-235.

Teffo, L. J. (2010, August). *The role of governance and democracy in promoting community innovations in the bio-economy.* Paper presented at the Regional Symposium on Indigenous Knowledge and Community Innovations in the Biosciences and Biotechnology in Southern Africa, KwaMaritane Game Lodge, North-West, South Africa.

The World Bank. (1998). *World development report, 1998–99.* Washington, DC, USA: Author. Retrieved from http://web.worldbank.org/WBSITE/EXTERNAL/ EXTDEC/EXTRESEARCH/EXTWDRS/0,,contentMDK:22293493~pagePK: 478093~piPK:477627~theSitePK:477624,00.html

The World Bank. (2004). *Indigenous knowledge: Local pathways to global development: Marking five years of the World Bank Indigenous Knowledge for Development Programme.* Washington, DC: Author. Retrieved from http://www.worldbank.org/ afr/ik/ikcomplete.pdf

UNDP (United Nations Development Programme). (2000). *Namibia human development report, 2000.* Windhoek, Namibia: Author.

Warren, D. M. (1987). Linking scientific and indigenous agricultural systems. In J. L. Compton (Ed.), *The transformation of international agricultural research and development* (pp. 153-170). Boulder, USA: Lynne Rienner Publishers.

Warren, D. M. (1991). Using indigenous knowledge in agricultural development. *World Bank Discussion Papers No. 127.* Washington DC, USA: The World Bank.

Questions for students

INDIGENOUS KNOWLEDGE GENERAL

1. What is science? What do you understand by the terms 'ethnoscience' and 'indigenous science'? What is the relationship between indigenous knowledge and science?

2. Indigenous knowledge is the local knowledge that is unique to a culture or society. Other names for it include: 'local knowledge', 'folk knowledge', 'people's knowledge', 'traditional wisdom' or 'traditional science'. This knowledge is passed from generation to generation, usually by word of mouth and cultural practices, and has been the basis for agriculture, food preparation, health care, education, conservation and the wide range of other activities that sustain societies in many parts of the world. Discuss how indigenous knowledge:
   a. helps to improve ways of living together and using resources sustainably
   b. helps to maintain the sustainability of a community
   c. is undermined by 'modern' education.

3. Discuss the following questions regarding indigenous knowledge:
   a. Is indigenous knowledge empirical and rational?
   b. Do you think older citizens would be willing to share their indigenous knowledge with younger people?
   c. What are the advantages and disadvantages of sharing indigenous knowledge with other people?
   d. Is it appropriate for traditional healers to share their indigenous knowledge of medicinal plants?
   e. Discuss the merits and disadvantages of promoting the use, teaching and learning of indigenous knowledge given the current age of globalization.
   f. South Africa's new blueprint for science and technology puts indigenous knowledge at the centre of all activities. Discuss the reasons for this new emphasis on indigenous knowledge.

4. Discuss ways and means through which local people can benefit from the intellectual property rights of their indigenous knowledge.

ETHNOMEDICINE

1. The fields of ethnobiology and ethnomedicine are growing in recognition. Discuss the nature of these fields and their importance.

2. Why are plants targeted by scientists as sources of new drugs?

3. Weight loss pills have been developed by pharmaceutical companies from the plant, *Hoodia*, following the indigenous knowledge of the San people that use the plant for suppressing appetite during hunting expeditions. How could the San benefit from their indigenous knowledge?

4. What is biopiracy? How can we protect IK from biopiracy?

5. Why is it important to document traditional ethnomedicines and what risks do we run by not doing so?

6. What scientific skills are needed to identify and validate ethnomedicinal plants?

Ethnomedicinal practice

1. Name any two traditional medicinal plants that you know for healing ailments that are common in your area and indicate how it is administered to the patient.

2. Describe the different categories of traditional healers.

3. Discuss why traditional healers find it difficult to share their traditional healing knowledge with the larger community. Suggest ways of encouraging them to share this knowledge with others.

4. Why do people prefer herbal medicines over allopathic medicines?

5. Traditionally, ethnomedicine is used in the treatment of cancers:
   a. Name three plants used for palliation of cancer. How would you valorize these plants to increase their acceptability and reduce stigma associated with their use?
   b. Plants from similar families may have similar biochemical pathways; name a plant used to treat solid tumours in the Kavango regions and the family it belongs to.

6. Discuss factors that contribute to new HIV/AIDS cases in Namibia.

7. What measures can help lower the prevalence and incidence of HIV/AIDS infections?

8. Assume your classmate is suffering from HIV and has come to you for advice. Will you advise your friend to seek help from a traditional healer or to go to the medical doctor at the hospital? Explain your response.

9. List five ways of preventing malaria transmission.

Development of allopathic drugs

1. Describe three approaches to selecting plants for discovering new drugs.

2. Do you think Namibia should conduct drug discovery and development based on medicinal plants for cancer treatment or cancer palliation? Give the reasons for your answer.

3. Important antimalarial compounds that were originally isolated from plants:
   a. Give the names of the plants of origin and where they are found.
   b. What are the currently recommended drugs for treating uncomplicated and severe malaria in Namibia?
   c. List five classes of antiplasmodial phytochemicals.
   d. Discuss the role of ethnomedicinal plants in malaria treatment in Namibia.

10. The Sondashi formula is believed to inhibit HIV integrase.
   a. With the help of diagrams, show how the Sondashi formula works as an antiretroviral drug.
   b. Discuss the advantages (and disadvantages) of the Sondashi formula in relation to current antiretroviral drugs.
   c. Do you think the Sondashi formula cures HIV and AIDS?
   d. Discuss the challenges of intellectual property rights encountered during the discovery of the Sondashi formula.

4. Describe the use of thin-layer chromatography in the analysis of a plant's chemical constituents.

5. Explain the concept of IC_{50} and its use in determining the efficacy of compounds against parasites.

Ethnoveterinary medicine

1. Discuss the limitations and challenges of using ethnoveterinary medicinal plants.

2. Ethnoveterinary medicinal plants are perhaps the most sustainable methods readily adaptable to rural communal livestock farming. Discuss.

3. Despite the fact that many communal farmers use plants to treat livestock diseases, there is no ethnoveterinary pharmacopeia and the current status of information on ethnoveterinary usage of plants is still scanty. Why?

4. Discuss whether indigenous knowledge can contribute to crop and animal breeding, how, and whether it would be of value to integrate it into crop and animal breeding courses.

INDIGENOUS FOODS

1. African leafy vegetables (ALVs) have been consumed by rural people in Namibia for centuries, but are now considered 'old fashioned':
   a. Can ALVs, however, be used in combating malnutrition? Discuss.
   b. Can ALVs be considered an important source of antimicrobials and pharmaceuticals? Discuss.
   c. What kind of interventions can be implemented to encourage people to eat African leafy vegetables?
   d. What would be the best method to prepare African leafy vegetables to preserve their nutritional value? Explain your answer.
   e. Which methods could be used to extend the shelf life of ALV-based products?

2. Traditionally fermented milk products continue to remain popular in Namibia:
   a. Name three types of traditionally fermented milk products found in Namibia.
   b. What is the main function of adding roots to milk during some fermentation processes?
   c. What are lactic acid bacteria?
   d. What are the socioeconomic values of traditionally fermented milk?
   e. What are the benefits of drinking fermented milk over fresh milk?

3. The giant African bullfrog (*Pyxicephalus adspersus*) is a popular food in central northern Namibia. The methods of harvesting the frogs, and cooking and eating them follow traditional practices:
   a. Briefly describe the methods of cooking frog meat in the communities of Okahao, Oshakati and Okalongo.
   b. What is '*oshiketaketa*'? Explain how it is prevented and why this works.
   c. The tongue, internal organs and viscera, as well as the whole of the upper jaw and palate of the frog are not considered fit for human consumption. Research and discuss two other situations like this, where parts of an animal are not included for consumption.

d. In most African village situations, there is a hierarchy in the family at meals, whereby certain foods are designated for men's or for women's consumption, respectively. In northern Namibia, elders (usually male heads of families) prohibit the youth and women from eating the frog when supply is scarce. Substantiate this practice with any anthropological background.

INDIGENOUS ECOLOGICAL KNOWLEDGE

1. What is indigenous ecological knowledge (IEK)?

2. How do farmers along the boundary of ENP use IEK in the management of conflicts with problem animals?
   a. To what extent, in your opinion, is the indigenous knowledge of problem animal behaviour significant in mitigating human–wildlife conflict (HWC)?
   b. Discuss the extent to which local knowledge can be integrated into HWC management approaches and strategies targeting farmers along boundaries of protected areas in Namibia.
   c. Describe other indigenous knowledge practices that you know of relevant to addressing HWC.
   d. Explain whether it is possible to sustain and preserve traditional methods practised by communal and freehold farmers to minimize HWC problems in Namibia.

3. The Basubiya inhabit the floodplains of Zambezi Region in north-eastern Namibia.
   a. Why would the chief of the Basubiya liken his people to hippos?
   b. Discuss how the Basubiya people predict the size of the coming flood.
   c. How do the Basubiya cope during floods?
   d. What are the advantages and disadvantages of staying on the wetlands during the floods? What is your opinion: Do the disadvantages of the floods outweigh the advantages? Why do the Basubiya stay in the wetland?
   e. What advice would you give the Basubiya that do not to want to leave the floodplains for higher and drier lands?

4. Climate change is becoming an increasingly important topic worldwide:
   a. How is climate change likely to affect Namibia?
   b. How is gender relevant to climate change in rural Namibia?
   c. In what ways are climate change events exacerbating disadvantages that women experience in rural Namibia?

d. What can be done to systematically integrate gender issues in strategies to deal with climate change in Namibia?

TRADITIONAL RITES OF PASSAGE IN MODERN NAMIBIA

1. During premarital counselling or advice sessions, couples are not expected to respond to any of the advice given to them. Such sessions form one of the stages of the wedding ceremony – a time that would be difficult for one to change one's mind. What then, is the purpose of the counselling? How could tradition be modified to make counselling more valuable?

2. Tradition and culture play significant roles in shaping human beings throughout life. It is therefore important that traditions and culture include lessons that help people to deal with national and global challenges. HIV/AIDS is one such challenge that seems to be excluded from traditional life-skills programmes despite their known devastating impacts. How could culture and traditions help people prevent HIV/AIDS?

INDIGENOUS KNOWLEDGE AND EDUCATION

1. It is generally accepted that African communities followed a particular philosophy of education before the arrival of Western education.
   a. Discuss what this might have been and what it covered.
   b. Why did African communities embrace the Western system of education at the expense of their own?
   c. Foucauldian theory sees power and knowledge as intertwined entities, and in this way power may limit what is acceptable to be known and in turn knowledge can develop as response and resistance to the limits set by the powers that be. Explain how this scenario manifested itself between indigenous knowledge practitioners and colonizers.

2. Namibians identify strongly with their ethnic group or tribe.
   a. Discuss why this is so.
   b. Would these strong ethnic and tribal identities be a help or hindrance for the integration of indigenous knowledge into the school and university curricula?

3. Learners from marginalized communities in Namibia, such as the San and Ovahimba, have high dropout rates, especially from secondary schools.

    a. What do you think are some of the good practices for helping to retain learners from marginalized communities in schools?

    b. If you were appointed as a consultant to develop guidelines to help a particular San community overcome barriers they experience with education and bring them on par with the rest of Namibian society, what principles would you put in place, considering the diversity in views? Discuss these issues with a group of educationists and formulate your conclusions.

4. Currently, there is a strong push towards integrating indigenous knowledge into formal education.

    a. Why integrate indigenous knowledge in school and university science curricula?

    b. How can indigenous knowledge reclaim its place in formal education in modern Namibia?

    c. Discuss the problems that curriculum developers and science teachers would encounter in attempting to integrate indigenous knowledge in formal Namibian education curricula.

    d. What would be the best mode of teaching indigenous knowledge in science classrooms in Namibian schools? Give reasons for your answer.

5. Reflect on the merits and demerits of the use of indigenous languages in school instruction.

Glossary

Aawambo	ethnic group of African origin occupying the central northern parts of Namibia and southern Angola
ACTs	or artemisinin-based combination therapies, are artemisinin derivatives in a fixed or loose combination with partner drugs used to treat malaria
aestivate	to pass the dry season underground during which time the animal's metabolic rate is lowered
aetiology	the cause, set of causes, manner of causation or study of causes of a disease or condition
Afrikaners	ethnic group of White natives of Eurocentric origin in Namibia (and other areas of southern Africa) whose mother tongue is Afrikaans
AIDS	or acquired immunodeficiency syndrome, is a disease caused by HIV in the body of a human being
alkaloid	a naturally occurring nitrogen-containing compound; as a group alkaloids have diverse and important physiological effects on humans and other animals, e.g. morphine, strychnine, quinine and nicotine
allopathic medicine	conventional medicine
alternative medicine	any treatment or palliation of a disease or condition, which is not part of conventional medical curricula, such as acupuncture, faith healing, homeopathy, etc.
amphibian	any animal of the class Amphibia, such as frogs and toads
anaemia	condition in which there is a deficiency of red cells or haemoglobin in the blood, resulting in pallor and weariness
anthrax	infectious disease of livestock caused by the bacterium *Bacillus anthracis*
antibacterial	effective against bacteria; usually an agent that stops the growth or kills bacteria

387

antimalarial	a medicine that is used to prevent and/or treat malaria
antimicrobial	effective against microbes; usually an agent or chemical that is capable of destroying or inhibiting the growth of microbes
antineoplastic	acting to prevent, inhibit or halt the development of a neoplasm (tumour)
antioxidant	any substance that prevents molecules from being oxidized by free radicals by reacting with the free radicals, thus preventing their deterioration
antiplasmodial	an agent or substance that is used to kill or inhibit the growth of *Plasmodium* parasites
antiprotease	a substance that can inhibit the digestion or degradation of proteins
antiretroviral therapy (ART)	a combination of antiretroviral drugs given as treatment for HIV/AIDS, which maximally suppress HIV and stop the progression of the disease
apartheid	the official government policy of racial segregation in South Africa (1930s–1992) that was also enforced in Namibia during its South African colonial rule; under apartheid, races were separated and Blacks were discriminated against, including being denied voting rights
apartheid education	a system of education in South Africa and Namibia that was designed along the policy of apartheid ideology and racially segregated; the education system for Black students under this system was inferior to that for Whites
aqueous extract	a water-based preparation of a plant or animal substance containing the biologically active portion of the plant or substance without its cellular residue
backslopping	practice of using a small portion of a previous batch of fermented foods to start the fermentation process in a new batch of food
bacteriocide	an agent or substance capable of killing bacteria, such as antibiotics, antiseptics, and disinfectants
bacteriocin	antibacterial proteins that are produced by bacteria that kill or inhibit the growth of other bacteria
bacteriostat	an agent or substance that inhibits the growth or reproduction of bacteria, but does not kill them
benefit sharing	a commitment to channel returns gained through indigenous knowledge back to the identified communities or holders of the knowledge

bifidobacteria	gram-positive, rod-shaped, non-spore-forming, non-motile anaerobes that belong to the genus *Bifidobacterium*, which ferment carbohydrates and produce acetic and lactic acids
bilharzia	a disease of humans, also known as schistosomiasis, caused by worms carried by a snail host; it causes acute inflammation to the internal organs, especially the urinary tract
biocatalysis	the chemical process through which enzymes or other biological catalysts perform reactions between organic components
biofortification	a process of increasing the level and/or bioavailability of essential nutrients in edible parts of crops by conventional selective plant breeding or genetic engineering
bioinformatics	a new science that combines the power of computers, mathematical algorithms, and statistics with concepts in the life sciences to analyse and interpret biological data
bioprospecting	the systematic search for useful biological sources of chemical compounds or other valuable products and genes from microbes, fungi, plants and animals for further development into useful products, especially medicines
biotechnology	the commercial use of living organisms or their components to improve animal and human health, agriculture and the environment
bushmeat	also known as game or wild meat; meat harvested from non-domesticated animals, which have been hunted in their wild habitats
cancer	a group of diseases that are characterized by the development of abnormal cells which proliferate uncontrollably, which tend to infiltrate and destroy normal body organs
Caprivians	term describing a number of ethnic African groups occupying the far north-eastern parts of Namibia, formerly known as Caprivi Region, now called Zambezi Region
cattle post	a place away from the homestead where livestock is herded by pastoralists to access fresh grazing resources and a water source
CD4 count	marker of immune cells that define stages of HIV infection; a low CD4 count of less than 200 means severe immune deficiency, characteristic of AIDS
chemoprevention	the use of chemical-based medicines to prevent disease
chemoprophylaxis	the use of chemical substances to prevent humans from infectious diseases

chemotherapy	the use of chemical-based drugs to fight diseases as opposed to herbal medicines
clay pot	indigenous container handmade from clay soil and baked; it is normally used for storage, cooking or fetching water
climate change	is a statistical change in the earth's weather patterns (i.e. changes in temperature, wind and rainfall patterns) over an extended period of time
commercial farmer	a farmer that produces goods (livestock and/or crops) on a scale large enough for marketing; these farmers typically occupy freehold land in Namibia
communal farmer	a farmer that occupies communal state land under the jurisdiction of a traditional authority; their farming activities are typically for subsistence use
conservancy	a community management body concerned with the conservation of a common property; the community has rights to manage and utilize wildlife and tourism in a defined area of land, which is registered with the Ministry of Environment and Tourism
coping strategies	the specific efforts, both behavioural and psychological, that people employ to master, tolerate, reduce, or minimize stressful events
culture	is a way certain groups with shared values and characteristics do things; it includes language, childrearing practices, expected roles of men and women, etc.
Damara	ethnic group of African origin occupying the central and north-western parts of Namibia
decoction	an extraction containing the concentrated essence of a water-soluble substance, produced as a result of boiling; used in medicinal and herbal preparations especially
diaphoretic	a chemical substance that promotes perspiration
diviner	a traditional healer that has and uses special or magical powers to resolve a physical, spiritual or emotional problem or disorder
drought	low rainfall conditions over a prolonged period relative to long-term rainfall statistics
dysuria	difficult or painful urination; can be caused from eating bullfrogs when they first emerge from aestivation
efuma (sing.), *omafuma* (pl.)	local name in northern Namibia for the giant African bullfrog(s), *Pyxicephalus adspersus*

efundja	the seasonal flood of slow-moving water that flows along the shallow drainage network (oshanas) of the Cuvelai drainage system, northern Namibia
epidemiology	a discipline of medicine concerned with the incidence, transmission and control of epidemic diseases
ethnic group	people of a specific culture, having characteristic traditions and racial, linguistic and other traits in common; Namibia has several indigenous ethnic groups, including the Aawambo, Ovaherero, vaKavango, Lozi, Damara and Nama
ethnic minority	a group of people with the same culture and traditions, which differ from the majority of other people, and are therefore considered distinct or unassimilated
ethnobotany	the study and knowledge of the traditional use of plants, especially for medicinal and food purposes
ethnocentrism	chiefly concerned with or concentrating on a particular ethnic group or culture and the belief in the intrinsic superiority of that ethnic group; failure to recognize the importance and value of other cultures
ethnomedicine	the art and knowledge of traditional healers in diagnosing and treating conditions and ailments using local plants and other resources
ethnophytomedicine	ethnomedicine derived from plants
ethnopractitioner	a person actively engaged in ethnomedicine
ethnoveterinary medicine	ethnomedicine applied to domestic animals
Eurocentric	chiefly concerned with or concentrating on Europe and European culture and the belief in the intrinsic superiority of it above other cultures
exopolysaccharide	a carbohydrate (e.g., starch, cellulose, or glycogen) whose molecules consist of a number of sugar molecules bonded together
fermentation	the anaerobic conversion of carbohydrates to simpler substances, such as organic acids, alcohols and carbon dioxide, by yeasts, bacteria and other microbes
first-line treatment	the initial therapy recommended by allopathic practitioners to treat a specific type and stage of cancer
flood	temporary condition of partial or complete inundation of normally dry land area

floodplain	a flat area of land adjacent to a stream or river that becomes flooded during periods of high flow
food security	a 'situation that exists when all people, at all times, have physical, social, and economic access to sufficient, safe, and nutritious food that meets their dietary needs and food preferences for an active and healthy life,' the Food and Agriculture Organization (FAO)
forest resources	resources – fruit, fuelwood, timber, shade, etc. – derived from a naturally wooded area
Foucauldian theory	based on the theories of Michel Foucault; power and knowledge are intertwined entities, as such power might limit what is acceptable to be known and, in turn, knowledge can develop in response and resistance to the limits set by those in power
furunculosis	deep infection of the hair follicle leading to the formation of a boil
gender	the state of being male or female, typically used with reference to social and cultural differences rather than biological ones
gene bank	a biorepository that preserves genetic material, such as plant genetic resources, for future food and agricultural applications
geographic coordinates	the degrees of latitude and longitude that define the position of a point on the earth's surface
germplasm	the living genetic resource, such as seed or tissue, that is maintained for the purpose of animal and plant breeding, preservation and other research uses
green diamonds	a term coined by Dr Kazhila C. Chinsembu referring to the medicinal potential of Namibia's green plants for development into antiretroviral drugs to treat HIV/AIDS
Green Revolution	the increase in crop production in developing countries achieved by the use of artificial fertilizers, pesticides and high-yielding crop varieties
heads of agreement	the first non-binding step to the development of a legal contract that outlines a mutual understanding between different persons or organizations
herbal remedy	a chemically undefined tonic or medicine produced from plants to treat an illness or condition
herbalist	a traditional healer who prepares and administers herbal remedies to treat patients

HIV	human immunodeficiency virus; the cause of acquired immunodeficiency syndrome (AIDS), which attacks the immune system in human beings, rendering them to progressive illnesses with potentially fatal consequences
HIV-positive	a person infected by human immunodeficiency virus (HIV)
human–wildlife conflict	any interaction between humans and wildlife that results in negative impacts on human social, economic or cultural life, on the conservation of wildlife populations, or on the environment; the negative consequences that result from the interaction of humans and wild animals when they compete for resources and habitat
hyperlactataemia	increased concentration of lactate in the blood
hypoglycaemia	low level of glucose in the blood
inclusive education	an approach by which all children and youths are allowed and enabled to learn together in the same classrooms as their peers, irrespective of their physical, social, intellectual, socioemotional condition, or any other characteristics; it further refers to creating welcoming learning environments for all children and youths
indigenous ecological knowledge	cumulative body of knowledge, practices and beliefs, evolving by adaptive processes and handed down through generations by cultural transmission, about the natural environment and the relationship of living beings with their environment
indigenous knowledge	cumulative body of knowledge, practices and beliefs that is unique to a given culture, society or community and has evolved by adaptive processes and handed down through generations by cultural transmission; this local knowledge is mostly undocumented and contributes to the survival of the community, the protection and use of the local environment, and food security
indigenous knowledge system (IKS)	different ways in which indigenous peoples attempt to describe and explain events in nature based on careful observations and cultural ways of interpreting human experience
infusion	the liquid resulting after the extraction of chemical compounds from plant material in a solvent, such as water, oil or alcohol, by allowing the material to soak in the solvent
initiation school	a traditional school in which both boys and girls (usually separately) are taken through the rites of passage into adulthood and taught the associated skills by community elders; ceremonies might include circumcision

isoelectric point	the pH at which a particular molecule carries no electrical charge
Kaposi's sarcoma	lesions on the skin and mucosal surfaces that originates in lymph nodes and blood vessels and is caused by human herpesvirus in immune-compromised individuals, such as those with HIV/AIDS
kraal	a traditional enclosure for livestock
kraaling	the practice of keeping livestock in a kraal overnight
lactic acid bacteria	a group of phylogenetically diverse, gram-positive bacteria characterized by some common morphological, metabolic and physiological traits; they produce lactic acid as the major end product of carbohydrate fermentation
lactic acid fermentation	a biological process by which sugars, such as sugar, glucose, fructose and sucrose, are converted into energy and the metabolic product lactate
Lactobacillus	a large genus of lactic acid bacteria with over 100 species and subspecies
life orientation	the study of self, in relation to others and society; it has to do with an individual's personal, intellectual, social and physical growth and development and how individuals use these to express themselves in their daily lives
life skills	a set of abilities and psychosocial (including reflective and interpersonal) skills and behaviours needed by an individual in order to function effectively with the demands of everyday life as an accepted and acceptable member of society
living with HIV/AIDS	infected with HIV
lobola	an amount of money or property or certain number of livestock paid by a prospective husband to the bride's family shortly before marriage
mahangu	local name for pearl millet (*Pennisetum glaucum*) grown on sandy soils of northern Namibia where it is a staple food; it is usually ground to a meal or flour
maize meal	cornmeal; ground from corn (*Zea mays*); a staple food
marginalized community	a group that is deprived of certain services, privileges or standing in society by virtue of their culture, tradition or belief systems
metabolic acidosis	a condition in which the body produces too much acid, or when the kidneys are not removing enough acid from the body

minimum inhibitory concentration	lowest concentration of plant extract, or drug, that halts the growth of microorganisms in a culture
morbidity	the relative incidence of disease or poor health
mortality	the death of a person or animal; the number of deaths that occur in a time or place
nematicide	chemical substance used to kill nematodes
neoplasm	a tumour or abnormal growth of tissue
omuhongo	local name for *Spirostachys africana*
omuuva and *oshipeke*	local names of two trees (*Pterocarpus angolensis* and *Ximenia caffra*, respectively) whose twigs are used to line cooking pots before cooking bullfrogs in northern Namibia to prevent dysuria (*oshiketaketa*)
omwoongo	local name for the marula tree, *Sclerocarya birrea*
ondungu	local name for chilli
organic extract	an organic solvent-based preparation of a plant or an animal substance containing the biologically active portion of the plant or substance without its cellular residue
organoleptic	normally refers to a property of a food product that involves the use of a sense, such as taste, smell, consistency (touch) or sight
oshanas	the system of shallow, interconnected water channels, ponds or pools that make up the seasonal Cuvelai waterways in northern Namibia
oshifima	local name for thick porridge made from *mahangu* meal
oshiketaketa	the local name for dysuria that results from eating bullfrogs too soon after they emerge from aestivation
Ovaherero	ethnic group of African origin occupying the north-western and central parts of Namibia, coinciding with the Damara in the west
overexploitation	overuse and/or unsustainable, damaging or destructive utilization of a resource, which can lead to local extinctions
palliative care	acts and efforts of lessening the symptoms and stress of a serious illness, thereby making living with the disease easier
pap	local name for porridge
paradigm shift	a fundamental change in approach; a revolutionary concept when a person or society moves from one way of doing things to another; a major change in how a process is accomplished

perception	view, insight or intuition gained on interpretation of information
personpower	the power provided by a person; gender-neutral term for manpower
pet trade	illegal trade of wildlife; trade of high-value wild animals and products
pharmaceutical drug	therapeutic medications developed through scientific and chemical processes
phenomenological research	a study that attempts to understand people's perceptions, perspectives, feelings and understandings of a particular situation (or phenomenon)
phytochemical	chemical compound that occurs naturally in a plant (*phyto*, meaning plant); used by the plant to aid survival and capable of conferring pharmacological properties
phytochemistry	the study of chemicals derived from plants or secondary metabolic compounds found in plants
plant biotechnology	the application of knowledge obtained from the study of the life sciences to create technological improvements in plants
poultice	soft and moist mass of plant material applied to the body to relieve soreness and inflammation and kept in place with a cloth
prebiotic	a non-digestible carbohydrate that, when ingested, is digested by bacteria in the gut of the host
precursor	a compound from which another compound is derived
prevalence rate	the proportion of people in a population who have a particular disease at a specified point or period in time
probiotics	live yeasts and bacteria that confer a health benefit to the host
problem animal	a wild animal or animal species involved in human–wildlife conflict
prostration	extreme physical weakness or emotional exhaustion
psychosis	a severe mental disorder in which thought and emotions are so impaired that contact is lost with external reality
reverse pharmacology	the use of indigenous knowledge to shorten the drug discovery process by providing leads on which plants to screen for antimicrobial properties and toxicity, for potential drug development
riverine	riparian; associated with or living along the river

scaffolding	a process by which a person experienced in a particular area shows the way to a novice
scaffolds	in drug design, the fixed part of a molecule on which functional groups are substituted or exchanged
screens-to-nature assay	an assay that is simple, portable and predictive, which can be performed in a field setting
secondary metabolite	an organic compound that is not directly involved in the normal growth, development or reproduction of a plant
septicaemia	a potentially life-threatening infection caused by pus-forming bacteria in the blood
socioeconomic	of, relating to, or concerned with the interaction of social and economic factors
spoor	the physical footprint of an animal
starter culture	a pure culture or mixture of known microorganisms – usually in a medium, of grains, seeds or nutrient liquids – that performs a fermentation process to produce a particular food or drink
steam bath	vapour consisting of volatile compounds produced by placing plants in boiling water, to be inhaled under a blanket as a therapy
subsistence agriculture	farming for self-sufficiency; agricultural production focused on meeting individual family food and clothing requirements by cultivating crops and raising animals using simple low-input techniques
sustainable	in ecology, the endurance of natural systems and processes that maintain a productive, healthy and diverse environment
tadpoles	the aquatic tailed, limbless larvae of frogs that hatch from the eggs
taxonomy	the science of classifying plants, animals and microorganisms into increasingly broader categories based on shared features
terrarium	a cage or enclosure for keeping small terrestrial (land) animals
tincture	a liquid extract made from plants, which is taken orally as a therapy; plant extract prepared by macerating plant material in alcohol
traditional healer	a practitioner of indigenous medicine or ethnomedicine, usually using animal and plant parts and products; men or women within a specific community who are viewed to possess the knowledge and skills to treat or heal different ailments and diseases

traditional medicinal plants	local plants used to cure a variety of sicknesses
traditional medicine	a medical practice developed aside from modern medicine that is based on beliefs and practices developed in a particular cultural group, which are passed down from one generation to another
traditional practice	a customary action of a particular culture or ethnic group that has been handed down from one generation to the next; includes traditional medicine, agriculture, food preparation, etc.
ubuntu	a southern African moral code or philosophy that stresses the importance of community and not self; literally translates to 'human-ness'; it is an African view of life, collective consciousness of the African people, their own religion, their ethical values, their political ideologies, alms-giving, sympathy, care, respect, patience and kindness
ukadhinahanya	local term 'small ones', referring to small or sub-adult specimens of the giant African bullfrog
umami	a category of taste in food, corresponding to the flavour of glutamates, especially monosodium glutamate; derived from Japanese, meaning 'deliciousness'
validation	the act of verifying the acclaimed properties of traditional medicines using scientific methods
vulnerability	the potential for disruption or harm due to an environmentally hazardous event
Western	relating to, or characteristic of the western part of the world, especially the Americas and Europe
wetland	a land area saturated with water, either permanently or seasonally, such that it takes on the characteristics of and is considered a distinct ecosystem
xenograft	a transplant or graft of tissue from one species to another
zoopharmacognosy	a term used to describe the behaviour of wild and domestic animals that apparently self-medicate by selecting and ingesting or topically applying plants, soils, insects and other natural products to treat or prevent illness

Contributors

Margaret N. Angula is a Geography and Environmental Studies Lecturer, Department of Geography, History and Environmental Studies, at the University of Namibia. She is an environmental scientist with over 15 years of research experience in environmental management. Her current research focuses on vulnerability and adaptation assessments, gender and climate change, pastoralists' knowledge of environmental change and human–wildlife conflicts.

Joyce Auala is employed by the Ministry of Health and Social Services' National Vector-borne Disease Control Programme. She previously worked as a Postgraduate Research Fellow at the University of Namibia's Multidisciplinary Research Centre, on natural antimicrobial products from medicinal plants, and on malaria epidemiology.

Ronnie Böck completed his Bachelor's and Master's degrees at Saarland University in Germany, majoring in Genetics (Genetic Engineering), Botany and Biochemistry. He went on to gain his PhD in Biomedical Sciences at Oklahoma State University in the USA. He has researched extensively in the area of infectious diseases in the government service of Namibia, before he joined the Department of Biological Sciences, University of Namibia (UNAM). He established the Malaria and Biomedical Research Laboratory at UNAM, together with Dr Davis Mumbengegwi. This laboratory has assisted the Government of Namibia in their campaign to eradicate malaria from Namibia and has attracted major international support and collaboration on the African continent and abroad.

Ahmad Cheikhyoussef is a senior researcher and coordinator of the Indigenous Knowledge System Technology (IKST) Food and Beverages Programme under the Science, Technology and Innovation Division of the University of Namibia's Multidisciplinary Research Centre. He has a PhD in Food Science. His research focuses on ethnobotanical knowledge of traditional fruits and vegetables; development of food-grade supplements with biological activity for product safety and potential applications, and the nutrition and safety of traditional foods and beverages.

Grace M. Mukumbo Chinsembu was a part-time Lecturer in the University of Namibia's (UNAM's) Department of Lifelong Learning and Community Education, Faculty of Education. She taught comparative education, youth and family life, and programme planning. She has a Certificate in Primary Education (Solwezi Teachers' Training College, Zambia), Diploma in education (Chalimbana College/University of Zambia), and a Bachelor's and a Master's degree in Adult Education from UNAM. Over the past 15 years, she has taught in various schools in Namibia and Zambia. She has also conducted research on indigenous knowledge and how to mainstream indigenous knowledge into university education.

Kazhila C. Chinsembu, PhD, is a double professor: He is Associate Professor of Microbiology and Molecular Biology at the University of Namibia and Honorary Professor of Public Health at the University of Lusaka, Zambia. An award-winning scientist, Prof. Chinsembu works and writes on medicinal plants. Author of a highly cited research article in PubMed's *Journal of Ethnobiology and Ethnomedicine*, Prof. Chinsembu teaches in the Department of Biological Sciences, University of Namibia. Formerly, Prof. Chinsembu taught in the Department of Biological Sciences, University of Zambia and worked for the International Centre of Insect Physiology and Ecology, Nairobi, Kenya. Prof. Chinsembu is the author of another book, *Green Medicines: Pharmacy of Natural Products for HIV and Five AIDS-related Infections*. He and his wife Grace have two daughters, Wana and Lusa.

Iwanette du Preez is a Researcher at the Science, Technology and Innovation Division of the Multidisciplinary Research Centre (MRC) at the University of Namibia (UNAM). She is also a PhD candidate in UNAM's Department of Biological Sciences. In 2012, she graduated with a Master's degree cum laude, and was awarded best overall student at UNAM and the best postgraduate research student in the Faculty of Science. In 2010, she was awarded best postgraduate research fellow at the MRC. Her research focus is on evaluating antimalarial activity of plants using lab-based models of malaria and cell-based assays, for which she received training at the Kenya Medical Research Institute (KEMRI-Wellcome), Kilifi.

Florence Dushimemaria is a Postgraduate Research Fellow at the Science, Technology and Innovation Division of the Multidisciplinary Research Centre. She is also conducting research in the Biomedical Research Laboratory towards a PhD in the Faculty of Science. Her research work focuses on indigenous medicinal plants in Namibia and evaluating their antineoplastic properties and their potential for use in the treatment of cancer, or palliation of the disease. She is an alumnus of the University of Namibia having graduated with a BSc (Hons) in Microbiology and Biochemistry as the best undergraduate research student in 2011. She is also a double recipient of a German Exchange (DAAD) Fellowship for her MSc and PhD studies.

Werner Embashu is a researcher in the Science Technology and Innovation Division of the Multidisciplinary Research Centre, under the Indigenous Knowledge System Technology (IKST) Food and Beverages Programme, and is enrolled as a PhD student in Biochemistry (Food Biochemistry and Microbiology). His research project is on the biochemistry and microbiology of *oshikundu*, and its shelf-life extension and sensory evaluation. His educational background includes a BSc (Hons) in Biochemistry and Biology and an MSc from the University of Namibia. He received an award for the best postgraduate research student in the Faculty of Science for his MSc.

Cynthy K. Haihambo is currently a Senior Lecturer in the Department of Educational Psychology and Inclusive Education in the University of Namibia's (UNAM's) Faculty of Education. She has done extensive research and consultancies in the areas of special needs and inclusive education; early childhood, gender and HIV/AIDS; street children and other marginalized children; indigenous knowledge systems; and orphans and vulnerable children. She serves on various national and international education-related committees and platforms. Haihambo holds a Bachelor of Education (Hons) from UNAM, an MPhil (Special Needs Education) from the University of Oslo, and a Doctorate in Education (Inclusive Education) from the University of South Africa.

Miriam Hamunyela is the Head of the Department of Lifelong Learning and Community Education in the University of Namibia's (UNAM's) Faculty of Education. She holds a Bachelor of Pedagogics from the University of Fort Hare, South Africa; a Master's degree in Teacher Education (with distinction) from the University of Umeå, Sweden; and a PhD in Community Education and Development from the University of Pretoria, South Africa. She was identified as a high-achiever research student at the University of Pretoria (2008) and thus awarded a Certificate of Excellence by the university Chapter of the Golden Key International Honour Society, in recognition of her insight and outstanding performance in research. She has an interest in training community development workers and practitioners, thereby building their capacity towards alleviating poverty in Namibian communities.

Lusia Heita is a nutritionist at the Family Health Division of the Ministry of Health and Social Services. She has a Master's degree in Food Science. Her research area is the antimicrobial activity of lactic acid bacteria of traditional milk products from northern and north-eastern Namibia. Her educational background includes BSc (Hons; Food Science and Technology) from the University of Namibia.

Gladys K. Kahaka is a Senior Lecturer in the University of Namibia's (UNAM's) Department of Chemistry and Biochemistry (Faculty of Science). Her educational background includes a BSc (Biology and Chemistry) from UNAM, and an MSc (Plant Genetic Manipulation). She earned her PhD in Plant Science Biochemistry from the University of Nottingham (UK). She is the first Namibian to be awarded the L'Oréal–UNESCO International Fellowship for Women in Science (2012). This award is given to women under the age of 35 years who are moving science forward. Her current research involves the application of genetics and biotechnology towards the conservation of various endangered Namibian species.

Martha Kandawa-Schulz has worked at the University of Namibia (UNAM) since 1996 and is currently Deputy Dean of its Faculty of Science and a Senior Lecturer in the Department of Chemistry and Biochemistry. She is also the National Focal Point on Biosafety and a member of the Biotechnology Alliance (NABA). She earned her PhD from the University of Rostock, Germany. She has also published various peer-reviewed journal articles together with students working on her various projects, which are funded by the European Union, Carnegie-RISE, United Nations Environment Programme–Global Environment Facility, Swedish International Development Cooperation and others.

Lineekela Kandjengo is Head of the Department of Fisheries and Aquatic Sciences at the Sam Nujoma campus of the University of Namibia. He has conducted research on the fisheries of the Cuvelai drainage system in northern Namibia. After obtaining his BSc (Hons) and MSc from the University of Cape Town, Kandjengo's scope expanded to the marine sciences. He has presented many papers at both national and international conferences on the systematics of the Ulvaceae (green algae) of southern Africa.

Alex T. Kanyimba teaches Environmental Education, Education for Sustainable Development, Policy Studies in Education, and Economics of Education at the University of Namibia. He has published extensively in the areas of environmental education, education for sustainable development, environmental management and climate change education.

Hileni Magano Kapenda has over 28 years of experience as a teacher educator in the Namibian education system. She is currently a Senior Lecturer of Pedagogy in the University of Namibia's (UNAM's) Department of Mathematics, Science and Sport Education. She is also UNAM's Deputy Research Coordinator, in the Research and Publications Office. She received a meritorious award for *best academic performance* in 2014 from the Faculty of Education. With 16 years of experience in university teaching and research, she enjoys empirical research and has published over 20 articles and papers in peer-reviewed journals and proceedings at national and international levels. She earned her BSc from the University of Fort Hare, a post-graduate diploma in education (PGDE) from UNAM, MEd (Maths) from Ohio University (USA), and PhD from the University of the Western Cape (South Africa). In April 2015, she completed a graduate certificate in tertiary education management with the University of Melbourne, Australia.

Choshi Darius Kasanda, former Deputy Dean in the Faculty of Education, is currently a Full Professor of Mathematics Education at the University of Namibia (UNAM), and Deputy Director, Teaching and Learning Improvement Unit. He is actively involved in the teaching of undergraduate and postgraduate students. He holds an MSc and a PhD from the University of Wisconsin (Madison) in the USA, in addition to a BSc (Ed) from the University of Zambia. He was the founding Head of the Department of Mathematics and Science Education at the University of Zambia and at UNAM, respectively. He has been involved in the delivery of higher education pertaining to mathematics and science education for over 30 years. He is a recent recipient of UNAM's sabbatical merit award. He has published extensively in the areas of mathematics education, science, and information and communications technologies.

Martha M. Kashea worked as a teacher for more than ten years before joining the Ministry of Education as a Science and Technology Officer. Currently, she is serving at the National Commission for Research, Science and Technology as a Programme Officer. She works in the areas of research statistics, educational management and policy analysis.

Lawrence Kazembe is an Associate Professor at the University of Namibia (UNAM). He joined the university in 2012, having served much of his career at Chancellor College, University of Malawi. He previously served as Senior Biostatistician at Malawi–Liverpool Wellcome Trust Clinical Research Programme (Blantyre, Malawi), 2010–2012, and as a Research Fellow at the Medical Research Council of South Africa (Durban) in the Malaria Lead Research Programme, 2005–2007. He has published extensively in malaria research and population health, with over 40 peer-reviewed publications. His work has been recognised by the Malawi National Commission of Science and Technology, the Academy of Sciences in Developing Countries, and the Sub-Saharan Network of International Biometrics Society (SUSAN-IBS). He obtained his PhD in 2007 from the University of KwaZulu-Natal. His main research interests are in Bayesian statistical modelling and spatial analysis with applications in population health.

Selma M. Lendelvo is a Researcher and Programme Leader of socioecological systems in the Life Sciences Division of the University of Namibia's (UNAM's) Multidisciplinary Research Centre, focusing on research on livelihoods, rural development, socioecological and community-based natural resources management. She has a BSc (Botany and Zoology) from UNAM, and an MSc (Natural Resources Management and Sustainable Agriculture) from the Agricultural University of Norway.

John Makala Lilemba is a researcher, scholar and a winner of the Pamwe literature award in siLozi short stories. He is a Lecturer at the University of Barotseland in Zambia and was previously Head of Department of Educational Foundations and Management at the University of Namibia (UNAM). With 18 years of university teaching and research, he has read and researched widely, including reviewing journal articles, book chapters, conference proceedings and essays in educational sciences. He obtained a Bachelor's degree and a University Education Diploma at the University of the North (now the University of Limpopo, Polokwane, South Africa), a Master's degree in Educational Studies at the University of Manchester (UK), and a PhD at UNAM. He is the author of three books used in secondary schools and one novel prescribed by the UNAM Language Centre.

Anthony Mashego-Brown is a Lecturer in the University of Namibia's (UNAM's) Centre for External Studies. He has lectured in the field of Inclusive Education and Educational Psychology for the past nine years. He has carried out research in the fields of San education; sensory disabilities; disabilities and distance education; and HIV/AIDS education. He holds a BEd from UNAM, MA (Special Education) from Leeds University (UK) and EdD (Educational Disadvantage and Special Education) from the University of Birmingham (UK).

Yonah Hisbon Matemba is a Senior Lecturer in Social Sciences in the School of Education, University of the West of Scotland (UK), where he has been teaching since 2011. He obtained his first degree in Education in 1991 from Andrews University (USA) and then in 2000 completed two Master's degrees: an MA (History) from the University of Botswana and an MA (Theology and Religious Studies) from the University of Malawi. In 2011 he was awarded a PhD in Education at the University of Glasgow. He taught in secondary schools in Malawi, Botswana and the UK before subsequently taking up lectureship positions in universities and colleges of education in Botswana and Malawi. He is also a professionally registered teacher with the General Teaching Council for Scotland (GTCS) and a fellow of the UK's Higher Education Academy (HEA). He is author of more than 20 peer-reviewed articles, book chapters, reviews and books.

Nchindo Richardson Mbukusa is an upcoming researcher and scholar with an interest in flood studies. He is currently a Lecturer at the University of Namibia's (UNAM's) Centre for External Studies. Previously, he served as Head of Department at the former Rundu College of Education. Over the past 15 years, he has focused on supporting and teaching educational research to distance students. A few of his papers are on supporting distance education students in rural areas. Mbukusa earned a BA and PGCE from Andrews University, a BPhil (Ed) from the University of Exeter, an MA (Distance Education) from London University, and a PhD (Distance Education), University of South Africa.

John Kazgeba E. Mfune is currently a Senior Lecturer in the University of Namibia's (UNAM's) Department of Biological Sciences; Coordinator of the International MSc Biodiversity Management and Research, jointly run by UNAM and Humboldt University (Berlin, Germany); and Coordinator of the UNAM Faculty of Science Mentorship Programme. He has served as Dean of the Faculty of Science, Coordinator of MSc Environmental Science Programme, and Deputy Director of Postgraduate Studies, all in the Faculty of Science of Chancellor College (University of Malawi). He has been an accomplished lecturer, researcher and environmental consultant for over 20 years and has published many peer-reviewed journal articles, book chapters and conference proceedings. His research expertise includes: terrestrial ecology, especially of small mammals and large ungulates; environmental and natural resource management; local adaptations to climate change; human–wildlife conflicts; and ecology of macroparasites of mammals and their medical importance. He holds BSc and BSc (Hons) degrees from the University of Malawi, and an MSc and a PhD (Animal Ecology) from the University of Aberdeen (Scotland).

Pempelani Mufune (deceased) was Professor of Environmental Sociology at the University of Namibia's Department of Sociology. He passed away at the Windhoek Roman Catholic Hospital on 7 March 2015. May his soul rest in eternal peace.

Davis R. Mumbengegwi joined the University of Namibia's (UNAM's) Multidisciplinary Research Centre (MRC) in 2009 as a Researcher, establishing the pharmaceuticals programme in the Science Technology and Innovation Division (STID) and the Malaria and Biomedical Research Laboratory with Dr Ronnie Böck. He is now a Senior Research Scientist, Head of STID and Deputy Director of the MRC. A pharmaceutical scientist, he received his doctorate from the University of Manchester (UK) and was a Postdoctoral Research Fellow in the Department of Pharmacology at the University of Alberta (Canada), and in the Department of Anatomy and Cell Biology (Carver College of Medicine) at the University of Iowa (USA). His current research focuses on medicinal and veterinary drug discovery from indigenous knowledge and use of small animals for drug development. He leads the Drug Discovery and Development Programme, which conducts research on documentation and valorization of indigenous medicinal and veterinary plants in Namibia. Passionate about research training, he has supervised 13 MSc and PhD students (including co-authors for this book) as well as over 30 undergraduate project students and interns.

Lynatte F. Mushabati is an MSc student at the University of Namibia's (UNAM's) Department of Chemistry and Biochemistry. Her research project focuses on the namibian leafy vegetables from Zambezi Region and their phytochemistry, and antioxidant and antimicrobial activities. Her main academic interests centre on biological pathways.

Sylvia Nafuka is a University of Namibia (UNAM) graduate with a BSc (Hons) in Microbiology and Biochemistry and an MSc. She worked as a Postgraduate Research Fellow at the Science, Technology and Innovation Division of the Multidisciplinary Research Centre. Her research focuses on indigenous medicinal plants in Namibia, evaluating their antimalarial activity, and identifying the phytochemical basis of the activity. She was the recipient of an International Atomic Energy Agency (IAEA) fellowship and received training in analysis at the renowned National Food Technology Research Centre (Kanye, Botswana). She is currently a lecturer in the Department of Biological Sciences in the Faculty of Science.

Daniel O. Okeyo is a scientific authority in love with lacustrine and riverine animal (mainly fish) diversity, which has been his professional field for 25 years. He is currently the coordinator of Aquaculture, Aquatic and Marine Sciences of the University of Fort Hare (Eastern Cape, South Africa). He has served as Coordinator of Aquatic Sciences at Kenyatta University (Nairobi, Kenya), 1987–1995; Head of the University of Namibia's Department of Biological Sciences, 1995–2001; and Executive Dean of the Faculty of Science at the University of Fort Hare, 2001–2007. He authored *A Photo Guide to Freshwater Fishes of Kenya: Including Riverine and Lacustrine Haplochromines*, available online free of charge, as a 'thank you' contribution to African fish lovers from around the world.

Nguza Siyambango is a Researcher at the University of Namibia's (UNAM's) Multidisciplinary Research Centre, under the Life Science Division. Her research area is climate change and disaster risk management, focusing on community-based adaptation strategies, vulnerability and risk assessments. A Namibian with a BSc majoring in Environmental Biology and Molecular and Physiological biology from UNAM, she completed her Post Graduate Diploma and Master's degree in Environmental Management from the University of Queensland in Brisbane, Australia.